Praise for *Adolescents, Families, and Social Development*

"Few scholars have influenced the contemporary study of adolescent–parent relationships as much as Judith Smetana. I highly recommend this book to anyone interested in the ways in which family relationships are transformed during this stage of life."
Laurence Steinberg, Temple University

"In this very thoughtful book Judith Smetana provides deep and insightful understandings of adolescence. Smetana masterfully positions adolescence in explanations of difficulties and developmental progress during these years. This splendid book is indispensable for anyone interested in adolescence, social, and family relationships, moral theory, culture, and development."
Elliot Turiel, University of California Berkeley

"Drawing on much of her own creative and highly influential research, Smetana has produced a compelling account of adolescent development. The book is scholarly and engaging, a "must read" for any developmentalist."
Joan Grusec, University of Toronto

"This is an extraordinary book. Dr. Smetana has given us a compassionate account of the teen years – an account that is respectful of both the youth and their parents and an account that is respectful of the dynamic processes characterizing the relationships between youth and their parents at this point in human history. Dr. Smetana provides us a nuanced picture of this very important period of human development – a balanced picture that provides a much needed correction to the very negative stereotypes prevalent in Western culture about this difficult transitional period of life. The struggles of both parents and their adolescent children come to life, making us more fully aware of the true dignity of our youth and their families as they cope with the transition from childhood into adulthood in extremely complex and challenging social and political contexts. The book is a delight to read whether one is a developmental scientist, a counselor, a teacher, a parent, or just an interested observer of human nature."
Jacque Eccles, University of Michigan

"Smetana effectively highlights how adolescents are active members in their own socialization, striving to assert their own goals at the same time as integrating them with the norms and values of their families and broader cultural context."
Andrew Fuligni, University of California Los Angeles

D1379005

Adolescents, Families, and Social Development
How Teens Construct Their Worlds

Judith G. Smetana

A John Wiley & Sons, Ltd., Publication

This edition first published 2011
© 2011 Judith G. Smetana

Blackwell Publishing was acquired by John Wiley & Sons in February 2007. Blackwell's publishing program has been merged with Wiley's global Scientific, Technical, and Medical business to form Wiley-Blackwell.

Registered Office
John Wiley & Sons Ltd, The Atrium, Southern Gate, Chichester, West Sussex, PO19 8SQ, United Kingdom

Editorial Offices
350 Main Street, Malden, MA 02148-5020, USA
9600 Garsington Road, Oxford, OX4 2DQ, UK
The Atrium, Southern Gate, Chichester, West Sussex, PO19 8SQ, UK

For details of our global editorial offices, for customer services, and for information about how to apply for permission to reuse the copyright material in this book please see our website at www.wiley.com/wiley-blackwell.

The right of Judith G. Smetana to be identified as the author of this work has been asserted in accordance with the UK Copyright, Designs and Patents Act 1988.

Library of Congress Cataloging-in-Publication Data

Smetana, Judith G., 1951–
   Adolescents, families, and social development : how teens construct their worlds / Judith G. Smetana.
       p. cm.
   Includes bibliographical references and index.
   ISBN 978-1-4443-3250-6 (hbk. : alk. paper) – ISBN 978-1-4443-3251-3 (pbk.: alk. paper)
 1. Adolescence.   2. Parent and teenager.   3. Social interaction in adolescence.   I. Title.
   HQ796.S545 2011
   305.235–dc22
                            2010021919

A catalogue record for this book is available from the British Library.

Set in 11/13 pt Dante by Toppan Best-set Premedia Limited
Printed in Malaysia by Ho Printing (M) Sdn Bhd

1   2011

Contents

Preface

Adolescents have been a source of both fascination and irritation for adults for centuries. Much has been written about adolescence as a difficult developmental period and as a time of storm and stress. It has also been said that teenagers today are lacking in moral values, that they reject their parents' standards, and that they are rude, disrespectful, and lazy. But developmental scientists are much less pessimistic about the state of youth today and believe that the perils of adolescence are overstated. Adolescents do not reject their parents, nor are they rebelling against parental and societal values. At the same time, though, the path to adulthood is not smooth. Adolescents face many risks and challenges that must be met before adulthood is achieved. Typically, there are minor disruptions in their relationships with parents, although, for adolescents who are fortunate enough to live in stable, supportive, and cohesive families, these challenges lead to positive changes in family relationships and in the adolescents themselves.

My colleagues and I have been conducting research on these issues for many years. My focus has been on how adolescents and parents – of different ethnicities and in different cultures – construct their social worlds and create meaning out of their social interactions. I view adolescents' conflicts and disagreements with parents and their attempts strategically to manage information about their lives as a reflection of ongoing concerns with autonomy, personal choices, and agency. Some culture theorists have asserted that these concerns are emphasized primarily in individualistic cultures, whereas in collectivist cultures individuals are primarily concerned with duties, obligations in interpersonal relationships, and harmony and interdependence in the family. These views of culture ignore newer definitions, which emphasize autonomy in the context of ongoing relatedness to parents. And they provide an overly simple and stereotyped view of adolescents' lives in different cultures.

In this book, and drawing on a theoretical framework and research over the past 25 years, I examine both the universal and the context-specific aspects of adolescents' social development in family contexts. Adolescents worldwide are concerned with the stage-salient task of becoming more independent, although the pacing of this process and the types of issues over which autonomy is sought may vary in different cultures. Adolescents also develop a deep understanding of moral matters, including concerns with justice, others' welfare, and human rights. These concerns develop alongside adolescents' growing awareness of societal conventions, norms, and standards. Self and morality, defined in this way, are not of concern only to those growing up in individualistic societies; nor are social conventions the exclusive concern of youth in collectivist cultures. In this book I demonstrate that having such preoccupations is part of everyday social interaction for youth in different cultures. These are universal issues because they develop from social interactions that are common to individuals worldwide and reflect ways of thinking about self, society, and interpersonal relationships. Yet the differences in understanding them reflect the different circumstances and social environments of different groups and cultures.

My approach to social development considers how all of these separate strands of development – concerns with autonomy, rights and justice, society and social convention – change, conflict, and become increasingly integrated in adolescent social development. I argue that successful parenting involves a consideration of how parents draw boundaries between issues that are legitimately of parental concern and adolescents' claims for greater autonomy and personal choice. The balance varies in different cultures and contexts, and it also shifts during development.

Drawing on extensive data from my research with middle-class African American and European American families and with lower-class Chinese adolescents, I examine the different ways in which adolescents and parents think about, negotiate, and resolve disagreements in their relationships – disagreements that are primarily about these boundaries. I also discuss adolescents' sometimes more subversive routes to autonomy – including their attempts to manage and conceal information from parents. Although I draw on a wide range of sources, from public opinion surveys and movies to scholarly writings from anthropology and history, my focus is on theorizing and research from developmental science. The book describes the results of research on adolescent–parent relationships, parenting beliefs, and parenting practices among ethnic majority and minority families in the United States and elsewhere.

I am extremely fortunate in having, as close friends and inspiring colleagues, a group of scholars who share the theoretical perspective outlined in this book. Although we work on somewhat different research topics, our lively exchanges, warm and supportive interactions, and deep friendship over many years have enriched my thinking enormously and have encouraged and inspired me in my endeavors. This book reflects the research and influence of Elliot Turiel (my mentor, and an ongoing role model in terms of what serious, engaged scholarship ought to be), Larry Nucci, Melanie Killen, Charles Helwig, and Cecilia Wainryb, as well as that of many younger scholars who have joined the group along the way. It also reflects the influence of many talented graduate students, who over the years have pushed me to expand my thinking and have become close colleagues and friends, too. I especially thank Judith Braeges, Nicole Campione-Barr, Susan Chuang, Joseph Crockett, Christopher Daddis, Aaron Metzger, Marina Tasopoulos-Chan, and Jenny Yau. I owe a debt to Myung-Ja Song, who introduced me to cross-cultural research over 20 years ago. Cheryl Gaines was an invaluable guide, a good friend, and an inspiring source of support in studying African American youth.

I am extremely grateful to Melanie Killen, Larry Nucci, Elliot Turiel, and Chris Daddis, as well as to the graduate students in my current research group, Jessamy Comer, Marc Jambon, Wendy Rote, and Myriam Villalobos for their very careful reading of the manuscript. They read it more thoroughly than I could ever have hoped for, and their thoughtful comments and questions helped me to revise and clarify my thoughts. (Any remaining faults are entirely my own.)

The research described in this book was supported by many sources, including the National Institutes of Health, the National Science Foundation, the William T. Grant Foundation, and the Fetzer Institute. I am truly grateful for their support. The University of Rochester, where I have worked for many years, has been a lively and rich environment for developing my thinking and conducting research. I greatly appreciate the opportunities to grow as a researcher and the sabbatical time to write this book. I also wish to thank Chris Cardone, Constance Adler, and Manuela Tecusan at Wiley-Blackwell for their encouragement and assistance with this project.

No book on social development would be complete without mention of parents. My parents, Helen and Ernest, endured many hardships to provide a secure and loving home. This is in their memory. Finally, I am grateful to my family – Ron, Joshua, and Jeremy – for their love and support and for the possibility of constructing our worlds together.

1

Introduction

Perspectives on Adolescents and Their Families

There is a great deal of interest, ambivalence, and confusion about today's adolescents and their role and place in contemporary society. Social commentators are perennially trying to understand "what makes adolescents tick," as a 2008 cover story in *Time Magazine* illustrates (Wallis, 2008, September 26). This question has been answered in many ways, in part due to scientific advances in knowledge, but also as a reflection of the various preoccupations of different eras. At different times, explanations for teenagers' behavior have focused on teenagers' character (or lack thereof), the negative influences of their peers, and raging hormones. Currently, as showcased in the *Time Magazine* article, explanations are being sought in adolescent brain functioning. The claim is that adolescents misbehave because their brains are not yet mature. But why does adolescent behavior raise these questions? After all, we would not expect to see a cover story focusing on "what makes adults tick." The question highlights a societal unease about the very nature of adolescence.

Popular Views of Adolescence

Some public opinion surveys reveal that prevailing attitudes towards teenagers are largely negative. Public Agenda, a national public interest research organization, conducted a multi-year national survey a decade ago to examine the American public's attitudes regarding the nation's youth. Duffet, Johnson, and Farkas (1999) reported that "[m]ost Americans are deeply disappointed with "kids these days." More than seven in ten adults resort to words such as 'rude,' 'irresponsible,' and 'wild' to describe today's teens, and more than half also describe young children disapprovingly" (p. 3). According to Public Agenda's findings,

Adolescents, Families, and Social Development: How Teens Construct Their Worlds.   Judith G. Smetana
© 2011 Judith G. Smetana

both parents and the general public agree in these observations. Less than 15% of randomly sampled adults participating in this survey viewed positive characteristics as good descriptors for today's youth. Moreover, a surprising 58% of the general public and 57% of the parents surveyed agreed with the statement that "today's children will make America a worse place or will make little difference" (Duffet et al., 1999, p. 3).

Yet, despite these negative findings, the survey also found that most Americans acknowledged that it is much harder to be a parent now than before. Nearly 70% of the adults sampled viewed abuse of drugs or alcohol and too much sex and violence on TV as very serious problems facing today's youth. In 1999, nearly half of the adults surveyed blamed the problems that teenagers face as due to irresponsible parents who fail to do their job. A smaller percentage – less than a third – blamed the fact that there are perilous circumstances for today's youth on social and economic pressures on parents. This represented an increase from the previous survey, conducted 2 years prior, in the proportion of Americans willing to hold parents rather than broader social and economic circumstances responsible for the situation of American youth.

Some prominent commentators and moral educators also have promoted negative perceptions of adolescents. For instance, the former United States Secretary of Education William Bennett (1992, 2001) argues that there is a rising tide of juvenile delinquency, homosexuality, adolescent drug and alcohol use, and teenage pregnancy and child bearing that reflects a breakdown in the moral fabric of society. No matter that current statistics do not bear this out. (In fact, for the past decade, rates of teenage child bearing and juvenile delinquency have been on the decline.) In Bennett's view, as well as in that of some other prominent moral educators (Lickona, 1991, 2004), adolescents are rejecting parents' moral values and resisting adult authority. In their opinion this has led to widespread societal moral decay.

Another way to explore whether parents are failing in their parental roles is to examine the advice child-rearing experts offer. Parent advice books both reflect and shape the way adolescents and their growth and development are perceived. Americans are enamored with self-help books. Bookstores devote voluminous shelf space to books by child-rearing experts dispensing advice on parenting. The findings of psychological research studies and of large opinion surveys are echoed in child-rearing books. Books devoted to the special perils of raising a teenager typically are located apart from the volumes devoted to rearing infants and younger children. This physical separation is paralleled by marked differences in the tenor of the titles. Books geared towards parents of newborns and infants generally convey the joy and optimism that parents feel at bringing a new baby into the family. Of course, there are many books reflecting the difficulties of parenting infants and explaining how to cope with lack of sleep, cranky babies and the like, but the overall tone of the books imparts a view of parenting a young child as a happy and rewarding experience, of the role of parents as facilitating their children's creativity and development, and of babies as enjoyable, adaptive, and responsive.

The advice books for parents of children in middle childhood are more sober and straightforward. The majority of titles reflect a greater emphasis on how to discipline children and on how to manage their behavior effectively, as well as on how to instill self-esteem, good moral character and values, and positive attitudes. The books suggest that parenting during middle childhood is serious business, requiring effective and appropriate disciplinary techniques and behavior management strategies.

But child-rearing books on adolescence reflect a cultural anxiety that is not apparent in the books providing advice about parenting younger children. Whereas some of these books focus on more positive themes, a majority of the advice books on parenting teenagers portray adolescents as characteristically willful, unresponsive, and disrespectful. At the same time parents are depicted as bewildered, stressed, and overwhelmed. Both the tone and the titles depart from those of books about earlier ages, even when the same expert writes about different developmental periods. Thus one expert, who offers "magic hints for effective discipline" during middle childhood, views adolescence as something parents need to survive, as the title suggests: *Surviving your adolescents: How to manage and let go of your 13–18 year olds* (Phelan, 1998). And many more examples abound. The titles are catchy: *Teenagers! A bewildered parent's guide* (Caldwell, 1996); *Get out of my life – but first would you drive me and Cheryl to the mall? A parent's guide to the new teenager* (Wolf, 2002), *How to survive your teenager* (Gluck & Rosenfeld, 2005), and *"I'm not mad, I just hate you!" – A new understanding of mother daughter conflict* (Cohen-Sandler & Silver, 2000). Indeed, adolescence today has been considered so problematic that even one's pet's adolescence is to be feared – consider the recent addition to the canon, *Surviving your dog's adolescence: A positive training program* (Benjamin, 1993). But the sentiments these books convey about parenting an adolescent or engaging in a relationship with an adolescent are decidedly negative, even towards "normal," run-of-the-mill teenagers and their everyday problems. Why is there such a drastic shift in attitude, from the unconditional love and bonding reflected in the advice books to parents of babies to the ambivalence and hostility about parenting and parent–adolescent relationships expressed in these titles?

Of course, titles sell books, and, to some extent, the anxiety expressed in these titles, no matter how cute they are, may be "pitched" to match the prevailing beliefs about parenting and adolescence. But I believe these titles reflect more than shrewd marketing. If these books did not appeal to parents' concerns, the books would not sell. They would quickly disappear. And there is a market for such books, as their proliferation suggests. Beyond the clever titles, the contents of these books dwell on similar themes. They cover topics such as "how to bridge the gap," "emotional blackmail," "a different planet," "conflict," and "controlling your teenager."

There is a smaller but parallel set of advice books by child-rearing experts, which are geared to the teenage audience. Again, the titles are instructive. They are meant to convey the impression that parents' behavior is inscrutable and that parents are not listening to teenagers. Consider the following: *Teenage survival manual: Why parents act that way and other mysteries of mind and matter* (Coombs, 1998), and *Why can't we talk? What teens would share if parents would listen: A book for teens* (Trujillo, 2000). Are these titles accurate reflections of adolescents' views of their parents and of the adult world?

Adolescents' Views of Adolescence

When American teenagers are asked to characterize the general nature of adolescent–parent relationships, their responses are similar to those of adults. For instance, 60% of the teens surveyed in the Public Agenda national opinion poll – as compared to 58% of the general public and 57% of parents – also agreed with the statement that "today's children will make America a worse place or will make little difference."

Surveying a sample of college youth, Grayson Holmbeck and John Hill (1988) found that, prior to taking a psychology course on the psychology of adolescence, most students strongly believed that adolescence is typically a time of storm and stress. More than half of them endorsed, as being often or more frequently true, views such as that adolescents have identity crises, that adolescents are rebellious, that adolescents frequently fight with their parents, that adolescents prefer to talk to peers rather than parents, and that adolescence is a stormy and stressful time. Indeed, this last item was endorsed as being often or more frequently true by nearly three quarters of the sample studied by Holmbeck and Hill (and more so by girls than by boys). They were asked about the typical frequency of fights with parents over trivial issues (such as how to dress, what kind of music to listen to, cleaning one's room, spending money, and doing homework) and over nontrivial issues (such as attitudes, basic and religious values, educational and occupational plans, and respect for parents). Students reported that the typical teenager has about seven fights per month with parents over each nontrivial issue and over nine fights per month with parents over each trivial issue. Therefore the participants in this survey believed that the average teenager has over 40 fights per week across the different issues sampled! And these were students who were barely out of adolescence themselves.

Despite this situation, students typically did not believe that parents are disappointed in their adolescent offspring, or that children do not cooperate with their parents. They also rejected the notion that there is a generation gap between parents and children. These findings led the researchers to conclude that college students tend to view adolescence as a developmental period characterized by disruptions in relationships with parents rather than by a complete rejection of parents. Among the youth being queried, the perceptions were that college students viewed adolescence as a time typified by problems of identity, by a tendency to argue with parents, and by the rising influence of peers. This picture of adolescence as a relatively calm developmental period, characterized by generally positive relationships with parents, predominated over the view that adolescence typically involves oppositionalism and noncompliance. As we shall see in Chapter 2, this accords well with the conclusions drawn from recent psychological research to the effect that, when families are warm and close, moderate levels of conflict can have positive functions for adolescents' development.

Other research shows that, if adolescents and parents expect to have more "storm and stress" during adolescence, then this is what they experience (Buchanan & Hughes, 2009). When African American and European American 11- and 12-year-olds expected to be more involved in risk-taking and rebellious behavior during adolescence, they reported more of these behaviors in the next year than if they had not had these expectations. Likewise, early adolescents who expected to become more alienated from parents reported greater alienation later on. One year later, they reported less close and more conflictual relationships with their parents. They also were more susceptible to peer influence. The same was true for mothers; their perceptions became reality. Children and mothers who expected behaviors to be consistent with the stereotypes of adolescence as a period of storm and stress were more likely to experience those behaviors as the child transitioned to adolescence. This could reflect the fact that a perceptual bias towards the view that storm and stress behaviors are the norm stands a good chance of becoming a self-fulfilling prophecy. Indeed, in her earlier research, Buchanan (2003; Whiteman & Buchanan, 2002) found that general expectations about storm and stress had an influence on adolescents' behavior above and beyond the specific characteristics of the child. To some extent, adolescents behaved in ways that were consistent with their own and their mothers' earlier expectations.

Recently, sociologist Reginald Bibby (2009) reported the results of a decades-long large-scale survey study of 15- to 19-year-old Canadian youth. Every 8 years for over 30 years, he surveyed different cohorts of teenagers on a range of topics that included values, sexuality, their troubles, and global issues. He also surveyed them about their attitudes towards their parents. He found that Canadian youth today reported stronger ties to their parents than any cohort in the past 30 years. The picture that emerged is that adolescence is a time of relative calm and respect for parents. Relatively fewer adolescents than in earlier cohorts (although still over 50%) thought that their parents misunderstood them. Reports of squabbling with parents, although still substantial, also decreased by comparison with findings from earlier cohorts. Bibby's interpretation was that today's parents are doing a better job of parenting. They have become better at balancing careers and families than earlier generations of parents were. They make more time for their children, and their teenagers are happier because of this.

But others have criticized Bibby's "good news" interpretation of these findings. Lisa Belkin, a parenting blogger for the *New York Times*, quotes others, who suggest that today's parents are pushovers (Belkin, 2009, May 14). Belkin believes that, instead of being more competent, parents are more indulgent than earlier generations of parents. They give in to every whim. Teenagers may be happier and enjoy their parents' company more because parents are not doing their job. They are not parenting their children effectively and not holding them to reasonable standards. The emergence of "helicopter parents" is another manifestation of this phenomenon. It provides further support for this more negative interpretation of Bibby's results. Helicopter parenting refers to parents who pay extremely close attention to the successes and failures of their children (typically, college students) and attempt to buffer them from negative experiences. Helicopter parents do not let their children grow up and handle difficult experiences on their own. Instead, these parents inappropriately continue to manage their children's lives right through college.

Anthropological Surveys of Adolescence and Parent–Adolescent Relationships

Reports of conflict and disagreements in parent–adolescent relationships are not limited to Americans, nor are they limited to industrialized countries. Schlegel and Barry (1991) drew on the standard cross-cultural sample of 186 pre-industrial societies worldwide (Murdock & White, 1969; Murdock & Wilson, 1980) to draw conclusions about the variations in adolescent–parent relationships. The societies included in the sample were selected to be broadly representative, and the samples ranged widely in terms of their geographic location, type of subsistence technique and social organization, and level of modernization. Cultures that had a great deal of close contact with other cultures were excluded, so that the effects of cultural diffusion could be minimized. Schlegel and Barry coded these largely ethnographic accounts for different facets of adolescent–parent relationships, which included amount of contact (for instance the proportion of waking time spent together), intimacy, and adolescent–parent conflict. They also examined many other issues pertinent to an understanding of adolescence across cultures.

Several aspects of their findings are illuminating. First, with the exception of girls in one of the societies, all of the cultures in the standard ethnographic sample distinguished a social phase of life for both boys and girls that is distinct from childhood and adulthood. Schlegel (2009) notes that social adolescence has a biological basis, its onset being signaled by the physical signs of puberty. However, the expectations for young people's behavior and the way they are treated during this period differ from the behavior and treatment of younger children and adults. This led her to conclude that a distinct social stage of adolescence, which is separate from both childhood and adulthood, is a constant across cultures for both boys and girls. Schlegel notes: "Its absence rather than its presence requires explanation" (p. 574). Many but not all of the cultures had a specific label for this developmental period. But, according to Schlegel, the absence of a specific term does not negate the social reality of adolescence.

Second, Schlegel and Barry concluded that, overall, the ethnographies indicated that adolescents' relations with family members are generally harmonious – a conclusion that can be drawn about contemporary American families as well (Laursen & Collins, 2009; Smetana, Campione-Barr, & Metzger, 2006). Conflict between generations was found to be widespread, but generally mild in intensity. Again, these findings accord well with what is generally known about conflict in contemporary American families with adolescents. The amount of obedience, deference, or subordination in parent–child relationships in different societies was not associated with either intimacy or the extent of conflict with mothers or fathers.

Nuclear-family households, where husbands and wives live with their unmarried offspring, are the norm in Western societies. But they are not the preferred form in much of the pre-industrial world. Extended family arrangements, where several married couples live together (most typically, married parents and two or more of their adult, married sons and their wives, plus all unmarried children), are more common among tribal people. Households consisting of married parents and an adult child are more common in peasant societies. Schlegel and Barry (1991) had expected to find that there would be less conflict in larger households than in nuclear ones. This is because, in the former, there may be a need to suppress conflict in order to maintain harmony and the father's authority. But this was not the case. Across the wide array of the societies they studied, the type of family structure was not associated with the amount of conflict they experienced.

Schlegel and Barry drew distinctions between antagonism and conflict. Conflict "can often be petty, the bickering or mild disobedience that indicates discordance but not necessarily fear or dislike" (1991, p. 61). In contrast, antagonism does imply fear and dislike and may arise because of different interests of adolescents and parents (for instance in the case of inheritance of property or succession). Specifically addressing the issue of parent–adolescent conflict, Schlegel and Barry wrote:

> The impression one gets from reading many ethnographies is that conflict and antagonism between adolescents and parents in most traditional societies are not, in fact, serious problems. Adolescents do not struggle to individuate themselves from the family to the degree that Western young people do: their dependency on their families, or their spouses', will continue after they reach adulthood, and much of their economic well-being is likely to come from their contribution to group effort rather than from independent action. Nevertheless, conflict and antagonism can arise, so predictably as to be part of the cultural pattern. (Schlegel and Barry, 1991, p. 62)

This cultural pattern varied according to the social organization, including the means of production and control over property. This factor, in turn, determines the extent to which adolescents are required to become independent from their families. Schlegel and Barry's analysis suggested that individuals who move out of their parents' homes, who, in adulthood, are no longer economically dependent on their parents, and who have an extended period of adolescence before they are economically and socially independent experience more conflict with parents. But everyday and often petty disagreements appear to be an inescapable feature of adolescence across a wide variety of cultures. Disagreements and squabbling are not just a characteristic of adolescents and parents in modern North American families; they are found worldwide, and in very different types of families living in diverse circumstances. In this book, I describe adolescent–parent relationships, including conflict, in Western (primarily North American) families and in families from other, non-Western cultures.

Historical Perspectives on Adolescence

Earlier on I noted that adolescents' negative behavior towards their elders has been seen as reflecting a decline in parental authority. This attribution is nothing new. Laursen and Collins (2009) describe Plato's presentation of Socrates' lament about the youth of their day: "They have bad manners, contempt for authority: they show disrespect for their elders and love chatter in place of exercise." More than 2,000 years later, a child development expert formulated a similar concern:

> It must be confessed that an irreverent, unruly spirit has come to be a prevalent, an outrageous evil among the young people of our land [...] Some of the good old people make facetious complaint on this [...] "There is as much family government now as there used to be in our young days," they say, "only it has changed hands." (Cited in Demos & Demos, 1969)

Along with the words attributed to Socrates, this observer's sentiments (if not the language) is very similar to what current commentators like William Bennett are saying about today's youth. Yet this quotation is not from a modern observer. It is a typical example from a child-rearing manual from the period between 1825 and 1859. According to Demos and Demos, these manuals typically stressed the disobedience, licentiousness, and indulgence of youth. A recent *New York Times* article by Parker-Pope (2009, January 26) addressed the same issues. In fact, the point of Parker-Pope's article was that, in contrast to widespread public perception, teenage promiscuity is on the decline. In a *New York Times* blog following the appearance of this article, Judith Warner (2009, January 29) noted that two sociologists interviewed for Parker-Pope's article had to struggle hard to get people "out of their 'moral panic' mindset, and make them understand that teens are not 'in a downward spiral' or 'out of control.' 'They just don't believe you. You might as well be telling them the earth is flat,' the sociologists noted."

The Current Book

As these examples suggest, our feelings about adolescents have been shared by many generations of adults, going back to the ancient Greeks and extending across many different (and diverse) cultures. Why is it that we struggle so hard to understand adolescents? Why is it that they pose such a conundrum for adults of each generation? The answers to these questions are complex and can be answered in many different ways. In this book I provide one set of answers, from the lens of a developmental and constructivist perspective on adolescents' social and psychological development. I consider the mutual influences between parents and adolescents as adolescents move towards adulthood. I draw on anthropological, historical, and sociological sources, but my focus is on detailed psychological analyses of adolescents and their parents. In numerous studies conducted over the past 25 years, my students, colleagues, and I have researched different aspects of adolescent–parent relationships. We listened to the voices of parents and adolescents as they discussed their relationships with each other. We also mulled through piles of questionnaires and watched adolescents and parents as they interacted together, both in my university lab and on their sofas and around their kitchen tables in their homes. We investigated both beliefs about parenting and parenting practices in a wide variety of families. Much of the research discussed in this book focuses on North American families of various ethnicities, but I also draw on a large corpus of research (my own and others') consisting of families from other cultures. Issues of culture and ethnicity are discussed extensively here.

Part of my focus is on the kinds of issues that predominate in parenting books – the disagreements, squabbles, and conflicts that are common in the lives of adolescents and their parents. Why concentrate on some of the difficulties of adolescent–parent relationships? Does examining some of the frustrating and thorny aspects of social life perpetuate stereotypes of adolescence as a challenging developmental period? After all, a number of influential psychologists have called for a new science of positive psychology, which advocates a step away from "repairing the worst things in life" (Seligman & Csikszentmihalyi, 2000, p. 5), to increased focus on "the study of strength and virtue" (p. 7). Does paying attention to the sometimes rocky road to autonomy and adulthood reflect an unwarranted emphasis on negatives, on the difficulties of raising adolescents? Why not deal with the positive sides of adolescence? In a similar vein, some feminist psychologists have asserted that developmental psychologists' tendency to focus on the negative – on aggression, conflict, separation, and strife – betrays male domination in psychology. They argue that a more feminine orientation would focus on the positive aspects of human relationships, including strivings for peace, harmony, compassion, and cohesion.

In my view, we must apply ourselves to both. We must focus on the positive, negative, and grey areas of adolescent–parent relationships, because simple dichotomies do not do justice to the full range of social life – either for the adolescents or for the important adults in their lives. Social life is complex and often convoluted. Interpersonal relationships may entail intense feelings of connection and evidence of cooperation, as well as conflict and disagreements. Autonomy exists – and thrives – in the context of relationships with others. (And I will argue in Chapters 6 and 7 that autonomy is not only a developmental task in Western or individualistic cultures, but is a salient developmental task for youth worldwide.) These conflicting positive and negative feelings and goals can occur in the same relationships at different times, as well as – in varying degrees –in different relationships. And they can be inextricably intertwined in ongoing interactions. For instance, observational and discourse analyses of young children's social interactions have revealed that play that is cooperative and friendly may lead to momentary conflicts over the possession of toys, which in turn involve substantive disagreements over fairness and rights. Such disagreements often are fleeting and may be resolved without intervention from adults. Thus conflict and cooperation may be evident in interactions with the same participants. Likewise, although conflict, oppositions, and disagreements may elicit strong emotions, they do not elicit only negative ones. Various researchers (Dunn, 2006; Shantz & Hartup, 1992) have noted that, although conflicts may be bound up with feelings of anger, fear, or sadness, they may also involve feelings of excitement, satisfaction, or even glee.

In addition, different participants may have very different responses to the same social interaction and, sometimes, not in the way we might anticipate. Laurence Steinberg (2001) conjectures that parents are more bothered by the squabbling that takes place with their offspring during adolescence, and more likely to hold on to their negative emotions after a conflictive interaction, than teenagers are. As he notes, "[t]he popular image of the individual sulking in the wake of a family argument may be a more accurate portrayal of the emotional state of the parent than the teenager" (p. 5).

And, although disagreements and squabbling do seem to be a relatively regular feature of adolescent–parent relationships, it is not the defining feature. The national public opinion survey conducted by Public Agenda, mentioned earlier, also found that the overwhelming majority of the teenagers surveyed reported that they trust their parents to be there when they need them and that they have other grownups besides their parents to go to if they need to talk to an adult. This is very similar to the results of more detailed psychological research asking similar questions, which will be discussed in the next chapter. When asked about their own experiences and feelings, teenagers are connected in important ways to the adults in their lives.

Studying adolescent–parent relationships also sheds light on wider issues of concern to social scientists. It provides broader insights into child development and into the processes that facilitate it. For many years, developmental scientists advanced models of social development that provided a "top down" view of child socialization. Children's development has been described as the acquisition of cultural norms and standards. Parents teach children the norms, values, and expectations of their culture, which are acquired in successive elaborations through parental molding. This process allows for the "reproduction" of culture in succeeding generations. This view suggests that adolescent–parent disagreements are evidence of incomplete socialization – a lack of compliance to parental wishes and a failure to endorse parental values.

This top down model provides a limited view of adolescent–parent relationships and of children's social development more generally. It does not reflect the current thinking of most developmental scientists. The perspective taken in this book reflects a different perspective, one that is embedded in a more interactive and reciprocal view of adolescent social development. My interest is in the different and often conflicting meanings that adolescents and parents construct from their social interactions. These meanings are part and parcel of the different ways in which individuals create their realities and come to understand their social worlds. They can be understood in terms of the different types of social knowledge that adolescents and parents bring to bear on their day-to-day interactions. This perspective is described in detail in Chapter 4 and Chapter 5. It is elaborated in the context of adolescent–parent relationships, but we shall dwell on the broader issues of social development as well.

Before delving in, some definitions are in order. Much has been written about the complexities of defining adolescence. Although the notion seems straightforward, there are ongoing debates about when adolescence actually begins. And it is even more challenging to say with precision where it ends. Adolescence has been defined biologically as the period encompassing the onset of puberty and going on until individuals are capable of sexual reproduction. It has also been defined sociologically as the period when individuals begin training for adult work and family roles. According to this definition, adolescence ends when individuals fully attain adult status and privileges. There are also legal markers of the onset and termination of adolescence (that is, for the attainment of juvenile status, and then of adult status). All of these definitions and specifications are useful to some extent, but they also have limitations, particularly in considering when adolescence concludes. For instance, adolescents are capable of sexual reproduction (and indeed they are at the peak of their fertility and biological readiness for child bearing) well before most of us would feel comfortable about concluding that adolescence has ended. And, increasingly, adoption of adult work and of family roles is delayed well past the twenties and even into the thirties for some youth.

Therefore, along with many other researchers, I adopt a simple chronological definition of adolescence as roughly the period spanning the second decade of life.

A great deal of physical, psychological, and social change occurs during these years, however. Psychologists and practitioners have found it useful to divide this period further, into different phases. In this book I follow those conventions. I refer to ages 11 to 13 as early adolescence. The phrase "middle adolescence" refers here to ages 14 to 17, whereas "late adolescence" refers to ages between 18 and 21. For American readers, this corresponds roughly to adolescents' transitions through different educational institutions (that is, middle school, high school, and, for those going on in higher education, college).

Increasingly, researchers have come to refer to the early and mid-twenties as emerging adulthood. While this is by no means a universal phase of life, for many youth it is the period when transitions to adulthood occur. Schlegel (2009) notes that many cultures worldwide denote a similar second social stage beyond adolescence, often referred to as youth, which provides a transitional link on the route to full adulthood. With these definitions in mind, we begin in the following chapter with a discussion of how adolescent–parent relationships have been viewed historically from the lens of developmental psychology.

2

Studying Adolescent–Parent Relationships from the Lens of Developmental Psychology

Adolescent–parent relationships have been a topic of considerable interest among North American and European developmental psychologists over the past century, and it is instructive to understand how they have conceptualized adolescents' relationships with their parents. The prevailing view has alternated between two extremes. At one extreme, adolescence has been viewed as period of developmental disturbance, and relationships between parents and their teenagers have been seen as characterized by rebellion and conflict. At the other extreme, adolescence has been viewed as a relatively placid period, entailing warm and close relationships. As elaborated upon in this chapter, these dialectical views have been replaced in recent years with more moderate and multidimensional views. These include recognition of the continuity between childhood and adolescence in terms of the overall emotional quality of relationships and awareness that relationships change over the course of adolescence. These views also acknowledge that parent–adolescent relationships are transformed towards greater adolescent autonomy.

G. Stanley Hall's Contributions

The scientific study of adolescence began more than a century ago with the work of G. Stanley Hall. Hall, a professor at Johns Hopkins University and later the President of Clark University, championed the idea of systematic child study as a means of deepening an understanding of human development. His aims were both to inform the public better and to contribute to scientific knowledge (Demos & Demos, 1969). Beginning in the 1880s, Hall began to articulate a theory that

Adolescents, Families, and Social Development: How Teens Construct Their Worlds. Judith G. Smetana
© 2011 Judith G. Smetana

described adolescence in terms of severe crisis and storm and stress. The essence of his arguments was evident in his early writings. In a paper on the moral and religious training of children, Hall stated: "Before this age [12 to 16] the child lives in the present, is normally selfish, deficient in sympathy, but [is] frank and confidential, obedient upon authority" (Hall, 1882, January, p. 44). But, according to Hall, the biological changes of puberty lead to upheaval. He noted that, "[although] pubescent insanity is comparatively rare, the feelings, which are yet more fundamental to mental sanity, are most often perverted, and lack of emotional steadiness, violent and dangerous impulses, unreasonable conduct, lack of enthusiasm and sympathy [ensue]" (p. 45).

Hall and his students continued to elaborate upon these views, a process that culminated in the publication, in 1904, of his encyclopedic work, *Adolescence: Its psychology, and its relations to physiology, anthropology, sociology, sex, crime, religion, and education*. As the title suggests, this two-volume work created a grand theory of adolescence. Hall's views were strongly informed by Darwinism and by an evolutionary (and genetic) point of view. According to him, development can be described in terms of a series of stages. These stages involve recapitulations; each individual progresses through the different epochs that characterize the evolution of the species. Adolescence occupied a special position in this developmental history of the individual, as it was seen to recapitulate the most recent developmental advances of civilization. Standing on the brink of future achievements for the species, adolescence was seen as the most malleable developmental period and one with enormous potential for growth and change. In Hall's words, "early adolescence is thus the infancy of man's higher nature, when he receives […] his last capital of energy and evolutionary momentum" (1904, Vol. 2, p. 71). At the same time, Hall believed that adolescence was a time of significant and continual upheaval, characterized by many contradictory impulses, personality traits, and conflicts. In the physical realm, these conflicts were characterized by periods of extreme exertion and energy, which alternated with periods of fatigue and apathy. In the psychological realm, Hall asserted that adolescents vacillate between selfishness and altruism, vanity and self-doubt, virtue and vice, sensitivity and imperturbability, curiosity and lack of interest. These conflicting impulses were seen as partly biological, but they also were "suggestive of some ancient period of storm and stress" (Vol. 1, p. xiii). These were universal features of adolescence that had their origins in biological and evolutionary processes.

Hall acknowledged that individual differences and the immediate environment could influence the expression of storm and stress. "In short, the previous selfhood is broken up like the regulation copy handwriting of early school years, and a new individual is in the process of crystallization. All is solvent, plastic, peculiarly susceptible to external influences" (Hall, 1882, January, p. 45). In fact, Hall viewed the storm and stress of American society at the turn of the twentieth century as being aggravated by growing urbanization. He railed against what he perceived as its dangers.

Never has youth been exposed to such dangers of both perversion and arrest as in our own land and day. Increasing urban life with its temptations, prematurities, sedentary occupations, and passive stimuli [...] the mad rush for sudden wealth and the reckless fashions set by it's [*sic*] gilded youth – all these lack some of the regulatives they still have in older lands with more conservative traditions. (Hall, 1904, Vol. 1, pp. xvii–xviii)

Beyond the florid language, Hall's notions were a reflection of the thinking and beliefs of the time, which he amplified and to which he gave broader exposure and scientific legitimacy. His work captured the public imagination – even though, in the evaluation of at least one family historian, the work was "feverish, recondite, and at times, incomprehensible" (Kett, 1977, p. 6). According to several social historians (Demos & Demos, 1969; Modell & Goodman, 1990), Hall integrated those popular beliefs with the most exciting and novel ideas in science (primarily, evolutionary theory) and presented his own ideas persuasively, both to scientists and to the lay public. Most importantly, Hall popularized the notion of adolescence as a discrete developmental period. His work was read widely, and it broadly influenced psychology, education, child rearing, and books on religious training and vocational guidance. Although numerous prominent psychologists quickly came to reject many of his most central ideas (particularly the physiological orientation of his stages), his portrayal of adolescence as a period of storm and stress has had a lasting impact on how adolescence is perceived.

Contributions of Psychoanalytic and Neo-Psychoanalytic Theory

Notions of adolescence as a developmental phase of storm and stress were also advanced from the somewhat different perspective of psychoanalytic and neo-psychoanalytic theory. At the same time as Hall, and at the turn of twentieth century, Sigmund Freud (1953) challenged the conventional wisdom of the day by his provocative assertion that human sexuality begins in infancy, not at puberty. Freud located what he viewed as the most significant intrapsychic conflict for personality and moral development – the Oedipal crisis – in early childhood development. With this principle well established within psychoanalytic circles, Anna Freud, Freud's daughter, focused on the "upheaval in the psychic life" (1966, p. 138) that she believed occurred during adolescence. In her view, the conflicts that are aroused by puberty had received inadequate attention in her father's theory.

Like other psychoanalytic writers, Anna Freud believed in the crucial role of early infantile sexuality in development. However, she linked infantile sexuality and pubertal maturation, viewing them as similar in that they both were a source of intense intrapsychic conflicts entailing "a relatively strong id confront[ing] a relatively weak ego" – or, stated more strongly, a "vigorous" id encountering an "enfeebled" ego (1966, p. 140). For Anna Freud, pubertal maturation entails a recapitulation of infantile sexuality. That is, it leads to a resurgence of sexual impulses, accompanied by a reawakening of Oedipal desires that lay dormant during the earlier period – one of latency. She described the resurgence of these impulses as leading to intrapsychic storm and stress.

Anna Freud postulated that adolescence differs from the earlier Oedipal conflict in terms of the defense mechanisms that adolescents bring to bear on their unruly instincts. In describing various defense mechanisms that are prominent during adolescence, she subordinated both cognitive and emotional development to adolescents' attempts to gain control over their sexual impulses. Those defense mechanisms included increased asceticism, which secures the control of the ego over the id, as well as intellectualization. If not used in excess, these defense mechanisms provide adaptive ways of deflecting the force of sexual impulses. And they also provide a way of handling the problematic nature of adolescents' fixation on their parents, the primary love objects of childhood.

Consistent with psychoanalytic theory, Anna Freud believed that, prior to puberty, children harbor incestuous fantasies towards their parents. As Oedipal feelings resurface during adolescence, incestuous feelings towards parents give way to feelings of antagonism, resulting inevitably in adolescent–parent conflict. Therefore conflict and rebellion were considered necessary to resolve these Oedipal feelings towards parents successfully. Distancing oneself from parents accomplishes the dual goal of resolving Oedipal feelings and of facilitating adolescents' move towards more acceptable love objects. Resolution of these conflicts gives rise to new, initially "passionate," "evanescent" and fickle romantic relationships, which pave the way towards more adult romantic attachments. Central to Anna Freud's theory is the view that this process results in a period of inevitable developmental disturbance: "I have so often compared the peculiar characteristics of that period with the phenomena of grave disease" (1966, p. 171). Freud viewed adolescent–parent conflict as both inevitable and healthy for adolescent development. Furthermore, she proposed that healthy emotional autonomy entails separation or detachment from parents, a notion that has been perpetuated in popular views of adolescence.

Neo-psychoanalytic theorists further elaborated upon Anna Freud's views. The most prominent among them was Peter Blos (1962, 1979). Like her, Blos viewed development during adolescence as a recapitulation of childhood intrapsychic conflicts brought about by the biological changes of puberty. In contrast to Freud, however, Blos focused more on the adaptive functions of conflict, treating adolescence as a "second individuation period" (Blos, 1967, p. 162). Blos believed that important distinctions between self and non-self are made during early childhood. During adolescence, these issues are revisited in a more complex form – a process resulting in the achievement of a sense of identity. However, the route to identity, according to Blos, is through "oppositional, rebellious, and resistive strivings, the stages of experimentation, the testing of the self by going to excess" (Blos, 1962, p. 12). This is necessary and useful in defining a mature self.

Blos further posited that, in order to cope with the stress arising from the biological changes of puberty, adolescents must detach themselves from parents and channel their libidinal impulses in the form of sexual relations with peers. In his view, adolescents must give up their infantile love objects (the parents) in favor of new love objects (peer romantic partners). Thus, like Anna Freud, he viewed detachment from parents as necessary to the individuation process. However, the notion that this process results in a less idealized and more realistic view of parents was central to Blos's theorizing. He stated:

> While previously the parent was overvalued, considered with awe, and not realistically assessed, he now becomes undervalued, and is seen to have the shabby proportions of a fallen idol. The narcissistic self-inflation shows up in the adolescent's arrogance and rebelliousness, in his defiance of rules, and in his flouting of the parent's authority. (Blos, 1962, p. 91)

Therefore Blos regarded the rudeness, disrespect, and bad manners that scholars and commentators have attributed to adolescents since Socrates' time as characteristic of development. Such a conception reflects a transition towards a more realistic view of parents. Blos considered that separation and emotional distancing from parents facilitate the development of sexual attachments in late adolescence and young adulthood. He focused less on the behavioral storminess of this period and more on the ways in which individuation proceeds. Changes in adolescents' views of parents (like those just described) and of the self give rise to a unified and integrated self-system. Such a system facilitates adolescent individuation and resolves questions of identity. (These ideas were further expanded in Erik Erikson's notions of adolescence as a period of inevitable crisis entailing the resolution of fundamental issues of identity.) Furthermore, Blos, like Freud, viewed these processes as being inevitable. Those who experienced a conflict-free adolescence were described as being immature or as delaying the developmental tasks of adolescence. As he put it, "[s]ome children do not experience any conflict in relation to their parents; they have either repressed the sexual drive, or else their drive endowment is low and therefore the ego possesses the capacity to master it" (p. 76).

Although their theories differed in some important ways, Freud, Blos, and Hall all believed that youthful rebellion and conflict with parents were normal, regular features of adolescence. Such features were seen as psychological manifestations of the biological changes of puberty. These theorists also viewed the nature of adolescent–parent relationships as fundamentally discontinuous with that of childhood. The type of relationship children had with parents prior to adolescence could not be expected to predict the quality of those relationships in adolescence. Children who were good-natured and even-tempered were supposed to develop into moody, unpredictable, and contentious adolescents. Not only was this normal and expected, but conflict and rebellion were desired. This represented the course of healthy development and separation from parents.

Blos's and Freud's theories were derived from basic tenets of psychoanalysis. As with other psychoanalytic theories, empirical validation for these views was sought in the case studies of patients in therapy. And, while Hall did conduct research, it was largely unsystematic. It was collected from parents who were acquainted with his views through reading. All these theories painted a disturbing portrait of adolescent development in the family, and they continue to have an enormous impact on popular views of adolescence. They were not, however, immediately tested through systematic research focusing on samples of typically developing youth. Initially, psychologists who sought to examine these ideas conducted their research by using psychiatric patients or juvenile delinquents. The assumption was that findings from deviant groups would generalize to normal teenagers and would present the same basic conflicts as more clinical samples (Offer, Ostrov, & Howard, 1981).

Survey Studies of Adolescent–Parent Relationships

These assumptions have not proven to be valid. Community samples of families differ in their patterns of parent–adolescent relationships and conflict from samples of families who have been identified as having, and are in treatment for, psychological problems. They also differ from samples of families of adolescents experiencing behavior problems. Not surprisingly, clinically referred families have higher rates of conflict, and they demonstrate dominance and less communicative clarity than families drawn from community samples (Jacob, 1975; Prinz, Foster, Kent, & O'Leary, 1979; Robin & Foster, 1989).

High levels of adolescent–parent conflict have been consistently associated with poor psychosocial adjustment for adolescents, as assessed on a wide range of outcomes. These include externalizing behaviors such as marijuana and alcohol use, delinquency, early onset of sexual relationships or promiscuity, and running away from home. Highly conflictive or disrupted adolescent–parent relationships also are implicated in depression and suicide attempts. However, this does not necessarily mean that intense conflict always leads to poor outcomes for youth. Careful analyses using longitudinal data show that associations between adolescent–parent conflict and adolescent behavior problems are bi-directional (Maggs & Galambos, 1993). Adolescent–parent conflict predicts problem behaviors, but adolescent problem behaviors also predict subsequent conflict with parents, controlling for prior levels of conflict. Therefore, although severe or frequent conflict may adversely affect adolescent development, adolescent behavior problems also affect family functioning.

Eventually, the methodological problems inherent in generalizing from clinically referred families to the wider population were recognized. Accordingly, in the 1960s and 1970s, a number of large-scale research studies employing much more representative samples of adolescents were initiated. These studies attempted to test the notions of storm and stress promulgated by neo-analytic theorists. The focus of the research and the choice of questions also reflected concerns arising at that time about "the generation gap" and about adolescent alienation from adult society. The 1960s and 1970s in American culture were a time of significant societal change and disruption. This included student revolts on college campuses, youthful opposition to the Vietnam War, and significant societal debate and struggles over civil rights. It is no wonder, then, that researchers were concerned with whether adolescents were rejecting their parents' moral, religious, and political values and creating a distinct and separate youth culture. This was an idea that sociologist J. S. Coleman (1961) had proposed in his earlier and highly cited writings. On the basis of an extensive study of 10 American high schools, Coleman argued that the age segregation of American schooling has led to the rise of a separate peer culture that strongly influences adolescent development. For instance, Coleman asserted that peer culture, with its disdain for academic success, leads adolescents in the wrong direction (that is, away from academic achievement and towards problem behavior).

The findings of several large-scale and largely atheoretical studies contradicted the assertions of the psychoanalytic and neo-analytic theorists. They also pushed the pendulum in the other direction. These studies found that, for the majority of adolescents, extreme alienation from parents, intergenerational conflict, and youthful rebellion were the exception. Close, warm, and supportive family relations during adolescence were the norm. For instance, in a questionnaire study, Douvan and Adelson (1966) examined the attitudes of approximately 3,500 American teenage boys who were primarily 14 to 16 years old (girls, who ranged from 6th to 12th grade, were interviewed in a separate study). These researchers found that middle adolescents generally admired and trusted their parents. They believed that their parents' rules were, for the most part, fair and just. Adolescents not only agreed with their parents but also looked to them for advice. Douvan and Adelson's widely cited research, like a great deal of other research, has shown that adolescents and their parents agree on basic values.

Likewise, in their comparative study of nearly 2,000 mother–adolescent dyads in the United States and Denmark, Kandel and Lesser (1972) sought to examine the validity of Coleman's idea of a distinct youth culture and of the broader notions of alienation and generation gap. They investigated different spheres of adolescents' lives – peer relationships, schooling, and family relations. Their analyses were quite detailed and focused primarily on comparisons between the two cultural contexts. In the family sphere, the results were clear-cut. The majority of American and Danish adolescents sampled reported that their relationships with both mothers and fathers were either "very close" or "quite close" and that they depended "very much" or "quite a bit" on their parents for advice. A smaller but still substantial proportion of the teenagers sampled indicated that they talked over "most" or "all" of their problems with their mothers (and less than a quarter of American and Danish adolescents responded in kind about their fathers). Kandel and Lesser also found some differences between their Danish and their American teenagers; these included greater emphasis in the United States than in Denmark on the teenagers' responsibility to and reliance on the family. The researchers attributed this difference to a longer period of adolescent dependency in American than in Danish families.

Finally, in a landmark investigation, Michael Rutter and his colleagues (Rutter, Graham, Chadwick, & Yule, 1976) combined an epidemiological study of parents and teachers in the entire population of 2,303 adolescents on the Isle of Wight in Great Britain with more intensive studies of smaller, selective samples of adolescents. These studies included a random community sample of middle adolescents, as well as a small sample of adolescents who were identified as having deviant scores on the behavioral questionnaires. Rutter and his colleagues found that the majority of parents approved of their adolescents' friends. Moreover, parents reported very little adolescent alienation or withdrawal. (This was examined in terms of whether adolescents physically withdrew to their rooms, stayed out of the house, or just did not do things with the family.) Nearly a quarter of the number of parents reported that they had experienced some emotional withdrawal on the part of their adolescent children, or had difficulties "getting through" to their teens. For the most part, though, parents who reported difficulties indicated that these difficulties and poor relationships were present prior to adolescence. Therefore the two researchers concluded that parent–adolescent alienation was a myth.

The findings from Douvan and Adelson, Kandel and Lesser, and Rutter and his colleagues' detailed studies have been frequently and appropriately cited as stressing the closeness of parent–adolescent relationships. This research was widely seen, both then and now, as refuting the claim that parent–adolescent relationships are normally rebellious and marked by intense conflicts with parents. Rather, these authors concluded that having intense conflicts during adolescence was not the obligatory path. Adolescents who experienced high levels of conflict had had problems earlier in development. This contradicted the claim that development during adolescence is discontinuous with that of childhood. Later reviews of this research have emphasized the usually close, warm, and supportive nature of teenagers' relationships with parents. They also stress the continuities in the quality of relationships between childhood and the second decade of life. But each of these researchers presented a more complex and varied view of adolescent–parent relationships than more recent reviews of their work have acknowledged.

For instance, among their many findings, Douvan and Adelson (1966) reported that the youngest adolescent girls in their sample typically displayed a childlike dependence and submission towards their parents, which changed, with age, towards greater assertion and independence. Douvan and Adelson also found that many teenagers reported having disagreements with parents about such issues as choice of clothing, dating, and being allowed to go out. They described parent–teen disagreements as occurring in waves or arcs that peak at different ages, reflecting the growth of autonomy during adolescence. Among early adolescent girls (the researchers did not have a comparable sample of early adolescent boys), disagreements about clothing and personal grooming predominated; then they declined with age. Disagreements about dating, choice of friends, and driving in cars tended to arise, prevail, and become resolved during the middle adolescent years. Late adolescence was characterized by conflicts over ideology. Douvan and Adelson also found few differences in family functioning, parental authority, or use of discipline among girls who had reported low, moderate, and high proportions of disagreement with their parents. Therefore they viewed these types of parent–adolescent disagreements as an obligatory feature of family relationships. Such features would reflect the development of autonomy during adolescence. However, the two authors did not approach parents so as to obtain their views.

In their study of Danish and American youth, Kandel and Lesser (1972), too, found significant areas of disagreement between the generations. Adolescents placed more importance on their involvement in peer groups and less importance on their families than mothers thought they should. Mothers and youth in the two cultures did not differ in their long-term goals (for instance, the importance of attaining a college education). They did differ, however, on the importance of the immediate steps that needed to be taken to attain those goals. Adolescents placed less importance than their mothers wished on participating in activities or on engaging in schoolwork that could be seen as preparation for these future goals. And, like in more recent research, Kandel and Lesser found that, for some issues but not for others, teenagers relied on their parents or friends for advice. Teenagers sought advice from their friends regarding personal problems and friendship issues, whereas they relied on their parents (and particularly on their mothers) for advice on career issues, morals, and values. On the basis of these results, Kandel and Lesser rejected the notion of a separate peer culture, which entails a rejection of the values of adult society. Instead, they found that whether teenagers looked to parents and peers for advice depended on the type of issue and on the cultural context.

Rutter also found that adolescent–parent relationships were characterized by "minor disagreements or clashes between parents and adolescents on mundane day-to-day issues involving hair length, clothes, music, and time to be in at night" (Rutter, 1980, p. 33). These disagreements were present in a substantial minority of families – ranging from a quarter to a third (for boys and girls respectively) for disagreements over clothing to approximately one half for disagreements over choice of hairstyles. These numbers closely paralleled the findings from another large-scale community study, conducted in Great Britain (Fogelman, 1976, as reported in Rutter, 1980). Rutter and his colleagues concluded:

Alienation from parents is *not* common in 14-year-olds, although it is probably more frequent by the late teens. Most young teenagers continue to be influenced by their parents and get on quite well with them. Most adolescents are *not* particularly critical of their parents, and very few reject them. On the other hand, although still occurring in only half the group or less, petty disagreements about clothes, hair and going out are reasonably common. Some of these disagreements may get quite heated and many adolescents would like their parents to be less strict. Even so, most continue to share their parents' values on other things and respect the need for restrictions and control. (Rutter et al., 1976, p. 40)

Researchers eagerly embraced the evidence showing that there is significant continuity in relationships from childhood to adolescence, that teenagers are not alienated from, or reject, most of adults' values or society, and that teenagers love and admire their parents. Other findings from this study have received less attention. In spite of the conclusion that alienation is not typical of adolescence, Rutter and his colleagues did uncover a surprising prevalence of unhappiness in their community sample of teenagers – unhappiness that was not evident in parents' and teachers' reports. The researchers conducted psychiatric interviews with a subsample of adolescents from the larger study. These revealed that nearly half of the subsample, with no differences between boys and girls, reported some significant degree of misery or unhappiness. Moreover, the proportion of teenagers who reported feeling sad or depressed was far greater than the proportion of teenagers whom psychiatrists identified as looking sad, anxious, or unhappy at the end of their clinical interviews. Rutter and his colleagues concluded that the unhappiness and anxiety expressed in the interviews achieved clinical levels of depression for only a small minority of these teens. The incidence of psychiatric disorders in the subsample was small and consistent with prevalence rates found at other ages. Nevertheless, these findings led Rutter and his colleagues to conclude that "inner turmoil," as indicated by feelings of misery and self-depreciation, is in fact quite common during adolescence.

Other contemporaneous researchers also disagreed with the completely rosy picture of adolescent–parent relationships drawn by Douvan and Adelson (1966), Kandel and Lesser (1972), and Rutter and colleagues (1976). Offer questioned their positive interpretation, stating:

This infighting is over issues that seem small or undramatic [...] adolescents of this generation do not rebel against the entrenched important values of the parents' generation. [Other] investigators say therefore the rebellion is insignificant. It is true that the rebellion we observe is microscopic in size as to the content of the issues; and it may easily seem to the adult outsider, especially if he happens to be a reformer as well as an observer, that the whole phenomenon is trivial and has no importance; that it connotes a complacency, conformity, and loss of autonomy or identity in the adolescent, terms that are more or less vaguely defined. We emphasize that the rebellion has vital and important meaning to the adolescent in this stage of his development. Even though violent emotions are not involved, the same emancipation is at stake as for the adolescent who proceeds in a more tumultuous manner. (Offer, 1969, p. 186)

These classic studies of adolescent–parent conflict in community samples of families may have underestimated the prevalence of adolescent–parent disagreements and conflicts, because the survey methods relied on the global assessment of family closeness, intergenerational tension, or independence. The research of the 1960s and 1970s did not examine actual family interactions, nor did its authors obtain detailed accounts of relationships in daily life.

The "New Look" on Adolescent–Parent Relationships

These studies led to further research during the 1980s and 1990s, which brought more detailed, intensive, and sophisticated methods to the study of adolescent–parent relationships. In contrast to the large-scale survey studies of previous decades, researchers brought to bear a variety of different methods. These included a more rigorous application of standardized measures as well as observational techniques, theoretically informed interviews, and time-sampling methods. This has resulted in a more moderate perspective, touted by Laurence Steinberg (1990) as a "new look" on adolescent–parent relationships. The "new look" contrasts with the psychoanalytic and neo-psychoanalytic perspectives of Anna Freud and Peter Blos, but is consistent with the survey studies of Douvan and Adelson (1966) and of Kandel and Lesser (1972). This perspective recognized that, during adolescence, emotional bonds between parents and children typically are maintained. However, the focus of the "new look" perspective was on the readjustments and realignments of family relationships that take place during adolescence.

This newer research shows that adolescents do not detach or fully separate from parents, as earlier researchers had claimed. However, most adolescents experience some decline in their feelings of warmth, support, and emotional closeness to parents (and also to grandparents) as they move through adolescence (Furman & Buhrmester, 1985, 1992). Relationships improve slightly once adolescents leave home. This decline in closeness to parents is accompanied by increasingly close, supportive relationships with same-sex friends and, later on in adolescence, with romantic partners. Teenagers come to rely less on parents and more on their friends and peers for emotional support. Although there is, overall, a decline in the level of warmth, support, and closeness to parents, these bonds are highly stable over time. Youth who reported feeling closer to their parents earlier in adolescence tend to feel closer as they leave adolescence (Smetana, Metzger, & Campione-Barr, 2004). They also report better psychological well-being, feelings of competence, higher academic performance, and increased self-reliance.

The "new look" suggested that teenagers rely on their parents for advice about their future. Parents remain a source of support throughout the teenage years. Yet a significant proportion of American adolescents and of their parents also experience minor but persistent bickering, squabbling, and conflict over mundane issues of family life. This was confirmed by several descriptive studies conducted during the 1980s. For instance, Raymond Montemayor (1983) noted that adolescents' conflicts with parents rarely occurred over "hot" topics such as religion, politics, sex, or drugs. Instead, he concluded, conflicts primarily pertained to everyday family issues such as schoolwork, social life and friends, general disobedience, chores, personal hygiene and appearance, and disagreements with siblings. So, despite changes in family life, Montemayor noted that "adolescents appear to have the same kinds of disagreements with their parents that their parents had when they, themselves, were adolescents" (p. 92). In turn, this suggests that, when adolescents become parents, their views on these issues change.

Bickering and disagreements do appear to increase both in frequency and in intensity during adolescence. Statistical analyses of the results of numerous research studies have clarified the developmental trends. Laursen, Coy, and Collins (1998) conducted a meta-analysis, which aggregates the samples and findings from the available studies to determine the robust trends. They examined the rate or frequency of conflict (that is, how many conflicts were registered and how often they occurred over a specified period, for instance the previous 2 weeks or 2 months) and their affective intensity (how "hot" they were). When examined across studies, these researchers determined that the frequency of parent–child conflict peaks in early adolescence and then slowly declines, with small decreases found at middle adolescence and again at late adolescence. These patterns were maintained when different family dyads (for instance, mother–son and mother–daughter) were examined separately. In contrast, conflicts between parents and their adolescents, and particularly between fathers and children, were found to increase in emotional intensity and negativity from early to middle adolescence and then to decline to a level somewhat higher than at early adolescence. Therefore the general picture that emerges is that parent–adolescent conflict occurs most frequently – but is not affectively very charged – in early adolescence. Conflicts become more heated – but less frequent – in middle adolescence. Conflict declines even more in frequency in late adolescence, but does not change substantially in "heat" or affective intensity from middle to late adolescence. Of course, this meta-analysis paid heed to the studies that had been done up to that point, which primarily included families of North American origin and families of middle-class European background.

Thus, according to the "new look," everyday disagreements between parents and teenagers are normal temporary perturbations that help to transform parent–adolescent relationships. They may lead to changes in the power balance of the family. In the 1980s and 1990s, researchers conducted detailed observations of family interactions to document these changes in family dynamics, sometimes as a function of adolescents' physical development. For instance, one claim was that, as adolescents went through the biological changes of puberty, parents would respond in new ways to teens' greater stature and physical maturity. In consequence, researchers intensively observed the quality of family interactions among teenagers at different stages of pubertal development. Studies by John Hill and Grayson Holmbeck (Hill, 1988; Hill & Holmbeck, 1987; Holmbeck, 1996), as well as by Laurence Steinberg (1987), indicated that conflicts increase as teenagers reach the peak of pubertal maturation. Before puberty, fathers occupy a more dominant position than mothers, who are, in turn, more dominant than their sons. As puberty progresses, though, adolescent boys become more dominant. They switch places with their mothers in terms of power in the family. After puberty fathers still remain dominant, but their mature male offspring sit just beneath them in the family dominance hierarchy. Mothers are less dominant than their post-pubertal sons. These types of findings led researchers to propose that increased disagreements and conflict are adaptive because they change the power balance of the family. They make disagreements overt, which, in turn, leads to increased adolescent autonomy and readjustments in family relationships.

A New Look at The "New Look"

In the 1990s, several new trends emerged in research on adolescent–parent relationships (and in research on adolescent development more generally). One is that there was an increasing recognition that the available research was limited in terms of the samples studied. The focus had been largely on European American (or European) middle-class families and only rarely on families from other cultures or ethnic minority groups in the United States. This recognition led to a shift towards studying more diverse populations of youth. Assumptions about studying culture and ethnicity and cultural as well as ethnic variations in development are discussed here in Chapters 7 and 8.

In addition to considering social development in a broader range of cultures, researchers also began to study adolescents across a range of neighborhoods and socioeconomic status backgrounds. Studying psychological risk among youth living in poverty is nothing new. But in the past several decades increased attention has been paid to how adolescents cope with adversity and to factors related to resilience. In addition, youth from lower-class backgrounds have been compared to adolescents growing up in affluent neighborhoods. The startling result from this research is that, although children who grow up in very prosperous neighborhoods clearly are privileged in some respects, they also face elevated risks for adjustment difficulties, including substance use, anxiety, and depression. Indeed, the risks are as great among affluent youth as among teens growing up in serious poverty. Affluent and poor youth are similar rather than different in terms of experiencing parents as sometimes emotionally and physically unavailable

(Luthar & Latendresse, 2005a, b). As these examples suggest, research on adolescents and their families has expanded greatly in its scope. There has been much greater consideration of diversity, and hence of the universal and relative features of adolescent development.

The greater focus on diversity was accompanied by a shift towards a much greater concern with and appreciation of the contexts of development. Adolescents and their parents live in particular neighborhoods, which may be serene or unsafe. This has implications for parenting and for the types of opportunities afforded to adolescents, as well as for the types of opportunities that parents may allow. Parents may work in stressful or supportive environments (or may be laid off and looking for work). Different work environments may influence their resources, their parenting, and their availability, as we have just seen.

At the same time, researchers have become much more attuned to the different relationships and mutual influences among different subsystems of the family. Adolescents interact differently with their mothers from the way they interact with their fathers; each relationship has its own dynamic. Then, apart from the relationship with their offspring, parents also have a separate bond and identity as a couple. The overall quality of this relationship, as well as its ups and downs, may influence the parents' responsiveness to their teens and the emotional quality of their bonding with the latter. Adolescents may be much more successful at negotiating greater privileges (and they may have different perceptions of how to handle conflict) if parents are in a warm, communicative partnership than if they are embroiled in conflict. In addition, a mother's or a father's relationship with one child in the family may be very different from the quality of their interactions with the other children in the family. As we shall see, being the first born (rather than the second or third) may have consequences for adolescent development. And developmental scientists also have begun to expand their notions of "family" and to consider differences in how families are constituted. Families may consist of two parents (married or unmarried, gay or straight) and their offspring, but they may also be single parents, multigenerational families (including grandparents raising children), or families with extended kin.

Finally, the view of adolescent–parent relationships has shifted yet again towards a somewhat more complex, but decidedly more pessimistic view. This shift originates in several sources in the psychological research literature. One source is the detailed portrait of the lives of middle-class families painted by psychologists Reed Larson and Maryse Richards (1994) in their book *Divergent realities: The emotional lives of mothers, fathers, and adolescents*. This volume describes the results of research conducted on nearly 500 working- and middle-class suburban early adolescents and on an additional, smaller family sample consisting of mother, father, and adolescent triads. The authors used a method of experience sampling. Research participants carried pagers for a week and were paged at random intervals during that week. When receiving a signal, participants were instructed to complete survey forms asking for information on what they were doing and thinking about before and at the moment of the signal and how they felt about it. This methodology garnered over 7,000 reports of daily experience.

Larson and Richards's findings pointed to how "out of sync" different family members are with each other. In their words,

> each family member comes home each night to a different "family." Mothers, fathers, and adolescent children experience dissimilar families – interacting, conflicting, tugging at each other [...] Present[ing] a postmodern image of family life composed of multiple, contending realities. (Larson and Richards, 1994, pp. vii–viii)

As found in earlier research using the experience sampling method (Csikszentmihalyi & Larson, 1984), mothers and adolescents in Larson and Richards's study were found to spend very little time together, interacting directly. And mothers, Larson and Richards reported, spent more time being engaged with their children directly than fathers do. Fathers spend remarkably little time alone with their teenagers, and most of this time is in the presence of mothers. If shared time is an indicator of relationship quality, Larson and Richards suggest that adolescents and parents have little opportunity for "quality time." More often, mothers and adolescents spent time together being engaged in different activities (for instance, mothers do housework while adolescents watch TV or play a game) or being together in the same physical space but not attending to each other (for instance, teenagers listen to music with headphones on). In the study, mothers often interpreted such episodes as time spent together, but teenagers frequently did not.

More importantly, when mothers and adolescents were together, their emotional experiences of their interactions differed. Larson and Richards found that, prior to adolescence (for instance in 5th grade), children generally report positive and uncomplicated feelings towards their mothers. But entering adolescence was associated with changes in subjective emotional experiences, which diverged considerably from those of pre-adolescence. Teens reported having a more mixed set of emotions when they were with their mothers. Although their feelings were still positive, they reported less warmth, friendliness, and happiness and more negative emotions. There was a clear deterioration in the mother–adolescent relationship. The two researchers attributed this phenomenon, in part, to the increased enjoyment that adolescents begin to take in being with their peers, but also to conflict over what adolescents increasingly perceive to be their parents' capricious and arbitrary rules. Thus tensions arose between adolescents' desires and parents' rules. This tendency was coupled with the adolescents' increased ability to see their parents as ordinary (and sometimes fallible) people rather than as omnipotent. Such perceptions, in turn, led to feelings of closeness that were rather conditional and situation-specific.

The adolescents' emotional states also diverged significantly both from the mothers' and from the fathers' emotional experiences in the same situations. Regardless of the children's age, fathers tended to report positive experiences when they spent time with their teenage children, even though their children did not. In Larson and Richards's words: "What this means is that Dad is often having a good time, but the teenager is not" (1994, p. 172). These discrepancies were evident both in the boys' and in the girls' relationships with their parents. Yet fathers were less positive when they interacted with their daughters than when they interacted with their sons. Girls reported feeling unhappy when they interacted with fathers, and more so than boys did. Likewise, mothers' emotional states did not differ as their children moved into adolescence. However, adolescents' moods worsened, which led to an increasing disparity between mothers' and adolescents' emotional experience of their relationships. Mothers reported both positive and negative emotions when they were with their children. They experienced frustration and irritability when they had to cope with apathetic or obstinate teenagers.

This latter point is echoed in other research findings, based on studies that focus on parents' experiences in parenting adolescents. In his influential early study, Daniel Offer noted:

> the great majority of the parents say that the early adolescent years (twelve to fourteen) are the most difficult time they have in raising their children [...] The adolescent becomes a general irritant to the parents. (Offer, 1969, pp. 186–187)

Although Offer's provocative claim has not been extensively researched, several studies have confirmed his observation. For instance, in studying primarily American white middle-class parent–adolescent dyads, Cornell University researchers Small, Eastman, and Cornelius (1988) found that parents reported that parenting an adolescent is stressful. This was particularly true for inexperienced parents (that is, parents of first borns, as compared to parents of later born children). It was also true for parents of early adolescents as compared to parents of older and younger children. More detailed analyses also revealed that the factors that led to stress differed somewhat for mothers and fathers. Fathers reported higher levels of stress when adolescents did not heed to their advice and when adolescents were involved in deviant activities. Mothers, on the other hand, reported higher levels of stress as a result of adolescents' desires for greater autonomy.

A later research study by Susan Silverberg and Laurence Steinberg (1990) found that entrance into adolescence was related to a variety of negative effects on the parents. (In this study entrance was measured both biologically, through more advanced pubertal maturation, and socially, through greater involvement in mixed-sex peer group activities and dating.) Parents expressed more mid-life concerns, reported lower life satisfaction, and described more frequent psychological symptoms of depressed mood, feelings of tension, and similar problems. These scholars hypothesized that the extent to which parents focused their lives around their teenagers, as opposed to focusing on having a fulfilling career, would influence the way they experience these changes in their teenagers. As they expected, the researchers found that the negative effects of parenting a teenager were more pronounced for parents who were not strongly invested in their paid work roles. They also found more negative effects for mothers of daughters than for mothers of sons.

Silverberg and Steinberg originally studied children ranging in age from 10 to 15 years old. They also followed this sample longitudinally over the course of a year. The boys' emotional autonomy predicted more intense mid-life identity conflicts in fathers. However, the fathers' identity conflicts did not predict the boys' emotional autonomy. For mothers, the effects were bi-directional. Mothers who reported more conflict with their daughters when they entered the study had more depressed moods and showed more psychological symptoms one year later. But it was also the case that mothers who expressed more intense mid-life identity concerns when they were first assessed reported more mother–daughter conflict later on. Thus conflict influenced, and was in turn affected by, mothers' well-being.

Findings such as these have led others to re-evaluate earlier positions on storm and stress. For instance, in an article titled "Adolescent storm and stress, reconsidered," Jeffrey Arnett (1999) noted that scholars have rejected this notion and treat it as a myth. Yet, as the title of the article suggests, Arnett argued for the appropriateness of the description of adolescence as a period of storm and stress. He proposed that researchers reconsider the notion. Arnett defined storm and stress as encompassing the idea that adolescence is a difficult period of life; that adolescence is a more difficult time than previous or later developmental periods; and that adolescence is troublesome not only for adolescents but also for the people around them. Arnett pointed to three potential elements whose presence might indicate increased storm and stress during adolescence. These were: increased conflict with parents; increased emotional volatility and mood swings (an element drawn primarily from Larson and Richards's 1994 book); and increased involvement in risk behaviors. Arnett concluded that, on all three dimensions, recent evidence supports the notion of storm and stress. Although his case – particularly regarding adolescent–parent conflict – may be somewhat overstated, the evidence does suggest that the pendulum has tilted again towards a more negative view of adolescence.

In a similar vein, in his presidential address to the Society for Research on Adolescence, Laurence Steinberg (2001, p. 5) concluded:

> I now question the wisdom of the assertion that the storm and stress view is entirely incorrect. At the very least, I think the story is a lot more complicated than this characterization. The answer to the question of whether adolescence is a time of conflict depends on what we mean by conflict and, more importantly, from whom you collect your data. This suggests the need for a new perspective on the family, one that emphasizes the different viewpoints and stakes that family members bring

to the kitchen table. We are now fairly certain that frequent, high intensity, angry fighting is not normative during adolescence. But to characterize the storm and stress view as entirely wrong – as many writers, including myself, have done – is not entirely true.

And it is clear that it is not just parents who walk away from the kitchen table with unhappy feelings about conflict. Kate McLean and Avril Thorne (2003) asked a sample of European American college students to recollect "self-defining" experiences in their relationships with parents or peers. These were identified as memories that were vivid, highly memorable, personally important, and more than a year old. The respondents' narratives of their experiences with parents focused much more on conflict than their narratives of peer relationships did. Indeed, conflict was highly salient and mentioned in nearly all of the college students' memories of important experiences with parents. And, contrary to expectations, the proportion of parent memories that focused on conflict did not decline across adolescence. Thus conflicts, even ones that had occurred years previously, were clearly highly salient in the college students' memories of relationships with parents.

Conclusions

The theorizing and research discussed in this chapter indicate that, for most families, adolescence is not a period of storm and stress and adolescent rebellion against parents. This conclusion has been supported by research studies comparing normal and clinic-referred adolescents. The studies reliably show that intense and angry conflict with parents is not the norm. Rather, it is a reflection of troubled adolescence and disturbed family relationships. And, despite persistent mentioning of a "generation gap" or youthful rebellion, the evidence suggests that teenagers do not rebel against their parents, nor do adolescents reject all parental values. Adolescents look to their parents for advice, typically hold similar values to those of their parents on political, social, and religious issues, and report that they admire their parents.

Overall, decades of psychological research suggest that both conflict and closeness are important aspects of the adolescents' relationships with their parents. Nevertheless, when the results of psychological research studies are aggregated, it does appear that adolescents' disagreements and conflicts with parents increase in frequency in early adolescence and increase in anger and intensity in middle adolescence, particularly between mothers and daughters. The adolescents' and the parents' emotional experiences become increasingly divergent. Although conflict occurs over mundane everyday issues, these small conflicts do have a larger significance in the lives of adolescents and parents. In the following chapter we consider what that significance might be.

3

Conflicts and Their Vicissitudes

Social psychologists who study close relationships assert that, to understand individuals' behaviors, it is necessary to find out how they represent their circumstances to themselves. Adolescents and parents have different roles, responsibilities, and statuses in the family, as well as in the broader society. As Larson and Richard's research discussed in the previous chapter suggests, parents and teenagers may have divergent perspectives and goals in their daily social interactions. Parent–adolescent disagreements are a particularly vivid and valuable context for understanding these different perspectives. They provide a window into family functioning that may not be evident when social interactions are proceeding smoothly. Ruptures or breaches in the smooth flow of family interaction, even brief ones, can bring parents' and teenagers' different perspectives into sharp relief and help to illuminate parents' and adolescents' different beliefs, goals, and desires.

To understand these conflicts and their meaning in adolescents' and parents' lives, it behooves researchers to listen to how both teens and parents talk about their disagreements and justify their perspective on disputes. Central to the approach elaborated in this book is the proposition that children are not just molded by parents' actions. Rather, they actively interpret their social experiences with parents, other adults, and peers and attempt to make sense of their social world. In situations of conflict or disagreement, children sometimes choose to ignore or reject parents' wishes. We need to understand why this is so and figure out what it means. These responses could reflect defiance, limit-testing, bad conduct, or problem behavior, or they could be indicators of poor socialization; but we cannot assume that this is so – and certainly not in all circumstances and for all teens. We must examine these responses without automatically presuming that they indicate that children are not "measuring up" to parental standards. As we will see later, parental prohibitions and exhortations provide information

Adolescents, Families, and Social Development: How Teens Construct Their Worlds. Judith G. Smetana
© 2011 Judith G. Smetana

about the social world and the kinds of expectations that apply, but these are not the only experiences that matter in social development. Children have different types of social experiences and interactions, and these lead to the development of different kinds of understandings and social concepts.

Young children are bombarded with many different rules, prohibitions, and expectations. As anyone who has cared for young children knows, statements like "don't hit," "stop teasing your brother," "don't run into the street," "say 'please,'" and "don't use your fingers to eat your spaghetti" – all occur with great frequency. A fundamental task of social development is to help children learn to follow these social rules and expectations. Thus, much research has examined how children come to adopt the rules and values of their society. There are different ways of understanding these processes.

To illustrate: one such way, which differs in important respects from the approach described in this book, comes from research on parental socialization. Despite some minor differences in their accounts, socialization researchers assume that the process of social development involves the child's internalization of adult rules. In this view, parents are "the local guardians of the moral order" (Much & Shweder, 1978) and, as such, they bear the responsibility of conveying societal rules and expectations to their children. And, in turn, children are expected to learn and comply with parents' rules. According to this account, children become socialized as they gradually adopt parental expectations. No differentiations are made in the rules that children are expected to follow. Issues, both big and small, are seen in a similar light – as adult expectations that must be internalized, and the focus is strictly on their acquisition.

For instance, in an ambitious program of research, Grazyna Kochanska has advanced the notion of "committed compliance" (see Kochanska & Aksan, 2004; Kochanska, Aksan, & Koenig, 1995 for examples). She has asserted that, to a greater or lesser degree, children take on parents' rules as their own. To test this notion, she has conducted detailed observations of young children engaging in structured tasks in laboratory situations. The "clean-up" task is one such task. Parents are instructed to get their young children to clean up toys that are littered on the laboratory floor. Detailed observations are made of parents' and children's behavior in this context. Kochanska has distinguished between children whose be-havior is governed primarily by parental directives and control and children who are more self-directed. Children in the latter group seem to "own" and take pleasure in the task. For Kochanska and many other researchers, the clean-up task serves as a prototype for much of social development. It is an example of a situ-ation where parents have an expectation – not necessarily a desirable one, or one they consider to be intrinsically interesting or motivating – for the child to follow. They focus on the parenting techniques that are most effective in guiding the child towards successful internalization. Thus, in this and other socialization research, compliance or obedience to parents' or other socializing agents' rules and expecta-tions is a key measure of whether successful socialization has occurred. It is assumed that, over time, parental expectations are internalized through parents' socialization practices, so that children willingly follow their parents' rules.

Beginning with the work of Bell (1968), there has been greater attention to children's contributions to their own development and to a more transactional perspective on parent–child relationships. In their influential review of research on parenting styles and responsiveness, Eleanor Maccoby and John Martin (1983) called for a change from rather unilateral models of parental influence to more bilateral and interactive perspectives. For instance, Kochanska considers the child's contributions to development by assessing children's temperament. She proposes that child temperament influences the types of socialization techniques parents employ. She has demonstrated that good matches between parenting practices and child temperament (for instance, the use of gentle parenting with temperamentally fearful children) facilitate the internalization of rules.

But we can ask whether compliance, committed or not, is a good measure of successful socialization. On the surface, it seems sensible and useful. After all, children must acquire an understanding of the rules of their society. But Maccoby and Martin's analysis also entails a shift away from viewing compliance as the goal of most parent–child interactions to considering parents' different goals. Several prominent researchers have also called attention to the fact that parents may have multiple goals in their interactions with their children (Dix, 1992; Grusec, 2008; Grusec & Davidov, 2007; Hastings & Grusec, 1998; Kuczynski & Navarra, 2006; Lundell, Grusec, McShane, & Davidov, 2008). For instance, parents may desire compliance, especially in the short term, but they may also wish to teach their children important lessons, especially when they focus on their long-term goals (Kuczynski, 1984). When a young child approaches a hot stove, parents' primary concern is to stop the child from getting burned. They may push the child away, or yell at the child to stop; explanations can wait until later. Other situations might offer "teaching moments," where greater explanation can be offered. Kuczynski has usefully shown that parents use different disciplinary strategies when they focus on short- versus long-term goals.

Other goals may be important as well. Sometimes parents wish to reduce their own discomfort, but they may also strive to satisfy children's emotional needs and to make them happy. This may lead parents to endorse other outcomes than aims purely pertaining to socialization. In some instances the parents' goal may be to promote close, harmonious, and loving family relationships. Parents may hold these different and competing goals as they interact with their children. In this revised view, compliance may be just one out of several goals that parents may have in their social interactions with their children. But these approaches still focus on the *parents'* goals in the socialization process. And, in considering adolescent–parent conflict, this would lead researchers, for instance, to focus primarily on parents' perspectives.

Almost by definition, a focus on adolescents' and parents' different interpretations of conflict involves an interactive perspective, which places equal emphasis on both parties in the dispute. Even when teenagers give in to their parents' wishes, focusing on the potentially discrepant perspectives of parents and teenagers entails a subtle shift in the frame of reference. It moves the focus away from compliance and from an assessment of whether adolescents are measuring up to parents' expectations. It shifts towards considering the different and sometimes competing points of view that parents and teenagers may bring to their interactions. In turn, this shift allows us to consider how these divergent views are elaborated upon and negotiated in social interaction, rather than viewing adolescents as failing to comply with parental demands and standards.

A focus on conflict, therefore, allows the voices and perspectives of adolescents to be fully heard. It changes the emphasis from evaluating adolescents in terms of how closely their behavior approximates their parents' desires and standards to viewing the parents' and the teenagers' perspectives as distinct and separate. And research suggests that this is important, because, even when adolescents fully expect that they will adhere to parental standards, they may express legitimate needs, desires, and goals that differ from those of their parents. Therefore it is important to understand parents' rules, goals, and expectations and how well children are meeting them. But this does not provide a complete account of social development. It is equally important to consider adolescents' understanding and interpretation of their parents' rules, expectations, and wishes, as well as adolescents' own goals, desires, and beliefs.

In studying adolescent–parent conflict, at least two aspects of the divergent views of parents and adolescents need to be considered. Robert Emery (1992) has made a useful distinction between the literal content, or topics of conflicts, and what the conflict conveys about the relationship. Studying the topics of conflicts is relatively straightforward and descriptively useful. Indeed, as noted in the last chapter, the topics of adolescents' disagreements with parents have been extensively researched over the past 50 years. The studies converge in showing that conflicts between teens and their parents are over the everyday, mundane details of family life, or what Hill and Holmbeck (1987) refer to as "hair, garbage, dishes, and galoshes." In the following section I elaborate on the topics of conflict that have emerged from my research. However, studying the topics of teenagers' and their parents' disputes does not reveal the function of these disputes in adolescents' social development. For this, it is necessary to understand their meaning to the participants.

According to Emery, such understanding involves an analysis of the underlying issues at stake in the dispute. For this, a more interpretive approach is needed. The theoretical approach taken here is elaborated upon in detail in Chapter 4, when the topics of conflicts will have been more fully described. In hundreds of interviews conducted between 1986 and 2002 and discussed here and in subsequent chapters, I have listened to parents and to their adolescent children as they voiced their perspectives on disputes. Two of the studies, both of them cross-sectional, focused primarily on middle-class European American families and are discussed in this chapter. (These studies were originally reported in Smetana, 1988b, 1989a; Smetana, Braeges, & Yau, 1991; Smetana, Yau, & Hanson, 1991; and Smetana, Yau, Restrepo, & Braeges, 1991.) Two other studies (Yau & Smetana, 1996, 2003a), also cross-sectional, focused on low socioeconomic status (including lower middle-class) Chinese adolescents in Hong Kong and mainland China and are discussed in Chapter 7. Another study, which was longitudinal and followed families for 5 years, focused on middle-class African American families. This study is discussed extensively in Chapter 8. In all, my research has yielded nearly 700 intensive, face-to-face, semi-structured interviews with adolescents about their disagreements with parents. These interviews were audio-tape recorded and transcribed verbatim. Nearly the same number of interviews about parent–adolescent conflicts was conducted with parents. In this and subsequent chapters, I quote from these interviews (all names have been changed, to preserve anonymity). Several of these studies also incorporated surveys and observations of family interactions as family members engaged in structured tasks. In different studies, approximately another 500 adolescents and their parents have responded to extensive questionnaires about conflicts, but were not interviewed. This constitutes a considerable corpus of data, rich enough to permit us to draw conclusions about the meaning of conflict to participants.

In several of the studies we invited community samples of families, recruited from different school districts, to visit my university lab. The families in the studies described in this chapter were recruited from a middle-class suburb bordering on an Upstate New York city; it is one of several suburbs that surround the urban center. Although there are several very large apartment house complexes in the suburb (sometimes referred to as the "Divorce Court" because of the prevalence of divorced, single-parent families renting in these complexes), the area consists mostly of single-family homes on quiet, tree-lined streets. The suburb is known for its fine school district and family-friendly atmosphere. With the school district's cooperation, we solicited the participation of parents of elementary (5th grade), middle school, and high school students. Interested families visited my university lab for an evening or weekend session lasting several hours.

The research discussed in this chapter includes 102 two-parent families with children ranging in age from 10 to 18. Teenagers, their mothers, and their fathers were all interviewed. In addition, 66 families, all with two biological parents, were compared to 28 more families that were headed by divorced mothers, not remarried. The children from this last lot had been approximately 7 years of age when their parents divorced. For all the families, the lab sessions began with introductions and a brief overview of the session, designed to help put families at ease. Then each family member was interviewed separately. The session ended with their participation in a series of structured, videotaped family interactions.

Many researchers have used the Issues Checklist (Prinz, Foster, Kent, & O'Leary, 1979; Robin & Foster, 1989) to measure adolescent–parent conflict. This checklist includes 44 different areas of day-to-day decision-making (for instance over curfew, clothing, or homework). Family members indicate whether each issue on this list has been discussed within the past 2 weeks. For those that have, respondents rate the frequency and intensity of the discussion. The advantage of this method is that all family members evaluate a common set of items while still allowing for individual variation in the issues that are endorsed.

Despite the widespread use of the Issues Checklist, there are some disadvantages to it or to related measures. One disadvantage is that the checklist may not accurately assess the issues that matter to different families. For instance, it may lead investigators to overlook infrequently discussed but highly salient issues. Indeed, it may well be the case that issues that are highly charged affectively come to be discussed infrequently, exactly because of their extreme emotional weight to the family. Using a predetermined list also may lead investigators to overestimate the importance to the family of issues that are discussed regularly over the two-week period.

Therefore we asked parents and teenagers to generate examples of the everyday disagreements they experienced with each other. With the interviewer's probing, teenagers generated exhaustive lists of the disagreements and conflicts they had with their parents. Parent generated lists of the conflicts they had with their teens. After the participants listed the issues that came to mind, they were probed in order for us to determine whether they had overlooked any issues. In this way we combined a more open-ended format, which allowed participants to focus on issues of salience to them, with more standardized methods. In most of the studies discussed here and in subsequent chapters, participants were then interviewed extensively about each issue, in order for us to obtain their interpretations of the issues.

What European American Middle-Class Families Do (and Do Not) Fight About

What kinds of issues cause conflicts and disagreements in European American families? The topics are similar to those reported almost half a century ago by Douvan and Adelson (1966), Kandel and Lesser (1972), and Rutter and his colleagues (Rutter, 1980; Rutter, Graham, Chadwick, & Yule, 1976). They are also similar to more recent, smaller-scale, descriptive, and more focused investigations of adolescent–parent conflict (Montemayor, 1983). Conflicts between European American middle-class teenagers and their parents were primarily over the everyday, mundane details of family life, such as doing the chores, getting along with siblings (and others), doing homework and getting good grades, and teenagers' choice of friends and activities. (As we shall see in later chapters, these kinds of issues are typical of conflicts among African American and Asian teenagers and their parents as well.)

Doing chores, which included such tasks as setting the table, doing the dishes, walking the dog, mowing the lawn, shoveling snow, or cleaning one's room, was the most frequent source of conflict mentioned by adolescents and parents. Sometimes teens just did not want to do their assigned chores. As one 7th grade boy stated succinctly, "I don't want to mow the lawn. I think somebody has to do it, but I don't know why it always has to be me." Thus, although some European American teens acknowledged that there was a need for help around the house or for chores to be done, some wanted to abdicate their responsibility for carrying them out. More typically, though, European American teenagers acknowledged the need to do the chores, but not necessarily in the particular way or at the particular time parents wanted them done. Christina, a 5th grader, put it this way:

> Well, I usually get home from school at 3:30, and then I have a baseball game to go to, because I play baseball and sports, and that doesn't really give me any time to play with my neighbors or anything ... and my dad will make me do the dishes because he and my mom want to talk.

Families with middle and late adolescents mentioned these types of conflicts more often than families with early adolescents did, no doubt because middle-class American teenagers are given more responsibilities in the household as they grow older. Very frequently, teenagers and their parents clashed over the condition of the teenager's room. (I will have much more to say about this particular issue later.) They also disagreed over when and how teenagers did other assigned chores, over whether they cleaned up after themselves, and over the messy condition of the house or shared space. Adolescents, mothers, and fathers did not differ in the frequency with which they mentioned these conflicts.

How teenagers get along with others was another frequent source of conflict in teenagers' relationships with parents. When European American adolescents argued with their parents about these issues, however, the disputes generally were about getting along with siblings, and less frequently with friends. Sibling conflicts typically revolved around issues such as hitting, hurting, teasing, quarreling, and invasions of privacy. Peter, a 9th-grade boy, described a typical conflict in the following way:

> Well, usually I find something, like a mess, and I say, "Will you pick it up?," and my brother is like, "No, I won't pick it up." Like, "It's your mess. It's in our bathroom. You've gotta pick it up." And he goes, "Leave me alone," or something like that. So I like force him to do it, like I make him pick it up. And then Michael will probably start crying, even if I didn't hit him or anything. He'll just start crying, then he'll call my dad, and he'll say, "Peter, Dad wants to talk to you." I'll pick up the phone. My dad will say, "You're right. He's probably wrong, but ..." You know, I tell him what happened and he says that he agrees with me, but he doesn't want me to do anything like that. He says I shouldn't do it.

As was often the case, conflicts between siblings eventually escalated to become disputes between parents and children when parents were called in (or more actively intervened) as third parties in disputes. The conflict initially arose between Peter and his sibling, but, when they failed to resolve it successfully between themselves, Dad was recruited to arbitrate. As the example shows, this tactic does not necessarily lead to a happy resolution.

Teenagers and their parents also had disputes and disagreements about adolescents' activities. Typically, these conflicts pertained to the timing of activities or to the amount of time spent on different activities. For instance, a frequent source of irritation in these middle-class European American families was the amount of time adolescents spent using the phone or watching television. Sometimes these conflicts pertained more to time use, as when parents believed that the adolescents should be doing one thing (practicing the piano), and the adolescent wanted to do something else (relax before dinner). And sometimes the conflicts pertained to the choice of the particular activity itself, such as playing videogames with violent content.

In coding the content, or topics, of conflicts, we made distinctions between conflicts that related to the types of activities just mentioned and to the parents' attempts to regulate teenagers' interpersonal activities, deciding for instance when their children could see friends, or whether adolescents could go to parties or out on dates. This category also included teenagers' choice of friends. Conflicts over the parents' attempts to regulate interpersonal relationships were less frequent than disputes over regulating teenagers' activities; nevertheless, they accounted for a fair number of the adolescents' disagreements with their parents. These issues, as well as adolescents' choice of activities, were more salient to European American adolescents, and were raised more frequently by adolescents than by either mothers or fathers. As noted in an earlier chapter, in most American homes, mothers have a more direct responsibility than fathers for managing such activities. In this study, mothers raised issues of this kind more frequently than fathers did.

Some family disagreements occurred over adolescents' personality or behavioral style. These disagreements were framed primarily in terms of a behavior or a personality trait that was particularly annoying or repeatedly manifested, such as being hyperactive, lazy, messy, disrespectful, or stubborn. Sometimes these conflicts were elaborated upon in terms of specific situations or contexts in which teenagers manifested the behavioral style or personality trait. But the concern was about the behavior or characteristic that the partner found particularly irritating or conflictive. Not surprisingly, mothers and fathers raised this issue more often than adolescents did. Adolescents may have perceived conflicts more in terms of the particular activities (such as watching television or talking on the phone). In contrast, parents may have framed the same conflicts more in terms of an overarching negative personality characteristic or behavioral style, which they attributed to the adolescent in different situations.

Conflicts pertaining to homework and academic achievement constituted a relatively small proportion of the topics raised in our European American families. (In later chapters we shall see that these conflicts are much more prominent in Chinese and African American families.) For teenagers, these conflicts were often discussed in terms of getting homework done on a schedule set by parents. Jessica, a 7th grader, described it this way:

> Well, my mom says that I have to come home and do my schoolwork right after school, and usually I want to watch my programs after school, and like after dinner I'll do my homework, but my mom has a rule about it. Because I have all after dinner, and it's like three hours or something, so you don't really have to […] do it right away when you get home from school.

As this example suggests (and so did the earlier one, regarding chores), the issue was not so much whether or not homework was completed, but when and how this was done. Adolescents wanted to have more of a say in deciding when to do their homework, and they resented parents' attempts to impose structure on their behavior.

Doing homework or getting it done on time, getting good grades, or maintaining an acceptable academic average constituted about 10% of all the conflicts raised in this sample. Conflicts over homework and academic achievement were raised more often in early adolescence, as compared to younger ages or to middle adolescence. This increase roughly coincided with the ages at which teenagers in this school district make the transition from elementary to middle school. Many scholars view the transition to middle school as stressful (Eccles et al., 1993), particular when it coincides with other developmental changes such as pubertal maturation. Whereas elementary schools are more concerned with developing students' competence, middle schools place more emphasis on competition, academic performance, and grades (Eccles et al., 1993). Therefore, the intensification of conflicts over homework and academic achievement in early adolescence may have reflected the teenagers' difficulties in adapting to a new school setting, with its increased emphasis on academic performance.

There has been much media attention to teenage fads and styles in dress and appearance. But conflicts over teenagers' choice of clothes, make-up, and hairstyles were relatively infrequent, and extended in equal measure to families with boys and girls. These conflicts typically came down to clashes of opinion over appropriate styles. Sara, a tall and neatly dressed 9th grader, explained:

> It's not like I wear bad clothes to school, but she would like to see me wear nice corduroys to school with this matching shirt, and, "Why don't you put nice shoes on?" and "How about your nice necklace?" and I just don't like to do that.

Concerns pertaining specifically to health and hygiene, although rare, were of greater concern to mothers than to adolescents. These disputes were over everyday grooming, such as combing hair, brushing teeth, and wearing warm clothes and mittens in the winter. For instance, as Sam, a 6th-grade boy stated: "When we're going to parties, he says my face isn't washed and my hair is not combed right, and stuff like that."

Four aspects of these findings deserve note. First, it is worth underscoring what disagreements were *not* about. Adolescents and their parents did *not* have disagreements over the issues thought to indicate a generation gap. That is, families rarely had overt disagreements over religious beliefs, family values, or political attitudes. This is not to say that such issues never arose – they did, in some indirect ways. For instance, we recorded occasional conflicts about whether it was permissible for a teenager to date someone of a different religion. Clearly this dispute reflects differences in parents' and teens' values, as instantiated in the context of dating choices. But, in general, there were few direct clashes over teenagers' and parents' expressed religious, moral, and political attitudes and values. These issues may have served as lively discussion topics at the dinner table, but they did not surface in the more contentious sphere of disputes between parents and teenagers.

Also, disputes rarely touched upon the types of problem behavior that are of frequent concern to parents, like teenage drug and alcohol use or precocious sexual behavior. In fact we specifically probed these issues, to make sure that they were not overlooked or ignored as sources of conflict. But both teenagers and their parents asserted that such topics rarely arose as sources of intergenerational disputes. This does not mean that the corresponding behaviors were absent among the teenagers in this sample. The results of national surveys indicate that, by middle adolescence, a very high proportion of teenagers have at least tried alcohol and "soft" drugs (Johnston, O'Malley, Bachman, & Schulenberg, 2005). Furthermore, by middle adolescence, more than half of all American teenagers have had sexual intercourse. Health-risk surveys of this particular community mirror the national trends. But these issues typically did not produce conflicts between teenagers and their parents. In most cases, teenagers who indulged in alcohol or drugs told us that they took care to ensure that their parents were not aware of these activities. (This issue is discussed in greater detail in Chapter 11.)

The second finding that deserves mention is that, although the teenage participants in this study ranged from 10-year-olds to late adolescents, there was very little variation across ages in the types of conflict that adolescents and parents mentioned. Apart from the differences related to age that were noted previously, the issues that led to conflict between parents and their teenagers were highly consistent across the entire age span. Although adolescents spend more time out of the home and are supervised less as they get older, conflicts among older adolescents were still about the mundane details of family life, much as they were among the younger ones. (The most likely cause is that these are the issues that are directly observable by parents and serve as irritants in daily life.)

Third, two-parent biological families and divorced, single-parent, mother-headed families did not differ with respect to the issues they fought about. Although the larger sample of two-parent families did include some step-parent families, these were not included in the comparisons because they were too few in number. Other researchers have found that step-parent families have particularly contentious relationships, as compared to married families with two biological parents. As the family is reconstituted, the lines of authority, particularly for the new step-parent, become blurred. But divorced and two-parent biological families struggled with the same everyday issues of family life.

Finally, there was a great deal of consistency in the reports from European American middle-class teenagers and from their parents concerning the issues that lead to disputes in their relationships. In their interviews, teenagers reported that approximately half of their conflicts were with both parents. But, out of the remaining half, more were with mothers than with fathers. Yet there were very few differences between mothers and fathers concerning the topics of the conflicts they reported in their interviews. In turn, this suggests that, even though teenagers may have had more disagreements with their mothers than with their fathers, fathers were aware of the issues disputed among mothers and teenagers. As discussed in Chapter 11, fathers often get their information about their teenagers' behavior from mothers, not from the teenagers themselves. Furthermore, analyses comparing the types of conflict reported in two-parent, biological families and in single-parent, mother-headed households also revealed no differences in the topics that led to disagreements. More strikingly, there were relatively few intergenerational differences in the topics that teenagers and parents discussed. Although, as we shall see, teenagers and their parents view the same conflicts in fundamentally different ways, European American middle-class parents and teenagers agree on what their disagreements are about.

Summary and Conclusions

In this chapter I have claimed that parent–adolescent disagreements are a useful context for understanding parents' and adolescents' different perspectives on their relationship. I have asserted that it is important for researchers to go beyond a focus on parents' perspectives and on compliance, to consider the needs, wishes, and desires that both adolescents and their parents bring to their social interactions. Studying disputes can shed light on ruptures or breaches in family functioning – aspects that may not otherwise be evident when social interactions are proceeding smoothly. Thus, studying conflicts can illuminate the parents' and the teenagers' different perspectives on various issues.

We saw here that European American parents' and adolescents' conflicts are over the everyday details of family life, such as doing the chores, doing the homework, the choice of activities, the question of how teenagers get along with others, and their appearance. Adolescents and parents generally agree on the issues that cause conflict in their relationships. Across adolescence, relatively few age differences are evident in these topics. However, a distinction was made between the topics of conflict and the underlying meaning of conflict. We turn to this meaning in the next chapter, and we shall consider it in the context of social domain theory, which is the theoretical framework of this book.

4

Parents' Voices:

Conflicts and Social Conventions

I would remind them of certain simple truths. Conventionality is not morality ...
These things and deeds are diametrically opposed: they are as distinct as vice from
virtue. Charlotte Bronte, *Jane Eyre* (1949, p. 3)

In the last chapter we considered some of the issues that cause conflict in European American middle-class adolescents' and parents' relationships. What do these conflicts mean to the participants? The topics of conflict are "on the surface," and thus relatively easy to describe and categorize. But, to understand their meaning, it is necessary to consider the parents' reasoning in a broader theoretical framework. The framework that has informed my research (and that I have contributed to over many years) has come to be known as *social domain theory*. Social domain theory was originally formulated by Elliot Turiel (1978, 1979, 1983) almost 30 years ago and grew out of his research on the development of adolescent moral judgment. However, the theory has expanded considerably since then and has been profitably applied to a wide range of topics in social development (many of which are far beyond the scope of this book). Social domain theory is a theoretical and empirical approach to describing the development of children's social knowledge and the manner in which individuals apply and coordinate their understanding of different types of rules and social regulations (as well as of zones of autonomy and personal jurisdiction) in different contexts and situations.

Before considering its relevance to adolescent–parent disagreements, we must consider the theoretical tenets of social domain theory in some detail. Accordingly, in the following sections I define the different types of social knowledge that have been studied from this perspective and discuss some of the research support for the theory. With the theoretical concepts firmly in hand, we will return later in the chapter to a discussion of parents' reasoning about conflicts with their teens. Then, in the following chapter, we will consider adolescents' perspectives.

Adolescents, Families, and Social Development: How Teens Construct Their Worlds. Judith G. Smetana
© 2011 Judith G. Smetana

Social Domain Theory: Distinct Domains of Social Thought

The starting point for our discussion is the (rather obvious) observation that the social world is complex. As was described at the beginning of the last chapter, children are bombarded with many different types of rules, prohibitions, and expectations, and they have many different types of social interactions. How do they view the rules they are expected to adopt? Do they view them as a largely undifferentiated category, as "things parents want me to do and rules they want me to follow," as most socialization perspectives assume?

According to social domain theory, the answer is no. Children actively attempt to make sense of their social interactions, including the rules they encounter and the transgressions they experience, observe, and even perpetrate. A basic claim is that children have both systematic and differentiated ways of thinking about their social world. These can be described in terms of three organized systems, or domains, of social knowledge. More specifically, the claim is that concerns with justice, welfare, and rights (considered to be moral issues) co-exist with matters related to authority, tradition, and social norms (which are viewed as social conventions) and with attempts to understand the self and others as psychological systems (referred to as the psychological domain). Social domain theory proposes that each of these organized systems of thought arise from children's experiences of different types of regularities in the social environment.

Moral concepts

We begin by considering moral issues. Studies reveal that young children's conflicts most frequently focus on aggression and on not sharing communal toys. These can be seen as *moral* matters, because they involve acts that may potentially be harmful to others or cause unfairness. For instance, when parents prohibit hitting or teasing, their concerns typically are with the potentially negative consequences of these acts for others' welfare or rights. Hitting or teasing are *moral* matters, and moral rules are designed to regulate interpersonal acts that have negative consequences for others, including harm (welfare), others' rights, and the fair distribution of resources. Moral concepts develop from children's social experiences of the consequences of actions for others' welfare or rights. Several examples of social interactions in the context of moral transgressions, examples drawn from previous research on preschool children's social interactions, will make this point clear.

> A group of children are playing on the floor with toy cars. David, who has been coloring nearby, approaches and sees Michael's bright red car. When Michael looks away, David grabs it. Michael begins to cry and screams, "Mine! Mine!" (Smetana, 1983, p. 134)

Lisa, Michael, and David are all rocking in the rocking boat. Jenny, who has been waiting nearby for a turn, finally approaches. As the rocking slows down, she bites Lisa in the arm. Lisa screams and then cries. (Smetana, 1993a, p. 112)

Well, I remember one thing about um someone, um a friend hurting me. I, it was just a little bit. He was a friend, his name was William, he hit me with his hammer in the middle of the head and it really hurt. It was plastic. (Wainryb, Brehl, & Matwin, 2005, p. 54)

The pain or perceived injustice the victim of each of these transgressions experienced is a salient feature of all of these interactions. Children have direct experiences of the consequences of transgressions for their welfare and rights, both as victims of and as observers to the transgressions. Children actively attempt to understand their experiences of physical and psychological harm, fair distribution, and violation of rights. Victims' negative emotional reactions to transgressions (for instance, David's and Lisa's screaming and crying and the observation that being hit in the head with a hammer really hurts, in the examples above) highlight the negative consequences of the child's actions for the victim. Observers, too, may respond with negative emotions and affective reactions. And parents may respond by empathizing with the victim's pain or unhappiness. Parents may become angry as well, and may punish the perpetrator or explain in various ways why the act is wrong. All of these reactions are part of social interactions. Much of the research on parental socialization has concentrated primarily on what parents say or do when children misbehave or on what parents do to try to avoid child misbehavior. But, as we can see, social interactions are rich and involve varied sources of information, of which parental response is only one. According to Turiel (1983, 2002, 2006), children's experiences help them to construct abstract notions of what is fair and unfair, right and wrong. Therefore children develop an understanding of moral matters from their direct experiences of harm or unfairness, as well as from others' communications highlighting the experience of harm. These form the basis of prescriptive moral judgments about how individuals ought to behave towards others.

Moral concepts develop from children's and adolescents' interpersonal interactions pertaining to welfare or harm, justice and fairness, and rights. Moral concepts regulate individuals' interpersonal relationships. These concepts are prescriptive. That is, they tell us how we ought to behave. They are also obligatory. *All* individuals are obliged to follow them. They are universally applicable, because they are seen to apply to everyone in individual circumstances. They are impersonal in that they are not based on personal preferences. And they are unalterable; in other words, they are normatively binding. These criteria (that is, that morality is prescriptive, obligatory, universally applicable, impersonal, and unalterable) are, all, criteria employed in social domain research to define acts as moral. But these definitions and criteria are not just applied from the researchers' perspective. As we shall see, these criteria, along with the individuals' reasoning or their justifications, are used in research to examine whether individuals evaluate different actions as moral or nonmoral.

Concepts of society and social convention

Not all rules and regularities are moral, however. Therefore it is important to distinguish moral issues from other types of social rules and expectations. In particular, moral concepts have been distinguished from social conventions. Social conventions are defined as consensually agreed upon regularities or expectations that organize social interactions in different social contexts. For young children, social conventions consist of a set of arbitrary rules or standards that must be followed. (The "clean-up" task described in Chapter 3 can be seen as social conventional in nature, although it is often used as an experimental analogue of how moral development occurs.) Children pay attention to social conventions because the latter are important to adults, but children attempt to understand them as well. For instance, children may note that conventional expectations vary in different contexts. Children may be expected to take their shoes off when entering their house, but to keep them on at other children's houses. They may say grace before meals at home, but not at preschool. They may keep their coats in their cubbies at daycare, but hang them in the closet (or drop them at the front door) at home. Other conventions, like saying "please" when asking for cookies, may apply more broadly. Children seek to understand these regularities and the contexts in which they apply.

Conventional violations are not intrinsically wrong. As defined by Elliot Turiel (1979, 1983, 2002, 2006), social conventions are arbitrary social norms. They pertain to issues like etiquette, manners, forms of address, and contextually relevant school and family rules (like where to hang your coat or put your toys). Consider the following examples, drawn from observations with young children and described in Smetana (1993a).

Children are greeting a teacher who has just come into the nursery school. A number of children go up to her and say "Good morning Mrs. Jones." One of the children says "Good morning, Mary." (Turiel, 1983, p. 41)

It is snack time, and the teachers instruct everyone to sit in their seats. Cindy is kneeling in her chair. The teacher tells her, "Cindy, bottoms have to be on the chair before children can have their snack." Cindy sits down; the other children pay no attention. (Smetana, 1983, p. 135)

It is a hot day, and the teachers decide to take the children outside to play in the baby pool. Jason has forgotten his bathing suit, so the teachers tell him to pick one from the box of discarded bathing suits. He picks a pink suit. The teachers tell him he can't wear that one because it's a girl's bathing suit. He persists and says that that is the one he wants to wear today. The teachers repeatedly attempt to dissuade him. After prolonged discussion among themselves, they decide to let him wear it. He proudly puts it on. The other toddlers are oblivious. (Smetana, 1993a, p. 112)

In all three examples, there is no intrinsic basis for knowing what is wrong: that it is wrong for children to address their teachers by their first name, or that children must be seated before a snack is served. Rather, as noted elsewhere (Smetana, 1993a), this knowledge is based on an understanding of social conventions and of the regulations that apply in particular contexts. Social conventional knowledge and, more generally, an understanding of social systems and social organizations are constructed from children's experiences with and recognition of the uniformities and regularities they encounter in their social interactions. These include differences in expectations across various settings and social contexts surrounding the same acts. Conventions are arbitrary in that alternate actions could serve the same function. Eating with fingers, forks and knives, or chopsticks all accomplish the same ends, but the form of eating may vary in different cultures or contexts. And agreements regarding such forms serve to coordinate social interactions. That is, they provide a consistent set of expectations for appropriate social behavior and thus for efficiencies in social interactions.

Children do not passively accept parental norms and social conventions. They try to make sense of them. Their understanding becomes progressively more sophisticated with age. As they grow older, children begin to affirm the importance of social conventions, on the basis of a concrete understanding of rules and authority expectations. Turiel (1979, 1983) has proposed that, during the course of development, children go through phases where they alternately affirm and then reject the importance of social conventions. Early adolescents believe that conventions are arbitrary and changeable, even if rules exist. They are defined in terms of social expectations. By middle adolescence, teenagers begin to develop more systematic concepts and understanding of social structure. They grasp the notion that there are social roles within society, that these roles can be ordered in a hierarchy (for instance, teacher–student or parent–child roles), and that there are certain expectations that are part of those roles. Thus they begin to view conventions as normatively binding, because these exist within a social system that has fixed roles and a hierarchical structure.

Late adolescents go through a phase where, once again, they negate the importance of following conventions. Early adolescents viewed social conventions as "nothing but" social expectations. In contrast, late adolescents understand that conventions are part of a broader social system, but they do not believe that these conventions need to be followed. They believe that uniformity in conventions is "nothing but" adherence to arbitrary societal standards, which have been codified through habitual use. Finally, young adults develop an understanding of conventions as uniformities that coordinate social interaction and facilitate the smooth functioning and operation of the social system.

These distinctions between morality and social convention are part of children's lived experience, but they are also relevant in moral philosophy. Indeed, the theoretical criteria that social domain researchers have employed to distinguish morality from social convention were initially taken from moral philosophers working within a rationalist tradition (Dworkin, 1978; Gewirth, 1978; Mill, 1968; Rawls, 1971). These criteria were refined, tested, and elaborated upon using empirical psychological analyses.

Here it is important to note that the social domain view differs from global stage theories of moral development, such as the well-known theories of Jean Piaget (1965) and Lawrence Kohlberg (Colby & Kohlberg, 1987; Kohlberg, 1984). The latter researchers also claim that morality and social convention are differentiated – but only later on in development, if at all. They propose that individuals develop broad, global structures of reasoning and that the process of moral development involves the gradual differentiation of principles of justice or rights from nonmoral concerns (for instance with conventions, or with pragmatic and prudential issues). In their views, concepts of social convention are an inadequate or less mature form of morality rather than a distinct form of social knowledge, which develops in early childhood alongside of (but separately from) moral concepts.

Psychological concepts

Moral matters and social conventions have been further differentiated from individuals' understanding of persons as psychological systems. When interacting with others and trying to comprehend social situations, we often attempt to understand where others are "coming from." Individuals often must make inferences and attributions about their own and others' behavior. For instance, when a child is jostled in line, he or she must quickly decide whether the act was intentional ("he did it because he hates me") or not ("it's crowded, he didn't mean to bump me"). For that matter, we may also reflect on why we acted in a particular way in interactions with others. ("I couldn't believe I was blushing and stammering so much when I talked to George – hmmm, does that mean that I have a 'crush' on him?"). As children mature, they come to understand that individuals may hold different and sometimes conflicting beliefs or emotional responses from their own. They may find that others may have unique psychological experiences, or that they have privileged access to information that others do not possess. A great deal of psychological research over the past 20 years has been devoted to understanding how children's psychological understanding, referred to as "theory of mind," develops – particularly during the preschool years.

Psychological knowledge, including, but not limited to, theory of mind, can be distinguished conceptually and empirically from morality and social convention. The psychological domain refers to children's developing understanding of self and others as psychological systems. It includes an understanding of self, identity, personality; attributions for, and an understanding of, the causes of one's own and others' behavior; and also the individuals' attempts to assert personal agency by claiming control over personal issues. I will have much more to say about personal issues and their distinction from moral and conventional concepts in Chapter 5. But here it is important to note that these issues are part of the psychological domain and that this domain constitutes a third, distinct conceptual and developmental system of social knowledge.

Prudential issues, too, are an aspect of the psychological domain insofar as they pertain to the self. For instance, the examples of parental prohibitions described in the previous chapter included dicta such as "don't run into the street," "don't touch the hot stove," and "wear your mittens when it's cold." These rules (and prudential issues more generally) pertain to notions of harm to the self, comfort, and health. Prudential issues encompass many of the risk behaviors of adolescence, including smoking cigarettes (although the issue of second-order smoking is a moral issue), drinking alcohol, and engaging in illegal substance use. Both moral and prudential matters involve harm and may have physical consequences for persons. But prudential matters differ from moral ones in that morality is concerned with interpersonal harm, or harm that occurs in interactions between people. Prudential harm refers to nonsocial harm, which only involves the self.

Evidence supporting domain distinctions

The claim that morality and social convention (as well as the psychological domain) are conceptually and empirically distinct in development has received support in extensive research with children, adolescents, and adults. Most of the early research from the social domain perspective focused on testing the proposition that children distinguish different social concepts in their judgments and justifications. Some of the most persuasive evidence comes from studies of young children's judgments. This evidence is particularly compelling because younger children have fewer opportunities to be directly socialized by adults. From early ages on, children make distinctions between moral and conventional rules, events, and transgressions by using different criteria. They judge that morality is generalizable across different social contexts, whereas social conventions are not. When children are asked whether it is wrong to commit different violations at home versus at school (or, for older children, in their own country versus in different countries), they generally respond that moral violations are wrong all across the board, but social conventional violations are not. This is consistent with the notion that moral dicta are broadly applicable, whereas social conventions are relative to the social context.

Conventions stem from regularities. Conventional acts should be followed because particular social groups or societies say so; but they are not judged to be morally right or wrong. Moral violations are wrong because they have negative consequences for others' welfare and rights, and thus they are wrong whether or not rules or authorities say so. Therefore it can be said that evaluations of social conventions depend on rules, whereas evaluations of morality are based on the acts themselves. Even young children appear to grasp this distinction. For instance young children, including preschool children between the ages of 2 ½ and 5, have been asked whether it would be wrong to hit if a teacher were not to see it, or if there were no rule about hitting in their school (Smetana, 1981; Smetana & Braeges, 1990). Moral acts are evaluated as wrong whether or not there is a rule or law (that is, acts are seen as independent of rules or authority), whereas conventional acts are evaluated as wrong only if there is a rule or law (that is, they are contingent on rules or on the commands of an authority). Conventional rules are generally seen as alterable or changeable (it would be okay to say that one could use fingers instead of knife and fork, albeit the result would be messy), whereas moral rules are not (it is not okay to change the rule so as to make hitting permissible).

Preschool children distinguish moral and conventional transgressions, at least in rudimentary ways. They make these distinctions when the stimuli presented in research are concrete, familiar, and relevant to their lives (for instance in the case of everyday moral transgressions like hitting, kicking, and teasing, as compared to familiar social conventional violations like eating ice cream with one's fingers, not saying "please" or "thank you," not putting toys away). Also, because young children have limited verbal abilities, they make distinctions in their evaluations of familiar moral and conventional transgressions only when they are asked questions that do not demand sophisticated verbal responses. As children grow older, they are more able to distinguish moral and conventional events and transgressions in their judgments, particularly when they are asked to evaluate abstract or unfamiliar events. They also offer different reasons why moral and conventional transgressions are wrong. Children reason about moral events in terms of others' welfare, fairness, and rights, whereas when considering conventional events they reason in terms of demands from authority, punishment that might result from violating the rules, consequences of the event for social order or for the social organization, the importance of social norms and customs, and the need for conformity to social expectations (for instance for the sake of the smooth functioning of the group).

These distinctions also are evident when children evaluate actual events. For instance, in several studies, young children were found to distinguish actual moral versus conventional transgressions they observed in their preschool (Nucci & Turiel, 1978; Smetana, Schlagman, & Adams, 1993), as was examined by using multiple criteria. This finding has been replicated in other research with school-age children. Turiel (2008) conducted extensive naturalistic observations in several contexts in different schools, to obtain school-age children's judgments regarding actual situations. Children of varying ages were interviewed about actual moral and conventional events shortly after these occurred. They were also interviewed about hypothetical moral and conventional events, about a month following the observations. Children of all ages distinguished actual moral from conventional events, but judgments about the hypothetical events were more clear-cut and uniform than judgments about the actual events. Variations occurred because transgressors and victims sometimes disagreed over who initiated a moral transgression or why a transgression occurred. When children encounter straightforward moral transgressions in everyday life, the situations may be more ambiguous, and the features of the events may not be as well specified and detailed as in the situations presented to them in hypothetical interviews. In addition, children may be more motivated in real-life situations to try to understand others' intentions and emotions.

Differences between morality and social convention are based on fundamental differences between the acts. They are not based on variations in the seriousness of conflicts (or rule violations), or on the importance of the issues being contested. Marie Tisak and Elliot Turiel (1988) demonstrated this convincingly in a classic study. Most moral transgressions are naturally more serious than conventional transgressions. But Tisak and Turiel showed that children are able to separate the severity of different transgressions from the qualitative criteria that differentiate moral concepts from social conventional concepts. Children ranging from 6½ to 12½ years compared a moral transgression that had minor consequences (stealing an eraser) with a moral transgression that had major consequences (hitting someone). They also compared the minor moral transgression with a major conventional transgression (wearing pajamas to school), which pilot testing had revealed to be viewed by children as a very a serious and disruptive transgression. Most children indicated that a person would be more likely to commit the minor moral violation than the major conventional offense. When they were asked what one *should* do, however, most children indicated that they would choose the major conventional transgression over either of the two moral transgressions. They also viewed the conventional event as less wrong than the moral transgressions, because the moral events would have negative consequences for others' welfare.

Young children also differentiate between moral harm to others and prudential harm to self, even when the events are described as having similar consequences. Marie Tisak (1993) asked young children to distinguish between moral situations involving a child pushing another child off a swing and prudential harm, such as when a child purposely jumps off a swing. In both situations, the hypothetical child was depicted as getting hurt. Young children judged moral transgressions to be more wrong than prudential transgressions, even when the consequences of the latter were depicted as being more severe than the moral rule violations, or when the consequences of moral violations were depicted as being minor. This demonstrates that children make conceptual distinctions between moral and prudential issues that do not depend solely on how much harm is depicted as resulting from their transgression.

Social experiences as the basis for distinguishing social acts

As the earlier examples suggest, the assertion that morality and social convention represent qualitatively distinct types of social concepts is based on the claim that they develop from qualitatively different social experiences. Conventional concepts are thought to arise from social interactions that highlight the rules, sanctions, and regularities appropriate in different social contexts. In contrast, children's experiences as victims and observers of transgressions, and particularly their experiences of the consequences of transgressions for the others' rights and welfare, facilitate the development of prescriptive moral judgments. This is much as Piaget (1965) and other developmental psychologists (Damon, 1977; Youniss, 1980) have proposed. They believe that the reciprocal nature of peer relationships allows for experiences of conflict, cooperation, and negotiation that may facilitate moral judgment development.

The emphasis on the role of reciprocity in peer moral interactions also led to the view, initially propounded by Piaget (1965) and later adopted by Kohlberg (1984), that adults are not an important source of influence in the development of moral judgments – or indeed that parents may even constrain moral judgment development. In their view, this is because parent–child relationships are hierarchical and parents hold a great deal more power in the relationship than children do. In contrast, my view is that interactions with parents (and, more broadly, with other adults) contribute in a meaningful and positive way to moral judgment development by providing a complementary source of information to children's more direct experiences of harm or injustice. Parents' domain-appropriate explanations of why actions are wrong (which are sometimes referred to as inductive discipline) and their responses and reactions to children's behavior are also important for development. Parents' comments, reactions, and responses to the child's behavior ("Look what you did – you hurt her and made her cry!") facilitate his or her moral development. They provide information about the nature of acts, highlight their salience, and stimulate children to think reflectively about their actions. They focus children on what they have done and why it is wrong.

Observations of children's naturally occurring social interactions in the home, in preschools, and in elementary schools all show that children's moral and conventional experiences differ. Larry Nucci and Elliot Turiel (1978) pioneered a protocol for observing moral and conventional transgressions in different contexts. Observers in preschool classrooms (or homes) reliably identified and classified observed transgressions as moral or conventional on the basis of particular behavioral definitions (for instance, object conflicts or aggression were examples of moral transgressions). Observers then examined who responds (the victim, other peers, or adults) and the different ways they respond to the transgressions.

When 2- and 3-year-old toddlers' interactions with mothers and familiar peers have been observed in the home using these standard methods (Smetana, 1989b),

I have found that children have different social interactions regarding moral and conventional issues. Toddlers' interactions with peers were primarily over moral issues, such as possession of objects, rights, taking turns, hurting, aggression, and unkindness. Although children's moral development may be of great concern to adults, this and other studies demonstrate that many moral conflicts occur among peers and are resolved in the absence of parents or other adults. In contrast, conventional conflicts – over issues like manners and politeness, rules of the house, and cultural conventions – occurred primarily in interactions with mothers. This is not surprising, as these issues are primarily of concern to mothers. Mothers expect obedience in these matters, especially as children grow older and become more competent to behave appropriately. Indeed, in my observational study, 3-year-olds were seen as committing more conventional transgressions than 2-year-olds were. This does not mean that children misbehave more as they grow older. The finding most likely reflects the mothers' increasing demands for conventionally appropriate behavior, and hence the increased likelihood that mothers treated toddlers' misbehaviors as transgressions.

Both adults and children (primarily the victims) responded to moral transgressions in ways that provided feedback about the effects of the actions for others' rights or welfare. For instance, mothers requested that children take the victim's perspective ("how do you think you'd feel if someone took your toy?"; "look what you did – you made her cry"). Mothers also evaluated the person whose rights were violated ("she had it first – give it back"). Children (usually the victims) typically responded with emotional reactions (crying, yelling) and statements of rights ("mine!"; "I had it first"). These responses are consistent with the notion that children's moral understanding can be derived from the acts themselves rather than from the rules that regulate the acts.

But, as these examples suggest, this was not the only source of information about the nature of the interaction. Children had other, complementary bases for evaluating the intrinsic consequences of moral violations for the others' rights and welfare. They had their own direct experiences as victims of moral transgressions. Children draw on their own emotional responses to events in making moral judgments. And transgressors (or, in other contexts, bystanders) may also observe the victims' negative reactions to events. Finally, mothers typically offered explanations as to why the acts were wrong. As all this suggests, children have available to them multiple sources of information, both affective and cognitive, to help them evaluate moral transgressions and judge why they are wrong. (The connections between emotional responses and judgments are discussed below.)

Mothers responded more frequently to conventional violations than to moral transgressions. Mothers (and other adults) respond to the children's conventional transgressions because they have a stake in maintaining conventional regularities. But, until about middle childhood, children rarely respond. Adults respond to conventional transgressions with commands that the children cease the misbehavior or with descriptions of the punishments that might ensue if they do not.

Such statements typically do not include explanations of why the acts are wrong. (The lack of explanations may be one reason why children's understanding of social conventions lags behind their understanding of morality.) In my observations, mothers also responded to children's conventional violations with statements about the disorder the acts created and with reiterations of the rules.

Observational studies show that social interactions in the context of moral transgressions also differ qualitatively from social interactions regarding prudential events, even among young children (Tisak, Nucci, & Jankowski, 1996). When preschoolers' naturalistic interactions were systematically observed, adults were found to respond to prudential rule violations with statements regarding the risks involved in the child's actions. They also provided rationales pertaining to safety or prudence. Less frequently, they uttered commands to stop and statements of rules (Nucci & Weber, 1995; Tisak et al., 1996). Thus the adult responses to young children's prudential violations focused these children on the consequences of their actions for their own health or safety. As in other observational studies, however, the responses to moral transgressions focused the transgressor on the consequences of his or her acts for others.

Emotions and cognitions

It is worth highlighting here how emotions and cognitions are intertwined in the development of moral and social judgments. William Arsenio and his colleagues at Yeshiva University (Arsenio, Gold, & Adams, 2006; Arsenio & Lover, 1995) have outlined four steps describing the influence of emotions on moral judgment development. In the first step, and as I have just described, children have experiences as witnesses to and participants in moral and conventional events. These experiences are plentiful in early childhood and can be highly emotional and affectively laden.

In the second step, connections are made between different emotions and different types of events. Arsenio and his colleagues propose that children's emotional experiences differ by domain. Moral and conventional acts vary in the extent to which they elicit emotional arousal. Highly arousing moral events are considered "immoral," partly because they are affectively more salient than less arousing events. But, in addition, moral and conventional interactions also evoke specific (and different) emotions, which become part of the individuals' cognitive representations of events. In turn, children encode moral and conventional events differently.

Research supports this notion. Studying kindergartners and school-age children, Arsenio (1988) found that children evaluated moral events as affectively negative; but conventional transgressions were seen as affectively neutral. And the connections went both ways. Young children could use information about the nature (domain) of different acts to predict what types of emotions hypothetical actors would experience. They could also infer the type of event that had happened when they were provided with affective information. Children used information about whether actors or victims were happy, sad, angry, fearful, or neutral to infer whether events were conventional or moral.

According to Arsenio and his colleagues, the third step in the chain is that children use information about the affective consequences of different events to anticipate the likely outcomes of different alternative behaviors. In the final step, affective knowledge is employed in the development of more generalized moral judgments. Individuals may vary in these last two steps. There also may be distortions and biases here, which may lead to problems in the development of moral judgment.

As the foregoing discussion suggests, the social domain theory view is that emotions are deeply embedded in the children's social judgments. This differs from a recent and popular view, which states that emotions play a central role in morality and that individuals respond to many social and moral situations in primarily affective and intuitive ways, leaving very little room for moral reasoning and deliberation in everyday social life (Haidt, 2001). According to this view, individuals typically react emotionally when moral situations arise and rarely stop to reason and reflect. The claim is that when moral reasoning occurs, it is post-hoc and used primarily to justify emotional responses. In contrast, in the view outlined here, emotional and cognitive responses are not so easily separated. They are intertwined, as affective responses become part of the process of making social and moral evaluations.

Overlaps and coordinations in reasoning

In many everyday situations individuals uphold moral principles just as in the hypothetical scenarios used in research. Indeed, one of the striking things about social life is how often moral principles are upheld. In his book *The moral sense* (1993), political scientist James Q. Wilson makes a similar observation. He notes that newspapers are filled with examples of violent crimes precisely because these fall outside the norm. They are exceptional events. If individuals regularly violated moral norms and these became everyday occurrences, they would not be so newsworthy. He asserts that most people uphold moral principles in their everyday life, and this is so much taken for granted that it is rarely noticed. Many social commentators choose to focus on – and exaggerate – the exceptions, when the really notable fact is the extent to which most individuals follow moral requirements and conventional norms in their everyday lives.

It may be quite easy to follow moral or social conventional principles when they do not conflict with other goals, motives, or values. But not all events or situations are strictly moral or conventional, or can be cleanly separated into moral or conventional components. Many events or situations are multifaceted and may be seen as involving elements from different domains. The focus of social domain research has shifted from examining whether children at different ages distinguish the domains in their evaluations of hypothetical, prototypical events; this is clear and well established. Instead, much current research now focuses on how children and adolescents reason about (and act in) more complex, multifaceted situations. Before returning to consider the parents' perspectives on conflict, I will offer two brief examples of the multifaceted nature of social events from other areas of research on adolescence.

Psychologists have a long-standing interest in understanding why individuals include or exclude others from their social groups, particularly when this is done on the basis of race or gender. Melanie Killen and her students at the University of Maryland (as reviewed in Killen, Margie, & Sinno, 2006) have shown that evaluations of peer exclusion can involve moral notions of fairness, conventional concerns with group norms and effective group functioning, and concerns with autonomy, personal choice, and identity. All of these different types of concerns may be involved in making judgments about peer and intergroup exclusion. When situations of peer exclusion are described in a straightforward way without any competing considerations, most children and adolescents view it as wrong to exclude others, and they do so on the basis of moral concerns with fairness and rights. It is not seen as acceptable to exclude a peer from a school group on the basis of race or gender. However, when different qualifications for group membership are introduced, children coordinate and sometimes prioritize conventional over moral aspects of the situations. For instance, when children are presented with stereotypal information that poses threats to group functioning (such as that boys or girls lack specific abilities, which might impede the group), early adolescents are more likely than younger children to emphasize conventional concerns. They reason about effective group functioning and group processes. They are also more likely to recognize and coordinate moral and social conventional concerns rather than to focus on one set of concerns or the other.

Stacey Horn (2003) also has demonstrated that adolescents treat exclusion from social groups as being multifaceted and as having moral and conventional components. Adolescents who belong to high-status peer crowds like "cheerleaders," "jocks," or "preppies" judge exclusion from peer groups as less wrong than do adolescents who either do not belong to a group or who belong to low-status high school peer groups like "dirties," "druggies," or "gothics." Therefore the moral aspects of the situation, as well as the adolescents' position in the social hierarchy, influence the latter's moral concepts of fairness and equal treatment.

In a similar way, Stacey Horn and Larry Nucci (2003) have found that adolescents have multifaceted evaluations of homosexuality. They bring to bear both moral and social conventional concerns in their judgments. These researchers found that adolescents who held more negative attitudes towards homosexuality reasoned on the basis of societal and religious conventions, norms, or rules. More positive attitudes towards gay and lesbian youth were based on moral concerns with fairness and rights. These were associated with evaluations that it is wrong to tease, harass, or exclude others on the basis of sexual orientation or gender nonconformity in school. However, all adolescents viewed excluding (but not teasing or harassing) as less wrong when the excluded individual was described as gay or lesbian than as heterosexual. Adolescents and young adults appear to distinguish between their personal beliefs about the permissibility of homosexuality and their conceptions of the fair treatment of others.

As these examples demonstrate, individuals' reasoning about social events can involve concerns from different domains. Sometimes individuals view these different concerns as in conflict with each other, and they vacillate between them. They may see different perspectives as having validity, and they may be unable to decide which one is right. At other times, though, individuals may coordinate the concerns, or subordinate one set of them to another. As this suggests, individuals may have varying interpretations of the social situations. Whereas one child may view peer exclusion as wrong on the basis of moral concerns with fairness or equal treatment, another child may view the same act as acceptable on the basis of social conventional concerns with group functioning. One or the other concern may be seen as carrying more weight in the situation, but the child also simply may not see the potential complexity of the situation and the competing concerns that are involved.

As Cecilia Wainryb and her colleagues at the University of Utah discuss in greater detail (Wainryb et al., 2005), just because individuals arrive at different conclusions about right or wrong, we cannot infer from this that morality is relative. Moral relativism is the notion that moral claims are relative to social, cultural, historical, or personal circumstances rather than deriving from more objective and broadly generalizable moral truths. We have seen that children construct prescriptive moral concepts out of their social interactions. There may be some variation or subjectivity in children's perception of situations and in their interpretations of the relevant features of those interactions, as well as in their understanding of the way things are. Children may attend to different features of the social situations and, to some extent, construct different realities. Their perspective, which may be informed by their individual circumstances, may lead to different construals or interpretations of situations. For instance, as we just saw, Horn's research shows that adolescents' position in the social hierarchy influences their judgments concerning exclusion from peer groups. Likewise, several other studies have shown that children reason differently both about hypothetical and about real-life transgressions, depending on their perspective on the situation (that is, on whether they are the victims or the perpetrators of the transgressions). In a later chapter we will consider the relevance of these notions for parenting.

Informational assumptions

Individuals also may vary in their descriptive understanding of the nature of reality. Many apparent cultural and ethnic differences are due to differences in factual beliefs, or to what has been referred to as informational assumptions. Social domain researchers have proposed that informational assumptions need to be distinguished conceptually and empirically from moral evaluations (Turiel, 1983, 2002; Wainryb, 1991; Wainryb & Turiel, 1993). The claim is that individuals consistently take into account both moral and factual beliefs in making judgments. Differences in informational assumptions may lead to apparent differences in moral and social evaluations. Informational assumptions may bear on how individuals construe social practices and act on their own beliefs. For example, whether one considers corporal punishment to be morally reprehensible or not depends on whether one believes that this is an efficacious or necessary way to teach children about societal expectations. Different groups vary in these beliefs, which sometimes leads to deeply contested arguments about best practices for child rearing.

Informational assumptions come from many sources, including science and religion. Many of our factual beliefs are taken for granted and rarely examined. But different groups within and across cultures may disagree in their informational assumptions. For instance, there are different religious beliefs about when a fetus becomes a person, different scientific theories about the causes of HIV/AIDS, and different lay theories about effective child-rearing practices. Moreover, these beliefs can change, as when scientific knowledge advances. For instance, recent scientific advances have made some of the theories of HIV/AIDS transmission less credible. We are continually bombarded with new and conflicting scientific evidence – is drinking red wine beneficial or harmful for health, does Vitamin C protect against colds, are childhood vaccinations a cause of autism? When new scientific evidence comes to light or information becomes more widely disseminated or politicized, they may change the nature of our understanding. For instance, when scientists confirmed that exposure to cigarette smoking was harmful to others, cigarette smoking became not just a prudential issue of health, but also a moral issue. Individuals began to recognize that smoking affects others' welfare in the form of passive smoking.

Informational assumptions account for some cultural differences. This is illustrated in the following lengthy example. Cultural anthropologist Richard Shweder and his colleagues (Shweder, Mahapatra, & Miller, 1987) conducted a cross-cultural study comparing the judgments of middle-class and upper middle-class adults from Hyde Park, Chicago with those of Brahman and Untouchable adults from the orthodox temple town of Bhubanswar, India. Participants evaluated the perceived permissibility, alterability, relativity, and seriousness of 39 acts. Judgments were considered conventional when participants rated the practice as both relative and alterable within one's group, whereas practices that were evaluated as relative but unalterable were seen as "context-dependent moral obligations." Using these criteria, the researchers found a virtual absence of conventional judgments in India and a much lower percentage of conventional judgments among participants from their American sample than previous studies have reported.

As Turiel, Killen, and Helwig (1987) noted, however, there were several problems with the methods of the study, including the lack of comparability of the samples and the way conventionality was assessed. But, most importantly for the present argument, Turiel and his colleagues (1987) suggested that moral evaluations and informational assumptions were not sufficiently differentiated. That is, many of the 39 practices studied by Shweder and his colleagues were events that involved assumptions about the natural order, and in particular about the afterlife. For example, one item revolved around a son eating chicken the day after his father's death. This would appear to be a clearly conventional practice (and, as such, it was not considered a transgression by American participants). However, Indian participants evaluated this practice as involving moral obligations. Other ethnographic data showed that this was because Indian participants viewed this act as causing the father's soul not to receive salvation. In fact, many of the conventional stimulus items included in the 1987 study of Shweder and his colleagues referred to the existence of nonobserved entities (like souls), which would experience harm if certain earthly activities were performed (or not performed). On the basis of a conceptual re-analysis of the stimulus items, Turiel and his colleagues asserted that most of the conventional items studied by Shweder and colleagues were either multidimensional events (domain mixtures or second-order moral transgressions) or moral items relying on various informational assumptions. The findings demonstrate differences between Americans and Indians in their informational assumptions about what causes harm or who may suffer it. At the same time, the study demonstrates similarities among the Indians' and the Americans' moral evaluations of the idea that it is wrong to cause harm.

In a further study conducted in India, Madden (1992) addressed these criticisms by directly examining informational assumptions among a group of priests from Bhubanswar, India (the same temple town where Shweder and colleagues conducted their research), as well as among local college students. He distinguished between prohibitions that were associated with religion and unobservable events in the afterlife and transgressions of conventions that were not mediated by "unearthly" beliefs (for instance, a wife kissing her husband in public or a husband cooking dinner for his wife and friends). In contrast to Shweder and his colleagues, Madden found clear evidence of conventional judgments in his study. Both the priests and the college students judged conventional transgressions to be less wrong than moral transgressions, more contingent on existing practices, more alterable, and more relative to cultural contexts, based as these were on conventional reasons. Judgments regarding transgressions that pertained to unearthly beliefs associated with religion were more equivocal, at least among the priests. Priests judged both these and the moral transgressions to be wrong; but the transgressions involving unearthly beliefs were seen as more contingent on existing practices, more alterable, and more culturally relative than the moral transgressions. In contrast, students unequivocally responded to the belief-mediated events in conventional terms and distinguished them clearly from moral events.

Priests also evaluated the transgressions on the basis of informational assumptions opposite to their own (for example, on the basis of the assumption that no harmful effects to souls would follow from earthly practices). Many of the priests refused to entertain the alternative assumptions. But those who were willing to consider different informational assumptions shifted in their judgment of the transgressions. When adopting different informational assumptions, they considered these transgressions to be acceptable. Therefore the results of this study highlight the importance of separating informational assumptions from moral and social judgments. They also demonstrate the heterogeneity of social judgments, and they show that Indian culture cannot be characterized as lacking in a concept of convention.

Cecilia Wainryb and her colleagues have convincingly demonstrated that informational assumptions influence our evaluations of social practices. Wainryb and her colleagues (Turiel, Hildebrandt, & Wainryb, 1991; Wainryb, 1991, 1993; Wainryb & Turiel, 1993) found that individuals generally have similar moral beliefs about the wrongness of inflicting harm on others. However, they may evaluate particular situations and different social practices in different ways, due to divergences in their informational assumptions. Individuals may disagree about what they believe to be true. Differences in factual beliefs informed moral evaluations of particular situations. Manipulating the informational assumptions led to changes in individuals' moral evaluations of the acts. (I will elaborate on this notion in Chapter 10.)

To summarize this lengthy theoretical interlude, social domain researchers propose that children's social knowledge develops within three distinct domains: the moral, the conventional, and the psychological domain. Moral matters pertain to individuals' prescriptive understanding of how they ought to behave towards others; such matters focus on reasoning about justice, welfare, and rights. Social conventions pertain to individuals' descriptive understanding of the more arbitrary, agreed upon regularities and norms that structure social interactions in different contexts. Social conventions help to provide expectations about appropriate behavior, in different social contexts and for individuals in different roles. Thus they facilitate the effective functioning of social groups. Psychological issues, including personal issues, pertain to our understanding of self and others as psychological systems. A great deal of research has shown that, from early childhood on, children distinguish different rules, events, and transgressions along the different dimensions (criteria) that are hypothesized to distinguish these domains. Moreover, children apply these different concepts in their reasoning about multifaceted situations. They weigh and coordinate different concerns in thinking about complex social issues.

We are now ready to return to a consideration of the parents' reasoning about conflict. Later we will see that these different ways of thinking are relevant to the way in which adolescents and parents construe their relationships with each other.

Parents' Perspectives on Conflict, Interpreted

Social conventional justifications for conflicts

We saw earlier that conflicts occur over everyday, mundane issues of family life. What are these conflicts "really" about? Social domain theory provides a way of understanding them, together with the types of reasons that parents (and, as we shall see in the next chapter, adolescents) give for their expectations. The finding of my studies show that parents justified their perspectives on conflicts primarily by invoking social conventions. Parents raised a variety of different conventional concerns. For instance, some of them referred to family rules and parental authority. We frequently heard refrains such as "if he lives in our house, he has to follow our rules," or "I'm the boss here." Parents also staked out the boundaries of their authority, which conflicted with their teenager children's perception. "She says it's *her* room but it's not, it's *my* house." Sometimes these appeals to authority referenced a higher authority ("it's against the law," or "the Bible says so"). Or, as one mother said in reference to keeping a clean room, "[c]leanliness is next to Godliness, and that's the way we were raised."

Parents also expressed conventional concerns with appropriate roles ("who do they think I am – the maid?"), the need for respect ("he needs to be more respectful – he shouldn't talk to his father like that"), and maintaining the effective functioning of the family social system. Both mothers and fathers talked about the family as a unit and about the need for adolescents to contribute to its functioning. Parents sometimes emphasized the need for different family members to coordinate their efforts, so that each family member would know what was expected of him or her and the family could function efficiently. For instance, in responding to a question about why it is important for her son to do his chores, Suzanne, the mother of 16-year-old Henry, talks about her son's responsibility to the family:

> Everybody has to do his or her part. I work. I come home. I'm tired. I can't stand it when Henry doesn't pick up. He walks in the door, drops his backpack and his jacket. Then he leaves a trail of paper and books up the stairs. He needs to pick up. He has to do his part as a member of the family and do his chores. Henry just doesn't want to do it.

The parents' awareness of the adolescents' increasing age and competence also contributed to their perception that these adolescents had responsibilities to fulfill. Agreements among family members were seen as facilitating social order and efficient organization.

Parents also instantiated this concern in their comments about mess and social order. Such comments arose in particular in reference to doing chores around the house and around the state of the adolescents' bedrooms. Mothers lamented: "It's such a mess. I don't know how she can find anything in there." Parents had other types of concerns as well. For instance, Lynn, the mother of 13-year-old Abby, was worried about the others' negative reactions to Abby's appearance. When asked what was wrong with the way Abby dressed, Lynn articulated several different themes.

> Well, it's really provocative, for one thing. She says that's the way everyone dresses, and that it isn't my decision. But as long as I buy the clothes, it is my decision. She just wants to fit in. But I'm afraid that other kids – especially the boys – will get the wrong idea. And I see other kids – they don't all dress that way. But she tells me that I'm just old-fashioned and that if she wore the clothes I pick out for her, all the other kids would laugh.

By describing her daughter's clothes as provocative, Lynn implicitly referenced social norms and suggested that Abby is flaunting existing standards. Moreover, Lynn noted that, despite Abby's protestations, her clothing choices were not consistent with mainstream norms or with Abby's peer culture. Lynn also asserted that, because she was paying for the clothes, she had the legitimate authority to make the final decision.

Concerns with first impressions were often evident. When asked about a conflict about which clothes to wear, Anna provides the following response – first from her own perspective and then from that of her teen's.

> I want him to look respectful, look presentable. I just want him to look good. Because he will have a better chance at people having first impressions of him. He wants to wear baggy clothes, baggy jeans, tennis shoes that aren't tied up and just have that city gangster look that I don't care for. He thinks it's stylish. It's the teen thing to do, and it's not necessarily ethnic because it's all of the kids that look that way. Black and White. But I don't care for it.

Parents also expressed the need for social conformity. Not to conform to social expectations was seen as having potentially negative consequences. This problem arose particularly in regard to adolescents' appearances. For instance, parents were concerned with the potential for embarrassment stored in their adolescent's behavior or appearance, and with the inaccurate or inappropriate attributions that others might make about their child (as was the case with Anna and Lynn, quoted previously, both of whom worried, for different reasons, that others might get the wrong idea). Parents also perceived the potential social costs, possibly to their own reputation ("What would Aunt Minnie think of us if she saw your room looking way?"; "Do you want to give your Grandma a heart attack?"). They worried even about the teenagers' peer groups and wondered whether their offspring's behavior would lead them to be ostracized or ridiculed by their peers.

As these examples suggest, parents articulated a number of different social conventional concerns with norms, authority, social order, social nonconformity, and social organization. Indeed, among my middle-class, primarily European American, families, appeals to social conventions were the modal response of mothers and fathers and accounted for, or justified, 50% of their disputes. The parents' appeals to social conventions reflected their efforts to maintain social order, promote social interaction, and enforce cultural norms and more idiosyncratic family rules and expectations. Their demands reflected the aim of helping adolescents acquire the psychological and social competencies required by society in order for people to lead productive lives. In other words, parents' appeals to social conventions serve a socializing function in adolescent development. They help to facilitate the adolescents' effective participation in family and society.

Moral justifications

But parents' reasoning about conflicts is not entirely social conventional. Parents expressed a variety of other concerns. They also reasoned morally about everyday conflicts, although these responses were relatively infrequent and accounted for only 15% of the parents' responses in the study of European American two-parent families (very similar findings were obtained in other studies as well). The parents' moral reasoning about conflicts reflected their attempts to facilitate interpersonal relationships and to work out differences within them. Parents reasoned morally about conflicts primarily when they were drawn in as a third party in the adolescents' moral disputes with their siblings and, occasionally, with friends. Parents were asked to referee and resolve conflicts. Therefore most of the conflicts that elicited moral reasoning from parents focused on their concerns that one sibling would physically harm another sibling, that teasing should stop because someone's feelings were getting hurt, or that siblings were not sharing resources in an equitable way.

Prudential and pragmatic justifications

Nearly a quarter of the parents' justifications for conflicts were prudential or pragmatic and pertaining to practical needs or consequences (prudential and pragmatic justifications were not differentiated in this study). Parents offered prudential arguments particularly when they had disputes with their adolescents over going to bed late or over the latter's choice of activities. When discussing bedtimes, parents were concerned about issues like tiredness ("He'll be tired tomorrow in school, and he needs to get his sleep"). In the course of discussing the choice of activities and of regulating the adolescents' behavior, worries about their health or safety frequently arose. For example Monica, the 36-year-old mother of Gabriel, elaborated on the theme of her concerns regarding Gabriel's health in relation to his choice of activities and to his manner of spending his free time.

MONICA: Well, it is that he likes to play the PlayStation. And the house could blow up around him and he could be into the PlayStation, and I try to get him to do some variety. I mean, there's time like – it's summertime. It's time [to] go out and enjoy the sun. Don't be cooped up in the house. If it's raining or something, then fine, come in. But just not for eight hours try to sit in front of a video game or TV. Do something different. I think video games are probably bad on his eyes. And TV doesn't always have the best things for the kids. Although at his age, they're watching a lot more risqué stuff that's right on TV. But just variety.

INTERVIEWER: In this situation, what does Gabriel want to do?

MONICA: Just leave him alone and let him do what he wants to do. He doesn't see that it's hurting him in any way.

As this example suggests, parents sometimes viewed as harmful behaviors that their adolescents did not.

Parents typically framed in prudential terms their concerns about lack of supervision and about knowing where their teens were. This is illustrated in the following example provided by Barbara, the mother of 14-year-old Tanya:

Again, it's the age thing. I think 14 is just too young to turn them loose right now … I know what happens [when kids are unsupervised]… I talk to students and work with students in her age group, and some kids say they don't have a curfew or that they can go and hang out and come home, and their parents don't know where they are. I can't imagine that. It's not safe.

Overall, there were very few differences between the mothers' and the fathers' reasoning about conflicts. Fathers, however, were more concerned than mothers with the prudential aspects of regulating their adolescents' activities and behaviors. In contrast, parents typically justified the need to get homework done and to do well in school by appeal to pragmatic considerations. Parents' pragmatic justifications focused on practical needs and consequences, such as the need to do well academically in order to ensure future success in life.

Summary and Conclusions

To discover the meaning of conflicts to different family members, we examined mothers, fathers, and adolescents' justifications, or their reasoning about their disputes.

This analysis was informed by a large body of psychological and developmental theorizing and research from the framework of social domain theory. A central claim of social domain theory is that individuals attempt to make sense of their social world and construct meaning from their social interactions. Social domain theory calls attention to the types of rules and expectations children are asked to follow, as well as to the areas that individuals see as extending beyond legitimate social regulation. More specifically, children distinguish between different forms of social regulation – including social conventions (the arbitrary, agreed upon rules and norms that structure social interactions in different contexts) – and moral issues (prescriptive judgments about how individuals ought to behave). Moral and conventional concepts are also distinguished from psychological concepts – which include personal issues (these will be discussed in greater detail in Chapter 5) and prudential issues (these pertain to individuals' safety, comfort, and health).

Using this framework, we saw that European American parents brought different social concepts to bear on their reasoning about their everyday disputes with their adolescents. Most frequently, parents treated conflicts as issues of social convention, but they also formulated moral, psychological, prudential, and pragmatic concerns. Social conventional claims were varied and included concerns with social order, authority, social coordination, the consequences of social nonconformity, and the need for respect and politeness. Although parents offered diverse reasons, these were seen as sharing a common underlying theme. The claim is that parents' appeals to social conventions reflect parents' attempts to socialize their adolescent children into the norms and standards of their families and of the broader society. Although they occurred less frequently, parents' appeals to prudence focused on keeping adolescents healthy and safe, and their pragmatic reasons focused on practical advice and on concerns designed to ensure future success.

So far, the focus has been on the parents' perspectives. Therefore the picture is incomplete. Do adolescents agree with their parents' perspectives on disputes? We must listen to adolescents' voices to find this out. Adolescents' characteristic responses to interviews about conflict are considered in the next chapter.

5

Adolescents' Voices

Autonomy and the Personal Domain

Kelly, an attractive 17-year-old, enters my university lab with her mother and father to participate in interviews. She clearly has a comfortable relationship with her parents. They talk and joke as they wait for their interviews to begin. After moving into separate interview cubicles, the interviewer asks Kelly about the disagreements she has with her parents. Despite the obvious warmth in her relationship with her parents, Kelly quickly brings up several areas of disagreement. A major issue for Kelly is the way she keeps her room. In response to the interviewer's probing regarding her messy room, she elaborates:

KELLY: It's my room and it's how I do things.

INTERVIEWER: When your parents complain, what do you want to do?

KELLY: In my room, I'm comfortable when it's messy. It's my space. My parents would like it to be neat and tidy like the rest of the house, which I can appreciate, but my room is my own. It's my space, so I should be able to keep it the way I want to.

INTERVIEWER: What do your parents want you to do?

KELLY: Clean it up. Most people think that it's better to be neat than messy. It gives a better outward appearance. You know, if I came to school with my hair still the same way it was when I got up, that gives a certain image [...] Nobody really sees my room except my good friends, and they don't care. They know me anyway, so I don't mind.

Kelly views her room as her private space. Kelly is not unlike many teens. She clearly understands that some actions, like whether her hair is messy, might lead others to make negative judgments about her. But she distinguishes between the type of public actions that might lead to negative appraisals of her and her room, which she views as her private space.

Adolescents, Families, and Social Development: How Teens Construct Their Worlds.   Judith G. Smetana
© 2011 Judith G. Smetana

The state of teenagers' rooms came up often in interviews. In this context, European American teenagers almost always expressed the view that the room was their territory, that its appearance or condition was their personal choice or an expression of their identity, that the issue is trivial or inconsequential, and that it should not matter to parents. These ideas were typically described as being in opposition to the parents' conventional concerns with social order and conformity to standards, or to the parents' prudential concerns with health and cleanliness.

But the bedroom was not the only battleground where teenagers expressed desires for personal choice. Steven, a 10th-grade boy, argues that doing chores is his business. In his case, he means this quite literally, because he has his own business cutting lawns for his neighbors during the summer. Although he recognizes the need for chores to be done, he views his parents' expectations about when to cut the lawn as arbitrary. When asked why he should be able to cut the lawn when he decides rather than on his parents' schedule, he asserts that he should be able to choose when and how to do the chores.

> It was my business and I was in charge of all these lawns, and they were saying, "Well, we want you to do them now [...]" I feel that if I am the one who has to cut it, I should do it when I have the time and when I want to do it, not when they want me to do it. If they want it done today, they can do it today, I am going to do it Friday or sometime [...] I might have other plans or just feel like relaxing that day, and since I am planning to do it at a certain time that isn't too far away, I don't see why that is not acceptable.

Teenagers, and especially older teenagers, asserted strongly that the issues were theirs to decide or control. Decisions that were appropriate for parents to make for younger children were no longer parental prerogatives. For example, as teenagers grew older, they asserted that they should be able to decide when to go to bed, even though they understood and agreed that parents may have legitimate concerns about whether they might feel tired the next day. When questioned about a conflict over bedtime, Becky, a 17-year-old, states this clearly.

> Bedtime is sticky. I think that at 17, they shouldn't be telling me what time to go to bed. I sort of pretty much know that if I don't go to be bed by 10 pm I'll be tired. But whether or not I can or choose to go to bed at 10:00, it's my concern now. They don't agree [...] If I'm not in bed by 10:00, there's a reason for it [...] If I have homework. If I've had a hard day, and I'm watching a good movie [...] [My mother] wants me to go to bed early, so that I'm not tired in school the next day. Her reason is valid. But I think at 17, I should be the one to decide. I mean it should be my final decision.

Some teenagers viewed conflicts as happening over unimportant issues. For instance Jodi, a 14-year-old girl, discusses a conflict she has with her father about how she spends her money. She is preoccupied with looking good and keeping up with fashion, but she also believes that how she spends her money is inconsequential. Therefore her spending decisions should be her own choice.

> I usually like to spend it [money] all at one time, and my dad wants me to save it because I'm not getting any more until spring. I like to keep up with the fashions, stuff like that. And it doesn't hurt anybody if I have nice clothes or anything. It doesn't hurt anyone, and it's important to me to look ok […] [My father] wants me to save it until I can […] until I find some really good deals, and I can save some money, stuff like that.

As in the previous interviews, Jodi draws a line between issues that cause harm to others and those that do not. She views how she spends her money as not harming anyone else. Therefore she sees it as being under her control. It advances her goal of keeping up with styles and being fashionable.

Adolescents also asserted that making personal choices allowed them to demonstrate their style or individuality. Again, these issues were seen as largely inconsequential and simply a matter of personal taste. Rick, a 17-year-old boy, discusses his decision to get an earring (he was interviewed well before earrings and piercings became common among males).

> When I first got it done, my dad was upset that his son wears an earring […] I just like it, I think it's kind of cool. I like it […] I think they [parents] are just conservative. Boys or men don't wear earrings. It looks weird. But I think it's kind of nice … Whether I wear an earring or not, it doesn't matter. If I like it, fine. If people like plaid, they can wear plaid. You know, it's the same thing for me as them. I think there's a certain style about it. I like the style.

Other teens focused on the need for privacy. Roberta, a 13-year-old, describes a conflict she has with her mother about talking on the phone. She asserts that talking on the phone is a personal preference, and she does not see any harm in her actions. She also wants more privacy:

> I want to talk [on the phone] longer, and usually I want it in private, too. You know, I don't like a lot of people around me when I'm talking […] [My mother] doesn't want me to talk as much […] [because] I could be doing homework. But I think she's wrong … I mean, what's so wrong about talking on the phone for an hour or so? There's nothing really wrong with that. I don't think she has the right to be mad.

This theme of privacy emerged in many of the interviews. Some teenagers talked about the need for personal space. They viewed their room as offering a physical haven for privacy. Fourteen-year-old Jessica offers a more dramatic example of privacy needs:

JESSICA: Well, she denies it [snooping around], but if she finds a bad test
                         grade, or she finds notes that I've written, or that my friend's
                         written back, and I see my desk drawer all cleaned out and I
                         know that she did it, I just get really mad about it. I don't know
                         why, it just bugs me really much, that I just get out of control
                         and I really mess up my whole room.
INTERVIEWER: You've told her not to snoop around?
JESSICA: Yes. Not to touch my stuff. Because it's my private stuff, she's got
                         no business there, and I don't go in her room and snoop around.

Jessica goes on to talk about privacy in reference to another conflict, about whether
she discloses information about her activities to her parents.

> I don't want to tell them things because I think it's none of their business, and I
> could talk to a more understanding person, like a friend, and I would just [...] I'll
> still get in a lot of trouble, when they find out about it, they'd get mad that I didn't
> tell them [...] Because it's none of their business, and they don't understand and
> they'll just get mad, so I just save a lot of trouble.

This issue of keeping information private, which emerged in the context of talking
about conflicts, is an important one for adolescent development and is explored
in more detail in Chapter 11 and in Chapter 12. But it is interesting to note that
the essence of this conflict for Jessica was that she should be able to keep things
private. Her mother's attempts at "snooping around" and finding out what is
going on are seen as unwanted intrusions into her personal space.

These examples, which are highly representative of the responses we obtained,
suggest that European American middle-class adolescents frequently framed their
arguments in terms of personal preferences and choices. Adolescents claimed that
the issues causing conflict were unimportant or inconsequential ("it doesn't
matter," "it's no big deal"), that their behavior was acceptable or permissible ("it's
okay,"), that their choices were a reflection of their identity and individuality or
an aspect of their personal expression ("it's part of who I am"), or that the issues
were personal choices. The constant refrain emerging from these interviews was
"it's my choice," "it's my decision," "it's up to me."

One interpretation of these findings is that they reflect the selfishness or ego-
centrism of American youth. As we saw in Chapter 1, this is an argument that is
made frequently – and not just about contemporary American youth. But another
interpretation is that adolescents' responses reflect legitimate concerns with personal expression and choice. In the last chapter I described the basics of social
domain theory, and I claimed that concepts of social convention and morality (as
well as prudential concerns) belong to distinct types of social knowledge. As the
foregoing examples suggest, adolescents' reasoning about their conflicts with
parents does not fit these categories. Instead, a central theme that emerged from
the responses was one of boundaries: where to draw the line between issues

parents legitimately could or should control and adolescents' personal preferences. Adolescents' responses indicated that, in their view, some conflicts arise
because parents want to regulate issues that teenagers believe should be under
their control. Rather than demonstrating a selfish or egocentric orientation, these
responses relate to personal choice and personal jurisdiction and can be seen as
falling within the psychological domain. As I argue in the following section,
concerns with personal choice and freedoms reflect an important aspect of psychological knowledge and are distinct from both moral and social conventional
considerations.

The Personal as a Distinct Domain of Social Knowledge

Larry Nucci has written extensively on the subject of children's reasoning about
personal issues. (From here on, I will adopt the shorthand of referring to personal
issues as the personal domain; but keep in mind that these issues are one aspect
of children's developing psychological knowledge. Prudential issues, which pertain
to the self, are also part of this domain.) Nucci (1981, 1996, 2001, 2008) has defined
personal issues as comprising the private aspects of one's life. Personal issues are
seen as lying beyond the realm of legitimate societal regulation and moral concern,
because they pertain to privacy (for instance, the content of one's diaries or journals), control over one's body, and certain preferences and choices. Among
American children, choices regarding friends, hairstyles, clothes, and leisure time
activities usually are treated as personal issues. The personal domain is not simply
what is left over – what is unregulated or not seen as conventional in different
contexts. Rather, it includes issues that are actively negotiated and claimed to be
personal.

For example, in her autobiography, *Red azalea* (1994), Anchee Min describes
her experiences as she grew up under the last years of Mao's rule in China. Born
in Shanghai, she was sent, at the age of 17, to work at a labor collective as a
member of the Red Guards. Her life there was heavily regulated. She was forbidden to speak out, to dress as she chose, to have contact with men, or to write to
friends and family. Min writes admiringly of another young woman, Little Green:

> She was daring. Dared to decorate her beauty. She tied her braids with colorful
> strings while the rest of us tied our braids with brown rubber bands. Her femininity
> mocked us. I watched and sensed the danger in boldness. I used to be a head of the
> Red Guards. I knew the rules. I knew the difference between right and wrong. I
> watched Little Green. Her beauty. I wanted to tie my braids with colorful strings
> every day. But I did not have the guts to show contempt for the rules […] We tied
> on brown rubber bands. The color of mud, of pig shit, of our minds. Because we
> believed that a true Communist should not care about the way she looked […] Little
> Green never argued with anyone. She did not care what we said. She smiled at

herself [...] She smiled, from the heart, at herself, at her colorful string, and was satisfied. (Min, 1994, pp. 51–52)

In this example, Little Green defies the social conventional expectations and makes her appearance a matter of personal expression. Min goes on to describe how Little Green "used remnants of fabric to make pretty underwear, finely embroidered with flowers, leaves, and birds" (p. 52). This example suggests that Little Green's rebellion, conducted both in private (her embroidered underwear) and in front of others (the strings on her braids), reflected her attempts to establish herself as a separate and unique individual.

Indeed, claims to personal choice and personal prerogatives are important in asserting one's sense of agency. They serve to enhance awareness of oneself as an initiator of action, as well as one's sense of the self as a separate, unique, and bounded individual. Philosophers and psychologists have struggled with the problem of describing and defining the subjective sense of "self" and of "agency." The pioneering American psychologist William James (1899) distinguished between what he referred to as the "I-self," or the actor as knower, and the "Me-self," or the actor as object of one's knowledge. In James's description, awareness of the "I" extends over the aspect the self that organizes and interprets experience. This includes the perception of continuity, in other words the perception that one is fundamentally the same person over time. It also includes awareness of agency and the sense that individuals have ownership over their thoughts and feelings. Finally, the "I-self" also includes the feeling that the self is a stable, coherent, and bounded entity and the realization that individuals are distinct from each other. Appeals to personal choice and control are ways of instantiating these different aspects of the self. Claims to personal choice provide opportunities for asserting agency. They also provide a means of self-expression, of developing an identity, and of expressing needs for privacy. This view of the personal domain is also consistent with the writings of other theorists from a variety of different perspectives, who have pondered about how to describe the self in psychological terms (Baldwin, 1906; Damon & Hart, 1988; Erikson, 1968; Kohut, 1978; Mahler, 1979; Selman, 1980). Most of these theorists assert that there is a close connection between personal autonomy and the formation of the individual.

Cultural anthropologists and psychologists, too, are much concerned with how individuals define the self and perceive personhood in different cultures. Cultural anthropologists have demonstrated that there are variations in how personhood is defined across cultures (Geertz, 1975; Markus & Kitayama, 1991; Shweder & Bourne, 1984). At the same time, though, anthropologists generally agree that notions of self and personhood are basic human concepts (Damon & Hart, 1988; Geertz, 1975; LeVine & White, 1986). As will be discussed in more detail in the following chapter, the boundaries of the personal domain may vary in different cultures – in particular how broadly it is defined and what is considered to be under the individual's personal jurisdiction. For instance, Anchee Min's description of life in a Chinese farm collective shows how many issues like wearing hair ribbons and how many decisions about whom to associate with and when became highly politicized conventional issues rather than being personal choices. In this case, the boundaries of the conventional domain include issues that, in other contexts, might be considered to be personal. Min also describes in great detail the aversive psychological consequences these restrictions had for individuals. Later, in Chapter 10, we will see that research has confirmed Min's observation that too much control of the personal domain can have negative consequences for individuals' mental health. Although there are cultural variations in the content and extent of the personal domain, all cultures treat some issues as fundamentally within the boundaries of the self and of personal agency. Nucci has asserted that creating an arena of personal freedom, with its concepts of personal control, is necessary for the establishment of the psychological self.

Although disputes over personal jurisdiction may take on new meanings and an increasing intensity during adolescence, appeals to personal choice are not solely a phenomenon of adolescence. Personal concepts emerge in early childhood. Psychological research demonstrates that, by 3 years of age, children identify a set of issues as being under their personal jurisdiction. They distinguish personal from moral and conventional issues. With age, preschool children increasingly categorize personal issues (both at home and in school) as being up to the individual to decide rather than as acts that are right or wrong. They also explain or justify their responses with claims that personal issues are personal matters, that they should be the actor's own business, or that the acts only affect the individual (Ardila-Rey & Killen, 2001; Killen & Smetana, 1999; Nucci, 1981; Nucci & Weber, 1995; Yau & Smetana, 2003b; Yau, Smetana, & Metzger, 2009).

There is compelling evidence that young children carve out a personal domain that involves their active claims to autonomy, choice, and control. Kristin Lagatutta, Larry Nucci, and Sandra Bosacki (2010) asked 4-, 5-, and 7-year-olds to evaluate stories describing an actor who wanted to do something that conflicted with parents' rules. The behaviors in question were personal matters and pertained to friend, activity, and clothing choices. For comparison purposes, the researchers also asked the children to evaluate a moral situation. With age, young children were increasingly likely to judge that the characters in the story would comply with moral rules and would feel good about doing so. But this was not the case for rules intruding on their personal domain. When asked to predict what the imaginary children would do about these situations, children in all three age groups typically said that the characters would disobey the rules and would feel good about their noncompliance.

Young children's understanding of personal issues is limited in some respects, however. In conformity with what is known about young children's developing theory of mind, most preschool children do not view it as permissible to have different perspectives on disagreements pertaining to personal taste. In a recent study, Cecilia Wainryb and her colleagues at the University of Utah (Wainryb et al., 2004) asked preschoolers whether individuals could have different beliefs about whether chocolate ice cream is yucky or yummy. Only a minority of preschoolers believed that two conflicting beliefs about personal tastes could be right. Young children (5-year-olds) did not understand that some individuals could believe that chocolate ice cream tastes yucky, whereas others might believe that it is yummy. Most children asserted that only one view (that chocolate ice cream is yummy) could possibly be correct. Seven- and 9-year-olds, though, clearly understood that individuals could vary in their preferences. In contrast, children across a broad age range rejected the notion that there is more than one right belief about moral and factual matters.

Like moral, conventional, and prudential concepts, personal concepts develop through social interaction. Children's experiences, communications, and negotiations with adults about preferences and choices are particularly important for their development. An observational study of American, middle-class, suburban mothers' negotiations with their 3-year- and 4-year-old children over personal issues in the home demonstrates this. Larry Nucci and Elsa Weber (1995) observed children's interactions with mothers around four periods of activity during the day. These started with early mornings, when children woke up, dressed, and had breakfast. The four periods also included a free play period during the day, when children played either with a sibling or with a friend. Next, children were observed during late afternoons, which typically included dinnertime, and at bedtime, which included bath time. Each child was observed during all four periods over several days. By making observations at these different times, the observers were able to capture a variety of different types of interactions.

The researchers found that personal interactions differed qualitatively from parent–child interactions around moral or conventional events. Mothers' responses to personal issues involved tacit forms of communication, including negotiation and opportunities for children to make choices. For instance, in discussing what clothes to wear to preschool, mothers implicitly offered their children choices. They made statements such as: "Which sweater do you want to wear – the red one or the yellow one?" These statements communicated to their children that they were able to make choices about certain issues. To a lesser extent, mothers also said such things as "That's up to you" or "That's your business." Mothers did not explicitly label these events as personal matters. Children were left to interpret this from mothers' communications.

This contrasted with interactions regarding moral and conventional events, which never entailed negotiation. (It is hard to imagine a mother saying: "Would you rather tease or hit your brother?") Mothers' statements regarding moral events were direct and explicit. By assuming control over the moral and conventional issues, mothers conveyed that these are events that require children to adapt to social expectations and meanings. In contrast, by allowing negotiation and implicitly providing choices regarding personal issues, mothers conveyed the tacit message that these are issues that the child could control. Mothers responded differently to personal events and recognized the need to grant children some personal discretion.

Importantly, however, Nucci and Weber (1995) noted that children did not just accept the adults' tacit social messages about what is personal. They actively negotiated with and challenged their mothers so as to gain more control and assert their perspectives on the issues involved. Again, this was in contrast with what happened with moral issues, where children rarely challenged their mothers. The limits of moral and social regulation, and hence the issues that should be under the individual's control, are actively negotiated and claimed. Mothers and their young children also had conflicts over personal issues. These reflected ongoing negotiations over how to draw the boundaries between what was personal and what was expected or regulated within a particular family (or in society, as the example from Anchee Min's autobiography suggests).

Melanie Killen and I (Killen & Smetana, 1999) conducted a similar observational study in preschool classrooms – one that also included interviews with teachers and young children. We conducted extensive observations in 20 preschool classrooms, half of them with 3-year-olds and the other half with 4-year-olds. We found somewhat similar patterns to those observed by Nucci and Weber. Teachers encouraged young children's autonomy by offering choices regarding food, activities, and participation in story time. As Nucci and Weber found in the homes, teachers were more indirect in their interactions regarding personal events than in those regarding moral and social conventional ones. Unlike mothers at home, teachers did not always support children's choices. They never negotiated with them over personal issues in the classroom. This is because teachers have many other goals besides fostering children's autonomy. They are also concerned with facilitating children's learning, maintaining social order, and promoting group activities and norms. Teachers may prioritize these other goals at the expense of fostering children's autonomy.

We also conducted interviews with the same 3-year- and 4-year-olds who were observed in the classrooms, as well as with an additional group of 5-year-olds. Children were interviewed about hypothetical situations where personal issues conflicted with teachers' directions. These hypothetical examples, including what to wear, what to eat at lunch, and what activities to choose during free time, were drawn from our observations. For instance, in one hypothetical scenario, the child wanted to draw pictures, but the teacher directed the child to play with blocks. Young children's understanding of personal discretion and choices in the classroom differed according to age. Less than half of the 3-year- and 4-year-olds thought that children, not teachers, should make choices about personal issues in the classroom. However, the majority of 5-year-olds viewed these decisions as legitimately made by the child. Likewise, when asked to give reasons for their evaluations, 5-year-olds gave more personal justifications than younger children did. Three-year- and 4-year-olds judged that children should be able to decide, but most children were not able to articulate a reason why. In contrast, the 5-year-olds were very explicit in their assertion of choices and prerogatives. The following example is from an interview with a 5-year-old as described in Nucci, Killen, and Smetana (1996, p. 19).

INTERVIEWER [teacher wants Jenny to wear her red sweater, and Jenny wants to wear the yellow one]: Should Jenny wear the red sweater?

CHILD: She should wear the yellow sweater because she knows what to wear and what is right.

INTERVIEWER: Who should decide what Jenny should wear outside, Jenny or the teacher?

CHILD: Jenny, because Jenny is the boss of herself.

INTERVIEWER: If the teacher didn't tell Jenny to wear her red one, would it be all right for her to wear the one that she wants to?

CHILD: Yes, because she's the boss of her own self.

We found similar responses to the other stories. By age 5, American middle-class children construct stable conceptions of the personal domain in different contexts, including home and preschool. They identify a set of actions (pertaining primarily to choices about food, clothes, and activities) as falling within the realm of their personal choice. Their justifications for their choices are based on personal prerogatives.

These findings accord well with other observations of early childhood development. Scholars from different theoretical traditions, including neo-psychoanalytic theorists like Erik Erikson (1968), Margaret Mahler (1979), and Renee Spitz (1957), as well as researchers from constructivist perspectives (Damon & Hart, 1988), have viewed autonomy as a central issue of early childhood, when important distinctions between self and others are made. During the second half of the second year of life, children demonstrate a growing capability for self-assertion. Most parents are very familiar with children's developing ability to say "no." Much to parents' chagrin, this is often one of the first words that children use, typically loudly and with great frequency. Indeed, saying "no" has become the hallmark of what many refer to as the "terrible twos." The terrible twos are so named because children often assert their own wishes, even when these conflict with parents' desires. Children may "test the limits" by choosing not to comply with parents. They actively disobey parents' requests and assert their own will. Many scholars claim that this early assertion of will represents an early attempt to establish control over the self. Children are not simply being disobedient. They are individuating and establishing independence (which may be of small comfort to parents in dealing with this behavior).

There are, however, different and distinct forms of early childhood self-assertion. Some are healthy and reflect the child's developing social competence and autonomy; others are not. The more usual forms of negative responses that parents typically encounter, such as saying "no" to mothers' directions or requests, represent healthy forms of self-assertion. These have been contrasted with defiance. Defiance involves strong resistance and a great deal of anger and aggression in response to mothers' requests. It may also include engaging in behaviors that are directly contrary to what mothers want, or responding to mothers' demands by "upping the ante" and intensifying the original misbehavior. In one study, Susan Crockenberg and Cindy Litman (1990) found that 2-year-olds who were able to assert themselves in a healthy way had well-developed negotiation skills, positive communication, and competent social behavior, and their mothers parented them by using guidance and directives. On the other hand, defiance may signal more problematic social development. Crockenberg and Litman found that defiance was associated with a distinctive pattern of practices that included highly controlling and power-assertive parenting and the use of threats, criticism, and anger in disciplining children.

Parents' beliefs about the personal domain

Parents of young children do believe that it is important for children to develop autonomy and personal choice. They support and facilitate their emergence. But they are also concerned with obedience and conformity to social norms, as well as with children's developing kindness and caring towards others. In other words, parents have a differentiated worldview, which includes these different kinds of concerns. Longitudinal studies of parents' rules for their infants and toddlers show that European American mothers are primarily concerned with communicating rules regarding their toddlers' safety, avoidance of damage to their property, and delay (that is, the inhibition of impulses; Gralinski & Kopp, 1993; Smetana, Kochanska, & Chuang, 2000). Mothers make few requests regarding personal issues, like choice of clothes, food, and playmates, because they do not view such requests as developmentally appropriate. Parents naturally constrain the choices of very young children. As their network of rules expands during the child's second year of life, mothers increasingly regulate personal issues, out of concern for their child's health, comfort, or safety, and – less often – for practical reasons.

Larry Nucci and myself have explored mothers' views on the personal domain in interviews with 40 working to upper middle-class mothers of 4-year- and 6-year-olds (Nucci & Smetana, 1996). Mothers were questioned in an open-ended way as to whether children should have decision-making authority and, if so, over what types of issues and why. They were also interviewed about the types of issue that cause conflict with their young children and about the ways in which they negotiate these conflicts. All of the mothers we interviewed believed that their young children should be allowed choices over some things, like clothes, type and amount of food, playmates, and play activities. They granted their children some decision-making authority because they wanted to promote their competence. Mothers also claimed that children should be allowed to hold and express their own opinions, as a way of fostering their self-esteem and agency. But children were not allowed to control all their activities. Mothers clearly set boundaries over what their young children could decide. They placed limits on activities that conflicted with conventional, moral, or prudential concerns. Occasionally they also placed limits on – and had conflicts over – exactly those issues over which they had indicated that they allowed their children to have control. For instance, although they allowed the children to choose their clothes, sometimes they limited or rejected their children's choices. As Nucci and Weber (1995) found in their observational study, these situations resulted in mothers' negotiations with their children.

There are some interesting parallels between children's assertions of self during the toddler years and early and middle adolescents' conflicts and disagreements with parents. As with the "terrible twos," it is important to distinguish between the relatively infrequent but more problematic forms of conflict and normal and healthy self-assertion during the adolescent years. As Rutter and his colleagues noted in their early studies in the 1970s, described in Chapter 2 (Rutter, Graham, Chadwick, & Yule, 1976), intensely angry, highly conflictual parent–adolescent relationships constitute only a small proportion of parent–adolescent disagreements. Research has consistently shown that very angry, intense, and unresolved conflicts are problematic for development. Teens fitting this profile typically have psychosocial problems prior to adolescence and are at increased risk of having problems in their social development. It should be clear that my focus here is on the more "garden variety" forms of self-assertion, which may erupt into everyday disagreements with parents.

There are also parallels between the types of issue that are contested between mothers and young children and the types of issue that lead to conflict with parents during adolescence. Both in early childhood and in adolescence, parent–child conflicts are often over schedules, routines, and bedtimes. (In adolescence, this latter issue morphs into conflicts over curfew.) In the early years, parents and their offspring had conflicts about "picking up," but, as children grew into adolescence, conflicts erupted over the cleanliness or general condition of teenagers' bedrooms, as well as over appearances and regulating activities. Of course, there are some differences between the content of parent–child conflicts in early childhood and in adolescence. Conflicts over homework are rare among mothers with young children but occur with some frequency during adolescence, whereas conflicts over children's food preferences are prevalent in early childhood but are infrequent in adolescence. Nevertheless, both during the toddler years and during adolescence, conflicts with parents regarding preferences, activities, and privacy reflect the status of these topics as prototypical personal issues in American culture.

Adolescents' Reasoning about Conflict with Parents, Interpreted

We are now ready to return to the examples of adolescents' responses to questions about their conflicts and disagreements with parents, which were described at the outset of this chapter. The account of personal reasoning given in social domain theory, as a distinct form of the children's developing social knowledge, helps to illuminate adolescents' responses. As the examples suggest, appeals to personal choices and jurisdiction predominated in European American middle-class adolescents' reasoning about conflict. Personal justifications accounted for about half of teenagers' responses (Smetana, 1989a).

This finding has proven to be remarkably robust. Personal reasoning prevailed among primarily European American teens from married, two-parent families, as well as among demographically similar teens residing in mother-headed, single-parent families (Smetana, Braeges, & Yau, 1991). Personal reasoning was also the most frequent response in studies where youth had been asked to rate or endorse different reasons in questionnaires rather than in interviews (Smetana & Asquith, 1994; Smetana & Berent, 1993). And, as discussed in detail in the following chapters, very similar findings have been observed in more ethnically and culturally diverse samples. Across different methods and samples, adolescents' perspectives on their disputes and disagreements with parents primarily involve appeals to personal choices and personal jurisdiction. But, although appeals to personal choice prevailed, these were not the only justifications teenagers offered for their perspectives on disputes.

Moral reasoning about conflicts

Paralleling the findings for parents, adolescents rarely engaged in moral reasoning about actual family conflicts. Moral justifications accounted for only about 10% of teenagers' responses in their individual interviews. As with parents, adolescents' moral reasoning primarily pertained to conflicts with siblings (and, less frequently, with friends). Parents only became involved when they had to adjudicate whose rights should prevail. This also has a striking parallel in the results of observational studies of young children's conflicts. These studies have shown that, although adults may intervene in moral conflicts, the conflicts themselves occur primarily between children. And, in turn, this conclusion is consistent with Piaget's (1965) contention that morality develops out of reciprocity between equals and near-equals rather than from more hierarchical parent–child relationships.

Psychological research on sibling relationships helps to clarify and provide a context for these findings. Researchers focusing on the developmental implications of siblings' shared and unique experiences in the family have argued that siblings essentially grow up in different families. Their parents treat them differently, due to their prior parenting experiences as well as to individual differences among children. A number of studies, using different methods, have examined the extent to which children perceive their parents as behaving differently towards them. This phenomenon is referred to as parental differential treatment. Children who perceive that their parents treat them differently generally have poorer quality relationships with their siblings (although newer research suggests that this depends on the siblings' understanding of parental differential treatment and on whether they think it is fair). In studying perceptions of parental differential treatment, Kowal and Kramer (1997) found that, for the most part, 11-year- to 13-year-olds and their siblings perceived that they and their siblings were treated similarly. However, perceptions of parental differential treatment were more common among earlier born children than among their later born siblings. And, in the majority of the instances where parents were seen as treating siblings differently (and particularly among first borns), this treatment was viewed as fair. Teenagers recognized that parents took into consideration age differences between siblings and the siblings' different needs, attributes, and relationships with parents. This suggests that children and adolescents do have some understanding of the reasons why parents treat siblings differently, and they see it as being justified under many circumstances.

However, Kowal and Kramer's study also shows that, even when early adolescents understand that their sibling have different needs, they may still view their parents' behavior as unfair. This was evident in our interviews too. The following examples suggest that teenagers often viewed parents as treating siblings preferentially and resolving sibling conflicts in an unfair or unjust way. Sometimes they felt that parents were not properly impartial (or not sufficiently partial in the desired direction!) in settling disputes or in distributing resources. Teenagers' moral conflicts were only rarely described as originating in the parent–adolescent relationship itself. In the following example, Mike, a 13-year-old, complains about how his parents treat him and his brother differently:

> And he [the brother] usually gets more privileges in the house, and I don't think it's because he's older, it's just because he's braver than I am. He stands up to them [...] But they usually just say, "[...] I want you to do this." And I usually end up doing whatever they want [...] They'll just say, "you're wrong," and they'll accuse me of being wrong, even though they don't know what we're fighting about. Or they'll say: "You have no right to say anything like that," and they don't even know what I said!

As this illustrates, parents have different (and sometimes unfair) expectations for their older and their younger offspring. In the following example, Ben, an older sibling, voices a similar perspective:

> It's just that they [the parents] feel, you're so much bigger, you're so much stronger, don't pick on him [the brother]. And I sit there and I get so mad sometimes, you

know. He's allowed to sit here and take his little plastic men, or whatever, and throw them at me and hit them at me, and chase me. I'm supposed to sit there and turn the other cheek and walk away. And it just seems to me, it's like – They see me standing there big, and they see him standing there smaller, and they never see the situation where he picks up something which could possibly do some destructive damage. They don't see that part. They see the end of it where he swings and misses and I go – WHAM – and hit him or push him, and they hear the end result. So that's what bugs them. But they have to hear my story too! I'm not going to say that beating on your little brother is a healthy release of nervous energy. I think there's better ways you can get rid of it. I just think there's some times when it's justified. So, I mean, it's like they're expecting too much.

Even when teenagers viewed their parents as acting wisely and fairly, they did not always like their choices. Beth, a 14-year-old, states that her mom acts as referee, and "she sometimes picks sides." Even though this adolescent acknowledges that her mother gives both siblings equal consideration and sides equally often with each, she hopes for an impossible resolution. As she also states, "I always want my mom to be on my side."

Adolescents' moral reasoning about conflicts declined in frequency during early adolescence. This is consistent with the trends observed in studies of sibling relationships, which have found that conflicts with siblings generally peak in early adolescence and then decline (Buhrmester & Furman, 1990). Siblings also report that closeness, affection, and companionship all decline after early adolescence. Typically, younger siblings in the dyad are the ones who report increased sibling conflicts in early adolescence, whereas older teens in sibling dyads begin to view their relationships with their younger siblings as more egalitarian (Buhrmester & Furman, 1990). But this is not always the case, as our interviews with European American teenagers demonstrate. Rick, a 17-year-old boy, discusses his conflict about getting along with his sister:

I think it's just more about the differences about how they treat each of us. My parents treat my sister and I differently. Like, they'll do something for her, they'll make something available for her, they'll give her something, they'll OK her to do something, and for me, they'll give certain opportunities for her and they'll never do them for me, and you know, it's a problem when it happens because [...] I think it is kind of unfair, just because we're different people, we don't get the same opportunities [...] You know, and that just doesn't seem right.

Rick understands that he and his sister have different relationships with their parents, but he views his parents' adjudication of those differences as unfair.

Teens' conventional reasoning about conflicts

The concerns with social conventions and parental authority, which preoccupy parents, are relatively infrequent in the adolescents' reasoning about their disputes with parents. They accounted for only about 13% of adolescents' responses, both in individual interviews and in family interactions. In a few cases the adolescents' reasoning was clearly conventional. For instance, in the following example from another of our interviews with European American two-parent families, the shoe is on the other foot. Dahlia, a 15-year-old girl, talks about her mothers' behavior, which she views as rude and disrespectful. Dahlia asserts:

> She is always late, always, always late. And you know I think that being late is so rude, I think it's just the worst reflection on you […] Because I think being late is the rudest thing and I don't like your lateness to be reflected on me.

This kind of response, where teenagers objected to parents' behaviors or characteristics on conventional grounds, was relatively infrequent among European American teens. As discussed in Chapter 7, however, it was more frequent among teens in other samples.

When teenagers voiced conventional arguments, their reasons primarily reflected a concern with peer group conventions. In the first interview example, Joannie, a very bright and academically successful 15-year-old girl, discusses a conflict she has with her mother about her reading choices.

> Well, I read certain books. Did you ever hear of the book *White Seas*, by Judy Bloom? It is her one adult book, and it is really dirty, and last year every girl in my school was reading it. So I was reading it. Everybody else was. It wasn't so terrible. I knew about all of the things that were in it. She [her mother] just spazzed out. She kept telling me how I was reading garbage. Everybody is reading them. You ask the average 15-year-old girl they are all reading those teenage romances. I mean they are good. I read them. I like books, that's what I have. I read them.

Joannie views her reading preferences as permissible because everyone is doing it. She grounds her argument in the need to follow peer group tastes and mores. Most of the concerns with peer group conventions were about clothes or style. Teenagers stated that they wanted to follow current fashions and dress like their friends. This is not very surprising, as hairstyles, make-up, and clothes are important markers of different peer groups and crowds during adolescence. But it is especially ironic that adolescents appealed to their reference group norms as a way of establishing what they viewed as their unique identity. Personal identities were seen as woven out of crowd values. Adhering to the particular peer group conventions regarding dress is one of the ways in which adolescents establish their identity.

Adolescents argued for the need to follow peer group norms as a way of differentiating themselves from parents and establishing an independent self. For instance, in the following lengthy example, Sara, a 14-year-old, argues that she wants to dress like her friends, not like her mother. Moreover, she states that not conforming to the peer group conventions would have negative consequences.

At the same time, though, she asserts that the styles also reflect her personal tastes (which clearly are shaped by the peer group). Another aspect of her claim is that she views it as important to do what she wants (a personal concern). And a further concern is that wearing what her mother wants would be uncomfortable, which raises prudential issues. So personal, conventional, and prudential perspectives are all intertwined in her reasoning.

SARA: My mother was brought up with preppy clothes with the nice pants and the nice shirt and she still wears them, and most parents wear them. I think she would like to see me like that, preppy like her and very nicely, nicely dressed. She would like me to be in nice things. "Why don't you put on a skirt?" "Well, mom, I don't want to wear a skirt." That is not what everybody wears, and I don't personally like wearing those clothes, it's very uncomfortable. I think she is entitled to her view, not that I will listen to it. She doesn't really get mad, she just has her little fits.

INTERVIEWER: Why do you think it is okay to wear whatever you want?

SARA: Because you are going to be around the people and I think that the people are going to look at you, and it has to be your problem if you are not wearing the right clothes. My mother doesn't understand that, but if I am not wearing the right clothes and then they might say something [...] I guess, just because she has to know that this is the "in style." She doesn't seem to realize that, because it is not what it used to be 20 or 30 years ago. So I think I should be able to be allowed to wear what I want to wear. I know what the other kids wear to school, because I have been around other kids and she hasn't. She has just been around the other people and other friends.

Peer group conformity typically peaks around the 9th grade, around the same age when crowds are most influential in adolescents' lives. This was reflected in the adolescents' responses, as this emphasis on peer group conventions was particularly prevalent in middle adolescence.

As these social cognitive analyses show, adolescents applied different modes of reasoning in their conflicts with parents. However, appeals to personal choice were by far the most characteristic.

Adolescents' and parents' counterarguments

As a further step in our studies, both adolescents and parents were also asked to provide counterarguments, or to take the other's perspective on the dispute. Counterarguments further illuminate teenagers' and parents' interpretations of conflicts, because they indicate how participants view the other's position. Consistency between adolescents' justifications and their parents' counterarguments (or vice versa) tells us whether the justifications given in the interviews are familiar and can be articulated by the other. If parents are aware of their teenagers' arguments, but adolescents appear to misinterpret or not to "get" their parents' perspectives, this also could potentially reveal developmental differences in adolescents' ability to understand their parents' points of view. And, more generally, misunderstandings on both sides could reveal personality or situational differences in bridging the parents' and the adolescents' divergent perspectives.

There was a strong convergence between the justifications parents and adolescents offered in their individual interviews and their perceptions of the other's reasons, as revealed by their counterarguments. Some of the examples at the outset of the chapter also include adolescents' counterarguments. For instance, in the first example, 17-year-old Kelly states that her parents thought she ought to clean up her room, because it gives "a better outward appearance." Having a messy room would project a negative image. In other words, Kelly's mother considered the negative social consequences of acting contrary to group norms. Most of the examples included in this chapter indicate that adolescents had a firm grasp of their parents' position in their disputes. But at the same time, when asked whether they agreed with the parents' conventional or prudential arguments, adolescents clearly rejected their parents' point of view. In some cases they conceded that there was some validity to parental arguments, although they disagreed with them. But in most cases they simply rejected them as wrong or misguided. Similarly, parents understood and were able to articulate clearly their teens' personal perspectives on disputes, but they strongly disagreed with them. Parents made statements like the following:

> They think their room is their own, that they can keep it any way they want. But they're wrong. The room is part of the house. As long as they live here, they have to follow my rules.

Indeed, parents frequently offered this "my house – my rules" retort to teenagers' claims that choices were theirs to make. Both the parents and the teenagers understood but rejected the other party's perspectives on disputes. Qualitatively as well as in terms of response frequency, parents' justifications and teenagers' counterarguments (and, likewise, teenagers' justifications and parents' counterarguments) were nearly mirror images of each other.

Reasoning in face-to-face family interactions

In addition to the individual interviews with mothers, fathers, and teenagers, families also discussed conflicts together, as a family, in a semi-structured social interaction task. They were instructed to pick three issues of disagreement that arose in their individual interviews and to spend about 10 minutes discussing each, working towards resolution. These conversations were videotaped and then transcribed, word for word, for later analysis. The justifications family members offered each other in the context of this structured, videotaped family interaction task were coded, so that they could be compared with the justifications obtained in individual interviews.

Adolescents' appeals to personal jurisdiction were less frequent in the context of family interactions than they were in their individual interviews. They accounted for about a third of their responses, as compared to 50% in individual interviews. Parents are highly familiar with adolescents' points of view. As the parents' counterarguments suggest, adolescents may not feel the need to reiterate their personal arguments explicitly when discussing a conflict with their parents. They were clearly treading on well-trodden ground!

Natural discourse is often fragmentary and elusive. Much is taken for granted rather than stated explicitly. But, even considering this, teenagers were much more opaque in expressing their claims to personal jurisdiction in the videotaped face-to-face interactions than they were in their individual interviews. They used more circuitous and less conflict-arousing strategies when discussing conflicts face-to-face with parents. In particular, adolescents focused more on the pragmatic and practical aspects of the situations. For instance, in family discussions they offered statements like: "I would take out the garbage, but it's just that I'm usually at football practice when it needs to be taken out." Even when they made claims regarding personal choice, they tended to bolster their arguments with statements negating the possible prudential or conventional consequences of their behavior. For instance, in considering their bedroom, they made statements like "why does it matter? It's not like I have week-old pizza in there," or "you may think it's a mess, but I can find everything I need. And besides, I like it that way!"

Adolescents were deliberate in these interactions. Sociologist Erving Goffman has elaborated upon this notion in his book *Strategic interaction* (1969). Goffman argues that individuals engage in strategic interactions when they reveal information for a purpose, such as besting a foe or gaining an advantage. This was, indeed, the flavor of many of the family discussions we observed. Although parents may support adolescents' desires for autonomy in general, the counterarguments suggest that they strongly reject their children's claims to personal jurisdiction in particular situations. In consequence, adolescents appeared to choose their words carefully, so as to appease their parents. They strategically framed their arguments in ways that could minimize overt conflict and help them get their way. And indeed, parents may be more receptive to this line of argumentation than when they are confronted more directly. Personal and conventional perspectives constitute fundamentally different, opposing, and therefore difficult to harmonize ways of conceptualizing the issues that cause conflict. Parents may be more receptive to adolescents' arguments when teens frame them in more pragmatic terms. As part of this tendency, teens may temper their appeals to personal jurisdiction when interacting and negotiating with parents in order to reduce the level of conflict in their relationships. Although their claims to personal jurisdiction are developmentally important, their direct expression in situations of conflict may not lead to the outcome adolescents desire.

In a similar vein, parents were less explicit about their conventional perspectives in family interactions than in interviews. They did not fully articulate the conventional bases for their expectations, most likely because their positions on the disputed matters were highly familiar. And adolescents' counterarguments in the individual interviews did indicate that parents' perspectives were clearly understood (but also roundly rejected) by teenagers.

It is important to note that disagreements are not the only means through which adolescents and parents renegotiate the boundaries of parental authority. Parents and children have many opportunities to make decisions together, and not all family decision-making is necessarily conflictive. There are many instances when teenagers disagree with parents' rules and limits but comply with parents' wishes. But, as described in Chapter 10, the extent to which conflicts are openly discussed and negotiated may differ according to the parents' characteristic modes of handling disciplinary situations. It may also vary in different cultures and among youth of different ethnicities. And, as discussed in Chapter 11, adolescents may take issues into their own hands and use more subversive tactics to get their way.

Discussions, negotiations, and decisions about how to handle details of adolescents' everyday lives, including what is permissible and what is not, contribute to subtle and gradual shifts in the boundaries of parental authority. Situations of conflict highlight tensions in everyday interactions.

The Role of Peers as Influences on Teenagers' Views

Close friends

Researcher Christopher Daddis (2008a, b) has proposed that friends are an important source of influence on adolescents' desires for more autonomy. Teenagers may look to their peers in forming their beliefs about what they can or should be able to control. Most parents have heard the claim that "everyone else is doing it." Teenagers may use this as an argument for why particular restrictions should be lifted or why teenagers should be allowed new freedoms. Adolescents may use friends as an important point of reference in gauging how much autonomy is appropriate. In dyads consisting of primarily European American, middle-class, early and middle adolescent close friends, Daddis found that close friends were indeed more similar than non-friends in their judgments and reasoning as to whether various issues are personal and beyond legitimate parental control or not. (Left open was the question of whether teenagers seek out teens who are similar in their strivings for autonomy or whether friendships influence autonomy desires.)

As part of one study, Daddis (2008a) interviewed teenagers about their perceptions of influences from friends and family on different types of actions. He also examined other sources of influence, including the self, other adults, and the media. Teenagers viewed their parents as the primary influence on their thinking about who should control conventional and prudential issues. For example, in discussing sources of influence for conventional issues, one 16-year-old boy stated: "Dad's house, Dad's rules." Another 15-year-old elaborated: "If they are responsible for you, you should follow their lead. They are teaching respect for later in life" (Daddis, 2008a, p. 92). In contrast, when it came to personal issues and issues that overlapped the domains (issues referred to as multifaceted), teenagers looked outside the family and viewed their friends as influencing their thinking in these areas.

When different sources of influence were compared, adolescents estimated that their friends had twice as much influence as their parents in deciding who should control personal issues. Teenagers who were still attending middle school were much more likely than high school students to view their parents as influential on personal issues. For example, when asked whom she looks to in making decisions about her appearance, a 12-year-old girl replied: "I look to my mom. I am always asking her what I get from the store and how to wear it. If I'm always doing this, then I'm probably not ready to choose what I wear yet" (Daddis, 2008a, p. 91). Teenagers also relied much less on their own judgments than on their friends. However, their reliance on their own judgments increased with age. As a 15-year-old girl stated: "You should choose what you wear. You choose who you are, what you do, and how you look – it is who you are" (ibid.). Interestingly, although much has been written about the negative influence of the media on teenagers today, teenagers did not view the media as a powerful influence on their thinking. This is not to say that the media does not have an effect, but teenagers do not perceive it as such.

Adolescents believed that their friends influenced their thinking about personal authority primarily by setting standards. They compared the amount of decision-making control they had with what their close friends were allowed to do. Compared to early adolescents, middle adolescents used their friends more as a standard for deciding what should be personal. Less often, but more among middle adolescents than among early adolescents, teens viewed their friends as offering advice.

Peer group influence

To test more directly the effects of peer influence on adolescents' autonomy-seeking, Daddis (in press, b) compared adolescents' perceptions of their own autonomy with their perceptions of how much autonomy their peers had to make decisions regarding different types of issues. He found that adolescents who believed that their peers had more autonomy to make decisions about multi-faceted and prudential issues than they had desired more autonomy for themselves, but only if their own levels of autonomy were low. When adolescents reported having considerable autonomy in their family decision-making, their peers' autonomy (relative to their own levels) did not influence their desires for more autonomy. The familiar saying that "the grass is always greener on the other side of the fence" was true in terms of their ideas about how much autonomy their friends had. They typically overestimated their peers' autonomy, particularly over moral, conventional, and prudential issues. They made more realistic assessments of their peers' autonomy over multifaceted and personal issues (although more so over personal than over multifaceted ones). Much of the push for greater autonomy occurs over prudential and multifaceted issues. All this suggests that adolescents' desires for greater autonomy come partly from their perceptions of the freedoms that their peers enjoy.

Crowds as sources of identity and influence

More broadly, adolescents may look beyond their close friendships, to their peer groups, as references for their emerging beliefs about greater personal control. Peer crowds may be particularly relevant in modifying these beliefs, because to identify with a particular crowd is a way of developing one's identity and autonomy from parents (Brown & Klute, 2003; Brown & Larson, 2009). Peer crowds – like the "brains," the "jocks," or the "preps" – are a prominent feature of American middle adolescents' social life. Crowds are defined, to a large extent, by their variation in personal expression. Crowds share similar personal tastes and predilections regarding clothes, make-up, and hairstyles, preferences for specific activities, and orientation towards school. In fact, adolescents are seen as members of a particular crowd to the extent that they endorse these characteristics and adhere to crowd norms regarding behavior, activities, appearance, and achievement. The different orientations of these crowds help to locate adolescents in the social hierarchy of the school. They channel adolescents into interactions with others, who share the same orientation and reputation, providing a context for developing one's identity. They also offer guides to appropriate norms and behaviors.

Parents' concerns that their adolescents will "hang out with the wrong crowd" reflect a belief that, despite parents' best efforts, adolescents will choose to affiliate with a peer group that does not meet with parents' approval. A prevalent concern is that the adolescents' associates will steer them in the wrong direction (whatever that might be). But there is evidence to suggest that the adolescents' desires to affiliate with different crowds are influenced by their upbringing. Bradford Brown and his colleagues (Brown, Mounts, Lamborn, & Steinberg, 1993) have shown that different aspects of parenting – including the parents' emphasis on achievement, the extent of their supervision and monitoring, and their style of family decision-making – all influence adolescents' interests, abilities, and orientations. Parenting impacts the formation of various individual characteristics, including the adolescents' academic performance, their involvement in deviant activity, and their emotional adjustment.

In turn, the adolescents' different orientations influence the likelihood of affiliation with different crowds. For instance, parents who emphasize academic achievement and stress its importance are likely to have adolescents who do well in school. Adolescents who are oriented towards academic success are more likely to join certain crowds, which value that orientation ("brains" or "populars," for instance) and eschew others, which do not ("druggies," for instance). Over time, identifying with different crowds is likely to accentuate the characteristics that initially drew them to that crowd. Teenagers who are drawn to the "brains" are likely to have friends who share their orientation and value a commitment to academic achievement. They are also likely to do well in school and to encourage and reward their peers for their academic success, which leads to an even greater investment in school and to stronger academic performance. Over time, this process is conducive to further differentiation among youth in different crowds. Identity formation is facilitated as different characteristics are selectively encouraged in different peer crowds. In Chapter 9 we shall see that different reference groups also have distinct patterns of beliefs regarding how much personal jurisdiction adolescents should have. But, from a social cognitive perspective, identification with a peer crowd may provide adolescents with opportunities to contrast and compare different orientations as they construct beliefs about the timing and content of their expanding personal domains.

Sources of Influence on Parents' Views

If American middle-class teenagers look to their friends to help them gauge when they should demand greater autonomy, how do parents determine when to allow children to make their own decisions? These evaluations are influenced by many factors, including the parents' beliefs about parenting and their previous parenting experience (which are discussed in more detail in Chapter 9 and Chapter 10). Parents are also guided by their assessments of their offspring's abilities and competencies. Early adolescence is a time of enormous change – physically, socially, and cognitively. Parents' appraisal of teenagers' competence may be particularly variable and divergent during periods of rapid developmental change (Collins, 1995). Moreover, the rapid changes of early adolescence and the processes of adaptation to those changes make it difficult to assess accurately whether teenagers are developmentally ready to take on more freedoms. The resulting discrepancies between adolescents' desires for more control and parents' changing estimations of their children's developing competencies may contribute to disa-greements about who should decide on various issues.

The developmental and social changes of adolescence typically lead to the formation of many new areas where limits must be renegotiated and autonomy may be sought (or feared). As adolescents grow older, they spend more time away from home, without supervision. This may cause increased parental concerns about monitoring, curfews, and teenagers' involvement in problem behaviors. Transformations of adolescent friendships into cliques, crowds, and romantic relationships also result in increased parental concerns about peer group influ-ences, dating, and too early sexual involvement. The emerging ability to drive and to work outside the home brings new opportunities and risks. All these social changes require parents to reassess adolescents' competencies, which are them-selves changing.

Parents' reluctance to grant adolescents more personal freedom stems in part from the desire to protect their teens and to keep them safe. The adolescents' counterarguments clearly demonstrated that they are aware of their parents' pru-dential concerns for their safety and health. They are also aware of their parents' social conventional concerns with responsibility, social order, and family and cultural norms. But teens discount these concerns, sometimes viewing them as misplaced or invalid. The examples from some of the interviews also show that, in other instances, teenagers may agree that parents' concerns are legitimate, but still believe that the choices are theirs to make. Some researchers have described teenagers as having a "personal fable," or a feeling of invulnerability that is char-acteristic of early adolescent thought. For instance, "other teens may get into car crashes, but not me," "other girls may get pregnant if they don't protect them-selves, but I won't," or "drinking alcohol may impair one's judgment, but I can handle it." The personal fable may enter into teenagers' eagerness to discount parents' concerns for their safety. But it is more likely that the teenagers' relative inexperience and immaturity (in a developmental sense) and their desires for greater autonomy combine to "put the pedal to the metal" in instances where parents are often putting on the brakes.

Parents clearly do put on the brakes and guide the eventual granting of greater autonomy. Christopher Daddis and I examined mothers' and middle adolesc-ents' expectations concerning when teenagers should be granted autonomy over various personal and prudential issues. We were interested in whether their expec-tations regarding the desired pacing of autonomy in different domains influenced family decision-making about these same issues 3 years later, in late adolescence (Daddis & Smetana, 2005). We found that the adolescents' autonomy desires did not influence how much autonomy they subsequently achieved, but mothers' expectations for the adolescents' autonomy did. In other words, adolescents push, but parents grant autonomy. Furthermore, the effects were domain-specific. When mothers expected adolescents to become more autonomous over personal issues at later ages, these adolescents had less autonomy over personal issues down the road. The same was true for prudential issues. But mothers' expectations for adolescents' autonomy in one domain did not influence how much decision-making autonomy the same adolescents achieved in another domain 3 years later. The one exception was in the desired pacing of autonomy over multifaceted issues (which, remember, include overlapping components from different domains and are the issues that typically cause conflict in parent–adolescent relationships). Here, mothers' expectations regarding the desired pacing of autonomy over personal issues – but not over prudential issues – influenced the adolescents' autonomy over these issues.

This suggests that, when parents and adolescents negotiate over conflicts, parents confront and perhaps re-evaluate the limits of their authority and the boundaries of adolescents' personal control. Teenagers' push for greater control and freedom can move parents to reconsider their limits. They may reconsider whether their expectations are appropriate, or whether adolescents have matured or developed new competencies that might permit some revisions of their rules. In interviews, parents in our studies have talked about how they were sometimes persuaded to let their teens take "baby steps" towards new freedoms, or how they sometimes felt that their teens' good behavior in one realm had earned them a chance for new privileges in another.

Over time, the parents' appeals to social conventions or to prudence, the adolescents' rejection of their parents' perspectives, and their reinterpretation of parents' wishes as being related to matters that fall legitimately under their personal jurisdiction form a continuous dialectic, which transforms the boundaries of parental authority. Parents shift from viewing a variety of issues as legitimately subject to their authority to granting adolescents autonomy over those issues. In turn, this leads to the outward reach of autonomy during adolescence. Family decision-making also shifts over time – from parental decision-making (perhaps with some input from the teens) to more shared forms of authority and from dependence to individuation in the family.

Within-family variations

In research on parenting and social development, families are usually studied in terms of the parents' relationships or interactions with a single child in the family. But with the possible exception of China, which for many years has had a one-child policy, families with only one child are not the norm. Most families worldwide have at least two children, and often many more. Researchers have only recently begun to explore the impact of ordinal spacing among children both on their development and on the parenting of adolescents who grow up in families with siblings.

Most research (including my own) has proceeded from an "individual development" model. That is, the implicit assumption is that developmental processes are similar for different siblings in the same family. But the family systems perspective pioneered by family therapist Salvador Minuchin (1974) reminds us that the whole family, not just the parents, provides a context for adolescent–parent relationships and development. As we saw earlier in the discussion of parental differential treatment, children in the same family may have different relationships with their parents as a function of their birth order. They may, in some sense, grow up in different families. This may be evident in their experiences of warmth or of conflict with parents and in the timing of their eventual attainment of autonomy. Parents with more than one offspring may learn from their experiences with their first born and adjust their parenting practices and expectations accordingly. And later born offspring also have opportunities to observe and interpret their siblings' interactions with parents, guiding their beliefs, expectations, and behaviors. The challenge is to describe how children's ordinal position in the family influences family dynamics.

Because the family is a system, we might expect that changes in one of its subsystems would influence the others. For instance, researchers studying marital relationships have demonstrated that marital conflict frequently spills over into parent–child relationships. Likewise, stresses that arise in parents' relationship with one sibling may spill over into their relationships with another sibling. For example, when the first born child transitions into adolescence and conflicts increase in frequency, parents may experience increased conflicts with their younger child (or children), too. But parents may learn from the experience of taking a child through the transition into adolescence. They may loosen their restrictions when their next child reaches this phase, so that the transition occurs more smoothly.

Researchers Lilly Shanahan and her colleagues at the Pennsylvania State University examined these different models. They investigated parent–adolescent conflict and warmth in a sample of American families – primarily middle-class and of European American origin – whose children were followed for 5 years, from middle childhood through to adolescence (Shanahan, McHale, Crouter, & Osgood, 2007; Shanahan, McHale, Osgood, & Crouter, 2007). Family dynamics were found to be complex. They had different influences on developmental processes during adolescence. For first born children, development followed regular patterns. That is, conflicts increased in frequency from early to middle adolescence. During this same time span, warmth between children and their parents diminished. But the increased conflict that parents experienced with their first borns in early to middle adolescence spilled over into their relationships with their second borns. Both kinds of siblings experienced increased conflict with parents at that time. So conflicts with parents increased in frequency as first borns transitioned from early to middle adolescence. And second born children in the family, who were no more than 4 years younger than their siblings and therefore were only in the later part of middle childhood, also experienced more frequent conflicts. For these children, conflict co-occurred with their older siblings' – but not their own – developmental transition. Second born children did not experience increased conflicts with parents as they transitioned into adolescence. In addition, they experienced a less pronounced decline in warmth in their relationships with their fathers than first borns did. So there was spillover from the first born to the second born child in the family. Moreover, parents may have learned from their experiences in raising their first born offspring.

As second borns have conflicts with parents at earlier ages than their older siblings, they may gain autonomy at earlier ages as well. This is what Nicole Campione-Barr and I (2009) found in a small sample of European American lower middle-class families. We studied early and middle adolescents, their mothers, and a sibling who was 1 to 4 years older or younger than the target child. In general, and regardless of their ordinal position in the family, all children expected to have autonomy at younger ages than their parents expected. But in addition, later born teens expected to gain autonomy at earlier ages than their first-born siblings did. No doubt they observed the freedoms their older siblings already had and wanted some of it for themselves.

Negotiations for greater autonomy may begin in early adolescence, but they are not realized until middle adolescence. Early adolescents who were either the oldest sibling (first borns) or a later addition to the family did not differ in their views of family decision-making. But middle adolescents who had older siblings reported having more input into family decision-making than did same-age teens who were first born (that is, the oldest sibling in the family). These effects were especially pronounced for girls, who seemed to benefit more than boys did from the parents' "loosening the reins" with their later born children. And their greater autonomy was domain-specific. Girls attained autonomy for conventional and prudential decisions at younger ages than their older brothers and sisters did. (Recall that, earlier in this chapter, we saw that peers also influence conventional and prudential decisions.) But we did not find differences for personal and multi-faceted issues.

Some research suggests that parents' greater permissiveness with their later born girls (as compared to boys) may have potentially detrimental effects. Younger sisters of childbearing adolescents are at higher risk than girls whose older sisters have not born children are. They are more accepting of nonmarital adolescent childbearing, they expect to marry and have a child at younger ages, they engage more in problem behavior, and they are more pessimistic about school and career goals (Cox, Emans, & Bithoney, 1993; East, 1996). And older siblings, too, have been found to influence younger siblings' dating and their sexual and problem behavior. For instance, siblings are more alike in their deviant behavior and sexual intimacy than one would expect them to be by chance (Rowe, Rodgers, Meseck-Bushey, & St. John, 1989).

Families in Campione-Barr's and my study also participated in a semi-structured family interaction task in our university lab, much like the one described in the previous chapter. Families spent eight minutes discussing a conflict together and working towards resolution. Trained observers rated mothers and adolescents for their support and involvement in the task. Immediately following the interaction, though, we also asked adolescents and mothers to rate themselves and their interaction partner on the same dimensions (Campione-Barr, Smetana, & Bassett, 2009). Family members' perceptions of their interactions provide an interesting comparison to observers' ratings. Trained observers have a more objective view of the family, but they lack an insider's perspective on family dynamics. They do not know the history of the family and the particular meaning that certain behaviors may have for parents and children. And, in our study, observers and family members rated differently the interactions of families with first and later born offspring, even though the teenagers were at the same age.

When parents interacted with their first born teens, they were rated (both by their teenage offspring and by themselves) as more supportive and involved in these interactions than parents of later born adolescents were. There were similar effects when adolescents rated their own behavior. First born adolescents saw themselves as more supportive and involved in their interactions than did same-age adolescents who had older siblings. Therefore the higher levels of conflict and autonomy striving reported by later born adolescents, as compared to those of same-age first born adolescents, appear to result in less positive and less cohesive family communication – at least as perceived by family members. Observers did not view families with first born and later born offspring as differing in their interactions. However, they did view mothers as being more supportive and involved in the task than adolescents were. This probably reflects mothers' and teenagers' different "stakes" in disputes. Mothers want to retain their connections, whereas adolescents are seeking more autonomy.

Laura Wray-Lake and her Penn State University colleagues (Wray-Lake, McHale, & Crouter, 2010) also studied within-family variations in family decision-making. They followed families longitudinally from when children were 9 years old to 20 years of age. They focused only on parents' reports of family decision-making. When siblings at the same age were compared, second born children had more autonomy in decision-making than the first born child in the family, although this greater autonomy was primarily in middle childhood. This situation suggests that parents learn from their experiences as parents. For academics, the title of a recent paper by researchers from the same research group (Whiteman, McHale, & Crouter, 2003) says it all. Their paper was entitled "What parents learn from experience: The first child as the first draft?" The argument is that, as parents gain parenting experience, they relax their expectations for their second born child. Also, younger children seek more autonomy, in an attempt to differentiate themselves from their older siblings. These studies demonstrate that there are variations in the regular developmental path to autonomy as a function of experiences within the family.

Summary and Conclusions

This chapter described adolescents' personal reasoning as part of a broader developmental and conceptual system of social knowledge. Personal concepts are part of children's developing understanding of self and of psychological issues. These concepts first emerge in early childhood and are constructed from social interactions and tacit communications regarding privacy, control over one's body, and choices and preferences. Claims to personal choice in the context of conflicts with parents during adolescence reflect adolescents' ongoing concerns with the construction of self, identity, and autonomy.

Different issues may wax and wane as sources of conflict during adolescence, but, at heart, conflict often reflects an ongoing negotiation over what adolescents claim to be personal and what adults view them as competent to control. Teenagers' claims to personal choice reflect their attempts to enlarge their sphere of personal action and discretion. Appeals to personal jurisdiction reflect adolescents' attempts to claim an arena of personal discretion and choice, assert their agency, and construct a coherent self-identity.

We saw in Chapter 4 that the issues that adolescents believe to be personal are viewed by parents as social conventional (or as prudential, pragmatic, or, to a lesser extent, moral or psychological). It is important to note that adolescents are not rejecting the legitimacy of adult conventions overall; in fact, as will be described in greater detail in Chapter 9, adolescents uphold most parental and societal values and social conventions. Adolescents view themselves as obligated to conform to most social norms. Rather, in situations of conflict, adolescents are attempting to coordinate their beliefs about the legitimacy of social conventions and about the validity of moral prescriptions with their desire to stake claims to areas of self-regulation and personal control that are required or desired in order to become an independent adult in their cultural setting. Therefore adolescents fully understand, but reject, parents' claims to social conventions (or other concerns) in these particular instances. Moreover, we saw in this chapter that appeals to personal jurisdiction are not just a manifestation of adolescence; rather these claims emerge in early childhood, although disputes over personal jurisdiction may take on new meanings and increased intensity during adolescence.

Although the majority of European American teenagers' conflicts are treated as personal issues, adolescents are also concerned with fairness and equal treatment, prudence and pragmatics, other psychological issues, and social conventions. Instead of pertaining to adult (family and societal) conventions, though, adolescents' conventional perspectives on conflict typically pertain to peer group norms.

Some theorists may wish to view adolescents' conflict with parents as indicating noncompliance, resistance to adult authority, and, more generally, failure in internalization. The claim made here, though, is that adolescents' appeals to personal jurisdiction serve an important function in social development. Parents' claims to social conventions, adolescents' rejection of those claims, and their appeals to personal jurisdiction form an ongoing dialectic, which leads to transformations in the boundaries of parental authority. Adolescents accept parental and cultural conventions in some instances, but they are also attempting to construct a coherent self and identity and to establish boundaries of personal jurisdiction. They attempt to negotiate those boundaries through transactional and constructive processes. Adolescents are attempting to redefine the hierarchical relationships of childhood into the more mutual relationships of adulthood. Parents also believe that these transformations should occur and they want to facilitate adolescents' autonomy, although perhaps more cautiously and at a slower pace than adolescents desire.

As the examples offered in this chapter demonstrate, there is no bright line separating issues that are viewed as legitimately controlled by parents and issues that are seen to be under adolescents' personal authority. This division varies within and across families over time, and within and across contexts (including different cultures and ethnic groups). Adolescents often look to their peer group to determine how much autonomy is appropriate. Middle adolescents, in particular, use their friends as a standard for evaluating whether they ought to seek more autonomy over different issues. However, adolescents often overestimate the extent of their friends' autonomy, particularly regarding moral, conventional, and prudential issues. There is also variation within families in granting autonomy. Comparisons between first and later born offspring at the same age reveal that later born adolescents are given more autonomy than first borns. More specifically, later born girls are granted more autonomy over prudential and conventional issues than first born girls are.

Later on we shall consider how beliefs about parental authority and parenting practices contribute to this differentiated notion of social development. But, first, in the following two chapters we shall consider cultural variations in these issues.

6

Autonomy, Conflict, Connectedness, and Culture

The psychological research on adolescent–parent relationships discussed in the last chapter focused primarily on European American middle-class families. But there has been an increasing and long overdue interest among developmental scientists in the cultural, ethnic, and ecological contexts of development. This expanded focus includes increased concern with the role of culture in social relationships and in social interactions (broadly considered). These issues were mentioned briefly in Chapter 1 in discussing Schlegel and Barry's (1991) cross-cultural analysis of the anthropological data on parent–adolescent conflict. But the different ways in which social relationships have been conceptualized cross-culturally deserve greater consideration. These issues bear on the research on adolescent–parent relationships described in the last chapter, as well as on research to be discussed in subsequent chapters. The issues are embedded in ongoing debates about how best to conceptualize the role of autonomy, parenting, and culture.

Conflict and Cohesion as Characteristics of Cultures

In one currently popular and influential view, harmony, autonomy, and conflict (as well as distance and alienation) in social relationships are seen as integrally related to the different ways in which cultures are organized. That is, harmony and conflict, each, have been associated with different behavioral patterns that are thought to organize (and differentiate) cultures. In particular, harmony and conflict have been described as integral aspects of individualism and collectivism. These are global dimensions that have been used by a number of psychologists to characterize cultures (for example, Hofstede, 1980; Markus & Kitayama, 1991; Markus, Mullally, & Kitayama, 1997; Oyserman, Coon, & Kemmelmeier, 2002;

Adolescents, Families, and Social Development: How Teens Construct Their Worlds. Judith G. Smetana
© 2011 Judith G. Smetana

Shweder et al., 2006; Triandis, 1995, 2001; Triandis & Suh, 2002). Individualistic cultures include the United States, most of Western Europe, Australia, and New Zealand. In contrast, collectivist cultures are seen as the norm worldwide and predominate in much of Asia, South America, and Africa. Distilling and summarizing a great deal of recent research, Triandis (1990, 1995, 2001) has proposed that individualism and collectivism can be defined in terms of four universal and interrelated features.

First, individualistic versus collectivist cultures differ in how the self is conceptualized. The self is defined as interdependent in collectivist societies and as independent in individualistic societies. Markus and Kitayama (1991; see also Marcus et al., 1997; Nisbett, 2003; Shweder et al., 2006) have elaborated on this notion. These scholars propose that individualistic cultures promote the development of independent construals of the self. This entails a view of the self as separate from others, from the social context, and from the larger collectivity. The self is described as unique, autonomous, and bounded. Personal achievement and self-reliance are strongly emphasized. This state of things has been contrasted with collectivist cultures, which are said to promote sociocentric or interdependent construals of the self. Interdependent construals entail connectedness with the social context, indirectness in social interactions, a focus on statuses, roles, relationships, and a concern with fitting in. Rather than stressing personal achievement, collectivist societies emphasize social integrity.

These contrasting notions of independence versus interdependence are related to the second feature differentiating individualism from collectivism. Individualistic societies are seen as emphasizing personal goals at the expense of collective goals, whereas collectivist societies promote group goals over personal goals. In stressing the subordination of individual goals to the needs of the larger group or society, collectivists are said to emphasize the importance of their ingroup and to focus on how their actions affect other members of their collective. Because they feel interdependent, individuals in collectivist societies are said to share resources with other members of their group. In turn, these values are seen to lead to particular child-rearing patterns, which produce conformity to group goals. Children are expected to subordinate their personal goals to family goals and needs. More broadly, parents in collectivist cultures are said to be primarily concerned with obedience, conformity (particularly in public settings), reliability, and appropriate behavior. In contrast, in individualistic cultures, where personal goals are highly valued, parents value self-reliance, independence, self-actualization, and creativity. These characteristics are seen as enhancing the complexity of the private self and as promoting the uniqueness and independence of the individual.

A third characteristic of the distinction between individualism and collectivism is that the underlying moral systems of the two types of society are said to differ. In collectivist societies, norms, role obligations in the social hierarchy, and duties are thought to guide social behavior. In contrast, individualist societies are described as structured in terms of personal autonomy, contracts, and rights

(Miller, 1994; Shweder, Mahapatra, & Miller, 1987; Schweder et al., 2006). Collectivist societies place a greater emphasis on differences in status among individuals, such as those based on gender, age, or social class. For instance certain castes in India are accorded greater power and prestige than others. Correspondingly, the rights and freedoms of those in the lower castes are severely restricted. Likewise, in most cultures, men are accorded more power and personal freedom than women are. Collectivist societies are oriented towards group goals, and their morality is structured by respect for authority. Therefore those at either end of the social hierarchy are seen to consider their roles and statuses within the social system as fixed and appropriate. Higher-caste individuals in India, or men in most cultures, view their greater freedom as deserved. Those at the lower end of the social hierarchies (lower-caste members or women, in these examples) accept their fate. In contrast, individuals in individualistic (Western) societies are seen as focusing on moral equivalencies among individuals. This attitude leads to a focus on individual rights and on the social contracts that provide the basis for rights.

Finally, collectivist cultures are said to prioritize relationships, even when they are disadvantageous to the individual. Collectivist cultures emphasize harmony in relationships, particularly among ingroup members. According to Triandis (1990), this emphasis on harmony stems naturally from the notions of hierarchy and from the promotion of group goals. When those in power promote harmony, there is less need to maintain authority or to stifle dissent or conflict. Instead, the group can focus on achieving their goals. Therefore harmony facilitates the accommodation of the individual to society. In contrast, by promoting an independent self, individualists are said to stress detachment from others. Individuals in individualist cultures are said to emphasize a more voluntary approach to relationships. Individuals continually evaluate the advantages and disadvantages of maintaining a relationship (Triandis, 1995).

The notion that individualistic cultures stress detachment, or even alienation, from others is a theme that has been strongly promoted by several prominent social commentators. For instance, in a highly cited book titled *Habits of the heart*, sociologist Robert Bellah and his colleagues at the University of California, Berkeley (Bellah, Madsen, Sullivan, Swidler, & Tipton, 1985) assert that American individualism has gone too far and reflects an alarming symptom of societal disintegration. They argue that mainstream American society is embracing a form of radical individualism that is characterized by isolation, separation, and a focus on personal fulfillment over the needs of the larger community. The result has been moral confusion and decline. According to Bellah and his colleagues, as well as in the opinion of others (Etzioni, 1993), this state of affairs needs to be remedied by renewing our commitments to community and society.

In his highly publicized book, *Bowling alone: The collapse and revival of American community*, Robert Putnam (2000) likewise takes a sociological perspective and examines data accumulated over time regarding Americans' propensity to engage in communal social activities like signing petitions, voting, reading newspapers, socializing with neighbors, joining bowling leagues, and other forms of civic mindedness. Putnam asserts that Americans, and especially teenagers and young adults, are less likely to vote, read newspapers, and engage in community activities today than they were in previous generations. For instance, he finds that Americans are joining bowling leagues in much smaller numbers than in previous decades. On the basis of this evidence, Putnam argues that Americans are becoming increasingly disconnected from family, neighbors, and community. He claims that they are much less civic minded and social; rather, they are "bowling alone."

But others have characterized social relationships in individualistic cultures in other ways. For instance, in a synthesis of research, Rothbaum, Pott, Azuma, Miyake, & Weisz (2000) described social relationships in individualistic cultures (or, more specifically, in the United States) as more conflictive and characterized by interpersonal tensions to a greater extent than in collectivist cultures. These researchers propose a developmental framework for understanding cultural differences in relatedness (Rothbaum et al., 2000), or the interpersonal ties (such as love, loyalty, care, and commitment) that typically occur between parents and children or other close relationships. These researchers focus, specifically, on distinctions between the American and the Japanese culture. As Japanese society has been described as prototypically collectivist and the United States has been described as prototypically individualist, their arguments can be seen to exemplify the broader distinctions between individualism and collectivism.

Rothbaum and his colleagues propose that all individuals have a biological predisposition towards relatedness, which may be observed in infants' proximity-seeking behaviors. This universal dimension is interpreted through different cultural lenses, which stress individuation and accommodation to varying degrees. Such lenses therefore open different developmental pathways of close relationships. Rothbaum and his colleagues assert that, in Japan, development emphasizes the accommodation of the self to others, which leads the child on a pathway of symbiotic harmony. For instance, in infancy, Japanese mothers are physically more present and maintain more body contact than American mothers do.

Also, Japanese infants explore less and orient to the mother more than is found to be the case in the United States. In middle childhood, the cultural emphasis on empathy and on meeting the others' expectations and one's obligations leads Japanese parents to avoid confrontation with their children. It also prompts them to expect compliance and conformity and to de-emphasize children's social initiative and verbal assertiveness. The pathway of symbiotic harmony in adolescence is described as resulting in a continuation of one's closeness to parents, which has been nurtured since birth. Conflict between Japanese parents and their adolescents is said to be infrequent (White, 1993). Peer groups do not assume the same importance as in the United States. Japanese teenagers have less recreational time to spend outside of the family and less desire for personal freedom outside the home.

Development in the United States is said to emphasize individuation, because the predisposition towards relatedness comes into conflict with the needs for separation and autonomy. This kind of development sets the child on a pathway that accentuates the tension between generations. In infancy, this means greater emphasis on the exploration of the environment, greater physical separation from the mother, and a greater focus on directing the infant's attention outward. These child-rearing patterns create competing desires – for separation and exploration on the one hand, for reunion and proximity on the other. The claim is that, in middle childhood, the American emphasis on asserting personal preferences and the expression of self are conducive to greater child noncompliance and to more oppositional behavior than in Japan. Children in the United States are encouraged to express their preferences, but parents exert a more direct control and use more commands and coercion than Japanese parents do. Therefore the tension between parental control and children's self-assertion is thought to produce a more habitual pattern of conflict between parents and children in the United States than in Japan. This trajectory of generative tension increases during adolescence. It creates heightened conflict between parents and adolescents and leads to a greater desire for personal freedom in spheres outside the home and to the ascendancy of the peer group over the family.

These descriptions raise several questions. On the one hand, the view that interpersonal relationships in individualistic societies are characterized by conflict and tension between generations differs from the conclusions reached by Triandis (2001) and by Bellah and his colleagues (1985). The latter researchers have asserted that interpersonal relationships among individuals in individualistic cultures are characterized by detachment and separation. Interpersonal conflict may pose less of a threat to the maintenance of relationships when these are more detached; but the stakes also may be lower, which leads to less conflict. Although Rothbaum and his colleagues' descriptions of relatedness in infancy are supported by a great deal of empirical psychological research on attachment relationships, there has been substantially less research comparing adolescent relatedness in the United States and respectively in Japan. More systematic research on Japanese adolescents is needed before firm conclusions about these two different pathways of development can be drawn. However, a recent study by Yamada (2009), which will be discussed in greater detail in the next chapter, suggests that, in middle childhood and early adolescence, Japanese mothers and their offspring do have conflicts, and that these are much the same as in the United States.

Markus and Lin's (1999) account of cultural differences in conflict is somewhat similar to the preceding view. This work expands on the authors' previous writings on "selfways" – that is, cultural differences in the construction of self. Markus and Lin coined the term "conflictways" to examine how culture and conflict intersect. They argue that conflictways vary dramatically in different cultural contexts. The way individuals raise children or negotiate and resolve conflicts are culturally patterned. They propose that individualistic cultures like that of the United States are oriented around the unspoken assumptions that individuals have the right to disagree and that they should be open and honest in expressing their perspective. This set of assumptions includes the view that there is a "correct" solution to a conflict and that this solution will prevail, if it is supported by reason and solid argument. In collectivist cultures, by contrast, relationships and their maintenance are given priority, because such cultures value interdependence. Accordingly, the ways in which conflicts are raised (that is, openly or not), negotiated, and resolved reflect an orientation towards solving interpersonal problems so as to give priority to maintaining the relationship.

Critiques of Global Cultural Orientations

These descriptions are useful by focusing our attention on the ways in which individuals in different cultures actively construct meaning from their social interactions. But there are reasons to believe that the view of collectivist cultures as emphasizing harmony in interpersonal relationships is too broad, stereotyped, and overly romanticized. Although harmonious relationships surely occur, a great deal of evidence also suggests that disagreements, strife, and even violence may sometimes prevail in intimate relationships in collectivist societies. For instance, in her 1999 book *Sex and social justice*, political philosopher Martha Nussbaum states:

> Conflicts for resources and opportunities are ubiquitous in families around the world, and women are often the victims of these conflicts [...] sexual abuse during childhood and adolescence, forced prostitution (again, often in childhood), domestic violence and marital rape [...] are all extremely common parts of women's lives. Many of the world's women do not have the right to consent to a marriage, and few have any recourse from ill treatment within it. Divorce, even if legally available, is commonly not a practical option given women's economic dependency and lack of educational and employment opportunities. (Nussbaum, 1999, p. 63)

Nussbaum provides many examples of extreme cruelty and mistreatment (typically directed towards women), which occur in the context of intimate interpersonal relationships in collectivist societies. Wife beating, abuse, sexual violence, abandonment, and even death are, all, taken-for-granted aspects of interpersonal relationships in traditional societies. Although Triandis (1990) argues that an emphasis on harmony stems naturally from the notions of hierarchy and of the promotion of group goals, hierarchical social relationships may have a much darker side as well. The power accorded to those in dominant positions may be accompanied by the subjugation of those in subordinate positions, often through violent or coercive means. This, too, can be seen to stem naturally from notions of hierarchy and can be functional in promoting and maintaining group goals. Violence and abuse in interpersonal relationships in collectivist societies should not be taken to be the norm (and, of course, it occurs in individualistic societies as well). But these examples highlight the somewhat stereotypical nature of global views of collectivism such as those of Rothbaum or Markus and Lin.

And the violence is sufficiently problematic for these issues to have formed the topic of the pope's "Letter to women," issued just before the Beijing Women's Conference (Nussbaum, 1999). In this letter Pope John Paul II affirmed the importance of freedom from sexual violence, including marital rape, and of equality in women's rights, and he declared that these issues should be cardinal human rights. This suggests that describing social relationships in terms of a general orientation towards harmony ignores a great deal of the variability that is evident in intimate relationships worldwide. As I noted in Chapter 1, harmonious social relationships co-exist with tensions, conflict, disagreements, strife, and even violence. These aspects of relationships (including adolescent–parent relationships) may be found in individualistic as well as in collectivist cultures.

Ting-Toomey (1994) provides a more detailed discussion of the contrasting ways in which interpersonal relationships are managed in individualistic and in collectivist societies. She proposes that such relationships are constructed according to differences in individualism versus collectivism as well as differences in the treatment of men and women. In her view, individuals in individualistic societies rely on relational equity to manage interpersonal conflicts. Interpersonal conflict negotiation among ingroup members in collectivist cultures is structured by a more communal orientation. Individualists emphasize outcomes (who wins) in resolving conflicts, whereas collectivists are more process-oriented and focus on equality (rather than equity) norms. They emphasize relational goals like maintaining harmony, keeping long-term obligations, the sense of indebtedness, and reciprocity among individuals. A large relational investment (which is associated with collectivism) is thought to lead to greater use of "constructive" conflict responses, such as discussing issues of concern and remaining loyal. Relational investments discourage the use of more "destructive" responses, such as leaving the relationship. Overall, collectivists are described as resorting to more passive responses such as neglect and loyalty to resolve conflicts and to value restraint in emotional expression. In contrast, individualists are said to use more active strategies in reducing conflicts and to express emotions more readily in intimate conflict situations. In Chapter 7 we will consider whether these distinctions are born out by the manner in which adolescents and parents resolve conflicts in different cultures.

The distinctions that Ting-Toomey (1994) has articulated between how conflicts are managed in individualistic and in collectivist societies have also been observed in different kinds of interpersonal relationships in the United States. Building on earlier work by Ellen Bersheid (1985), W. Andrew Collins and Brett Laursen (1992) distinguish between closed-field and open-field relationships. Closed-field relationships (such as relationships within the family) are defined or constrained by kinship or legal ties. Closed-field relationships share many of the characteristics ascribed to interpersonal relationships in collectivist cultures, including long interaction histories, investment in the relationship, reciprocity or mutual attempts to regulate interactions, and conflict management strategies that preserve relationships. On the other hand, open-field relationships (such as relationships outside the family) share a greater similarity with the characteristics of relationships that Ting-Toomey (1994) and Triandis (1995) have ascribed to individualist cultures. They are more likely to be short term and vulnerable to disruption.

This suggests that interpersonal relationships cannot be adequately characterized by an overall style that varies with the culture. There is variation, both within cultures and within individuals, in styles of interacting and of managing conflicts. The type of relationship appears to dictate the style of interpersonal interaction. Moreover, Collins and Laursen (1992) have proposed that closed-field and open-field relationships also change as a function of development. Therefore styles of interacting and of managing conflicts also appear to vary over time.

Dimensions such as individualism and collectivism are meant to capture a great deal of variation in the behavior of individuals within and between cultures. According to Triandis (1995), individualism and collectivism constitute cultural syndromes, or "a pattern characterized by shared beliefs, attitudes, norms, roles and values that are organized around a theme and that can be found in certain geographic regions during a particular historic period" (p. 43). Therefore, for Triandis, culture consists of a set of behavioral patterns. There are many other ways in which culture has been defined. For instance, cultural anthropologist Clifford Geertz (1973) defines cultures in terms of plans, recipes, programs, or instructions. Others have defined culture more in terms of symbolical representations. Regardless of the definition, most culture theorists share a common assumption that culture shapes the behaviors, thoughts, and emotions of individuals within its sphere and that culture is organized around a dominant pattern, such as the dimensions that define individualistic or collectivist cultures. These homogeneous and integrated patterns are seen to have a formative influence on the conceptions of self, morality, and interpersonal relationships of individuals within a given culture.

On the surface, this notion of the existence of homogeneous and all encompassing cultural patterns such as individualism and collectivism is powerful. But scholars from several different perspectives have questioned these views. Cultural anthropologists have asserted that cultures may not be quite as monolithic, homogeneous, internally consistent, and externally distinctive in their orientations as these views suggest. Lila Abu-Lughod, a cultural anthropologist, has argued that such generalizations essentialize cultures and cultural differences in ways that cannot be defended. She states:

> Besides being theoretically unsound, this erasure of time and conflict is misleading because it makes what is inside the external boundary set up by homogenization seem essential and fixed. The appearance of a lack of internal differentiation makes it easier to conceive of groups of people as discrete, bounded entities. (Abu-Lughod, 1993, p. 9)

Sinha and Tripathi (1994) note that such dichotomies are convenient, but that they produce "stereotypical and distorted pictures of complex social reality" (p. 123). Subtle nuances are glossed over in favor of caricatures. The complexities and qualitative differences that constitute the society are overlooked. Echoing a similar theme, Claudia Strauss (2000), another cultural anthropologist, has noted that, whereas dichotomous characterizations of cultural differences have become increasingly prominent among psychologists, the majority of cultural anthropologists have overwhelmingly rejected such views on different grounds. Cultural anthropologists have become wary of "stark 'great divide' contrasts" (Geertz, 1994, April 7, p. 3), which lump all of Asia, Africa, and Latin America into a single category and then compare "the West versus the rest." Cultural anthropologists are quite willing to consider Western psychological theorizing to be too limited and ethnocentric. The predominant emphasis in cultural anthropology on cultural uniqueness makes the "lumping" of such diverse cultures into a single category unacceptable.

In response to criticisms, some have acknowledged that, while individualism and collectivism represent ideal types, cultures may vary along a continuum (Greenfield & Cocking, 1994; Triandis, 1995). In this view, different cultures may strike different balances between individualism and collectivism. For instance, Triandis and his colleagues (1995; Triandis & Gelfand, 1998) have expanded their description of individualism versus collectivism so as to include horizontal and vertical dimensions. The horizontal dimension emphasizes equality, whereas the vertical dimension emphasizes hierarchy. The crossing of these dimensions with individualism and collectivism produces a more differentiated, four-category scheme. Triandis and Gelfand describe horizontal individualists as wanting to become unique and distinct from the group, whereas vertical individualists would want to acquire status through individual competition with others.

In 2002, Oyserman and her colleagues published an extensive and detailed meta-analysis, which covered all of the research literature published in English using the constructs of individualism and collectivism from 1980 on (Oyserman et al., 2002). The team examined the thesis that Westerners (and particularly Americans) are more individualistic than members of other cultures. They considered the predominant orientation of the research participants in those studies (who, as it turns out, are primarily college students), who came from different ethnic groups in the United States and in other countries and cultures. As part of their analyses, they broke down the constructs of individualism and collectivism into smaller components. In their analyses, individualism included the dimensions of independence, goals, competition, uniqueness, direct communication, privacy, and self-knowledge. Collectivism included dimensions such as relatedness, belongingness, duty, harmony, advice, social contexts, hierarchy, and preference for groups.

The results of these analyses undertaken by Oyserman and her colleagues are complex, but several findings are of interest here. Americans were found to be more individualistic than individuals in most, but not all, Asian countries. Results suggest that dichotomous notions of "East" versus "West" are far too global. Some of the overall country comparisons were surprising. For instance, Americans were found to be more collectivist than the Japanese and no different from Koreans in respect of this same feature. Analyses performed with a view to examining differences along various components of the two global orientations yielded some unexpected results. For instance, Americans were lower in individualism than the Japanese when the assessments did not include the dimension of personal uniqueness. Americans did not differ from Hong Kong Chinese when collectivism scales did not include items pertaining to hierarchy and to valuing group goals. It seems that, when belonging to one's ingroup is assessed, Americans were higher in collectivism than Hong Kong Chinese. Oyserman and her colleagues concluded that their analyses support their general hypothesis that Americans are more individualistic than others. However, the picture they paint is much more complex and nuanced than general expectations would allow, and sometimes it conflicts with those general expectations.

Other scholars have gone further and acknowledged that individuals within a society may have diverse orientations. These different orientations have been associated with differences in ethnicity, social class, gender, education, religion, and ideology. This view parses the global notion of culture into one of smaller cultural communities, which share some sets of common characteristics that lead to similarities in orientations among its members. The differences are thought to stem from different social experiences, which in turn may have different psychological effects (Harwood, Scholmerich, & Schulze, 2000; Strauss, 2000). This perspective preserves the notion of a dominant cultural orientation, but calls into question how broadly that orientation can be applied. Therefore proponents of this approach assert that variation within a culture may result from the many ways in which societies (and individuals within them) differ and are stratified.

These theorists offer little specificity, however, and little guidance on how broadly or narrowly a cultural community is to be defined. Cultural communities can encompass broader social categories, like ethnicity or gender. But they have also been defined as small, local, and based on special interests (like playing soccer or following a particular rock group). Also, individuals may simultaneously be members of different cultural communities. Such pluralism can potentially lead to an endless proliferation of cultural communities – a situation that minimizes the role of society or culture as a collective unit or structure. Therefore proponents of this view have claimed that there are some overriding intrasocietal similarities in patterns, which result from the shared economic, political, and social environments (Strauss, 2000). The dominant orientation of the culture is seen to bind together individuals from different subgroups within a society.

But, as the examples offered earlier suggest, several scholars assert that individualism and collectivism co-exist within individuals and cultures. For instance, Sinha and Tripathi (1994) are of the opinion that dichotomies like individualism and collectivism are inappropriate to describe Indian culture and social reality.

They assert that Indian social reality is complex and consists of contradictory elements, some of which can be described as collectivist and others of which can be described as individualist. Moreover, they assert that these different elements may exist in paradoxical relationships, which are not easily reconciled by simply characterizing cultures according to dichotomous categories.

Turkish psychologist Cigdem Kagitcibasi (1996, 2005) offers another view. Kagitcibasi criticizes both the individualism/collectivism framework and the conceptually similar independence/interdependence framework of Markus and Kitayama (1991) as confounding two distinct dimensions. She asserts that interpersonal distance (emotional closeness versus separation) and agency are logically and empirically distinct dimensions of autonomy that should not be confused. Interpersonal distance and agency can "load together" in some cultures, such as the United States, where, she claims, being both separate and autonomous are valued. However, other cultural contexts may value closeness and connectedness (low interpersonal distance) but still appreciate autonomy (that is, agency). Thus she argues that agency and individual control are central features of all cultures, as is relatedness. This is an important clarification of the meaning of autonomy – and one that, as we shall see, is consistent with the view taken here.

In her book *Always separate, always connected: Independence and interdependence in cultural contexts of development*, Catherine Raeff (2006) also rejects the preponderantly dichotomous approach that has characterized much of the research on culture. She offers an alternative view. She asserts that characterizing cultures as having one or the other orientation obscures both within- and cross-cultural variability. Using the terms "independence" and "interdependence" rather than "individualism" and "collectivism," Raeff asserts that independence and interdependence are simultaneous and inseparable processes rather than two ends of a continuum. In her words, "inseparable cultural independence and interdependence meanings are enacted in the structuring of multifaceted and inseparable independence and interdependence activity dimensions as children participate with others in varied cultural approaches" (p. 47). In other words, individuals are simultaneously separate from and connected to others. Independence and interdependence are mutually constituted, and they are part of every social action. They need to be examined within cultural contexts. Raeff offers little guidance as to how this can be accomplished in empirical research. But the notion that individuals rather than cultures are heterogeneous is consistent with more recent views emerging from cultural anthropology.

Heterogeneity within and between Cultures as Seen in Anthropology

As these examples suggest, there appear to be variations in orientations within as well as between individuals. These variations are not easily explained by accounts that describe cultures as having a dominant, homogeneous orientation or pattern. The examples suggest that we must consider the diverse orientations of individuals within cultures. Different types of concerns may co-exist in individuals' judgments and behaviors. Individuals – for instance adolescents and parents in all cultures – may be collectivist in some situations and individualistic in others. They may value autonomy while at the same time stressing the importance of maintaining traditions and group goals. They may seek the fulfillment of personal goals (although perhaps covertly), even while they uphold their society's demands for conformity.

These assertions are consistent with an emerging trend in cultural anthropology, away from viewing cultures in terms of their coherence, consistency, and uniform orientations (such as those implied by individualism or collectivism) and towards viewing them in terms of their diversity, oppositions, and conflicts (Abu-Lughod, 1993; Holloway, 1999; Nussbaum, 1999; Strauss, 1992; Wikan, 2002). As Abu-Lughod stated, "[t]he effort to produce general ethnographic descriptions of people's beliefs or actions risks smoothing over contradictions, conflicts of interest, doubts, and arguments, not to mention changing motivations and historical circumstances" (1993, p. 9). A number of anthropologists have described individuals within cultures, including traditional ones, in terms of their conflicts, struggles, and attempts to transform social practices or the ways in which cultural understandings "may be conflicting, contested, and resisted by members of society" (Holloway, 1999, p. 61). These researchers claim that cultural psychology has focused too much on individuals in dominant positions, to the neglect of individuals in subordinate positions (Abu-Lughod, 1993; Turiel, 2002; Turiel & Wainryb, 2000; Wainryb, 2006). In turn, the focus on individuals at the bottom of the social hierarchy has revealed that cultural orientations seen to be dominant may be questioned or contested by those not in power.

Cultural anthropologists have illustrated this issue through many detailed examples. For instance, Abu-Lughod (1993) has provided an ethnography drawing on several years of living among the Awlad 'Ali Bedouin, a Bedouin society on the coast of Egypt. The Bedouin are a polygamous, patrilineal society, where marriages are matters of arrangement rather than of personal choice. Abu-Lughod describes how one of the older women in the community, Migdim, came to marry her husband. As Migdim recounts it, her father first promised her to her paternal first cousin. His relatives came to their home to conduct the marriage negotiations. As was the custom, the marriage agreement was sealed with the slaughtering of some sheep. But Migdim decided she did not want to marry this man. He was a first cousin and lived with her family; Migdim felt he was too old and too familiar ("we ate out of one bowl"). She cried and protested over a period of days, but to no avail. The relatives brought her wedding trousseau and the tent in which she and her husband were to live. Her protests intensified, and she manifested her opposition by fasting and by throwing a pot of black dye (which was destined to be used for dyeing the top of the tent). Finally, she ran away to her uncle, who intervened by asking her father to delay the marriage just a bit. After a period of months, the subject of the postponed marriage was raised again. But she protested again and the subject was dropped. No one spoke of the wedding again. Migdim described two more failed attempts at arranging a marriage. They involved similar episodes of crying, protesting, throwing food, and the like. The family's fourth attempt to marry off Migdim was successful and met with her approval. It led to a long marriage and many children.

As Abu-Lughod's (1993) ethnography demonstrates, the Bedouin women she studied used a variety of covert (and not so covert) procedures to subvert their subordinate positions and to attain their desired goals. Although Migdim's father had arranged her marriage (without her consent), she engaged in a number of strategies (such as overt protest, crying, throwing food and dye, running away, and enlisting the aid of sympathetic relatives) to avoid entering it as long as she found it unacceptable. And, although her father and other relatives initially ignored her resistance, her views eventually prevailed. She was not married until she found a partner who was acceptable to her.

In other words, against the odds, she asserted her personal choice in selecting a marriage partner – a notion that is difficult to integrate into accounts of collectivism. Abu-Lughod's aim in describing this incident was not to point out an exceptional case. Rather she claimed that, when the social conventions of Bedouin society denied women personal choices, they often asserted them in more covert ways. In a recollection of her childhood as she was growing up in a Moroccan harem, Fatima Mernissi (1994) has similar examples of the numerous ways in which women subverted the traditional social order to gain their desired ends (for an extended discussion, see Nucci & Turiel, 2000, or Turiel, 2002). This trend in cultural anthropology, towards considering the position of those in nondominant positions, has led to the recognition that cultures are considerably more diverse than has been acknowledged so far.

Recent literature, including biographies, provide similar examples. (Recall Anchee Min's autobiography of growing up in China during the Cultural Revolution.) In her best-selling memoir, *Reading Lolita in Tehran*, Azar Nafisi (2004) describes her experiences during the Iranian revolution and the subsequent period of the Iraq–Iran war. A literature professor at the University of Tehran, she was expelled for her unwillingness to wear a veil. She began a private literature class in her home with a group of women students, where she taught Western classics by authors like Nabokov, F. Scott Fitzgerald, and Jane Austen. In Nafisi's words,

We started reading *Gatsby* in November [...] I was taking some risks in teaching such a book at such a time, when certain books had been banned as morally harmful. Most revolutionary groups were in agreement on the subject of individual freedoms, which they condescendingly called "bourgeois" and "decadent." This made it easier for the new ruling elite to pass some of the most reactionary laws, going so far as to outlaw certain gestures and expressions of emotions, including love. Before it established a new constitution or parliament, the new regime had annulled the marriage-protection law. It banned ballet and dancing and told ballerinas they had a choice between acting and singing. Later women were banned from singing, because a woman's voice, like her hair, was sexually provocative and should be kept hidden. My choice of *Gatsby* was not based on the political climate of the time but on the fact that it was a great novel. (Nafisi, 2004, p. 108)

Nafisi uses her decision both not to don the veil and to teach Western literature as examples of resistance – and as expressions of personal choice – in response to an increasingly repressive society.

Along with the criticisms offered earlier, these examples suggest that the focus on unitary and global cultural orientations (like individualism and collectivism) must shift. We need a more differentiated view, which takes into consideration the heterogeneity and diversity of individuals' orientations within cultures. (In an interesting twist, another Iranian literature professor, Fatemeh Keshavarz, author of *Jasmine and stars: Reading more than Lolita in Iran* (2007) has criticized Nafisi's book on these grounds. She claims that Nafisi has presented a one-dimensional view, which does not accurately capture the depth and humanity of Iranian culture.) The psychological research and theorizing described in Chapters 4 and 5 provides such a differentiated view. It characterizes individuals – both children and parents – within cultures as having diverse understandings of morality, self, and society. These differentiated understandings may be applied in different ways to individuals' social interactions and interpersonal relationships.

Social Reasoning within and across Cultures

The social knowledge domains (moral, conventional, and personal) described in earlier chapters are applicable and useful in considering the orientations of individuals in different cultures. They provide a way of understanding individuals' social reasoning in different contexts. Children, adolescents, and adults in different cultures develop concepts of justice, rights, and welfare (moral concepts); ways of understanding society, hierarchical roles, duties, authority, and normative expectations (conventional concepts); and concepts of self, including a focus on personal goals, entitlement, autonomy, and fulfillment (personal concepts). These concepts may be applied in different ways in different situations, or may be coordinated in individuals' judgments.

The claim that cultures are organized around a dominant and homogeneous cultural orientation entails a particularistic notion of morality. That is, it assumes that concerns with social contracts, welfare, and individual rights are restricted to persons in individualistic societies and that concerns with duty, role obligations, norms, and conformity to authority structure the thinking and behavior of individuals only in collectivist societies. However, many other psychologists (Helwig, 2006; Killen & Wainryb, 2000; Nucci, 2001; Turiel, 2002; Wainryb, 2006) have proposed that there are similarities across cultures in individuals' social experiences and social interactions, including their experiences of welfare, harm, and the distribution of goods. These different concerns arise in interpersonal interactions. They regulate interpersonal relationships in a variety of cultures. Therefore they represent aspects of individuals' social reasoning in different cultures.

For instance, conflicts are ubiquitous in young children's social interactions with peers and siblings. Much research indicates that conflicts in young children's social interactions in free-play settings occur over the distribution of resources, including possessions, rights, and taking turns, as well as over hurting, aggression, psychological harm, and unkindness – all moral issues of rights, welfare, and fairness. This research has focused primarily on North American children. Yet very similar conflicts have been observed among children in cultures that are typically described as collectivist and where morality has been characterized in terms of an understanding of norms, roles, and hierarchical systems (which I have described earlier as elements of social conventional understanding). For instance, in their observations of young children in a preschool outside of Tokyo, Killen and Sueyoshi (1995) found that Japanese preschoolers' conflicts with peers were over object disputes, turn-taking, and (less frequently) physical and psychological harm. These types of social interactions facilitate the development of moral concepts.

The claim that reasoning about fairness, welfare, and rights is universally applicable may seem to suggest that moral practices are similar across cultures. Yet there is compelling evidence – both scientific and nonscientific – for variations in moral practices across cultures. But the existence of variations is not sufficient to prove that morality is culturally relative, or that concepts of rights are restricted to Western societies. Much of the variation in social practices that has been the mainstay of cultural anthropology (for example, Benedict, 1934) can be seen as social conventional in nature. Moreover, evidence for variations in cultural practices does not automatically translate into an explanation of how different moral concepts are acquired or transmitted (Hatch, 1983; Spiro, 1984, 1986; Turiel, 2002; Turiel, Killen, & Helwig, 1987). Both the variations and the continuities in social practices need to be explained. We would expect that individuals in all cultures develop an understanding of social conventions, although the specific conventions that organize social interactions would, by definition, be expected to vary across cultural or subgroup contexts. These specific conventions develop along with an understanding of fairness and rights. The claim that individuals across a range of cultures develop an understanding of social conventions as arbitrary, consensually agreed upon, and contextually relative social norms, together with an understanding of moral concepts as obligatory, generalizable, and nonalterable has been examined and confirmed in a variety of cultures, which include children and adolescents in different countries in Africa, Asia, the Middle East, and South America.

Empirical evidence for moral and conventional concepts across cultures

Researchers have examined whether children in different cultures worldwide distinguish morality and social convention along the dimensions described in Chapter 4. That is, they have examined whether children and adolescents judge morality to be prescriptive, generalizable, and independent of authority and whether they evaluate conventions as contextually relative, alterable, and contingent on rules and authority. In these studies, moral transgressions generally pertained to similar types of acts (for instance harming another or stealing), whereas the conventional transgressions were culturally specific. For instance, in a study pursued in Nigeria, it was revealed that the conventions included eating with the left hand (Hollos, Leis, & Turiel, 1986). In a study undertaken in Korea, the conventional items included taking off one's shoes before entering a room and eating with fingers instead of using chopsticks (Song, Smetana, & Kim, 1987). The evidence provides strong support for the claim that moral and conventional concepts co-exist in different cultures.

Children in almost all of the cultures studied distinguished between moral and conventional rules by using different theoretical criteria. Moreover, these distinctions have been found among the very young, including preschool children in Hong Kong (Yau & Smetana, 2003b) and Colombia (Ardila-Rey & Killen, 2001). Some cultural differences have been observed, but they pertain primarily to the types of justifications children used. For instance, in explaining why conventional transgressions were wrong, Korean children and adolescents used more justifications related to social status, social roles, appropriate role behavior, and courtesy. Such concerns are less common in American children's reasoning (Song et al., 1987). Ijo children and adolescents in Nigeria (Hollos et al., 1986) and Arab children in Israel (Nisan, 1987) affirmed the importance of customs and tradition to a greater degree than American children did. And young Chinese children in Hong Kong (Yau & Smetana, 2003b) offered moral justifications focusing on welfare and fairness at earlier ages than we have observed this kind of reasoning to develop among middle-class children in the United States.

Some recent empirical studies have also examined young children's judgments about authority in Western cultures, as well as in more hierarchical, non-Western cultures. This has been of interest, given the emphasis on obedience to authority and on the importance of hierarchical relationships in Asian cultures. In a series of elegant studies, Marta Laupa (1991; Laupa & Turiel, 1986) showed that American children's views of adult authority depended on whether the authority occupied an appropriate social position and the individual was competent and had the requisite knowledge to fill the role. For instance teachers were seen as having legitimate authority, whereas former teachers were not. Competent teachers were seen as more legitimate authorities than incompetent teachers. Interestingly, although we tend to associate the notion of "authority figure" with adult status, simply being an adult was less important in American children's evaluations than being knowledgeable or occupying the appropriate social position. Moreover, children also coordinate their evaluations of the position of given authority figures with the social context in which these figures issue their commands. For instance, in schools, teachers are seen as more legitimate authority figures than mothers.

Studies of children in Korea, Macao, and Hong Kong (Kim, 1998; Kim & Turiel, 1996; Laupa & Tse, 2005; Yau, Smetana, & Metzger, 2009) demonstrate that Asian children differ from American children in how they weigh these various authority attributes. Children in Korea, as well as Chinese children in Macau, emphasize adult status and knowledge over social position more than American children do (Kim & Turiel, 1996; Laupa & Tse, 2005). However, Korean children viewed both adults and peers as having legitimate authority when their commands were consistent with the children's understanding of the acts. Children recognized actors' social standing, but gave priority to morality. In all of these studies, Chinese children differentiated between the legitimacy of authority and obedience to authority as children from Western cultures did. However, they showed a greater focus on the avoidance of punishment and sanctions when they reasoned about obedience. These studies provide a nuanced view of how different elements of social conventions and moral concepts interact in evaluating authority.

Concepts of rights across cultures

More directly, research studies have examined the claim that children and adolescents in collectivist cultures subordinate rights to duties. But, first, it is important to note that, even in individualistic cultures, where an orientation towards rights is said to predominate, individuals have complex and shifting views and do not endorse rights in all circumstances. Survey studies have shown that the extent to which individuals uphold different rights varies according to whether rights are presented in the abstract (freedom of speech) or in particular contexts (whether Nazis should have the right to free speech in a local town hall). Charles Helwig (1995, 1997, 1998) has conducted programmatic research to examine age-related changes in North American children's and adolescents' conceptions of specific civil liberties, like freedom of speech and freedom of religion. These particular rights were chosen because, in philosophical writing, they are often considered to be prototypical examples of rights.

In one study, Helwig (1995) examined teenagers' judgments about freedom of speech and freedom of religion when these were presented abstractly (for example, whether the law should allow people to express their views). He also examined judgments when these freedoms were presented in a more specific, contextualized way. For instance, in one condition, the vignette described a resident of a surrounding neighborhood as giving a speech in a designated area of a park. This was referred to as an unconflicted application, because the right to free speech was described in a more contextualized way, but with no other competing moral concerns. Finally, the same freedoms were described as being in conflict with other moral concerns. To continue with the previous example, one description presented an individual making a public speech in the park, but his speech contained racial slurs aimed at a minority group. In other words, rights were presented as conflicting with psychological harm. This was referred to as a multifaceted application. In these multifaceted applications, freedom of speech and religion were depicted as conflicting with psychological harm, as just described, and also as resulting in physical harm or inequality.

Helwig found that nearly all (primarily White, middle-class) adolescents in his study viewed freedom of speech and freedom of religion as universally applicable rights. They considered that these rights were not contingent on existing rules or laws (for instance, that it would be wrong for the government to prohibit them). They made these judgments both when the two rights were presented abstractly and when they were presented in contextualized situations where there were no competing moral concerns.

These same rights were much less likely to receive unqualified approval, however, when the freedoms concerned were presented as coming into conflict with competing moral concerns. This was particularly the case when physical harm was seen to be a consequence. One may conclude that North American teenagers subordinated rights to other moral concerns, such as the prevention of harm or the promotion of equality. As they grew older, teenagers demonstrated an increased ability to coordinate different principles and concerns in their judgments. Early adolescents were more likely than older ones and than college students to view issues of equality as overriding civil liberties. For instance they were less accepting of speech that advocated the exclusion of low-income people from political parties. They were also less likely to uphold civil liberties when these conflicted with a law. Younger students could evaluate laws and social systems by using abstract concepts of rights. But nearly half of the participants used a purely legalistic perspective in order to evaluate the legitimacy of violating existing rules in situations where the social system was described as restricting individuals' civil liberties. And, in turn, these results suggest that the notion that persons in individualistic cultures uphold rights is far too simple. Individuals do uphold rights, particularly when presented abstractly, but they also consider other concerns and features of situations. They consider the social context, and they coordinate their concerns with rights with other concerns.

Similar patterns have been observed among teenagers in other cultures. Like North American youth, adolescents in other cultures endorse rights and freedoms in some situations, but subordinate rights to other moral and social concerns in others. An interesting and timely example comes from Verkuyten and Slooter (2008). These researchers examined reasoning about freedom of speech and minority rights among Dutch 12- to 18-year-old adolescents. Of course, Dutch teenagers are considered to be members of an individualistic culture. However, the interesting feature of Verkuyten and Slooter's study was that they compared the responses of Muslim minority and non-Muslim majority adolescents. (Immigration, particularly from Middle Eastern countries, is currently a controversial issue in the Netherlands.)

Unlike Helwig,, these researchers did not include in their study an assessment of abstract situations. They examined judgments given only in concrete and realistic situations. Instead they varied several features of those situations, including the type of situation, whose rights the participants were asked to endorse, these participants' own group affiliation, and the affiliation of the actor depicted in the hypothetical vignette. Participants were only moderately accepting of freedom of speech and of minority rights. Their endorsement of rights varied according to the specific features of the situations. Muslims were more likely than non-Muslims to reject freedom of speech that pertained to Islam or that was described as offending God and religion. Non-Muslims rejected minority rights that entailed separate schools and the burning of the national flag in a demonstration, particularly when depicted as performed by Muslim actors. Thus, as with previous research, the study demonstrated that individuals apply different forms of social reasoning to evaluate complex social issues of free speech and minority rights. These results also added another wrinkle of complexity by showing the importance of considering individuals' social identities, including their group memberships and the intergroup context.

Children and adolescents in different cultures have also been queried about their conceptions of the fairness of different political systems. In one study (Helwig, 1998), they evaluated different forms of democracy, such as consensual, direct, and representative; oligarchy, which is rule based on the wealth of a few people; and meritocracy, where the most intelligent and knowledgeable individuals make decisions. Not surprisingly, North American children viewed all three forms of democracy as more fair than either oligarchy or meritocracy. By early adolescence, teens also came to view direct democracy as more fair than other democratic systems, on the basis of appeals to democratic principles such as majority rule and representation. This is much as one would expect, given that the participants grew up in a democratic system. The changes brought by age appeared to reflect a more nuanced understanding of the participants' own governmental system.

But, more surprisingly, similar results have been obtained in comparisons made between Mainland Chinese and Canadian adolescents (Helwig, Arnold, Tan, & Boyd, 2007). There were very few differences in the judgments and reasoning of urban middle-class teens in Canada and respectively in Nanjing, China. In both cultures, these adolescents viewed representative democracy as being most fair; this was followed by direct democracy, on the basis of appeals to democratic principles. But, as emphasized, both the Chinese and the Canadian youth were drawn from similar environments. Therefore the researchers also compared urban Chinese youth with teens from two additional locations in China. The locations varied in their degree of modernization and exposure to Western influences, and in whether they were urban or rural. Teenagers in Canada and China, including Chinese youth in rural, less modernized villages far removed from Western influence, all judged democratic systems to be better and fairer than either oligarchy or meritocracy. These judgments were based on rationales such as that people should have a voice or a "say," that democratic systems allow different segments of society to be represented in governance, and that these systems provide accountability. Moreover, Chinese youth considered representative democracy to be better than democracy by consensus on the basis of concerns with practicality and utility. This suggests that adolescents in different cultures evaluate the features of political organizations independently of official cultural ideologies and connect them to judgments of political fairness.

The results of these studies support the view that there is a mixture of social judgments, actions, and concerns of persons within cultures. Social judgments are heterogeneous. Even in collectivist cultures, where individuals are said to value duty rather than rights and interdependence rather than independence, different social concepts co-exist, which include justice, interpersonal obligations, conventions, personal choice, and personal entitlements.

Empirical evidence for personal concepts across cultures

The proposition that individuals in all cultures have heterogeneous social orientations entails a related claim: individuals in all cultures develop notions of the person that include concerns with personal expression, choice, and privacy. These concepts relate to issues that individuals view as going beyond the boundaries of societal regulation or of general morality. (And we shall see, this thesis is central to my claims about adolescent–parent conflict in different cultures.) Again, it can be seen that this view differs from that of culture theorists, who have proposed that a conception of the self as unique, autonomous, and bounded and a focus on self-sufficiency and the attainment of personal goals are restricted to persons in individualistic cultures.

At a general level, culture theorists agree that notions of self and personhood (Damon & Hart, 1988; Geertz, 1975) and a sense of agency (Markus & Kitayama, 1991; Miller, 1997) are basic human concepts. They are sensitive to the universal existence of notions of self and of a sense of agency. However, they have given more emphasis to the extent to which agency is embodied in culturally variable forms, particularly in representations of the self as an individual (Miller, 1997), and to the ways in which definitions of personhood vary across cultures. For instance, the anthropologist Clifford Geertz (1984) claims that the sense of self as a bounded, discrete social being is a peculiarly Western construction. He argues that in many other cultures, such as among the Balinese, notions of self are unbounded in the sense that people perceive themselves to be part of selves blended in social relationships. Miller (1997) claims that both how the sense of agency is expressed and the contexts in which it is expressed are culturally variable.

But there is evidence that concepts of personal choice and personal freedom have a broader psychological reality, which can be applied cross-culturally (Killen & Wainryb, 2000; Nucci, 1996, 2001; Turiel, 2002; Wainryb, 2006). Nucci proposes that all cultures treat some issues as falling within the boundaries of the self and personal agency. This is because both the establishment of an arena of personal freedom and notions of human agency are necessary for the formation of the self and for the development of the social individual. Thus appeals to personal choice fulfill basic psychological needs (Nucci, 1996; Nucci & Lee 1993). Theorists who study human motivation from the self-determination perspective have made similar claims (Ryan & Deci, 2000). They argue that, along with competence and relatedness, autonomy is one of three basic, universal psychological needs.

In this chapter I have emphasized the universal dimensions of the personal domain. But, as I noted in Chapter 5, there are cultural variations in the boundaries that constrain or define the personal domain (Nucci 1996; Nucci & Lee 1993; Smetana, 1995b), and hence in what is considered to be under the individual's personal jurisdiction. Individuals develop personal concepts in all cultures; but these concepts are elaborated in cultural contexts that define their scope and content. And, although there are cultural variations, the evidence suggests that there is a great deal of overlap across cultures in the types of issues that are treated as personal.

Cecilia Wainryb's research (Wainryb, 1995; Wainryb & Turiel, 1994) offers a detailed example. Her programmatic research examined how individuals in a traditional, hierarchically organized society reason about justice, interpersonal obligations, and personal entitlements. This research is particularly useful because it specifically examines the proposition that concepts of fairness and rights, as well as concepts of personal entitlement and personal choices, are evident in individuals' reasoning in collectivist societies. However, she also considered how cultural orientations affect social judgments. She expected that thinking about personal goals and entitlements would take a different form in traditional societies, due to differences in social arrangements. Wainryb and Turiel stated this as follows:

> We propose that irrespective of the type of social arrangements – of the type of hierarchical relationships – interpersonal relationships are multifaceted and dynamic, and involve mutual expectations, conflicts, and negotiations over issues of personal preference, rights, and fairness. All relationships, however authoritarian, involve more than just the fulfillment of established or fixed duties and obligations. Relationships, even in hierarchical and authoritarian contexts, involve instances in which certain individuals (those in dominant positions) impose their own personal choices and decisions on others, as well as instances in which certain individuals (those in subordinate positions) attempt to pursue their own goals and desires, try to assert their rights and entitlements, and arrive at compromises. (Wainryb & Turiel, 1995, pp. 304–305)

These propositions are supported by several studies examining judgments from children, adolescents, and adults about fairness, rights, and personal entitlements among the Druze Arabs in Israel. The Druze are a small, highly inbred Arab community founded in the eleventh century. Druze society is hierarchically organized. There are specific duties associated with particular roles, as well as traditions that require adherence by all. The Druze are a patriarchal and patrilineal society, and this results in many restrictions on the behavior and activities of women and girls.

In one study (Wainryb & Turiel, 1994), adolescent girls and boys, as well as adults, evaluated several situations of conflict that were presented in the context of family relationships. The situations depicted one family member objecting to the activities of another family member. In one set of conditions, the father or husband (who usually occupies a dominant position in the family) objects to the activities of his son, daughter, or wife (who occupy subordinate positions in the family). In the other set of conditions, these situations were reversed: individuals in the subordinate position objected to the activities of the person in the dominant position. Overall, a great deal of authority and power was attributed to husbands in relation to their wives, and to fathers in relation to their daughters. Most frequently, justifications for granting husbands and fathers decision-making authority over their wives and daughters were based on concerns with status, roles, and duties. Some justifications directly referred to the father's position in the social hierarchy ("she must obey him because she's his wife"). Other justifications referred to the father's role-related obligations to care and be responsible for his family. These findings accord well with the propositions put forward by Triandis (1995, 2001) and others (Shweder et al., 2006) about individuals' orientations in collectivist societies.

But the findings were considerably more complex. They also reflected a concern with personal autonomy, if only for those in dominant positions. Appeals to personal choice and personal jurisdiction were embedded in the notion of hierarchy. Again, these appeals were made on behalf of those in dominant positions. For instance, both males and females appealed to personal choice and personal needs in justifying why husbands and fathers could impose their views on their wives and daughters. Such justifications included statements like "the daughter should do it because her father wants it done now," or "he can tell her what to do because he owns her." Justifications for why fathers could not impose their will and assert decision-making authority over their sons most frequently involved appeals to personal choice and rights.

To a great extent, females accepted the legitimacy of males making decisions about their activities. They acquiesced, recognizing their subordinate position in the hierarchical social order and the personal entitlements granted to those in dominant positions. They also acknowledged that serious consequences could result from their disobedience. These consequences were seen as another justification for affirming men's power over women. But females' responses also reflected a critical stance on the existing social arrangements. Even though they supported the legitimacy of men's authority, the majority of girls and women also viewed their husbands' or fathers' decision-making control over them as fundamentally unfair and as violating their rights. Thus reasoning about these situations involved concepts of duty, authority, and obligation, as one would expect from descriptions of this culture as collectivist. But the same situations also evoked notions of personal entitlements, personal choices, and personal jurisdiction, as well as moral concerns with fairness and rights.

This research indicates that children's, adolescents', and adults' evaluations of the fairness of different social arrangements depend on where one stands in the social hierarchy. This conclusion is very similar to the results of Stacey Horn's research on American adolescents' evaluations of exclusion from peer reference groups, described in Chapter 4. Those in subordinate roles (that is, females) experienced greater restrictions in their choices and freedoms as a function of their social position. And they evaluated certain social practices as being more unfair than did those in dominant positions, who were accorded more entitlements and choices. On the basis of these findings, Wainryb and Turiel (1993) concluded that the broad interpretations of cultural differences as reflecting global individualistic and collectivistic orientations are overstated. Rather, the findings support the proposition that individuals' judgments within cultures are heterogeneous and contain diverse social orientations.

The ethnographic, anthropological, and psychological research converge in studies of individuals' social reasoning in different cultural contexts. The result has been an attempt to shift the discourse on culture from its focus on unitary and global orientations (like individualism and collectivism) to a more differentiated view, which pays heed to the heterogeneity and diversity of orientations within cultures. Attempts to examine how cultural meanings are subverted and contested have focused primarily on the subordinate role of women and on their attempts to challenge cultural practices. However, this view can be fruitfully applied to an understanding of parent–adolescent relationships as well, as I will elaborate in the following chapter.

Summary and Conclusions

This chapter has examined different ways in which culture has been conceptualized in psychology and cultural anthropology. One currently popular tendency is to differentiate cultures along the global dimensions of individualism and collectivism. Individuals in individualistic cultures have been characterized as stressing autonomy and personal goals, making moral judgments on the basis of rights, and seeking individuation and separation from others. On the other hand, individuals in collectivist cultures have been characterized as stressing interdependence and group goals and duties rather than rights, and as developing along a pathway of relatedness.

Although highly influential, this view has been criticized as providing an overly stereotyped and too simple view of culture. There are variations within as well as between cultures. One response to these criticisms is to propose that cultures vary along a single continuum of individualism and collectivism. Another response is to assert that individualism and collectivism exist within individuals in all cultures. A third response is to argue that different dimensions of autonomy have been confounded. Recently, cultural anthropologists proposed that views of culture have been derived largely from individuals in dominant positions. A different picture results when one studies the perspective of individuals in subordinate positions in society. From this vantage point, cultural understandings may be contested and resisted. Cultural anthropologists have obtained this alternative narrative by focusing on women, who usually occupy subordinate roles in society. As elaborated in more detail in the next chapter, I suggest that a parallel shift occurs when we focus on children's rather than parents' perspectives.

Research shows that individuals in different cultures develop concepts of fairness, welfare, and rights, along with concepts of social convention and society. Adolescents assert rights, even in cultures that are considered to be collectivist. Social conventions may vary in different cultures, but all individuals develop an understanding of social conventions as structuring and organizing social interactions in different contexts. Concepts of personal choice and personal freedom also are found cross-culturally, although the boundaries and content of the personal domain may vary. These concepts fulfill basic psychological needs of self and agency.

In the following chapter we shall consider some cross-cultural support for this claim. We shall examine mothers' beliefs about personal freedoms, before turning to research on adolescent–parent relationships in different cultural contexts.

7

Adolescent Relationships and Development within and between Cultures

As a topic of study, adolescent–parent relationships may seem somewhat removed from the types of concerns with cultural orientations considered in the last chapter. Indeed, relatively few connections have been made between the developmental literature on adolescent–parent relationships – which has focused primarily on American youth and, until relatively recently, on mainstream middle-class youth (see Graham, 1992; McLoyd, 1990) – and theorizing and research about cultural orientations. But the nature of adolescent–parent relationships and the conceptualizations of these relationships bear on the cultural issues elaborated in Chapter 6 in several interesting ways.

First, an obvious but frequently ignored fact is that, like relationships between men and women in traditional societies, parent–child relationships are mostly hierarchical. Most of the time, parents are in dominant positions; children have subordinate roles. This is an issue that has been explicitly considered by several researchers and theorists (Hartup, 1989; Piaget, 1965; Youniss & Smollar, 1985). Of course, this is as it should be, at least in early development. A prolonged period of dependency is necessary to ensure the young children's survival and, more broadly, for them to acquire the norms, values, and expectations of society. But modern society has prolonged the transition into adulthood well beyond the point when biological and cognitive maturity is attained. Indeed, some theorists have proposed that the period of youthful dependency extends far beyond the chronological period of adolescence. They consider young adulthood (referred to as "emerging adulthood") as a distinct developmental stage (Arnett, 2000, 2004, 2007).

Moreover, American society is ambiguous about when the transition from the subordinate status of childhood to the relatively equal status of adulthood is achieved. The staggered timing for conferring the legal status of adulthood (for example the legal ages for driving, drinking alcohol, the draft, and voting) is a

Adolescents, Families, and Social Development: How Teens Construct Their Worlds.   Judith G. Smetana
© 2011 Judith G. Smetana

vivid demonstration of this. The extended delay in achieving adulthood is fraught with many of the same tensions and contradictions that cultural anthropologists have noted when focusing on individuals in subordinate positions in more traditional cultures. Of course, it is important to note that not all of the parents' and children's interactions reflect the hierarchical nature of their relationships. In some of these interactions the power differential is suspended, and parents and children deal with each other as equals. For instance, in playful exchanges, parents may engage the child at a more equal level and behave more like peers than as parents. And research has shown that parents also strive to maintain loving, trusting bonds and to make children happy (Hastings & Grusec, 1998), goals that may not necessarily rely on emphasizing hierarchy.

In Chapter 5 I described European American adolescents' reasoning about personal jurisdiction in situations of conflict with parents. In light of the perspectives discussed in Chapter 6, some might wish to characterize the adolescents' responses as reflecting the individualistic orientation of American culture, with its focus on personal goals, individual rights, and personal agency. These responses might also be seen to attest to the hedonistic desires for personal fulfillment or for the selfish achievement of personal needs and goals, which Robert Bellah and his colleagues (Bellah, Madsen, Sullivan, Swidler, & Tipton, 1985) considered to be endemic to American culture, given its overly individualistic orientation. In addition, these descriptions could be viewed as consistent with Markus and Kitayama's (1991) characterization of independent construals of the self. Indeed, in describing the cultural features of the American self, Markus, Mullally, & Kitayama (1997) stated:

> choice – picking one's favorite, having it your way, the availability of a wide variety of styles, favors, colors, and so on – is central to many domains of U.S. life. Choice is important because it allows people to selve – to manifest their individuality, to express themselves, to be active agents who control their own actions. Choosing involves knowing, revealing, and making good on one's constituting preferences and attitudes. (Markus et al., 1997, p. 24)

This statement appears to be an apt description of European American middle-class adolescents' assertions of personal choice in situations of conflict with parents. Indeed, the mere fact that parents and adolescents have disagreements can be seen as a reflection of the individualistic orientation of American society and of ongoing debates about whose rights should predominate. But, before drawing this conclusion, it is worth considering whether the responses of European American youth generalize to ethnic minority youth in the United States – and, more broadly, to youth in other cultures.

Several studies have examined conflict and conflict resolution among culturally diverse youth in the United States. (I will take up this issue in more detail in reference to African American youth in the following chapter.) These studies are well cited as illuminating ethnic variations in adolescent–parent relationships, and they do show that relationships among diverse groups of American adolescents vary in some important and interesting ways; but they also show surprisingly few cultural and ethnic differences when it comes to conflict. Differences are primarily in beliefs about relationships and in the ways conflicts are resolved. For instance, in studying American adolescents from Mexican, European, Filipino, and Chinese backgrounds, psychologist Andrew Fuligni (1998) found that there were strikingly few ethnic differences in these adolescents' willingness to disagree with their parents. Filipino students were less willing than others to disagree with both of their parents, and Mexican students were less willing than others to disagree with their fathers. Over a 2-year period, however, all youth became willing to express disagreements with parents. But the ethnic groups did not differ either with respect to the frequency of conflicts between children and parents (which was generally low) or with respect to children's feelings of cohesion with their parents (which were generally quite high). Fuligni notes that American adolescents from different ethnic and cultural backgrounds had strikingly similar relationships with parents. Fuligni, Hughes, and Way (2009) concluded in their recent review that "the overall picture of dyadic interactions between parents and adolescents during the teenager years [is] fairly similar across ethnic and immigrant generational groups" (p. 529).

But American adolescents from different ethnic backgrounds say that they would handle conflicts with parents in different ways. Researcher Jean Phinney and her colleagues (Phinney, Kim-Jo, Osorio, & Vilhjalmsdottir, 2005) studied responses from American adolescents – coming from European, Korean, Armenian, and Mexican backgrounds – to hypothetical vignettes about conflicts. Six vignettes were selected to represent issues that might have different cultural meanings; the object of investigation was particularly whether these issues were considered to be matters of personal choice among individuals from different ethnic groups. For instance, one of the vignettes raised the problem of whether adolescents can date someone from a different group. This taps into cultural variations in (social conventional) beliefs about whether dating and the choice of a dating partner are personal matters. In some immigrant groups, dating partners are seen as a matter of concern to parents, and parents are expected to be consulted. In addition, families also vary in the extent to which they expect children to marry within their own ethnic group. Assessing differences in beliefs about obligations to the family, another vignette focused on whether adolescents can choose to attend a party with friends rather than be present at a weekly family dinner. Then, some groups (particularly Armenian families) expect children to live at home until they marry. Thus another vignette examined whether adolescents can choose to move out of the house to live on their own.

The results were surprising in light of the researchers' hypotheses about cultural and ethnic group variations. Regardless of ethnicity, the type of action that adolescents preferred in most cases and most frequently endorsed was self-assertion (that is, the option of following their own wishes), which the authors viewed as an expression of autonomy. This choice did not differ according to ethnicity, but there were some age differences. Older adolescents from Mexican and Armenian backgrounds endorsed self-assertion more than did younger teens from the same ethnic groups. In other words, self-assertion was preferred more by older than by younger adolescents, even in groups that are considered to be collectivist. The next most frequent action choice was negotiation; and it was followed by compliance. The major difference in action choices was that European American adolescents endorsed complying with parents' wishes less than other youth.

The researchers also examined adolescents' different reasons for their choices. What the researchers referred to as self-interest was by far the most frequent reason adolescents articulated. The examples in their coding indicated that this category reflected personal choices (for instance, "it is what I want," "it is my right," "it is my life, so it's my choice"). Other reasons – such as fear of parental punishment or force, concern with mutuality, or concern with the family and with maintaining family harmony – were much less frequent. Again, the expected ethnic differences failed to materialize; only age differences were found. The study also included a college sample. College students focused more on concerns with the family and less on personal choices. And, although European Americans are characterized as individualistic, concerns with the family were greater among older (college-age) students than among their youngest peers.

In this study, ethnic variations were most pronounced when adolescents gave their reasons for compliance. More than other youth, European American adolescents focused on trust in their interpersonal relationships. They also gave more self-interested responses (invoking the argument that their actions might benefit them in the future). Armenian adolescents focused more on feelings of warmth and closeness as a reason to comply with parents' wishes. Korean adolescents were more likely to talk about the importance of family and the need to respect and obey one's parents. More than others, Mexican American youth expressed care and concern for family members. In sum, there was some evidence that ethnic minority youth endorsed complying with parents more out of concern with, or respect for, their parents, whereas European American youth endorsed compliance on the basis of self-interest. But, notably, the responses from European American teens focused predominantly on the importance of trust in their relationships with parents.

The sample for this study included immigrant youth as well as youth born in the United States. The different ethnic groups varied in the proportion of youth who were also immigrants. Phinney and her colleagues did not examine the extent to which this influenced adolescents' responses. But adherence to cultural values is clearly influenced by whether adolescents immigrated to the United States from another country (these are referred to as first-generation immigrants), whether they were born in the United States but their parents were not (second-generation immigrants), or whether both they and their parents were born in the United States (third-generation immigrants, or beyond).

More specifically, when families from different backgrounds immigrate to the United States, their successive generations increasingly adopt American values. They become less likely to endorse the cultural values of their original culture. They come to adopt the perspectives and beliefs of mainstream or majority American culture. Children often find it easier to adapt to majority American culture than their parents do, and therefore they acculturate faster. They certainly learn the language faster and more easily, and they experience greater exposure to American cultural values through their interactions with peers. Indeed, some research has shown that immigrant children become "culture brokers" for their parents, navigating American culture and speaking English or translating it for their parents. These differences in levels of acculturation may lead parents and adolescents to have different expectations of their relationships. In particular, the second generation (where youth were born in the United States but their parents were not) may experience a larger acculturation gap than adolescents and parents who were both born in the same country (that is, the United States, for third-generation youth, or elsewhere, for the first generation). For instance, researcher Ruth Chao (2001) found that, compared to first-generation Chinese adolescents, the second generation perceived their mothers as less warm than they wanted them to be. Andrew Fuligni's (1998) study, discussed earlier, also indicated that the belief that disagreeing with parents is acceptable and behavioral autonomy is desirable was stronger among Mexican American adolescents from later generations, as compared to those from earlier generations.

The results from these studies highlight the complexity of making sweeping claims about individual behavior on the basis of cultural orientations like individualism or collectivism. Indeed, the results of a recent study of Japanese children highlight this complexity. Yamada (2009) asked 7-, 9-, and 11-year-old urban Japanese to evaluate hypothetical situations where a child's personal desire was in conflict with the parents' moral, conventional, or personal demands. The results for the conventional stories are particularly illuminating, as they mirror the types of situations that cause conflicts for American adolescents and parents. In one story, the child wants to watch TV, whereas the father wants the child to clean up the table after dinner. In the other conventional story, the mother demands that the child do a household chore (clean the entranceway to the house), whereas the child wants to play with friends.

Yamada found that nearly all (about 80%) children and early adolescents believed that these parental demands were acceptable on the basis of conventional and practical reasons. But, when asked who should make the decision, about half of the children judged that the child should decide what to do. Only one third thought that the parent should decide. (The remainder indicated that both parties should decide.) Children reasoned that, although these were assigned jobs, it was up to children to decide when and how to do their chores. Remember, this is very similar to what American children said about doing chores. And a substantial number (corresponding to two thirds of the children) also considered that parents did not have the legitimate authority to make this decision. Yamada argued that Japanese mothers encourage children to take charge of their belongings and to feel responsible for tasks. Therefore he speculated that children may view doing chores as an issue legitimately under their control, just like other personal issues.

Furthermore, in hypothetical situations where parents' and children's personal choices were in conflict, children (and especially early adolescents) viewed parents' demands as unacceptable and the decisions as being up to the child, on the basis of personal reasons. And they overwhelmingly rejected the parents' authority over these issues. Again, these results suggest that conclusions about broad cultural orientations regarding conflict may be premature and must be considered more broadly. As we shall see in the following section, several studies have shown that parents in different cultures do endorse the view that an arena of personal control is important for their children's development.

Mothers' Beliefs about Children's Personal Freedoms

Several studies conducted in diverse cultural and ethnic contexts have examined mothers' beliefs about granting children personal freedoms. Although the studies were conducted by different scholars, they all employed a similar interview to investigate the issues that mothers (and in some cases fathers) in different settings believed to be personal and up to the child to control. These studies also examined how parents decide when an issue should be personal and what their reasons are for allowing independent decision-making. Nucci and Smetana's (1996) study of European American middle-class mothers of 5- and 7-year-olds and, to some extent, Nucci and Weber's (1995) study of European American middle-class mothers of 3- and 4-year-olds have already been described in Chapter 5. These works illustrate the European American point of view. But further evidence in support of the claim that autonomy and personal choices are valued universally comes from other studies. These deal with African American middle-class mothers of early adolescents studied longitudinally over 2 years (Smetana & Chuang, 2001), Taiwanese–Canadian mothers of 6- to 8-year-old children (Chuang, 2006), Chinese American mothers (from the Peoples' Republic of China) with young children (Xu, 2000), Japanese mothers in Tokyo (Yamada, 2004), and Brazilian mothers of children and adolescents from two different regions and social classes in Brazil (Nucci, Camino, & Sapiro, 1996). Because cultural norms and values influence parents' beliefs (Goodnow & Collins, 1990), examining beliefs about areas of personal discretion among mothers from different cultures or ethnicities can illuminate both universal values and culture-specific orientations.

Mothers' evaluations of children's independent decision-making

Mothers from these different cultures all claimed that there were issues that they believed should be up to children to control. They had markedly similar ideas about the types of issues they believed the child should be able to decide, and their responses were consistent with descriptions of the personal domain. Mothers asserted that it was permissible to allow children to make independent decisions about their choice of clothes, their activities or play choices, when and what to eat, and, less frequently, their choice of friends or playmates, and control over daily routines. When variations in responses were found, they appeared to be due more to age differences than to cultural characteristics. For instance, as I noted in Chapter 5, the issue of homework features as a personal issue only in the studies that include adolescents. Children must demonstrate a certain level of developmental competence before they are allowed to make independent decisions in this arena.

Mothers also constrained children's personal choices when the children's behaviors involved (or were seen to involve) environmental risks. This fact was reflected in judgments from Brazilian mothers according to their social class. Like mothers from the other cultures, middle-class Brazilian mothers claimed that children should be allowed to make decisions about some things. But lower-class Brazilian mothers of 6- to 8-year-olds and, to a lesser extent, lower-class Brazilian mothers of older children rejected this notion completely. Mothers – especially of the youngest children – expressed concerns about their offspring's health or safety. Such concerns led them to think that children should not be given any say in decision-making. They also expressed doubts about their child's developmental readiness to chose and decide. In sum, delays in granting children personal choices reflected lower-class Brazilian mothers' assessments of the dangers present in their physical environment and of their children's lack of maturity to handle making choices. This was not the case for middle-class Brazilian mothers. As will be elaborated in the next chapter, worries about safety are a concern also for African American mothers.

Mothers' justifications for permitting independent decision-making

Mothers had different ways of explaining why various issues should be up to the child to decide: they offered several reasons or justifications. Despite the variety of this assortment, their justifications were conceptually similar. Most of the responses referred to the importance of developing the child's competence and of developing autonomy, a sense of individuality, independence, and the child's uniqueness. As we saw in Chapter 5, formulating choices and manifesting individuality are often seen as expressions of individualistic cultures. However, mothers from collectivist cultures – for example Taiwanese–Canadian mothers,

Japanese mothers in Tokyo, and lower- and middle-class Brazilian mothers – all emphasized autonomy as a reason for allowing independent decision-making. This reason accounted for a large majority (about 70%) of responses in each group. Mothers also appealed to personal reasons, to the developmental appropriateness of the act, or to the developmental readiness of the child. All of these can be seen as closely related and pertaining to aspects of the child's psychological or self-development.

Nevertheless, there were cultural variations in the specific ways in which mothers reasoned about personal choices for their children. Some researchers have claimed that the way in which European American mothers discipline their children reflects their concern with establishing and enhancing the latter's self-esteem (Wiley, Rose, Burger, & Miller, 1998), whereas Chinese mothers rely heavily on narratives of young children's transgressions in order to induce guilt and shame (Miller, Fung, & Mintz, 1996). (But as we shall see in Chapter 10, children do not necessarily view mothers' use of shaming in a positive light.) As one might expect on the basis of these findings, concerns with fostering the child's sense of agency or self-esteem were more evident among European American middle-class mothers than among mothers from other cultures. However, they did not predominate in European American mothers' responses, nor were they absent from those of the other mothers. And mothers from each of the cultures studied viewed independent decision-making as important in fostering their children's autonomy, agency, competence, and self-reliance.

Miller and her colleagues' (1996) conclusions were based on observations of mother–child interactions, whereas the cultural comparisons discussed here are derived from interviews with mothers and focused on their beliefs. But the interview studies just described also show that in situations involving children's misbehavior, European American middle-class mothers are not necessarily more concerned with protecting and enhancing their children's self-esteem than are mothers in other cultures. In four of the studies, which dealt with European American mothers, Chinese mothers from Taiwan and mainland China residing in North America, and Japanese mothers, mothers were also questioned about their children's motivations in situations where they resisted what their mothers asked them to do. Japanese mothers, especially mothers of young children, viewed their children's resistance to their wishes as selfish or egocentric. Some Chinese mothers offered a somewhat different explanation for children's resistant behavior. They regarded their children as being defiant or as testing the limits. These latter views were infrequent among European American mothers and absent among Japanese mothers. On the other hand, only European American mothers thought that their children were seeking attention when they disobeyed their mothers' wishes. And only mothers from the People's Republic of China cast child resistance in a positive light and indicated approval of the child's behavior: they viewed parents as being bossy and thought that situations of resistance offered positive learning opportunities for children. So, in contrast to Japanese mothers,

Chinese mothers appeared to encourage resistance to their wishes (at least to some extent).

Again, these responses cast some doubt on the claim that cultural orientations differ substantively and substantially. The overriding themes are similar, but there are nuances and variations in how they are expressed. And, although several of these studies focused on mothers with young children, the studies of mothers' beliefs about the behavior of their adolescent children produced similar results.

We shall turn next to the adolescents' reasoning about conflicts.

Adolescent–Parent Relationships in Hong Kong and Mainland China

As I noted earlier, one interpretation of the European American adolescents' appeals to personal jurisdiction in situations of family conflict is that these would solely be reflections of the individualism of American culture. This interpretation is not supported by the findings of research on adolescent–parent conflict in different cultural contexts.

Chinese cultures have been described as prototypically collectivist (Markus et al., 1997). The meta-analyses carried out by Oyserman, Coon, & Kemmelmeier (2002), cited in Chapter 6, show that the Chinese, when examined along multiple dimensions of individualism, are considerably less individualistic than the Americans. In many studies, Chinese family life is seen as strongly influenced by Confucian values (Chao, 1995; Chao & Tseng, 2002). This involves a hierarchical structure, clearly defined roles and responsibilities, deference to parental authority, and reverence and respect for fathers in particular (filial piety). Chinese families are said to emphasize affiliation, cooperation, and harmony in interpersonal relationships and in children's obligations to the family. They are thought to place greater emphasis on social and moral values than on personal values and on competence in the accomplishment of individualistic goals (although, as we have just seen, Chinese mothers' beliefs about their children's independent decision-making do not necessarily conform to these descriptions). Jenny Yau (who worked at the Chinese University of Hong Kong and then at the Hong Kong Institute of Education) and myself examined whether Chinese adolescents' reasoning about conflict reflected the types of concerns ascribed to individuals in collectivist cultures. Our studies focused on reasoning about adolescent–parent conflict among Chinese adolescents in Hong Kong and mainland China.

These studies used the same methods described in the previous chapters to examine reasoning about adolescent–parent conflict. The first one (Yau & Smetana, 1996) focused on Chinese lower and lower to middle socioeconomic status 10- to 19-year-olds living in Hong Kong. We intentionally sampled lower socioeconomic status families, in order to study teenagers who were less westernized and more traditional than adolescents growing up in middle-class families. Trained inter-viewers conducted individual interviews in Cantonese, the Chinese dialect spoken in Hong Kong, with adolescents in their secondary schools.

In 1994, when this study was undertaken, Hong Kong was still a British colony, with a population of 6 million people. Hong Kong is one of the world's major centers of trade and finance. It is highly industrialized and westernized, but it is also strongly influenced by traditional Chinese culture. Nearly all of the popula-tion speaks Chinese. Moreover, research has shown that the values of Hong Kong Chinese parents differ significantly from those of European American parents in the United States (Feldman, Rosenthal, Mont-Reynaud, Leung, & Lau, 1991).

Recently, researchers have begun to focus on the heterogeneity found among the Chinese living in different countries (and, more generally, among children and adolescents treated as part of a single cultural or ethnic group: Parke & Buriel, 2006; Tardif & Miao, 2000). Within Chinese culture, for instance, there is a great deal of diversity in language and in ethnic backgrounds, as well as in adherence to religious and cultural beliefs. There are regional differences as well. For instance, research conducted in mainland China has found that urban Chinese youth believe more strongly that it is acceptable to disagree with parents than rural Chinese adolescents do (Zhang & Fuligni, 2006). These studies suggest that it is worthwhile to examine heterogeneity within cultures if one is to understand differences in parenting and in parent–adolescent relationships.

This led us to compare adolescent–parent relationships in two different Chinese cultural contexts, in a subsequent study. We examined the responses of primarily lower and lower middle-class 10- to 19-year-old Chinese adolescents in Hong Kong and compared them with adolescents of the same age in Shenzhen, mainland China (Yau & Smetana, 2003a). Again, students were interviewed in their schools and in their native languages (Cantonese for youth in Hong Kong and Mandarin for youth in Shenzen). As in our earlier study, most parents had a high school education at the most and were employed as skilled or semi-skilled laborers.

Shenzhen is within striking distance of Hong Kong. It is located to the south of Guangdong Province, on the border between Hong Kong and the People's Republic of China (PRC). Shenzen is one of the centers of mainland China's recent economic growth. It has become a model for the rest of China's economic reform. It is now a major manufacturing center in southern China, and part of Shenzen has become a Special Economic Zone. These factors have led to an enormous influx of population from other parts of the country.

By the time we conducted the second study, Hong Kong had become part of the People's Republic of China and a Special Administrative Region. But Shenzen and Hong Kong are very different. They have different histories and political systems, and their citizens espouse different values. Due to recent modernization and industrialization, the living standard in Shenzhen is higher than in other regions of mainland China, but it is still substantially lower than in Hong Kong. Moreover, like much of mainland China, Shenzhen has experienced enormous political and economic change. The parents of the Shenzhen teenagers who participated in our study grew up after the Cultural Revolution of the 1960s and 1970s. This means that they were raised under the Communist system but spent most of their adult years in a society that placed a great deal of emphasis on pursuing material success and a better life.

Rates and topics of conflicts

The picture of Chinese youth that emerges from these two studies is similar in many ways to the image of European American youth described in the previous chapters. As in European American families, teenagers in Hong Kong and Shenzen reported having the greatest number of conflicts with mothers and fewer conflicts with fathers. Teenagers had conflicts with both parents only infrequently. Teenagers in Hong Kong reported more conflicts with their mothers than youth in Shenzen did. We believe that this was due to the greater number of mothers in Shenzen than in Hong Kong who worked outside of the home. Mothers who stayed at home have more of an opportunity to monitor their adolescent children's activities and have more occasions for disagreement.

As found among American youth, Chinese girls reported more conflicts with their parents than boys did. Conflicts were relatively frequent, but they were only moderately "hot" or intense. Chinese and European American adolescents' responses were not directly compared, but it appears that Chinese teenagers generated a smaller number of conflicts than their European American peers and that conflicts were less frequent and less intense among the former than among the latter. This points to potential differences in the expression of conflict between Chinese and European American teenagers.

As with European American teens, Chinese adolescents' conflicts with parents were over the mundane, everyday issues of family life. The greatest number of conflicts, accounting for more than a third of Hong Kong adolescents' responses, occurred over regulating adolescents' activities. Such issues came up far more frequently than we have observed among middle-class European American adolescents. This could be ascribed to cultural differences; but we believe that it is due to the living conditions in Hong Kong. Hong Kong is a very large, dense, and crowded urban environment, and families live in very small, cramped spaces. Conflicts about activities generally occurred because teenagers wanted to do things out of the house, whereas parents worried about their children's safety in an urban setting that was perceived as unsafe.

Teenagers also reported conflicts with their parents over chores, as well as over doing homework and getting good grades in school. Reflecting the high value placed on academic success among Chinese families, conflicts over homework and academic achievement occurred among Chinese teens in Hong Kong at twice the frequency they were observed among the European American teens I studied.

They were also more prevalent among youth in Shenzen than among youth in Hong Kong, particularly among 7th and 12th graders. These grades coincide with the ages at which Chinese students (both in Hong Kong and on the mainland) must prepare for, and participate in, highly competitive public examinations. The results of these exams are used to place students on different academic tracks. Therefore they have enormous implications for further schooling and for the development of future vocations. But the pressures of doing well in those exams are even greater in Shenzen than in Hong Kong. In Shenzen, the results of these exams are more influential in determining further education, which in turn increases the students' chances for personal and economic success. This also explains why conflicts over chores were greater in Hong Kong than in Shenzhen. Because of the one-child policy in mainland China, parents have only one opportunity to promote their child's academic success. Therefore many parents from the mainland relaxed their demands regarding their children's participation in chores around the house, so that their offspring may have more time to study and do well on exams, thereby increasing their chances of future academic and financial accomplishment.

Less often, conflicts were about interpersonal relationships, health, and appearance. Conflicts also occurred over the parents' behaviors – for instance their smoking, the types of leisure activities they chose, or their relationships, either between the two of them or with other siblings. These types of issues were very infrequent among European American families (although recall the example of Dahlia in Chapter 4, who described conflicts with her mother over her mother's lateness), but they were more evident in Chinese families.

Reasoning about conflicts

The most striking thing, however, was that Chinese adolescents primarily reasoned about conflicts in terms of personal choices and preferences. Personal reasons were the most frequent response in both studies. They accounted for half of the justifications for conflicts in Hong Kong, and the result was just slightly lower when responses from Hong Kong and Shenzen teens were compared. Appeals to personal choice predominated in conflicts over activities and over doing homework.

There were some qualitative differences in the way personal choices and preferences were expressed among Chinese youth, by comparison to the responses of European American teens described earlier. Chinese teens typically did not assert their uniqueness, nor did they claim that a preference or a choice was "their business," as Kelly, Lisa, and Jody, among others, did in the examples provided in Chapter 5. But Chinese teens consistently referred to their personal preferences and choices. This is in keeping with the results of Oyserman and her colleagues' (2002) meta-analyses, which likewise found that Hong Kong college students used more personal preference terms to describe the self than European American college students did.

Chinese teenagers clearly stated their own preferences and choices, which they saw as running contrary to their parents' wishes or expectations. They also stated that parental expectations pertained to issues that they viewed as unimportant or inconsequential and that, therefore, their choices were permissible. In discussing a conflict about watching TV, 12-year-old Bao-yu, a girl, stated: "I watch TV when I'm bored, when I have nothing to do. Besides, there's nothing wrong with watching TV." Similarly, when asked why he has conflicts with parents about not having enough pocket money, 14-year-old Fa states:

> I think it is not enough. I want more – I like to go to play the TV game, so I need more money. Also, I want to save some money, so that I can buy the things that I like [...] It's for entertainment.

In the third example, Fen, a 14-year-old girl, indicated that she had conflicts with her mother about getting up late. She also said that sleeping later is permissible:

> Because there is nothing important waiting for me to do. Therefore, I take a little while longer in bed. She [her mother] wants me to help her out with something or she wants me to study [...] We think differently.

These teenagers asserted that watching TV, spending pocket money one way or another, and getting up late are minor, inconsequential decisions, which should be up to the teen to settle. Teenagers also appealed to the need for privacy. The interviewer questioned 13-year-old Hong about situations where she feels like being alone but her parents disturb her. She declares:

> Because I just want to be alone to think or do my own things at that moment. They think they have something to discuss with me. However, I don't want to discuss the matter, for I have some other things to do. Usually those are private matters.

Finally, another theme that emerged from the interviews is that teens saw themselves as mature and competent enough to make their own decisions. In discussing conflicts with her mother about doing her homework, Min, a 17-year-old, expressed it in the following way.

> I do the homework. I can mange that, but my mom bugs me to do the homework. That is very annoying ... My homework is ok; there is no need to bug me about that. I am mature enough to manage that. I will plan some time to do the homework. She doesn't just ask me to do the homework, she asks me to study hard. She would like to see that I enter the university. She keeps on bugging, and she also feels annoyed. Then she will keep silent. I won't listen to her. At night, I pretend to do the homework, so as not to be bugged by her. She thinks that I am studying, when in fact I am reading fiction.

This response is strikingly similar to 17-year-old Becky's response ("I think that at 17, they shouldn't be telling me what time to go to bed. I sort of pretty much know [...] it's my concern now"), described in Chapter 5.

We did not interview Chinese parents, but we did obtain Hong Kong teenagers' counterarguments. Recall how we saw in Chapter 5 that teenagers' counterarguments closely mirrored their parents' justifications. Therefore such counterarguments can provide some clues as to how Chinese parents reason about the conflicts in question. Adolescents in Hong Kong viewed their parents' arguments as being mostly pragmatic. They asserted that their parents wanted them to use their time more wisely, study harder, and do well in school in order to get ahead and achieve personal and financial success. Adolescents claimed that their parents exhorted them not to waste money (or time). The high frequency of pragmatic counterarguments was directly linked to their conflicts over homework and academic achievement. Parents' concerns regarding these issues were almost always described as pragmatic. But, as the foregoing examples suggest, Chinese adolescents portrayed themselves as responding to strong pressures for achievement from their parents by treating their school and academic achievement, or decisions about when to do homework, as personal matters.

Although such occurrences were relatively low in frequency, Chinese teenagers did view their parents as reasoning conventionally about conflicts, particularly those over doing chores. But again, by their own account, adolescents rejected parents' appeals to tradition, authority, and social coordination. This is shown in the following example about a teen not making the bed upon getting up in the morning.

TEEN:	No one will see it. So why bother?
INTERVIEWER:	Do you think there is a need to do so?
TEEN:	No [...] But it is a traditional way of thinking that one has to take good care of one's belongings.
INTERVIEWER:	That means that it is your responsibility to do so?
TEEN:	Yes.
INTERVIEWER:	Will you insist on not making the bed?
TEEN:	Yes.

Among Hong Kong adolescents, nearly a quarter of the justifications for conflicts focused on psychological concerns. These were more common among Chinese girls than among Chinese boys. Girls sometimes couched their desires for independence in the context of interpersonal concerns (as desires to see friends), emotions (feeling bored at home), and personality faults ("I'm lazy"). All of these were coded as psychological reasons. In contrast, boys revealed their interest in gaining independence more directly, by appealing to personal choice.

The emphasis on personal choice and preferences that we observed among Chinese youth in our two studies is consistent with the claim that conflict facilitates the development of autonomy in adolescence even in cultures considered to be collectivist and oriented towards interpersonal obligations and harmony. Some researchers view age differences as reflecting the deepening influence of the process of socialization. According to this view, the responses of older children and adolescents more closely approximate the cultural goals, ideals, and expected endpoints of successful socialization. But both in Hong Kong and in Shenzen, contrary to what the picture of collectivism might suggest, older adolescents expressed greater desires for autonomy and they appealed to personal choices and preferences more than younger teenagers did.

Other researchers have similarly found that Chinese youth desire more autonomy as they grow older. For instance, in a series of studies, Shirley Feldman and her colleagues have investigated the desired pacing of behavioral autonomy among Chinese youth in Hong Kong, as compared to that of Western teens. In these and other studies of expectations for autonomy (Daddis & Smetana, 2005; Feldman & Quatman, 1988; Feldman & Rosenthal, 1990; Feldman & Wood, 1994; Fuligni, 1998), parents and adolescents have indicated the specific ages at which they think that teenagers should be able to make decisions about, or engage in, different activities. Although not categorized or labeled as such, many of the issues included in these assessments, like choice of clothes, hairstyles, how to spend their own money, and what books or magazines to read, are personal. Other issues, like when teens should be able to decide whether to smoke cigarettes, drink coffee, beer, or wine, or have sex, are prudential. And a third category consists of a mixture of personal, conventional, and prudential issues (for instance, how late teenagers can come home at night, and when they can go out on dates).

Feldman and Rosenthal (1990) found that the pattern of autonomy-seeking was relatively similar among Chinese youth residing in Hong Kong and among Chinese youth who had immigrated to Australia and to the United States. However, the desired pacing of autonomy was different. For some items (such as attending boy–girl parties, staying home alone at night when parents are out, and choosing one's own friends even if parents disagree), Chinese teenagers residing in Hong Kong expected autonomy at later ages than Chinese immigrant children did. The latter, in turn, expected autonomy at later ages than teens of European descent did. But, like the more Westernized Chinese teens, Chinese adolescents residing in Hong Kong also expected autonomy at earlier ages than their parents thought it appropriate. Responses did not differ according to acculturation for other items, such as going out on dates, choosing what clothes to buy in the face of parental opposition, and preferring to do things with friends instead of families. Over most of the issues raised in our studies, Chinese parents and adolescents expected autonomy to be attained by the end of adolescence or young adulthood.

Recently, Zhang and Fuligni (2006) examined adolescent–parent relationships and expectations for autonomy in a large sample of 10th through to 12th graders in Shandong Province, China. China is in the midst of a transition to a market economy, but families living in rural areas are peasants who lead an agricultural life. They have little opportunity to travel and participate in the changing economic system. These researchers compared adolescents who were living in rural areas with adolescents from urban cities in the same province. Thus the youth in the study were growing up under the same political system and shared the same language and culture. Boys living in the urban city environment had earlier expectations for autonomy (and less cohesive relationships with their mothers) than urban girls or rural youth of either gender. This indicates that, among Chinese youth, disagreements with parents may provide a framework for autonomy negotiations to proceed, although there are contextual differences in the desired pacing of the growth of autonomy and in the appropriate means for obtaining it.

Resolutions and discussions regarding conflicts

Of course, this assumes that the Chinese youth Jenny Yau and I studied in our research actually raised conflicts directly with their parents. Another possibility would be that they disagreed with their parents but did not openly express those disagreements; instead, they may submit to their parents' desires to maintain harmony in the family. But this did not seem to be the case. We asked youth in Hong Kong and Shenzen whether they should be able to express openly their disagreements with their parents (Yau & Smetana, 2003a). The responses were nearly unanimous in favor of being able to communicate their disagreements and their choices to their parents. This is similar to what Zhang and Fuligni (2006) found when they asked rural and urban teens from mainland China to rate the acceptability of disagreeing with their parents. Urban teens were more willing to disagree openly with their parents than rural adolescents were, but all youth believed that explicit disagreement was acceptable.

In addition, in our studies, Yau and I interviewed the Chinese adolescents about the types of issues they believed they should be able to discuss openly with parents. The issues that teens wanted to raise explicitly with their parents were the same ones – choice of activities and schoolwork – that caused most of the conflicts in their relationships in the first place. (Recall that this finding is similar to what Larry Nucci and myself, 1996, observed in our interviews with European American mothers of young children, discussed in Chapter 4.) When asked what types of issues they would prefer *not* to discuss with parents, Chinese adolescents (and particularly teens in Shenzen) expressed reluctance to discuss their interpersonal relationships, such as their opposite-sex friendships and dating. They believed that their parents would not listen or understand, and they also wanted to avoid punishment. We shall see in Chapter 11 that these concerns are central to why some teens do not want to talk to their parents about dating and romantic relationships. Chinese culture strongly emphasizes the need to preserve harmony in interpersonal relationships. But Chinese adolescents very rarely gave this as a reason for avoiding open and frank discussion of their disagreements with their parents.

Although Chinese adolescents indicated that they openly expressed conflicts with their parents, raising the issues did not guarantee that they got their way. When asked how the conflicts discussed in their interviews were resolved, Chinese teenagers reported that most of the time (in just over half of their disputes), parents had the final say. Chinese adolescents reported getting their way in nearly a third of their conflicts. The rest were resolved through joint resolutions or compromise. Much like in Zhang and Fuligni's (2006) study, we found that, at least among urban teens, older adolescents (and boys) gave in to their parents less than younger teens (and girls) did.

In European American families, too, we found that parents typically had the final say in resolving conflicts. And, as with Chinese teens, older adolescents gave in to their parents' wishes less than younger adolescents did (Smetana, Yau, & Hanson, 1991). But among European American families this age-related decrease in giving in to parents was accompanied by a corresponding increase in the frequency with which adolescents' views prevailed. As European American teens grew older, the number of conflicts resolved in favor of teens getting their way multiplied. In contrast, although a small proportion of Chinese adolescents did get their way in disputes, this did not increase with age: in other words, older teens did not get their way more than younger adolescents did. Instead, there were more compromises and joint resolutions among older adolescents than among early and middle adolescents. One can conclude that, in European American families, there appears to be some transfer of authority from parents to children during adolescence (although European American parents still decided the outcomes of disputes for the most part). However, Chinese parents retained their authority among older teenagers while acknowledging adolescents' increasing role in decision-making.

Although Chinese teenagers typically did not win in their conflicts with parents, they thought they should. When asked to identify the best solution for each conflict, Chinese adolescents said that their views should prevail. Adolescents rarely stated that giving in to parents was a desirable outcome. Therefore, although Chinese adolescents submitted to their parents' wishes in resolving conflicts and felt that the solutions were relatively fair, this was not an ideal state of affairs in their opinion. They clearly wished to get their way and they expressed desires for greater autonomy and power of choice.

Other researchers have found that Chinese youth in Hong Kong perceive parents who rely heavily on dominating control as being less warm and more distant (Lau & Cheung, 1987). Among Hong Kong youth, we also found that perceptions of Chinese parents' warmth and use of control were associated with variations in the rate and intensity of conflicts. Chinese adolescents who perceived their mothers as lower in warmth had more frequent conflicts with their mothers. They also reported a greater number of conflicts when both parents were rated as lower in warmth. And teens who viewed their parents as more controlling had more intense, angrier conflicts with their parents. In a nutshell, individual differences in Chinese adolescents' perceptions of the rate and intensity of conflicts with their parents were connected to their perceptions of use of control and degrees of warmth in their parents. This is consistent with the notion that autonomy and relatedness are basic human needs (Ryan & Deci, 2000) that, when thwarted, lead to conflict.

The results of these studies paint a more complex portrait of Chinese adolescent–parent relationships than notions of individualism versus collectivism suggest. An emphasis on maintaining harmony in interpersonal relationships was reflected in the relatively small number of conflicts generated and in the relatively moderate frequency of those conflicts. It was also reflected in the trend towards compromise or joint resolutions rather than towards age-related increases in teens getting their way or "winning" in their conflicts with parents. At the same time, the predominant orientation towards personal choice in Chinese adolescents' reasoning about conflict, as well as their desires to have their own views prevail in conflicts, also reflect prototypical aspects of the independent self. The mixed pattern of these findings is congruent with the proposition that cultures do not have unitary orientations and that individuals cannot be simply categorized as individualistic or collectivistic. It is also consistent with the notion that needs for autonomy and agency are universal and separable from interpersonal distance (Kagitcibasi, 1996, 2005). Chinese adolescents clearly desire and attain greater autonomy with age. These studies suggest that such attainment may be negotiated, at least in part, in the context of everyday disagreements and through the adolescents' assertions of personal choice.

Summary and Conclusions

In this chapter I claimed that independent construals of the self, which are seen to be characteristic of American (and Western) adolescents, apply more broadly to youth from other cultures too. Studies conducted in different cultures have examined mothers' beliefs about granting children and adolescents personal choices and freedoms. Mothers from Brazil, China, Japan, and Taiwan, and European American and African American mothers in the United States all identified a similar set of issues (like choice of clothes, food, clothes, and friend choices) that children should be able to control or decide about. Across contexts, mothers' reasons for allowing children choices focused on the development of autonomy and competence.

American teenagers from different ethnic and cultural backgrounds have strikingly similar relationships with their parents. Conflict and cohesion with parents do not seem to differ according to ethnicity (Fuligni et al., 2009). Also, there are few differences in the types of reasons that adolescents give for asserting their choices when they want to have it their way. American adolescents from different ethnic backgrounds do appear to differ, however, in their willingness to disagree with parents, in their outward compliance with parents' wishes, and in the reasons they give for that compliance.

Research on Chinese adolescents in Hong Kong and Shenzen provides further support for the claim that autonomy and personal issues are important aspects of social life in different cultures. Chinese adolescents have conflicts with their parents over everyday issues, like their choice of activities and doing homework. Like European American teens, Chinese teenagers reasoned about conflicts in terms of personal preferences and choices, and these justifications were more frequent among older than among younger adolescents. This is surprising, in light of claims that socialization reflects a greater internalization of cultural values and that Chinese culture emphasizes interpersonal harmony and deference to parental authority.

Chinese adolescents also claimed that they raised conflicts directly with their parents. Chinese adolescents, like European American youth, reported that conflicts were resolved primarily by giving in to parents' wishes. But, with age, European American adolescents were more likely to get their way in conflicts. This was not the case with Chinese youth. Instead, among the latter there was a modest increase, with age, in joint resolutions or compromise with parents. Rather than a transfer of authority, then, there was a shift towards more joint decision-making. Overall, the studies reviewed in this chapter suggest that there are cross-cultural similarities as well as cultural shades of difference in adolescent–parent relationships.

In the following chapter we shall continue the discussion of cultural and ethnic variations by considering adolescent–parent relationships in African American families.

8

Adolescent–Parent Relationships in African American Families

In the previous chapter we considered issues of culture in adolescent–parent relationships. We saw that there are similarities across cultures in such relationships, particularly in the types of issues that cause conflicts and in the way adolescents reason about them. But there are also culturally distinctive nuances – for instance in the frequency with which specific issues of conflict arise, or in how conflicts are resolved. In this chapter we take a more in-depth view of adolescent–parent relationships in African American families.

In recent years, numerous scholars have called for more research on the typical development of American ethnic minority youth, including African Americans, and on the specific developmental issues and challenges they face. In response to this call, the number of studies focusing on ethnic minority youth has increased dramatically over the past 15 years. Despite this interest, much of the research has concentrated on youth growing up in poverty and their associated problems, such as crime, juvenile delinquency, drug abuse, precocious sexuality, and early child bearing. Less research has studied the typical development of African American adolescents, and even fewer studies have focused on middle-class African Americans. However, recent census data indicate that slightly less than half of African American children are growing up below the poverty line. This means that the development and adjustment of the remaining half are understudied. The sizeable and growing African American middle-class has been largely ignored.

The consequences of this state of things are two-fold. First, conclusions drawn from research focusing primarily on lower socioeconomic African American families may confound ethnicity and socioeconomic status, and thus they may attribute to ethnicity effects that are actually due to socioeconomic status. Furthermore, researchers often focus on middle-class European American samples when the prevailing concerns are with normal adolescent development, and they focus on

Adolescents, Families, and Social Development: How Teens Construct Their Worlds. Judith G. Smetana
© 2011 Judith G. Smetana

lower socioeconomic status African American adolescents when problem behaviors are of interest. This has led to a skewed perception of all African American youth as troubled. It has also led to a dearth of knowledge about normal development in a broad spectrum of African American families.

Research on ethnic minority children and adolescents often employs race-comparative designs, whereby ethnic minority children are compared to White middle-class children. Too often, White families have been seen as the gold standard against which differences are to be judged. The resulting judgments have promoted a picture of African American families as not measuring up to European American families. This "deficit" model has characterized a great deal of the early research (especially prior to the 1990s) on African American families. Differences have been viewed as deficiencies, without much regard for the confounding effects of socioeconomic status, family structure, community, or neighborhood and without adequate consideration of cultural values. As a consequence, some researchers have argued against conducting studies that involve comparisons between different ethnic groups. They have advocated instead focusing intensely on a single ethnic group (Phinney & Landin, 1998). And, as some scholars have reminded us (Hill, Murry, & Anderson, 2005), African American families are diverse and heterogeneous. One of the advantages of using a within-group design is that researchers can focus on this heterogeneity and describe the variations that exist within the group.

This is the strategy I have used in the research described in this chapter. I describe the results of a 5-year longitudinal study of middle-class African American families with adolescents. I consider in some detail, and in their own words, middle-class African American adolescents' and parents' descriptions of their relationships, including adolescent–parent conflict and closeness and how these change over time. The present chapter also considers a broader set of issues. The nature of parenting in African American families has been the subject of much debate, and is also discussed here. This topic is illuminated by parents' responses to interview questions about their goals on the matter of autonomy versus control. Parents also discussed how they handled the highly charged issues of race, prejudice, and discrimination. Finally, parents and adolescents were observed interacting together.

Brief Overview of the Study

The University of Rochester Youth and Family Project was initiated in 1996. A small but intensively studied sample of 96 middle-class African American families was followed longitudinally for 5 years and assessed at three points in time. At the first two assessments, held 2 years apart, we conducted face-to-face interviews and detailed observations of family interactions with adolescents and with their parents or guardians. At all three times, parents and teenagers completed extensive surveys. When the study began, adolescents (mostly first borns) were, on average, 13 years of age and ranged in age from 11 to 14 years old. There were nearly even numbers of boys and girls. Most parents had been to college, and most mothers worked outside of the home. Although much has been written about the prevalence of single parent, mother-headed households in the African American community, the incidence of single-parent families varies according to socioeconomic status. Single-parent households (and also multi-generational households) are much more common among families living in poverty. Among the middle class, rates of marriage are much higher. When the study was initiated, most (70%) of the families were two-parent households of married couples. The remaining were single-parent households consisting either of never-married women or of parents who were divorced. Twenty percent of the sample experienced a change in marital status over the course of the study, and mainly in the last 3 years. Families sometimes dissolved or reformed, and two of them experienced the death of a spouse.

Families were recruited from Rochester, New York and surrounding suburban areas. Like many Northeastern cities, Rochester has an urban core that is predominantly minority (mostly African American, but with a growing Latino population) and poor. Indeed a very high proportion of the children attending the city schools (over 85%) qualify for the federal free lunch program – an indicator of poverty status. The surrounding suburban communities are more middle class, but far fewer African American families reside there. This posed a challenge for the recruitment of a middle-class African American sample.

The Black church is the heart of the African American community. The Black church serves far more than individuals' spiritual and religious needs. It embraces traditional African American values, it typically offers a wide range of community and social services, it identifies with, and promotes, the political struggles of African Americans, and it serves as the bedrock of the community (Billingsley, 1992; Lincoln & Mamiya, 1990). Drawing on the results of the National Survey of Black Americans, Jacqueline Mattis (2005) notes that nearly all African American adults describe themselves as religious and as engaging in religious activities like praying, meditating, or reading religious materials. Most also report attending religious services. According to sociologist Andrew Billingsley (1992), they primarily attend Black churches.

Given the central role of the church in the African American community, families were recruited from African American churches (particularly ones noted for having a more middle-class base), with the cooperation of African American pastors. Most Black churches are located in primarily African American neighborhoods. But African American middle-class families who have migrated to the suburbs typically retain their association with an African American church, often as a way of preserving their African American identity. Indeed, for families who move to the suburbs and enroll in majority White schools, maintaining ties with the African American church is a way of promoting African American values by instilling them in their children.

Families were recruited through announcements made at church services and at church gatherings, as well as through social organizations that cater specifically to middle- and upper middle-class African American families (such as Links and Jack and Jill). The resulting sample was middle class, and ranged from lower middle class to upper class. We used yearly family income as a way of screening families, but then we obtained more complete measures of socioeconomic status. It should be noted that middle-class status masks racial disparities in wealth that are greater than the existing racial disparities in income. African American middle-class families are much less likely than their White counterparts to own their own homes, to have accumulated assets like stocks, or to transfer wealth across generations (Darity & Nicholson, 2005). This means that, because of the differential in wealth accumulation, middle-class status is more precarious for African Americans than for European Americans.

Moreover, because families were recruited from religious, social, and professional organizations rather than from schools, they came from diverse neighborhoods. Approximately half of the families lived within the city limits. The other half lived in the surrounding suburbs. But the families came from many different neighborhoods within the city and from a variety of different suburbs (indeed, from over 57 separate census tracts). We visited tiny homes in neighborhoods that could be considered blighted, as well as gracious homes with large, spacious curving driveways on large expanses of land.

We took several steps to ensure that our methods took into consideration the community we studied. We wanted to listen to our participants not just in the process of collecting data, but in formulating crucial aspects of the study as well. To accomplish this, we conducted focus groups before we began the study. Focus groups are a qualitative method originating from marketing research (Krueger, 1994). Focus group methodologies are quite well developed. They include procedures for sampling, the development of a focus group protocol designed to ensure that the topics of interest are covered, the use of skilled facilitators to run the groups, and specific methods for analyzing focus group discussions.

We used focus groups as part of an iterative process in designing our study. That is, we made some initial decisions about the sampling, the constructs we wanted to assess, and the methods and measures we intended to use. Then we conducted focus groups with middle-class African American parents. The groups provided a great deal of useful information. For instance, parents stated that "[s]chools don't care about our children." They indicated that they would be more likely to participate in the project if they were approached through their churches. This reinforced our decision to avoid schools altogether and to recruit mostly through churches, where our project would be more visible and would have more credibility for the community. Focus group responses were also instrumental in our choice of some measures, for instance in our choice of family interaction tasks.

We found that one of the commonly used tasks (where families plan a vacation together) had little ecological validity for these families. We changed the task on the basis of parents' responses. Focus group responses also helped us to generate items for a parental authority measure.

Most importantly, the focus group responses highlighted the importance of certain issues. As part of the focus group, parents discussed in a very open-ended way some of the pressures and problems they felt as parents. Several researchers and clinicians (Boyd-Franklin, 1989; Franklin & Boyd-Franklin, 1985; Garcia Coll et al., 1996; Garcia Coll & Pachter, 2002) have written about the importance of considering the effects of racism in understanding Black families. The importance of racism in families' lives was painfully evident in our open-ended discussions. We decided to include, in our semi-structured interviews, questions about how parents cope with racism and how they socialize their children around these issues. (When we began this project, relatively little had been written on this topic, although now the impact of racism and racial socialization has been much more thoroughly researched.)

We also enlisted the advice of a community advisory board throughout the project. Our community advisory board was composed of leaders of the community and parents. They served as sounding board for many aspects of our research. They enhanced our credibility in the community; they had many useful suggestions about recruiting our sample; and they gave ongoing advice on the project.

Interviews with family members, conducted by two African American interviewers, took place primarily in families' homes. Interviewers met for approximately three hours (and often more) with teenagers, mothers, and fathers. Sometimes other adults were present. Often enough, younger children ran through the rooms or were being watched by another family member. After introductions, paperwork, and an overview of the session, participating family members were individually interviewed in private areas of the house, while other family members completed paper and pencil surveys. Then family members gathered around a table or on their sofa and engaged in several structured family interaction tasks that were videotaped.

Interviews were repeated 2 years later. We were able to locate most of the families, and most of them agreed to be re-interviewed. Indeed, interviewers typically received a warm welcome into homes for these second interviews. They followed the same format as in the first round. Five years after the initial interview and 3 years after the second set of interviews, parents and teenagers were contacted separately and mailed surveys that they had to complete. We retained 83% of the sample over the 5 years of the study. Families were lost through attrition, mostly because they could not be located despite persistent efforts. At this point, the majority (69%) of the adolescents had left home, mostly to attend college, or, in the case of a few boys, to join the Armed Services. Most of the college students were in 4-year schools. Most of the teens remaining at home had been younger when the study was initiated and therefore were still completing high school. Only two adolescents who were over the age of 18 when the study ended did not graduate from high school; one of them had completed a GED (General Education Development test, which is equivalent to a high school diploma). Both of these teens were working. When contacted for the third time, all but one of the teens reported being single, unmarried, and not cohabiting with a romantic partner. One adolescent was living with a partner, and one had given birth. As this summary suggests, this was a very successful and high-functioning group of African American youth.

The within-group design of the study was meant to capture the particular values and practices of middle-class African American families. But what are these values? They are discussed in the following section.

African American Cultural Values

African American culture reflects a complex and unique blend of both cultural and historical influences. As one group of researchers aptly stated,

> the way in which these separate threads are interwoven is as distinctly African American as is jazz, rap, and the blues. The notes are universal, but the style and verve echo the African American historical and cultural experience and have a signature integrity of their own. (Cauce et al., 1996, p. 112)

African American culture has been described as strongly influenced by West African values such as the importance of spirituality, extended kin networks, and communalism. Many scholars believe that West African values have not survived intact in contemporary African American culture, although this is a somewhat controversial claim. Rather, they would have been transformed and made to take a distinctively American pattern by the history of slavery and by the ongoing experiences of oppression and racism. The slave trade destroyed family ties among those who were captured and sold into slavery (Billingsley, 1992), but even during the time of slavery family ties were revived and sustained by large numbers of African Americans. As Billingsley notes,

> the African American family was re-created and reconstructed during slavery. It was not the African family, it was not the European family, nor the American family. It was and is a more distinctive aggregation, the African American family. It is characterized now as then by its matricentrism, its extended families, and its remarkable flexibility, adaptability, and resilience. (Billingsley, 1992, p. 107)

During the long history of slavery and Reconstruction, African American culture was nourished and maintained by ties and attachment to the family. African

Americans place a high value on communalism and harmony in interpersonal relationships. Families are strongly hierarchical in structure, and obedience and respect towards elders is expected. Group concerns are said to take precedence over individual concerns. Cooperation and collective efforts prevail, and belongingness to the group is highly valued. In addition, African American families rely on kinship networks for strength and support. Among African Americans, kinship networks, the community, and the church function as significant sources of strength, resilience, and protection (Boykin, 1983; Boykin & Toms, 1985; Garcia Coll & Pachter, 2002; Hatchett & Jackson, 1993; McAdoo, 2002; Parke & Buriel, 2006; Winfield, 1995).

For the middle-class African Americans we interviewed, being part of the community and having a sense of community were highly valued. But, as the description of the sample suggests, this sense of community was not necessarily derived from living in close geographical proximity. Families lived in diverse neighborhoods. Families who lived in an urban environment were more likely to reside in heavily African American or racially integrated neighborhoods, whereas families who lived in the suburbs lived mostly in more homogeneously White neighborhoods. Therefore the sense of community tended to derive from having an abstract sense of belonging, which came from sharing certain interests, concerns, political experiences, and cultural values. One of those shared things was the families' concerns and experiences with racism and prejudice.

Coping with Racism and Prejudice

When interviewed about parenting practices and family conflicts, parents made few explicit references to prejudice and discrimination, but these was implicit in much of what they said. On the other hand, they had much more to say about these issues, explicitly, in another part of the interview. There they were asked in so many words about the challenges of raising an African American child and about their strategies for addressing those challenges. As I write this, in the early days of the Obama Administration, social commentators and journalists have debated whether the United States has become a "post-racial" society (Bai, 2008, August 6) – that is, a society in which race is no longer significant or important. Although the Youth and Family Project was conducted well before Obama's historic election, I am certain that the African American parents I studied would soundly reject this notion even today. Regardless of socioeconomic standing, race remains a significant feature of life for African American parents, including middle-class ones. All of the parents we interviewed strongly asserted that racism was alive and well in American society.

As we have seen, parents of different ethnicities face challenges in fostering their adolescents' autonomy and competence while they protect them from the increased psychosocial risks of adolescence. But for African American parents the challenge is substantially greater, due to the effects of prejudice and discrimination. In a Sunday *New York Times Magazine* article, Sara Mosle vividly described her experience as a volunteer mentor to a group of poor African American boys:

> When I first started seeing my kids, people would smile at us on the subway, as in "Look at the nice white lady with the cute little black children." Now I found, when I was standing at the center of a group of teenage boys, people sometimes shot me expressions of alarm, as in, "Are you OK?" In the public's eyes, my kids had morphed, in the matter of one or two years, from being "cute" to being potential super-predators. I often noticed as we walked around the Upper West Side [of New York City] how people gave us a wide berth, how store managers stiffened when we walked in, how people moved, when we sat down in a theater, how, if I hailed a cab and my kids stepped off the curb, it would screech away [...] I wanted to hit people when these things happened. My kids just shrugged. It wasn't news to them, and it shouldn't have been to me. But all I can say is that it's not the same until it happens to you. (Mosle, 2000, July 2, p. 54)

Although being middle class certainly shields families from many of the ills associated with poverty, it does not protect them from racism. All parents articulated concerns about racism. All affirmed its existence, although they differed in whether they believed or not that it could be overcome. They also differed in their views of how it should be addressed in raising their children. In the opinion of one mother, "African Americans will always struggle for equality and struggle for the same education and status. The struggle is going to be there all the time." But other parents were more optimistic and saw cause for hope and change. Concerns with racism and its injurious effects were particularly potent for parents of boys. As one mother stated: "But in particular for an African American male –there are going to be some judgments that are going to be made about him regardless of the kind of person that he is, before he opens his mouth."

Like Sara Mosle, some parents were concerned about how their now tall, mature-looking, post-pubertal sons would look to others. As one father put it in response to a question about the challenges of raising an African American child:

> Well, the fact that he is an African American male. The whole idea that he is quite large. He's physically large. Very large, but very gentle. And that in itself can be a problem for him, being so big and yet so caring and outgoing. The two sometimes pose problems because they are misinterpreted.

Another parent described African American boys as being seen as potential threats to others.

> I think the main issue is that I feel that the most dangerous person to the popular culture is an educated Black man because they may have to come under submission

to him. And more effort is put into blocking their progress than there is effort put into dealing with an uneducated Black man. I tell him that whatever is in his school environment most of the time, that his misbehavior is going to be magnified as opposed to the misbehavior of a White child, and that a lot of the impressions of him that his teachers may have is [*sic*] not based on him but is based on the media. So when they approach him, they approach him from the standpoint that he's a young gang banger. And the darker you are, the more feared you are. But I tell him once again that whatever God's plan is for you, there's no devil in hell that can stop it. But you always need to be on your best behavior and you have to give respect in order to get it. And you have to be careful how you talk to people.

Short or tall, from poor or wealthy families, African American boys face risks as a consequence of their race. The parents we interviewed tried to prepare them for those risks. In their book, Nancy Boyd-Franklin and A. J. Franklin (2000) provide practical child-rearing advice to African American parents. For parents of boys, they discuss how to prepare their African American sons for incidents where they are stopped by the police for DWB – "driving while black." This phrase refers to racial profiling, whereby cars driven by African American males are stopped by the police for no reason other than the race or ethnicity of the car's occupants. As this illustrates, the risks are very real for African Americans – especially males – of all socioeconomic strata. As one mother stated:

A lot of people act as if racism is dead. And the answer is no. They need to know it's there, and it's not always straight out someone calling you a n–. A lot of times its very subtle. A lot of times its unspoken, and I want him to be aware of it.

Some scholars have asserted that African American male–female relationships are egalitarian due to the history of slavery, where family relations were frequently disrupted and female-headed households became the norm (Billingsley, 1992). However, in contrast to this claim, many feminists have described African American women as sitting below European American men and women and below African American men as well, due to the "double whammy" of racism and sexism. Therefore African American girls face another set of risks. Their relatively powerless position makes them vulnerable. In addition, African American teenage girls must construct a positive self-image in a climate where their looks do not fit desired physical stereotypes (blond, blue-eyed, small-featured, and thin: Cauce et al., 1996).

Parents responded to these challenges by asserting that their children (both boys and girls) had to be self-confident, develop perseverance, be highly qualified, and become well educated. The same words were echoed repeatedly. One mother stated:

As an African American young lady, she is going to have to be twice as good as the competition, as the White folks. She is going to have to be at her very best at all times. Things that others might be able to get away with, she won't be able to get away with. She's going to have to work harder in whatever she does.

Jerome, the father of a 13-year-old girl, put it this way:

> There may be some stereotypes about how people perceive her. She's going to have to be more aggressive. And we talked about that. She's going to encounter racism. She's going to have the skills to deal with it. But she's not going to let it be an obstacle in holding her back and realizing her goals. She's just going to have to learn how to liberate herself from an oppressive environment she might find herself in.

As described earlier, approximately half of the families who participated in this study lived in suburban communities that were predominately European American. Families had moved to the suburbs so that their offspring could take advantage of lower levels of crime, safer streets, and better schools. But being in suburban schools raised another set of challenges. In most of these schools, there were only a few other African American teens to blunt the force of racism. As the following mother notes, being an African American in a majority White school can lead to more overt encounters with racism.

> Well, in this day and age, you have to be twice as qualified as the average Caucasian. You have to be well versed in what you know. You have to present yourself, sell yourself twice as hard [...] Actually, he's come across a lot of things when we lived out in [a suburb]. There were very few Blacks that were going to the school that he attended. And he would come home every day and ask me different things about why people call them names or this or that. And I explained to him that he is somebody. And no matter what they say, you have the ability to be anything you want to be.

Many middle-class parents discussed the challenges of raising their African American teenagers in a White or multi-racial environment. Parents acknowledged the presence of racism and tried to prepare their children for encountering it. They made certain that their adolescents had opportunities to absorb African American cultural values from different contexts. They interacted with other African American families by attending Black churches or social groups. However, most parents conveyed positive and encouraging messages about getting along with all types of people.

> [I try ...] to expose her to different people. She may go to a predominantly Black church. But for grammar school, she went to a predominantly White school. And that was a conscious decision. So we try to make conscious efforts to expose her to different types of people and encourage her even within her school and her other activities to not limit herself to just her folks.

These preoccupations with racism and with exposing their children to African American cultural values formed the backdrop against which other parenting concerns were expressed. The focus on community, on belonging to the group, and on the hierarchical structure of the family are, all, characteristics that are consistent with collectivist values, as described in the last two chapters. However, Oyserman and her colleagues' detailed meta-analysis (Oyserman, Coon, & Kemmelmeier, 2002), discussed earlier, concluded that African Americans do not differ from European Americans in overall levels of collectivism, particularly when assessments of collectivism included advice-seeking. (European Americans seem to use advice-seeking as a way to relate and connect, which heightens their level of collectivism.) And, despite the importance of characteristics associated with a collectivist orientation, African American culture also emphasizes individuality, for example by treating others as separate beings with unique thoughts and feelings. African Americans are said to value spontaneity and self-expression and to encourage self-reliance, individuality, and independence. Indeed, the results of their meta-analysis led Oyserman and her colleagues to conclude that African Americans are also more individualistic than European Americans are.

Parenting in African American Families

The results of this meta-analysis reflect the heterogeneity in orientations found among African American families. In interviews about their parenting beliefs, African American parents simultaneously emphasized the importance of teenagers' developing independence – at least about some issues – and focused on the need for teenagers to adhere to moral values and cultural conventions. As we saw in previous chapters, these are issues of concern to families in other cultures and ethnic groups too, although the way they are expressed and coordinated may be culturally distinctive. In their interviews, parents described the types of limits they set and the ways in which they decided when to set limits, as well as when, how, and over what types of issues they permitted independence. Parents drew boundaries between moral values and conventional norms, which were firmly enforced, and personal issues, where more independence – as well as more negotiation over independence – was granted. Betty, mother of 14-year-old Amber, explains:

BETTY: I guess the hottest issue in our house is the issue of freedom. And the freedom to – she thinks she should have more freedom to do whatever she wants to do. I think that's part of getting older – the need to have freedom [...] we think it's important that with freedom comes responsibility [...] We have certain core things we try to establish in our house, and in terms of good manners, in terms of respect for parents, honoring your parents and spiritual values, and so when it comes down to – I mean there are areas where she has freedom, like clothing, music, things like that. But certain core things like the way she's going to behave at home, as a role model to her brothers and sisters, there are certain things that we definitely affirm about [...] We believe that the Scripture has a lot to say about life and how we should live our lives. And so that really informs how we set guidelines for her [...]

INTERVIEWER: Do you encourage her independence?

BETTY: Well, I think it's sort of an ambivalent feeling because in one sense you want her to be independent, but in another, you don't want her to become so independent that she feels like she can be rebellious [...] So it's like you want to strike a harmonious balance where she knows that being independent is good, but it's also good to be interdependent and to never feel like because you have enough money, you can be on your own and be self-relying and never depend on anyone else. Because I think no matter how much money we have, there's a place in life where we all need other people and we need other people's advice and fellowship and friendship and that's important. So I would say that's where the independence goes [...] And I think we want her to be independent but receptive and teachable.

Betty distinguishes between her desire to set clear standards over social conventional issues, like proper demeanor and respect towards parents, and the need to allow her teen some independence over personal issues like music and clothes. But she also sets limits on independence, noting the importance of maintaining connections to others and the dangers of detachment. She also stresses that it is important that Amber should be a good role model for her other siblings.

Denise, mother of 16-year-old Taye, also discusses the way she decided when to restrict Taye's behavior.

DENISE: Just because he is 16 doesn't absolve me of my responsibility [to set limits]. Because, as children, I believe they need guidance. Even adults sometimes still need someone to guide them. And if I am not doing that, then he may become another statistic. Kids committing crimes [...] So I try to be Taye's friend as well as his mother.

INTERVIEWER: How do you decide when to be firm and set limits?

DENISE: It all depends on the issue. Some fights are worth fighting. Some are not. You just let it go. I try not to stress myself out too much about things that won't have a final impact on his life [...] some things like the way he dresses I don't think that has an impact [...] I encourage [independence] because there's no guarantee that I am going to be around. I encourage respectful independence [...] Because as I indicated earlier, I believe he needs to be a free thinker. And I try to stop thinking for him so much [...]

he should be allowed, within limits, to decide who his friends would be [...] what clothes he will wear [...] what job he's going to work [...] But he also should understand that he's still a kid [...] And 'til I'm gone, he'll still be my baby.

Like Betty, Denise believed that certain things, like style of clothes, choice of friends, and decisions about jobs, should be under Taye's control. To some extent, Denise defined personal issues as decisions that are inconsequential ("things that won't have a final impact on his life"). But, as her discussion of job choice suggests, she also articulated a broader notion of the personal domain that encompassed future life decisions. Both mothers emphasized the importance of developing self-reliance and considered that greater independence was a way to achieve this. Indeed, many parents viewed some degree of independence as necessary training for adulthood.

But both mothers also imposed limits on independence. For Denise, this was expressed as a need for "respectful independence." Betty formulated a distinction between being too independent ("you can be on your own and be self-relying and never depend on anyone else"), and being, in her words, interdependent ("we all need other people and we need other people's advice and fellowship"). Therefore these mothers advocated a form of "autonomy–relatedness," or independent decision-making that is guided or informed by the parents' guidance, support, and love. In the following chapter we shall see the wisdom of Betty's words, as this form of autonomy-granting is linked to positive adjustment, particularly among early and middle adolescents.

Denise asserted that some fights are worth fighting, while others, presumably about personal issues like the choice of clothes, are not. But, as we have seen in the studies described in the previous chapters, the issues that parents believed should be left up to their children to decide were precisely those issues that sometimes caused conflict in their relationships. African American parents frequently endorsed the importance of developing independence when they discussed parenting in their interviews. But the fights they chose to fight were often around these very same issues. African American parents and teenagers did not see eye to eye on the matter of what should be treated as being up to the adolescents to control.

Conflict and Closeness in African American Families

Comparing Black and White styles of conflict, Kochman (1981) has described African American interactions in conflict situations as emotional, animated, energetic, and even confrontational at times. Markus and Lin (1999) have suggested that, in situations of conflict, African Americans expect others to advocate for, and to become emotionally invested in, their own personal positions. They claim that, for African Americans, emotional expression rather than reason and argument are signs of commitment to a position. In resolving conflicts, African Americans work towards a resolution "by the compelling presentation of arguments rather than attempts to appeal to some objective truth" (Markus & Lin, 1999, p. 326). Individuals may persuade others to adopt their position, which in turn restores harmony in interpersonal relationships.

However apt, these descriptions focus on African American adults. They do not consider how differences in age, status, and generation influence negotiations about conflicts. Indeed, the cultural patterns described earlier lead to conflicting predictions concerning how adolescent–parent conflict might be expressed and resolved in African American families. On the one hand, these descriptions suggest that conflicts might be affectively charged and high in intensity. Because African American families have been described as encouraging self-reliance and independence, adolescents' self-expression in the context of conflict might be tolerated or even encouraged as a sign of individuality.

On the other hand, African American families are described as hierarchical. African American parenting has been presented as strict, harsh, and parent-centered (Kelley, Power, & Wimbush, 1992; Parke & Buriel, 2006). Furthermore, the few studies that have considered socioeconomic status suggest that both lower- and middle-class African American families are more authoritarian in their orientation to parenting than European American families are (Lamborn, Dornbusch, & Steinberg, 1996). This suggests that expressions of opposition or disagreement among African American youth might be strongly discouraged, that conflicts might be low in intensity, and that obedience to parents might be stressed. It also suggests that conflicts might be resolved predominantly in favor of the parents' point of view.

In the Youth and Family Project, African American teenagers and their parents indicated, each one in part, their three "hottest" topics of conflict from among 37 potential issues of disagreement taken from the frequently used Issues Checklist (Prinz, Foster, Kent, & O'Leary, 1979; Robin & Foster, 1989). These three issues became the basis for semi-structured individual interviews about conflicts. The interviews were similar in format to those used in the other studies discussed in earlier chapters. That is, adolescents, mothers, and fathers described their disagreements in their own words. These descriptions were then analyzed for their content, in order for us to determine the topics of conflict. Family members justified their perspectives on conflicts, provided counterarguments, and then described how conflicts were resolved.

Conflict in middle-class African American family relationships

As found repeatedly in the studies discussed in earlier chapters, conflicts in middle-class African American families centered on the mundane, everyday issues of family life. Conflicts were over doing the chores, getting the homework done, the right time for going to bed, the right time to come home at night, and the types of activities that were permissible. When families were first interviewed, in the children's early adolescence, helping around the house (doing chores) and cleaning the bedroom took pride of place as the two "hottest" topics of conflict for African American teenagers, mothers, and fathers. They remained tied as the two hottest sources of conflict for teenagers 2 years later, although chores dropped to a lower position in mothers' rankings. For the most part, discussions over these issues echoed the discussions found in European American families. However, there were some culturally distinctive notes.

Cleanliness and order   Historically, and in response to the stresses and strains of the outside world, African American families have viewed the home as a haven and a place where order can prevail. W. E. B. DuBois, writing in 1926 to Black parents in *Crisis* magazine, was observing:

> At least in your home you have a chance to make your child's surroundings of the best; books and pictures and music; cleanliness, order, sympathy, and understanding; information, friendship and love – there is not much evil in the world that can stand against such home surroundings. (Quoted in Jenkins, 1988, p. 122)

Jenkins claimed that African American parents attempt to create a positive atmosphere in relation to those aspects of the environment they can control – such as the home – as a way of fostering their children's sense of self, agency, and competence. In keeping with this claim, disagreements over helping around the house, doing the chores, and keeping the bedroom clean accounted for a full third of all the conflicts discussed by mothers and teenagers in the interviews across 2 years (Smetana, Daddis, & Chuang, 2003). The prevalence of such disputes suggests that house-related issues constituted a highly salient theme for African American middle-class families. (The same issues accounted for only about half as many, or 18%, of the disagreements encountered in our European American two-parent families.) But African American mothers' reasoning about these issues was even more striking than their frequency. Mothers' justifications for their conviction that teenagers should pick up, do their chores, and clean up their bedrooms echoed the conventional responses that predominated in European American mothers' reasoning. But here other, more psychologically oriented themes – about the role of doing chores in the development of competence, self-efficacy, and self-reliance – also emerged in mothers' discussions of these issues. Mothers clearly valued the acquisition of habits related to order and cleanliness as a way to teach conventional responsibility. But these achievements were also seen as a way for teenagers to take pride in their accomplishment, develop psychological maturity, and learn skills for the future. Karen, mother of 13-year-old Aisha, explains:

INTERVIEWER: Helping out around the house – what is it you want her to do?

KAREN: I think I want her to be a little adult and do the stuff she's supposed to do. We all know what it is we're supposed to do. We come up with all kinds of wonderful, elaborate ways to keep track of who's responsible for doing what. And so I mainly want her to do her chores consistently and well. So that she can learn how to do things well, whether it's washing dishes or doing the laundry or cleaning her room. She can learn how to do those things and do a good job at it. And she can understand that if each of us contributes to the maintenance of the household through chores and whatnot, it's a nice feeling to be a part of the team contributing to that. And it will give her a good feeling to have a house that is well maintained. A place that she wants to be in that she is comfortable bringing her friends to.

As her neat, carefully coordinated, and nicely decorated living-room suggested, Karen saw virtue in a well-maintained home. Her justification for the child's duty to do chores sprang from conventional concerns with developing responsibility and with the need for social coordination in managing the labor. But she also viewed daily routines – like keeping the house tidy – as contributing to a psychological sense of well-being and pride and as creating a welcoming context for social interaction. In other words, the home is a warm and welcome haven, protected from the outside world. Anita, mother of 15-year-old Janice, offers a similar response regarding the need to keep the bedroom clean:

> When I say clean it up, I would like for everything in that room to be in a position where I don't have to walk in and see it all on the floor. Dusting that needs to be done. Making sure that the bed has been changed weekly, meaning that she changed her linen and washed it. Only because if you are in that room and that's your own domain, when I walk in there I still think it should be like any other part of the house. Comfortable, respectable, and clean. I definitely have a hard time when I walk in and see clothes everywhere or things aren't hung up properly, and I just want her to understand that if she cleans up her one spot, then any other spot will be easier to get to. Because again, it teaches responsibility. I feel that if she learns to clean her room, she will be responsible in one area, if nothing else. Besides learning responsibility and knowing that's hers, cleaning her own room should give her some kind of joy about it, and when she walks in, she can see the neatness and [it] should make her feel good about herself and that she has done it.

Mothers often talked about how learning to keep the bedroom neat provides training for the responsibilities that girls will have to assume as grown-ups. In a world where many African American women raise families by themselves, mothers explicitly described trying to prepare their daughters to learn to care for themselves and others. But "cleaning up" was not strictly an issue for daughters. Families with girls reported more "hot" conflicts over keeping the bedroom clean than families with boys did, but families with boys had more "hot" conflicts over doing chores as a whole than families with girls did. In the following example, Brendon's mother Nancy more explicitly highlights the need for initiative, self-reliance, and training for adulthood. She also links the issue of chores to social norms within the African American community. She asserts that connections to the family can be expressed through sharing in the work of keeping the house clean. Nancy also expresses concerns about clashes of values between her community of origin and the one in which she lives.

NANCY:
Well, the goal is really to help. What I would like to see is him take more of an initiative in terms of doing those things without me consistently having to say that these are the things you need to do. I know that he is quite involved in school. But I guess sometimes I get the feeling I don't know how to connect how he feels to this home and that the things here are not just his father's and mine. But it's our home, and we all should take pride in picking up something or doing something. And sometimes I feel like maybe he really is not connected that way or kind of takes those things for granted […] And I mean, a couple of times he's mentioned, "Why don't we have someone come in and do it?" And I'm like, "Oh yeah. Gee. We can pay them out of the shoe box full of money under the bed." And I guess part of it, too, I know I really have to think about though, is the culture and the community he is growing up in is not one of where people have pitched out and people come home and have chores. So we've had some struggles about that as well.

INTERVIEWER: Why do you think Brendon should do that?

NANCY:
Well, I always feel like first of all, it creates a certain amount of – I don't want to say independence, but it's also some learning, for the times when he's out on his own. I mean having something to do, and it's almost like a mini-job. When I was growing up and we talk about doing something around the house or getting paid, and my dad was like, "Getting paid?" I mean, you've been fed. You've got a place to sleep. So I don't know. I just feel like it is something that is needed.

Nancy identifies cleaning up as a collective activity – and as part and parcel of African American cultural values. She views this emphasis as distinctive in relation to the culture of the broader White suburban community where her family resides.

Respect and obedience   Another distinctive theme in the interviews about conflicts was the importance of respect for grown-ups. Parents talked about the need for teens to be respectful and not to talk back to their elders, which reflected the hierarchical structure of African American families and elaborated on the parents' own beliefs about parenting. Their justifications for disagreements with their children about the latter's tone of voice, disrespect, or talking back typically were social conventional; but the theme was one rarely heard in interviews with European American families. Tanya describes it in the following way:

TANYA: I want her to learn to be quiet after I've said what I've said, instead of, "But mom, this is why [...]", and I want her to – OK, then I say, "Be quiet." Then that's what I mean. Lock your lips. I don't want to hear anything else about it. Later on you can come and talk to me in a calmer state. Right now I don't feel like hearing about it, because I told you to be quiet and that's what I mean.

INTERVIEWER: Why?

TANYA: First of all, respect. And to listen instead of running your mouth [...] Because if I let her do it to me, then she'll be disrespectful to other adults out there in the street, and I don't want that because I don't think any child should be disrespectful. I don't care – to any adult, no matter what they are saying. And that's what's wrong with today's society, because even with parents now, they don't go back to the old school. My child said this, and they were in a fight instead of this is what adults say, and you listen. And then they can talk amongst themselves, but not in front of kids. So that's how I feel because she'll get out there and be disrespectful.

For Tanya, being "old school" means having respect for adults. But Tanya goes further, to assert that parents should model respect by maintaining a united front; parents' conflicting perspectives on disagreements should be discussed and resolved privately and not in front of the children. In her view, adults should lay down the law, and children should listen. Other scholars, too, have found that respect is an important value for African American families (Tatum, 1987).

Jessica's mother, Shawna, was asked what she wanted Jessica to do when they had a conflict about talking back. She responded that having respect includes both what is said and the way in which it is expressed:

Probably adjust her tone of voice or the content of what she said. So if she gets really agitated in making inappropriate comments, not necessarily cursing or swear words, but just being very argumentative or combative. Verbally combative [...] Stressing the importance of the rightness of her view. And we would want her to consider that she might be right, or she may think that she's right but be totally wrong. Or to just be open to the parents' viewpoint [...] Because I think it reflects her honor of our views, and in honoring of us. I think when you talk back to your parents in a disrespectful manner, you're not really honoring your parents. And we try to let her know that we don't expect her to agree with us on everything. But we expect her to show respect to us even when she disagrees with us. And I think that's just a common courtesy, because that is something that she needs to learn, because if she goes out into the world, she's going to run into bosses that she might not agree with, and I think her future and her career, if she decides to pursue a career, it's going to hang [in] the balance based on the way she responds to a person who[m] she is not in agreement with. You can't just go back and back talk your boss and sass them and say, "Well, I don't need this job anyway." I think we want to teach her to be cooperative and tactful and wise.

Like Tanya, Shawna connects respect for parents with how one needs to behave in the wider world. For Tanya, respect generalizes to other adults. Shawna explicitly links the importance of learning respect with the need to learn and practice respect, tact, cooperation, and wisdom in the workplace.

When parents were first interviewed, their reasoning about conflicts was primarily conventional and accounted for nearly half of their justifications for conflicts. However, reflecting the decline in chores as an issue of conflict, parents' conventional reasoning about conflicts declined over time, particularly in families with boys.

Doing homework and getting ahead   For fathers, not doing one's homework, and, for mothers, getting low grades in school were ranked together as forming the third hottest topic of conflict when families were first interviewed, in their children's early adolescence. When families were seen 2 years later, getting low grades in school moved up the scale, to tie with matters about the bedroom as mothers' hottest topic of conflict. Middle-class African American parents are intensely concerned with academic achievement and educational attainment (Barbarin, McCandies, Coleman, & Hill, 2005; Billingsley, 1992; Tatum, 1987; Wilson, Cooke, & Arrington, 1997). Indeed, educational attainment has been described as almost "an obsession" for middle-class African American parents. Since Reconstruction, education has been seen as a pathway for future success; it is something you can always carry with you, and it cannot be taken away.

These attitudes were evident in our interviews with parents, as well as in teenagers' scholastic records. The students in our sample were high achievers. According to parents, nearly half of the early adolescent students in our sample were "A" students. Most of the rest were "B" students. Grades in school were modestly associated with family income. Open-ended interview questions about academic aspirations, asked in early adolescence, revealed that nearly all the students in our sample intended to go to college, and most of them to 4-year colleges. Most students also expected to become professionals such as doctors or lawyers. Although academic achievement generally remained high across the first 2 years of the study, school grades declined over time (Smetana et al., 2003). This was accompanied by some changes in the students' descriptions of their educational aspirations. By the time they reached middle adolescence, fewer students – although still a considerable number – aspired to professional careers.

In turn, this drop over time in grades and educational aspirations was accompanied by a significant increase, with age, in parent–teen disagreements over doing homework and getting good grades. Issues of this nature accounted for 10% of the conflicts in early adolescence and for 16% of the disagreements in middle adolescence. This intensification was paralleled by an increase in mothers' pragmatic justifications for conflicts (from 21% in early adolescence to 31% in middle adolescence). As in the Chinese families discussed in the last chapter, mothers' reasoning focused mostly on the importance of education for future success and for financial well-being. Prudential concerns with teenagers' health and safety were relatively infrequent in the interviews. But they increased significantly over time (from 5% to 11%) among mothers of boys.

Clearly, teenagers' academic performance was an important issue for African American parents. They encouraged their children to study and do well in school. Regardless of ethnicity, grades and school achievement are a persistent concern among middle-class, upwardly mobile families, where pressures for success can be acute. But, as we have seen, for African American parents, these issues are etched against a backdrop of concerns with racism and prejudice. These parents were quite explicit and vocal about their demands: children had to achieve and make something of themselves in a world where expectations for African American teenagers (particularly boys) are often low. Sometimes issues of race were implicit in what parents said regarding the importance of education for their children's future success, but these concerns were often expressed directly. In the following interview, Gwen, mother of 16-year-old James, discusses her worries about her son's getting low grades.

> I want him to get better grades [...] Because in today's world, in this man's world, education is something that's held in high esteem. And those people that don't get them are not looked at favorably. And when he's an African American male, if he doesn't have an education under his belt, they are not going to look at him.

Sheri's mother, Maisha, was even more explicit:

> I want her to take more care when she's doing her homework. She rushes through her homework because she doesn't want to do it. So she wants to hurry up and be through with it, and she makes simple mistakes that she shouldn't make. And sometimes she just doesn't do it, and it makes me very angry, because she's a very smart girl. And that's when I say she's lazy. Everybody says you shouldn't say she's lazy. I haven't come up with a better word, because she's smart. There's no question that she has the intelligence to do the work, but she doesn't want to. She has to do her work, and she has to do it to the best of her ability if she's going to succeed in school and later succeed in life. I mean this is the first training ground for her to learn how to follow through, and to be a good performer. If she doesn't do it in school, then it's going to be hard for her to do it when she's on the job [...] I want her to get better grades. I want her to take her education seriously ... Time for playing is over

with. And that's what I want her to understand [...] She has to improve her grades because she wants to go to Spelman [an elite college for women, historically Black], and Spelman is not going to take a girl who's got low grades. You know, I used to think that school was just stupid, which is what she probably thinks now, too. But as I got older, I realized, school really is a training ground for real life. At the time that you're in it, you don't think so. You think you're like in this ivory tower. This is not the real world. But a lot of the same principles apply, and if she can learn to master it now, she's going to be far ahead of the game [...] She can do well in high school at the level that she is [...] And she takes gifted classes, then that means when she gets to college, she will be able to compete with the White students. And she will not have to feel like she's inferior, that she's not prepared, that she's not ready. And so that's why she's got to stop playing. She's got to really take it seriously now.

Mirroring the greater decline in academic performance, over time, among boys than among girls, parents of boys reported more conflicts over homework and getting good grades than parents of girls did. As with doing chores, parents viewed studying and doing well as a "training ground" for later life. They clearly saw education as a route to a better life. One mother elaborates in the following example:

I can't accept low grades from any of my kids. It's unnecessary. You go to school from 8 to 2. There's no reason for you to get low grades. When you come home from school, you do not have a job to go to. Your job is to sit down and do your homework, study, prepare for a test [...] Like I said you don't have a job to go to. You might have chores, but all your chores come after your homework is done. It's no reason for low grades. I will not accept them [...] He'll tell you, the only thing that's accepted in here is As and Bs. Maybe a C, if I'm in a good mood. Because to me, school is very important. I did not finish school. I am currently taking the GED test. I have one part to pass and that's the math. I can't say I've struggled too bad, but I feel that, had I finished high school and went to college, I could have been doing better than what I am now. I don't want that for my children. I won't accept any low grades.

In their highly cited ethnographic and anthropological research, Signithia Fordham and John Ogbu (1986) asserted that, for many poor African American youth, doing well in school is equated with "acting White" or with being a "brainiac," and therefore is disparaged. Like many students who are highly committed to doing well in school (Tyson, Darity, & Castellino, 2005), bright African American children do not want to be perceived as striving towards achievement. This helps them to maintain their identity and their status with peers. Many families investigated in this study had moved to the suburbs, often explicitly in order to take advantage of better schools. Parents talked about the trade-offs of living in communities with excellent schooling, but then having their children in schools that were predominantly White. (And, ironically, recent research has shown that, when parents move their children from middle schools where they are in the ethnic majority to high schools where they are in the minority, they are much more likely to feel disconnected from school; see Benner & Graham, 2009. Thus parents may provide their teens with a better education, but at some social and motivational costs.) Parents living in the city often took advantage of magnate programs and private schools – for instance parochial schools, where educational achievement was highly valued. But not all teenagers escaped the stereotypes that undercut their achievement. As Jennette, mother of 15-year-old Bradon, explained,

> I want him to do his homework. I want him to really apply himself to his homework and to do what he's supposed to do. You check it and make sure it's correct. And then if he wants to be on the phone, then I don't care if he's on the phone, just as long as he stays within that time frame. I told him about phone calls. If he wants to watch TV, fine. Just do what's important first […] Because he's preparing himself for his future. He just wants to talk on the phone with his friends or go play basketball or go by one of his friends. Just sleep. That's another thing he likes to do. But just take time out to do what's important […] Because he thinks it's cool not to pass in school. It's cool to them. Just to be like the others. Just to thinking about the latest fashion and the latest haircuts. And the expensive sneakers. But there's more to life than that, because that won't last forever.

These issues were also elaborated upon in the interviews about parenting. As one parent described,

> Cheryl is a straight A student. She's a bookworm. Has always been. It's nothing that the others haven't been exposed to as well. But her older brothers get on her all the time about acting White. I said, "Why? [Are] White people the only people who can be smart? Talking White. Are White people the only ones who know how to talk proper English? You give them too much credit." All those kinds of things that for them to even look back and see how they treat their own, there are going to be enough people shooting you down and your family down. Don't you do that. I'm adamant about that.

African American teenagers' perspectives on conflict

Many teenagers, too, saw the topics of doing homework and getting good grades as causes of disagreement with parents. Their reasons for not wanting to do their homework had mostly to do with their attraction to other activities – wanting to watch TV, go out, or listen to music, or wanting to decide on their own terms how and when homework should be done. As 16-year-old Sean put it:

> Usually, it's like because I don't do my homework or I'd rather go out or something. I'd chill or rest, and I don't do my homework. I'd go to like every week to Boy Scouts and stuff. Like when I was getting low grades, I was in football practice until

5 or so. Then, when I come home, I'm tired, I want to relax. Just hang around … I just like to rest to get my body energy up for the next day, and the sort of thing I just do. My parents tell me to go in and do my homework, or make up any assignments that I need to do. They want me to do my homework for the next day. They know I can get good grades. I just don't want to do what I need to do to get those good grades.

For Sean, not doing homework entailed both personal preferences – the things he would like to do instead of doing homework – and prudential concerns about resting and regaining his energy. Most teenagers acknowledged the importance of getting good grades for future success. A few discussed peer group norms that differed from this attitude. Seventeen-year-old Tamara, a bright student who has not always excelled in school, noted:

I mean, I know now what I have to do, and I know that Ds and Es are not going to get me where I want to in this world. So, it's basically I just had to learn by experience. And in the summer of the 10th grade, before I went to 11th grade, I have come to the realization that I am not going to get anywhere with Ds and Es […] So I had to really buckle down and be more responsible about my grades and I had to cut out the average attitude by just getting enough work to get by or to pass […] Because like everyone else, it wasn't "cool" or "in" to make the honor roll, getting a 3.8 every marking period. It was lame, as some people said […] A lot of people thought it wasn't cool to get good grades in school.

Just as we found out in interviews with European American and Chinese youth, African American teenagers characteristically treated conflicts as issues of personal choice or preference (Smetana et al., 2003). Their personal justifications echoed the responses received in the other studies. For 14-year-old Anthony, cleaning the bedroom was primarily a personal choice, although he raised prudential issues as well:

I just don't want to do it [clean the bedroom] sometimes. Sometimes I am just too tired, or sometimes I feel it's pointless to do it. I just don't want to do it at all […] I think it's okay for me not to do my room because no one else is going to be in my room. Not like what anyone else wants it to look. Sometimes I should just be able to decide things like that. [But my mother] wants me to finish cleaning my room. She wants me to get off my butt and clean the room and be done with it.

Watching TV, using the telephone, and the choice of music also were seen as personal. Sixteen-year-old Tamica discussed the need for privacy in her telephone conversations. She connected this theme with her growing maturity:

Teenagers do talk on the phone a lot. But I think my mother exaggerates how much I am on the phone and all that. She should be letting me decide on that a little bit.

I understand that I shouldn't be on the phone late, especially on school nights. She should try to think about how I am doing good in school and getting myself together. [I want to] get my own line. My own private line. So when I get phone calls, for my privacy [...] I think I am old enough [...] I think I deserve some privacy [...] I just think it's OK. Basically, I think that having your own line is almost like showing that you're maturing. It's something that's yours. [But my mother] basically wants me to respect her and do what she says and get off the phone.

African American teenagers also treated their choice of friends, and doing things with friends instead of parents, as personal issues:

I want to do my own thing. Sometimes, like not going places with them. I don't like hanging with my parents, like going to a party with them, or go to the movies with them [...][Because] kids may have more fun with their peers. People in your own age who are going through the same things you are going through. And they can relate more and they might like the same things that you like. Like the same music. Because my mother, we don't really like the same things. Kind of music, for example. She likes soft rock. I like hip-hop and R&B things. She thinks it's just a bunch of trash.

Some African American adolescents also linked personal choices, such as that of clothes, to creating a personal style or identity, as the following excerpt shows.

I should be able to wear what I want to. And while I am young, I should be able to pick what I want, when I want to wear it [...] Because it's my own creative style. And it's my own money. So most of the time when I am buying these clothes, it's just OK because I should. It should be my choice. I should be able to have my own style.

As these examples illustrate, African American adolescents viewed a variety of issues as personal. They articulated the need for personal choices and preferences, personal expression, and privacy, and the desire to make their own decisions. Appeals to personal choice were the characteristic response among African American adolescents, and these claims increased over time. Personal justifications accounted for 44% of the responses when teenagers were first interviewed about conflicts in early adolescence. This percentage increased to 54% when teens were re-interviewed 2 years later, in middle adolescence. Although the interviews about parenting clearly indicated that parents viewed granting independence as an important developmental goal, conflicts arose when parents rejected adolescents' desires for more control over particular issues. Parents were concerned about the timing and pacing of autonomy.

African American families rarely had conflicts over moral issues. As with European American and Chinese youth, moral conflicts primarily pertained to fairness in sibling relationships. These issues accounted for a small but stable percentage of responses.

Conflict frequency and intensity

Kochman (1981) and Markus and Lin (1999) claim that African Americans' conflicts are distinctively animated, energetic, and emotional. One way of examining this claim is to consider African American parents' and adolescents' perceptions of the emotional quality of their conflicts. Teenagers and parents rated the frequency and intensity of each conflict discussed in the interviews. Much as we found among European American families, conflicts were relatively frequent, but only moderate in their intensity. Conflict frequency did not change from early to middle adolescence, and adolescents and mothers did not differ in these perceptions. As is typically the case with European American families, conflicts were more intense among African American families with girls than among those with boys.

As reviewed in Chapter 2, many scholars have viewed moderate increases in parent–adolescent conflict, particularly in the context of warm, supportive family relationships, as functional in transforming family relationships. Conflict that is extremely angry and intense, largely unresolved, and carried over from childhood is thought to have negative implications for later development. But when conflict is moderate and when it occurs in the context of supportive family relationships, increases in conflict from early to middle adolescence are not considered maladaptive. The interviews about conflicts were conducted, both, when teens were in early and middle adolescence. Adolescents and their parents also rated the positive (supportive) and negative (conflictive) quality of adolescent–parent relationships, as well as their attachment to each parent, on standard survey measures, at all three waves of the study. These survey responses show that African American adolescents perceived their relationships with their parents in very positive terms. They rated these relationships as highly supportive and very positive, and their ratings were highly stable over time.

Some sex differences also emerged. Boys who were more attached to their mothers in early adolescence reported more supportive, positive relationships with mothers in late adolescence. However, girls' attachment to mothers in early adolescence did not influence their perceptions of support from them later on. Sex differences in adolescents' perceptions of their relationships with their mothers were not simply in the adolescents' eyes; they were also captured in the observers' ratings of family interactions. During the home visits, families participated in family interaction tasks, which consisted of several eight-minute discussions of their conflicts. These tasks were conducted in mother–teen or father–teen dyads – as well as in triads, if there was a father or a father figure living in the home.

These discussions were videotaped and coded by highly trained African American observers. A coding system that had been developed and used with European American families was adapted so as to be culturally sensitive to the interactions and cultural values of middle-class African American families (Smetana, Abernethy, & Harris, 2000). This adaptation included determining whether the original codes had the same meaning in African American families; rewording certain codes to make them culturally appropriate and to achieve consensus for African American coders; and clarifying behavioral markers of the coding system. We also added new codes, in order to capture and represent more accurately modes of interaction in African American families. For instance, we added a scale to reflect the focus on family harmony and interconnection, which is characteristic of African American families.

Observers rated African American mothers as interacting differently with sons and with daughters. Mothers supported and validated their sons more than their daughters. They listened to and were more receptive to their sons' than to their daughters' opinions. They also supported sons more, were more understanding of them, and tolerated differences and disagreements with them more by comparison with their support, understanding and tolerance of daughters. African American boys are more likely to be victims of racism and prejudice than girls are. Therefore mothers' greater supportiveness may reflect attempts to prepare their sons to survive in a hostile world.

There were several other notable aspects of the adolescents' perceptions of their relationships with parents. First, their perceptions of negative, conflictive interactions in early adolescence, which were reflected in their ratings of the intensity of conflicts with their mothers or fathers, did not have long-term consequences for the overall quality of adolescent–parent relationships in late adolescence and emerging adulthood; nor did the changes in these ratings that occurred between early and middle adolescence. Although adolescent–parent conflicts are distressing, particularly to parents, they did not have long-term effects (Smetana, Metzger, & Campione-Barr, 2004).

The family interactions confirmed this conclusion in an interesting way. When family interactions were examined, the variables cohered into the same scales of positive communication, parental support and validation, and receptivity to parents in early and middle adolescence. But in early adolescence there also emerged a distinctive factor reflecting emotionally intense, angry, and conflicted interactions. In middle adolescence, this factor morphed into more light-hearted, warm, and engaged interactions characterized by humor and laughter. And the few changes that we observed in the quality of family interactions over time were consistent with this process. Communication with fathers became more positive over time. In addition, when teens, mothers, and fathers discussed conflicts together, fathers supported and validated their sons and daughters more as they grew older.

Therefore, in these African American families, conflict appeared indeed to be a temporary perturbation in their relationships. This is a finding well worth highlighting. Although we have seen that parents find parenting adolescents to be challenging, it is worth knowing that the everyday conflicts and disagreements that erupt in early and middle adolescence do subside eventually, without leaving a lasting mark on parent–child relationships.

Conflict did not have enduring effects over time, but the extent to which teens perceived the overall quality of their relationships as warm, trusting, and supportive did. More specifically, African American teenagers' perceptions, in early adolescence, of close, trusting relationships with either parent influenced their perceptions of closeness with that parent in middle adolescence. In turn, this influenced their feelings of closeness and trust with that parent in late adolescence. Positive feelings about the relationship were carried forward, to influence subsequent feelings of trust and support. Although having intense, angry conflicts did not impact either on the positive or on the negative quality of later relationships with parents, teenagers who reported more negative interactions with mothers in middle adolescence also reported more negative relationships in late adolescence. In other words, the intensity of teenagers' conflicts with parents in early and middle adolescence did not influence their later relationships with parents. However, greater general negativity in the relationships with parents, at least by middle adolescence, was reflected in greater negativity in those relationships as teenagers moved into young adulthood.

In addition, and not surprisingly, adolescents' relationships with their fathers were impacted by whether or not the latter were living with them. Teenagers who lived in two-parent families in late adolescence reported more supportive relationships with their fathers than adolescents who experienced a change in their parents' marital status did, or teenagers living in stable single-parent households.

Conflict Resolution and Parenting

Some scholars have claimed that, during adolescence, there is a transfer of authority from parents to teens (Youniss & Smollar, 1985). We saw in Chapter 7 that this appears to be an accurate description of developmental changes in middle-class European American families. Older European American adolescents were more likely than younger ones to win disputes with their parents, although most of the conflicts were resolved by adolescents complying with parents' wishes. But we also saw that this picture of transfer of authority does not accurately describe Chinese families. Compared to younger teens, Chinese late adolescents described a small increase in compromise and mutual solutions, but there was no evidence of a transfer of authority from parents to children. Likewise, in terms of conflict resolution, we did not see a transfer of authority in middle-class African American families.

Among the families we sampled, authority remained firmly rooted in parental territory. African American parents have been described as strict and parent-centered. In keeping with this description, middle-class African American families reported that teenagers characteristically submitted to their parents' wishes when there were disagreements between them. Almost two thirds of the disagreements discussed in the interviews about conflict were described as resolved in this way. For example, when asked how a conflict about loud music was resolved, one mother, Gwen, stated:

GWEN: I usually get up, and I go in there, and knock on that door. I have to get up and knock on that door, and I give her the eye, which is called "the evil eye." And she knows that she has to turn that music down.
INTERVIEWER: What happens then?
GWEN: She smiles and she just slowly takes the remote control and slowly brings the volume down.

In talking about conflicts over watching TV at bedtime, another mother explains:

It gets resolved by the parent making the final decision, and the TV needs to go off unless there's been an appeal. If it's just for staying up to watch TV, there's no discussion. It's just "go to bed," and that's it. And I'm thankful that, somewhere along the line, we did something so that at least there is respect for the decisions that we make in that regard.

As these examples suggest, teenagers not only did as parents expected, but they did so with little argument or backtalk. This focus on following parents' wishes in resolving everyday disagreements is in keeping with the importance of respect for parents in African American culture and with the hierarchical structure of African American families.

Similar responses also emerged when parents were interviewed about parenting. When asked how they defined firmness and how they decided about setting limits for their teens, most of the middle-class mothers we interviewed described firmness in terms of a need to define limits clearly and firmly, often without input from their child. Even when they advocated listening to their teenagers' point of view, many parents were of the opinion that parents should have the final say. Moreover, for some of the specific issues that parents sought to control, their notions of strictness were gender-differentiated. A large-scale study has shown that African American boys have more freedom, fewer rules, and a later curfew than African American teenage girls do (Bulcroft, Carmody, & Bulcroft, 1996). Parents in our study were concerned with controlling African American girls' sexuality and with protecting girls from the risks of early sexual involvement. In the following example, Debra, mother of 14-year-old Shanae, hints at these issues in discussing Shanae's interest in boys. Debra elaborated:

She wants a boyfriend. She wants to have a young man come to the house or she wants to be able to go to the movies, get dropped at the movies with boys and picked up and so forth, and that's not acceptable as far as I am concerned. She uses the excuse that all of her other friends' parents allow them to do that, and of course, I do the old saying that "I'm not their parent, I'm your parent." So we battle about that, but we don't really battle about it, because it's final. There's nothing left to discuss as far as that is concerned. Another issue is that she wants to wear make-up, and I told her that I don't think that it is acceptable for a 14–15 year old girl to walk around with their face painted, and she's beautiful enough as it is. That's another issue that's just final. When I'm ready to let her do it, then I'll let her know [...] She can choose to go the other way, but I'm the warden, as I've been called in the past. That's my nickname, and I'm here to try to assure that she doesn't get involved in the things that she shouldn't, and I think dating too young is going to cause problems. I see girls all the time walking down the street with strollers ... and it just sends chills through me.

Many mothers expressed similar concerns regarding their daughters' behavior. Parents monitored girls' activities more and regulated girls' friendships more than those of boys. Parents viewed their sons as having more legitimate authority than their daughters to control their own friendships. They also expected their daughters to start dating at older ages (typically, around 16–17 years of age) than their sons. Typically again, limits were described in terms of guidance. As one mother stated,

I think everyone needs some kind of guidance. They are not adults, and even some adults don't make the right decisions, so as a parent, I feel it's my responsibility to make sure she is following certain rules so that when she grows up and there are rules to follow, she will already have experience with rules [...] If it's something that I have really strong feelings about as far as staying out late, doing your chores, or something that is real important in my view, then I will be firm on that

Teenagers' responses paralleled parents' descriptions. Even when they disagreed, African American adolescents did what parents expected of them. They viewed parents' expectations as rooted in love and concern. Sixteen-year-old Tamica, who was quoted previously as wanting her own phone line, so that she could have greater privacy in her conversations with friends, articulated similar concerns when talking about conflicts over the time to go to bed. She further elaborated on why she follows her mother's requests:

I feel that especially since I am older now, it's my choice [when to go to bed]. How late I go to bed. I think I should be able to do it. I mean, that's how I feel [...] Basically, she wants me to go to bed at a decent time so that I can get my rest [...] She thinks it's wrong because she loves me. She knows once again that I need my sleep for school. She tells me that I need to go to bed and get ready for school the next day. I will respect that and go to bed. That's it. Sometimes I get kind of mad because I am still trying to do what I believe to be right. And she's telling me to go to bed. So, basically, I do what I have to do. Just go to bed.

In the context of the interviews about parenting, the majority of mothers also expressed some openness towards compromising or changing their minds, at least about some issues. They indicated that, if their teenagers could provide good reasons and negotiate respectfully, they would consider revising their positions. Joint resolution or compromise in the context of adolescent–parent conflicts and disagreements increased significantly from early to middle adolescence, but it was still relatively infrequent. In the following examples, which are drawn from interviews about conflicts, two mothers, Bree and Raye, described how they allow for discussion and compromise, at least within certain limits. Bree demonstrates her willingness to reconsider her position:

> Well, sometimes we have discussions where everyone can express why they are upset, and share stuff. And we try to come to some kind of understanding. But if a punishment has been leveled and she hasn't started doing it […] usually, she does it for a period of time and it might be suspended, but I think the resolution comes to discussion. Most of the time we'll talk about it. "What do you think the problem is?" And we can speak your mind freely. So there's room for communication.

In discussing how conflicts typically are resolved, Raye also indicates that she leaves room for discussion, and even for compromise:

> Usually it may be a compromise. Like I said, the compromise is whether or not she wants to do it. And if it's really something that's workable, we'll try to work with it. If it's something that's just out of place, like for instance, you're going to go out with somebody we don't know, that's not acceptable. Then, the decision is made [by the parent]. And that's what you abide by.

Conflicts were rarely resolved by parents giving in to their teenagers. There was some shift towards more joint modes of conflict resolution over time, but parents primarily had the final say. And sometimes conflicts remained unresolved.

Discipline and corporal punishment

African American parents have been described as employing harsh, punitive discipline, including corporal punishment. In fact, there is a great deal of heterogeneity in African American parents' choice of discipline strategies. They rely heavily on strategies that entail warmth, acceptance, and love. But numerous studies have shown that, from early childhood through to middle adolescence, African American parents also use physical punishment (spanking) more than European

American parents do (Dodge, McLoyd, & Lansford, 2005). Spanking is also used more frequently among single-parent than among two-parent families, and among families of lower socioeconomic status. Although this suggests that the use of physical discipline may be related to the stresses of parenting in certain environments, Dodge and his colleagues note that there are, still, ethnic differences in parenting – even when socioeconomic status and marital status are controlled. Interview studies have shown that African American parents view mild physical punishment as appropriate and acceptable. It is not used in place of other strategies, such as verbal reasoning or induction; indeed, it is unrelated to their use. As a method in its own right, it appears to be part of African American cultural values and, potentially, a response to the dangers that African American children face in American society.

When interviewed about conflicts in our study, 10% of teenagers reported that conflicts with parents were resolved through punishment. This included physical discipline as well as other forms of punishment, like being grounded or being sent to their room. Adolescents' reports regarding the use of punishment were mirrored in mothers' responses. As teens grew older, their mothers' reports of punishment as a way to resolve conflicts declined. Likewise, when interviewed about parenting, only a small minority of mothers reported using physical discipline. For instance, Shirley, mother of 16-year-old Jasmine, stated:

SHIRLEY: I've already set very strict limits. And when I feel that she's going over those lines, she knows it. And that's when I find it necessary to be really firm with her. No means no. Yes means yes. I was brought up in a home that was – the rules were very clear. She's able to voice why she disagrees, and if she can give me three valid reasons why she disagrees, then I can possibly consider changing my mind [...] if it is necessary to go to the next level, then I will go to the next level with her. I will get physical with her if I find it necessary.

INTERVIEWER: What is the next level?

SHIRLEY: I will whip her ... She has gotten too old for it. Corporal punishment, so to speak [...] when I was smaller, we always got whipped, and I don't want to always have to whip her to get through to her.

In keeping with this sentiment, some mothers indicated that they had used physical discipline when their children were younger, but not now. As Marcus' mother explained:

Well, now that he is 16, I don't spank Marcus or whip Marcus anymore, I haven't now for a very long time, because he is just too big and he has already made up his mind that either he is going to do it or he's not, and usually, if he disobeys me or his dad, there are consequences. Right now he is being put on restriction or some other activity is being taken away from him, but he pays for whatever the misdeed is.

Like Shirley, who experienced whipping as a child, some parents explicitly stated that their parenting choices were a result of their own experiences. Many parents described their approach to parenting as drawing on these experiences. They enforced standards in much the same way as they had been raised. Typically, parents described their own parents as enforcing strict rules and using firm discipline. But sometimes the choice of such methods meant, on the contrary, rejecting the models their parents provided. Indeed, parents talked in equal measure about using strictness on the basis of their own experience and about using their own experience as a basis for rejecting those models. Some parents who had been raised in very strict homes explicitly sought another, more responsive mode of parenting. This is evident in the interview with Karen, mother of 14-year-old Evan. Karen indicates that she developed her choice of disciplinary strategy in response to her own experiences:

> Because it was just the opposite for me. When I was raised, you didn't wear lipstick, you didn't play gym in gym clothes, you had to wear a skirt. A very long skirt. You never showed your forearm, never cut your hair. No kind of make-up – and on and on. I mean, there were a thousand rules […] I certainly enjoyed those rules coming up because it put you in a very good place with your elders that if you followed all the rules, everybody thought you were wonderful … But after I left home and went to college, I realized they had been debilitating to a certain extent because I didn't know how to do anything. Not even braid my own hair. So I decided then as I started seeking my own independence that I tried never to oppress anybody […] Children should make their own decisions as much as possible because they live in the real world, and the world is changing. And just the fact that men, especially African American men, need to be able to be prepared for the real world.

This example demonstrates how parents' ideas about independence can become bound up with notions of freedom and oppression.

Summary and Conclusions

Adolescent–parent relationships in middle-class African American families are similar in many ways to the patterns observed in European American families, but they also reflect African Americans' specific historical circumstances (including their history of slavery), cultural values, and concerns with racism and prejudice. Adolescent–parent relationships reflect the realities of dealing with racism and prejudice, which still pervade American society. This remains an issue for all African Americans, regardless of socioeconomic status. Parents discussed the challenges of raising their children so as to give them an awareness of – but also help them rise above – racism. They focused on teaching their children to survive and thrive in an environment that may be fraught with physical and psychological threats, especially for African American boys. And these concerns with racism were implicit in their discussions of conflict.

Middle-class African American adolescents' relationships with parents were generally warm and supportive; but children did have conflicts with their parents over mundane, everyday issues, much like teenagers from a range of other cultures and ethnic groups. At the same time, the topics that were raised and the way parents responded to conflicts also reflected the ecological and sociocultural context of middle-class African American families. Some of these conflicts, such as disagreements over cleanliness and order, respect for parents, and homework and academic achievement reflect the specific values of African American families. These values include the importance of community and extended kin networks, the hierarchical nature of the family, and (particularly for middle-class families) the importance of getting a good education.

The positive quality of adolescents' relationships with parents in early adolescence influences their relationships with parents in late adolescence and emerging adulthood, but conflicts in early adolescence do not. Like other adolescents, African American teenagers express desires for more control over personal issues in early and middle adolescence, and this leads to conflict in their relationships. But such conflicts are temporary perturbations without long-term negative consequences for parent–adolescent relationships.

African American families place great store by children's respect for adults, and conflicts with parents typically are resolved by complying with parents' rules and expectations. Yet the essence of African American parenting is not captured by the notion of authoritarianism; parenting is strict, sometimes strict and harsh (and may involve corporal punishment), yet it is warm and supportive. Strictness is used in the service of warding off the perceived threats, both from the physical and from the social environment.

In the following chapter we shall turn to issues of parenting, more broadly considered.

9

Beliefs about Parental Authority

A wise parent humours the desire for independent action, so as to become the friend and advisor when his absolute rule shall cease. Elizabeth Gaskell, *North and South* (1995, p. 110)

In this chapter we consider beliefs, both of adolescents and of their parents, about the parents' authority to control different areas of teenagers' lives. Parents have many beliefs about the nature of the child, the social world, the parents' roles, and their goals in child rearing. These beliefs are at the heart of parenting and disciplinary practices, just as children's beliefs and understanding of the social world inform their actions and reactions to parents. In this chapter we will look at all these beliefs in detail. We begin by considering normative, age-related changes in one set of those ideas – namely the adolescents' (and their parents') beliefs about the legitimate authority of the parents. Later in the chapter we will consider individual differences in the patterning of those beliefs.

Beliefs about Parental Authority

The studies of adolescents' and parents' reasoning about conflict discussed in previous chapters reveal that conflicts often involve struggles about who has the right to control different issues. Where should the line be drawn between the parents' authority to make rules and regulate different aspects of children's lives and the adolescents' emerging desires for more control and personal freedom? Studies of adolescent–parent conflict tell only a part of the story; they focus on the areas of disagreement. But there also are substantial areas of agreement on what parents can legitimately control and what they cannot. Disagreements pertain in most cases to a grey area, where the boundary between the regions of legitimate parental control and those of the adolescents' authority over the self is uncertain or difficult to establish. And because development is dynamic, that boundary is ever shifting and changing through reciprocal social interactions.

Beliefs about the parents' authority to control moral and conventional issues

Much research has examined parents' and adolescents' beliefs about the former's authority to regulate moral and conventional issues (Braine, Pomerantz, Lorber, & Krantz, 1991; Damon, 1977; Smetana, 1988a, 1993b, 2000; Smetana & Asquith, 1994; Smetana, Crean, & Campione-Barr, 2005; Tisak, 1986). The results of these studies are very clear-cut. When it comes to moral and conventional issues, middle-class American adolescents, mothers, and fathers agree. They are nearly unanimous in avowing that parents have the legitimate authority to regulate the application of moral standards and principles in the family – like the principle of not hitting siblings, breaking promises, or lying to parents. Likewise, they strongly recognize parents' authority to regulate prototypical social conventional issues such as doing the chores, using appropriate manners, not talking back to parents, and not cursing. Parents and adolescents generally do not differ in these beliefs.

Furthermore, parents' authority over such issues is typically seen to extend across adolescence. This is not surprising, given that much of parental socialization is geared towards teaching children the moral and conventional rules and expectations of society. As we saw in Chapter 4, moral and conventional standards are established very early in life and are maintained across childhood. By the time children reach adolescence, these standards are largely unspoken and taken for granted. Both parents and teens clearly view the parents as retaining the authority to regulate these issues.

As a result, as we saw in Chapter 5, families generally have few conflicts over moral issues. When they do, these conflicts are typically about how moral principles like fairness and equal treatment should be applied in given relationships (with siblings or friends). Such conflicts are infrequent, but they are often quite intense, which reflects their interpersonal nature. Parents may be called in to intervene in these disputes; but moral conflicts very rarely arise between parents and adolescents. Rules regarding most of these prototypical issues are a "given" in most families. Parental regulation is assumed.

Most of the research on European American parents' and adolescents' beliefs about parental authority has compared families with teenagers at different ages. But the results of cross-sectional research have been confirmed in longitudinal studies. Similar age trends have been found in the developmental pathways of African American mothers and adolescents who were followed over 5 years (Smetana et al., 2005). Across ages, parents are overwhelmingly seen as having the legitimate authority to regulate moral and conventional issues. Moreover, acceptance of the parents' moral and conventional authority does not change over time.

A slightly different question is whether parents *ought* to make rules about moral and conventional issues. That is, do parents have an obligation to make these rules? For moral issues, both parents and teenagers think they do. Parents are seen as highly obligated to make moral rules (for instance, rules prohibiting lying, dishonesty, and physical harm towards family members). Both parents and teenagers also believe that parents are obligated to make rules for conventional issues – but less strongly than for moral issues (Smetana & Asquith, 1994). Likewise, children believe that they are obligated to respond if they witness a conventional transgression; but, again, they are seen to have less of an obligation here than in cases where they witness a moral transgression (Tisak, 1986).

Reciprocally, we can ask whether children have an obligation to obey their parents, once rules have been established. Numerous studies show that children and adolescents generally view themselves as obligated to obey parents' moral and conventional rules (Braine et al., 1991; Damon, 1977; Smetana & Asquith, 1994; Tisak, 1986). For moral rules, this is true even among late adolescents and their parents. Prior to adolescence, nearly all children believe that they are obligated to comply with parental conventional rules and standards (Tisak, 1986). Although still quite strongly endorsed, this belief declines across adolescence (Smetana & Asquith, 1994). In other words, there is some flexibility in adolescents' beliefs that they must obey parents' conventional rules.

It is worth noting that, although adolescents believe that parents have the authority to make moral and conventional rules, there are limits on what adults can legitimately expect children to do. For instance, children do not believe that it is permissible for adults to ask children to behave immorally. Parents cannot legitimately ask children to steal or hurt others (Damon, 1977). Neither can the law. In an elegant study, Charles Helwig and Urszula Jasiobedzka (2001) from the University of Toronto asked elementary school children ranging from 6 to 10 years of age to evaluate hypothetical laws that were unjust. For instance, children had to consider laws that entailed age discrimination or denial of access to medical care or education. Children thought these laws were unfair and believed that it was acceptable to violate them. This shows that even young children are not simply bound by adult authority. They reject parental and adult messages that conflict with moral norms.

Moreover, adolescents' obligations to obey parents only go so far. Adolescents believe that it is permissible to engage in deception when parents ask them to act in morally unjustifiable ways (Perkins & Turiel, 2007). American middle-class adolescents evaluated hypothetical moral situations where parents were described as asking teens to behave immorally. Teens were either asked not to befriend someone of a different race or physically to confront someone who, hypothetically, has been teasing them. A large majority thought that it was unjustified for parents to try to impose restrictions in these situations. And when parents were described as enforcing those restrictions, adolescents believed that it is legitimate to deceive them, in order to prevent harm or injustice.

What if God requests that children violate moral rules? Is it permissible to violate moral norms then? Apparently not, even though nationally representative survey studies of American adolescents conducted over the past decade show that most of them are highly religious and have a positive orientation towards matters of faith, religion, and spiritual experiences (Smith & Denton, 2005). Adolescents of different religious faiths – including Catholic, Dutch Reform Calvinist Amish-Mennonite, Orthodox Jewish, and Conservative Jewish – have been queried about different moral and religious rules (Nucci, 1985; Nucci & Turiel, 1993). Teens of different faiths were asked whether certain acts were permissible when there was (or was not) a specific command from God. They were also asked whether God's commands could make acceptable moral violations like stealing. Regardless of their religious affiliation, most adolescents treated moral issues like stealing, hitting, and property damage as wrong even if God had not made a rule prohibiting them. Violations of religious conventions – such as day of worship, expectations regarding appropriate dress (for Amish participants), and diet (for Jewish participants) – were seen as acceptable, though. In addition, most children rejected the notion that God's commands could make a moral violation such as stealing morally right. Nearly all of the participants rejected the notion that God would give such a command. Therefore we can infer that children's judgments are based on their own evaluations of the acts, not on the rules.

Children's acceptance or rejection of adults' moral and conventional principles depends on their evaluations as to whether the adult rules, expectations, or demands are appropriate and believable (Grusec & Goodnow, 1994). Even when they are, though, children and adolescents also actively evaluate the way in which adults convey their social messages. They consider the domain-appropriateness of the latter. Children and adolescents are more likely to accept adult explanations that are consistent with the domain of the act (or domain-appropriate) and reject messages that are discordant with it (or domain-inappropriate: Killen, Breton, Ferguson, & Handler, 1994; Killen & Sueyoshi, 1995; Nucci, 1984).

When applied to moral transgressions, parental responses such as "Look at what you did, you hurt her and made her cry!" can be considered domain-appropriate, because this response refers to the consequences of the act for others' welfare. The same response would be considered domain-inappropriate if it were applied to a conventional transgression. By the same token, statements such as "You're making a mess!" or "You're wreaking havoc!" may be an appropriate response to a conventional transgression, because these claims refer to the disorder the conventional violation caused. But such statements would not be appropriate in response to a moral transgression. And responses such as "Stop it!" are domain-undifferentiated because they do not provide information about the nature of the events. In studying children of ages 8 to 14, Larry Nucci (1984) found that children aged 10 years and older rated domain-appropriate responses (and the adults who issued them) more favorably than domain-inappropriate or domain-undifferentiated responses (and the adults responsible for them). Children and adolescents do not always accept the messages they are given. It behooves parents to react and respond in a way that is consistent with the nature of the event, because then children are more likely to heed the message.

Beliefs about the parents' authority regarding prudential issues

Prudential issues can pertain to minor matters of comfort or health, like wearing mittens when it is cold, or bathing and brushing one's teeth regularly. But, during adolescence, risky behaviors are on the rise. Both large survey studies and smaller longitudinal investigations have shown that experimentation with alcohol is standard among American adolescents, particularly as they grow older. For teens aged 15 years or younger, this is considered high-risk behavior (Dishion, Nelson, & Bullock, 2004). Some degree of indulging in these behaviors becomes more normal after the age of 15. Many teens in the United States experiment with smoking cigarettes, drinking alcohol, and trying "soft" drugs like marijuana (Johnston, O'Malley, Bachman, & Schulenberg, 2005). Teenagers also face increased risks when they begin to drive. Therefore parents have cause to be concerned about their teens' involvement in these prudentially risky behaviors.

In some ways, adolescents' and parents' beliefs about the parents' authority to make rules both about major prudential issues (like smoking cigarettes, drinking alcohol, and driving with teen drivers) and about more minor ones (like eating junk food) mirror the responses we have observed in the case of moral and conventional issues. Adolescents across a wide age range, as well as their parents, strongly believe that parents should be able to regulate prudential behavior (Smetana, 2000; Smetana & Asquith, 1994; Smetana et al., 2005).

Prudential issues, however, differ from moral and conventional issues in important ways. By definition, prudential issues pertain to the individuals' safety, comfort, and health. Most of our everyday prudential decisions are fundamentally personal choices. We may think it is foolish or unhealthy to eat a lot of junk food, gain weight, or choose not to exercise, but the decision is ours to make. (It is interesting to note that, although childhood obesity has become a national political issue in the United States, it is still being framed as prudential and as belonging within the realm of personal decision-making. For instance, when First Lady Michelle Obama rolled out her campaign against childhood obesity, she was quoted in the *New York Times* as stating: "I haven't spoken to one expert about this issue who has said the solution is having government tell us what we can do": Stolberg, 2010, February 9).

On the other hand, the American legal system recognizes the adolescents' lack of the maturity required to make decisions about some of these health and safety issues: they become personal choices only when individuals mature. Adults are permitted to decide for themselves whether or not to smoke cigarettes or drink alcohol, even though cigarette smoking is unhealthy at any age and too much alcohol has well-known adverse consequences for health. In the United States, these activities are considered "status offenses" in that they are illegal during adolescence. They become legally permissible and therefore individual choices, however, after the ages of 18 (for purchasing cigarettes) and 21 (for drinking alcohol). Other behaviors, like smoking marijuana or using cocaine, are illegal in the United States regardless of age (in the case of marijuana there are some medical exceptions), although many individuals believe that the government should not regulate their use. In other countries, drinking alcohol is considered permissible for adolescents. And there are wide variations across different states (and in different countries worldwide) regarding the age at which adolescents are allowed to begin driving cars. Some states also have graduated drivers' licenses, with different ages for when teens may learn to drive, obtain a drivers' license, be able to drive at night, and drive with other teenagers in the vehicle.

Beyond the legal considerations, though, parents are concerned about adolescents' safety and well-being. Their beliefs as to whether adolescents are ready to make their own decisions on these issues may vary. They may depend on their perceptions of their teens' competence and developmental readiness to make safe decisions. Individual characteristics, such as the adolescents' temperament, as well as the quality of the parent–adolescent relationships may come into play. This suggests that there may be a great deal of age variability in what parents permit. Yet we may expect to see some decline in late adolescence (or as children move out of the house) in the belief that parents have the legitimate authority to regulate various prudential issues.

It is not yet clear when authority to regulate prudential issues transfers from parents to children. In one study, primarily European American parents of 12th graders ceded more authority to adolescents over risky prudential issues – although not a lot – than parents of 9th graders did (Smetana, Metzger, Gettman, & Campione-Barr, 2006). The 12th graders were getting ready to graduate from high school. Some were intending to move out of the house in order to work or to attend college. Therefore more autonomy over issues of prudential concern may have been seen as developmentally appropriate. However, in my study of African American families (Smetana et al., 2005), neither parents' nor adolescents' acceptance of the parents' authority to regulate prudential issues declined over time, even among youth who were over the age of 18. This may reflect the fact that autonomy is gained at later ages in African American than in European American families.

A contrasting perspective emerges from research on a large and diverse sample of youth in Chile (Darling, Cumsille, & Martinez, 2008). These researchers found that Chilean adolescents' endorsement of their parents' legitimate authority to make rules about substance and alcohol use declined sharply with age over a

4-year period. Chilean adolescents viewed themselves as having more control over these issues as they grew older. In fact, they believed that they were legitimately able to control prudential decisions altogether. This may seem surprising. Predominantly Catholic South American countries like Chile are often thought to be more conservative in their family values than the United States. But these researchers note that Chilean culture has changed rapidly over the past two decades, due to urbanization and foreign media influences. Particularly in urban areas, youth in Chile face many of the same problems and share many of the same values as youth in the United States. And, with respect to the adolescents' alcohol and substance use, they appear to be much more permissive than their North American counterparts.

More generally, we do not know when authority shifts from parents to children over different prudential issues. Food choices, even unhealthy ones, are seen as personal choices at much younger ages than other prudential decisions are – especially those regarding risk-taking behavior, such as alcohol or substance use. Indeed, some African American parents we studied believed that there never was an appropriate age for their teens to decide about alcohol use and sex (Daddis & Smetana, 2005)!

American parents and adolescents hold somewhat different beliefs about whether parents are *obligated* to make prudential rules. For instance, in one study (Smetana & Asquith, 1994), European American mothers uniformly thought that parents had an obligation to make and enforce rules about prudential issues. However, teenagers (and their fathers) were more equivocal. They, too, thought that parents had such an obligation, but they did not endorse it as strongly as that. Their judgments on these matters more closely resembled those delivered on conventional matters. Teenagers did not see themselves as being strongly obligated to comply with parental prudential rules, once these had been established. Moreover, their perception of having an obligation to comply with such rules declined with age. This was because adolescents primarily treated prudential issues as personal and as matters under their jurisdiction, whereas their parents viewed them as primarily prudential matters related to their children's health and safety. Only occasionally did parents see these issues as personal matters for teens (or as social conventions or moral issues). Indeed, mothers were approximately twice as likely as their adolescent children (and fathers a little less so) to focus on the prudential dimensions of these acts. In other words, even though adolescents believed that parents had the authority to make rules about prudential issues, they still viewed them as personal to some extent. They were personal, although perhaps foolish.

A recent and large longitudinal survey study of American 5th through to 12th graders helps to clarify some of the different concerns regarding prudential issues (Flanagan, Stout, & Gallay, 2008). The researchers examined adolescents' perceptions of individuals' right to engage in risky behaviors that are potentially harmful to health. In addition, they also assessed adolescents' beliefs about governments' right to intervene in potentially harmful health behaviors. Issues that were presented as individual rights (that is, prudential issues framed in terms of personal choices) included doing what one wants with one's body, smoking or drinking as a personal choice, and having a right to smoke because it is seen as only harming oneself. Endorsement of these individual rights was relatively low across ages, but it was lower among early than among middle and late adolescents. Late adolescents were higher in their endorsement of personal choices when initially assessed at the start of the study than other teens were, but middle adolescents caught up as they grew older. They endorsed individual rights (personal choices) more highly 1 and 2 years later than they had at the outset of the study. In other words, much as Darling and her colleagues (2008) found, beliefs about prudential issues as personal choices increased from 11 to 18 years of age.

Flanagan and her colleagues (2008) also assessed what they referred to as public health beliefs (for instance, that the government should make laws to protect society against drunk driving, or that, if something is bad for health, the government should tell individuals to avoid it). Inasmuch as these issues pertain to others' welfare, they can be seen as moral issues; but they also involve social conventional concerns with social systems. Public-health beliefs also changed with age, but in a different way from beliefs about prudential issues as personal choices. In the case of the latter, there was a curvilinear relationship with age in adolescents' beliefs that society could control risky behaviors. Middle adolescents endorsed these beliefs less than either younger or older adolescents did. Moreover, examined longitudinally, early adolescents' public-health beliefs declined between the second and the third year of the study (that is, when they reached middle adolescence), whereas those of middle and late adolescents remained stable over time. The researchers concluded that, by late adolescence, youth arrive at a more sophisticated conception, which involves a coordination or balancing between individual rights (the individuals' personal choice to experiment with substances) and "a recognition of the need for laws enacted by government that constrain individuals' rights in the interest of a larger public good" (Flanagan et al, 2008, p. 831). The results of this study suggest that middle adolescents have difficulty integrating their notions of personal choice with their understanding of normative and moral regulation. (We shall see in Chapter 12 that difficulties in coordination appear to be characteristic of middle adolescence.)

Research by Larry Nucci, Nancy Guerra, and John Lee (1991) provides further insight into the relations between beliefs and behavior. They hypothesized that the matter of whether adolescents viewed alcohol and illegal drug use as a strictly personal issue or as a prudential one, of health and safety, would be associated with their actual drug and alcohol use. They surveyed an ethnically, racially, and socioeconomically diverse sample of American high school teens about their use of alcohol and illegal drugs such as marijuana, cocaine, crack, heroin, and hallucinogens. They split the teenagers into two groups on the basis of their responses. Teens who were designated as low drug users had experimented with alcohol and "soft" drugs like marijuana but were not frequent users. Their pattern of use reflects the style of experimentation characteristic of American youth. Adolescents who were considered to be high drug users consumed alcohol and illegal drugs on a more regular basis and went beyond "soft" drugs in their use.

High drug and alcohol users were more likely than other teens to classify drug and alcohol use as a purely personal matter. They were almost twice as likely as the low drug users to view themselves as having legitimate authority over their drug and alcohol use. In fact, they saw themselves as the only legitimate source of authority over these issues. They did not believe that others, such as parents, teachers, religious institutions, or the law, had the authority to make decisions about, or to regulate, their drug and alcohol use. In contrast, low drug-using teenagers were more likely to classify drug and alcohol use as prudentially unacceptable because it causes harm to the self. These teens were almost three times more likely than their high drug-using peers to view parents as authority figures with regard to drug and alcohol use. We cannot tell from these results whether different beliefs lead to greater drug and alcohol use, or whether greater involvement leads to different beliefs. But adolescents' different experiences with drugs were associated with their beliefs about drug and alcohol use.

Therefore these studies show that, through much of adolescence, parents are seen to have the legitimate authority to make rules and to set standards regarding adolescents' behavior in prudential matters, even though adolescents tend to focus on their personal dimension. There is also some evidence to suggest that authority over prudential issues is seen to transfer eventually from parents to children in late adolescence or emerging adulthood. When it comes to risky behaviors, there also appears to be a period, during middle adolescence, when teenagers have difficulty coordinating these conflicting notions of adult versus personal regulation.

Beliefs about parents' authority to control personal issues

American middle-class teenagers typically reject parental control over hypothetical, prototypical personal issues such as what TV programs they can watch, what music they can listen to, how they can spend their allowance or earnings, how they can style their hair, what clothes they can wear, and what friends they can choose (Smetana, 1988a, 1993b, 2000; Smetana & Asquith, 1994). The responses are much like what we saw in adolescents' reasoning about everyday disagreements with parents. Adolescents treat hypothetical, prototypical personal issues as being up to the individual to decide. Adolescents see such issues as extending beyond the boundaries of parents' legitimate control. Like the young preschooler who claimed that she had the right to choose which sweater to wear because she was "the boss of me," adolescents see themselves as the boss of their personal domains. They judge that they – and only they – have the authority to decide about these issues. When asked whether other authorities – including friends, parents, other relatives, teachers, religious institutions, or the law – can decide about personal issues in the home, the answer is a resounding "no." Teenagers soundly reject the notion that anyone else can control or decide these issues for them (Smetana & Asquith, 1994).

Furthermore, in the study of deception towards parents, discussed earlier (Perkins & Turiel, 2007), most adolescents also believed that it was permissible to lie to parents about personal matters in situations like dating someone whom parents disliked, or joining a club that parents think is a waste of time. As with the (im)moral issues Perkins and Turiel studied, teenagers did not believe that parents had the right to make rules in such areas. And older adolescents were even more likely than younger ones to believe that it is legitimate to lie to parents in situations such as these. In contrast, adolescents did not believe that it was acceptable to deceive one's peers about either moral or personal issues, or that it was acceptable for peers to attempt to restrict their friends' moral or personal activities. Whether deception to parents was seen as acceptable or not was tied to the nature of parent–adolescent relationships and to the fact that teenagers have unequal amounts of control as compared to their parents.

Parents also treat personal issues as distinct from moral norms, conventional standards, and prudential concerns. They believe that teenagers should have some control over personal areas of their lives, but typically less than teenagers want. This results in wide divergences between parents and teenagers about who should make decisions about personal issues. Parents believe that there is some validity to their children's claims to personal control, especially as the latter grow older. But parents consistently lag behind in their evaluations of teenagers' personal authority over these issues.

The responses of African American mothers and adolescents followed over 5 years reflected this pattern, although these parents were somewhat more restrictive than the samples of European American parents we studied (Smetana et al., 2005). When African American teenagers were first studied in early adolescence, most of the mothers believed that it was permissible for parents to regulate personal issues. This conviction varied, though, according to adolescents' age when they first entered the study. Not surprisingly, mothers of older early adolescents granted their teenagers more discretion to decide about personal issues than mothers of younger teens did. Mothers' beliefs also shifted over time. As teenagers grew older, mothers were less inclined to believe that they, the mothers, should regulate personal issues. On the other hand, even after 5 years, when their teens reached late adolescence, African American mothers were still inclined to think that parents had the right to make rules governing the personal areas of their teenagers' lives.

Despite the emphasis, in African American culture, on respect for adults and obedience, African American adolescents did not share their mothers' relatively restrictive views. (Recall that Chinese teenagers also rejected the parents' authority to control personal issues.) When studied initially, African American early adolescents maintained that they, not their parents, should control their personal domains. This stance was sustained across adolescence; teenagers' views did not change over time. But, gradually, mothers began to acknowledge that their teens were entitled to have some control over personal issues. Thus African American mothers' and teenagers' beliefs diverged the most in early adolescence, when the frequency of parent–adolescent conflicts typically peaks. Over time, parents' and adolescents' beliefs became less discrepant with each other.

Beliefs about parents' authority to control multifaceted issues

In the research on beliefs about parental authority, the divergences we observed in teenagers' and parents' reasoning about conflict were captured in a set of items we labeled "multifaceted." Multifaceted issues are issues that overlap domains. They do not form a domain per se, but are at the intersection of different domains. For instance, teenagers typically see issues such as the cleanliness or condition of the bedroom, or whether it is permissible to stay out late or to get a tattoo or a piercing as matters of personal choice. In contrast, parents typically focus on the conventional or prudential aspects of these same issues. Therefore the matter of how adolescents keep their bedrooms can be seen as a multifaceted issue. In addition, there are many aspects of friendships and peer and romantic relationships that, at least for parents, involve prudential concerns. For instance, as we saw in Chapter 5, parents may fear that their teen will hang out with "the wrong crowd," or with friends of whom they do not approve. They may also worry about whether their teenager is unsupervised, or spends time alone with a boyfriend or girlfriend. These friendship or romantic issues can be seen as multifaceted, too, in that parents generally focus on the prudential dimensions of relationships, whereas teenagers view them as personal matters, up to them able to control. (As I described in Chapter 4, issues can also be multifaceted when an individual sees multiple components of an issue from more than one domain, and they are either in conflict or in synchrony.)

Adolescents and parents were most discrepant in their beliefs about the latter's legitimate authority to control multifaceted issues. Parents thought they could control them, although typically less than moral, conventional, or prudential issues. But parents always believed that they had more authority to regulate multifaceted than personal issues. Teenagers, on the other hand, believed that they should have more control over these issues than their parents were willing to grant them – but again, less than over personal ones. Both nonsocial multifaceted issues (like getting a piercing or watching violent or sexually explicit movies or TV shows) and friend- and peer-related multifaceted issues occupied the middle ground between moral rules, conventional standards, and prudential concerns on the one hand and personal issues on the other. The former category was seen as clearly under parents' control, whereas personal issues were seen by teens (and, to a lesser extent, by parents) as being under teens' control.

As teenagers grew older, parents' belief that they should retain authority over multifaceted issues declined, in a parallel fashion, for African American mothers and teenagers alike (Smetana et al., 2005). Mothers believed, however, that parents had more authority over these issues than teenagers did. The consistent discrepancies between parents and teenagers reflect their different beliefs, which are at the root of much parent–adolescent squabbling and disagreement. These are the issues that are often hotly contested. But the decline, over time, in the belief that parents have the right to control these issues also reflects the outward reach of autonomy.

Beliefs about Parental Authority among Diverse Youth

Typical patterns of authority beliefs

The studies just discussed focused on middle-class European and African American families. But there is persuasive evidence to suggest that developmental changes in adolescents' beliefs are more broadly applicable to youth of varying socioeconomic statuses, ethnicities, and cultures. (We do not know if such changes also generalize to parents' beliefs, as few of the available studies discussed in the following section included parents: these studies do not examine convergences and discrepancies in parents' and adolescents' beliefs.) For instance, researcher Andrew Fuligni (1998) found no differences in the authority beliefs of American adolescents from Mexican, Chinese, Filipino, and European backgrounds. Beliefs did not differ, either, according to whether adolescents or their parents were born in the United States. These researchers did not study moral and prudential issues. But, across the different ethnic groups, adolescents, particularly younger ones, viewed their parents as having the most authority over conventional issues and less authority over multifaceted issues. Parents had the least authority over personal issues, especially for older adolescents. These researchers also followed a small number of teens over a 2-year period. The longer the adolescents had been in the United States (that is, among later generations of youth), the less accepting they became of parental authority to control personal issues and the more willing they became to disagree with their parents.

Earlier in this chapter, and in connection with the discussion of prudential issues, I briefly mentioned a study of Chilean adolescents, which was conducted on a large and diverse sample (Darling et al., 2008). This research focused on a broader set of issues than just prudential ones, and endorsement of parents' authority to make rules about different types of issues declined over the 4 years of the study. Age and domain differences in beliefs about parents' authority mirrored the general patterns just described.

This means that, with age, adolescents came to view an increasing number of issues as rightfully theirs to control. Changes were most dramatic in early adolescence. Teenagers' views of parents as legitimate authorities, as well as their beliefs that they were obligated to obey their parents, declined sharply from early to middle adolescence. Changes were less dramatic as they transitioned from middle to late adolescence. Their endorsement of parents' authority declined mostly for prudential issues (like alcohol use) and least for multifaceted issues. Personal issues fell in-between. Teenagers who were relatively uninvolved in problem behavior when the study began, and who viewed their parents as more supportive and as monitoring their behavior to a greater extent, were more likely to maintain over time their beliefs in parents' legitimate authority and their obligations to obey parents. But the age-related declines in parental authority were not just due to differences in parenting and problem behavior. Rather, they reflected normal trends: they were found for most youth, regardless of their histories of problem behavior and of the kind of parenting they had been exposed to.

Similar patterns of beliefs regarding legitimate parental authority were also observed among youth in Chile, the Philippines, and the United States (Darling, Cumsille, & Pena-Alampay, 2005). Adolescents in these three countries all differentiated among parents' legitimate authority to control various issues – including prudential, multifaceted, or related to friendship – and their stance on personal issues, as well as on a mixed category referred to as parental expectations. Chilean youth made the sharpest distinctions among the different issues. Filipino and American adolescents differentiated the most between prudential and various multifaceted and personal issues. The researchers also examined adolescents' obligations to follow parental rules, and their perceptions of their parents' restrictiveness. The patterning of these ratings and beliefs differed in each country. The results indicated that differences in the timing and pacing of autonomy cannot be simply explained in terms of broad cultural orientations like individualism and collectivism. They reflected differences among cultures and their values, with varying patterns of adherence and rejection of parental authority in different domains and in the different countries.

These beliefs about parental authority and obedience are also associated with adolescents' willingness to obey parental rules. Another study conducted in Chile found that adolescents obeyed their parents more if the latter had clear rules and enforced them strictly (Darling, Cumsille, & Martinez, 2007). But adolescents also varied in whether they agreed with parents and in their beliefs about legitimate parental authority. Interestingly, these variations in beliefs influenced obedience.

As one might expect, teenagers obeyed their parents more when they agreed with them. Adolescents also obeyed them more when parents enforced rules and monitored adolescents' activities. But, beyond this, teenagers were more obedient when they believed that parents had legitimate authority to regulate the issue and when they felt obligated to obey their parents, even if they disagreed with them. Therefore this study provides an interesting link between parents' parenting practices and adolescents' willingness to follow their parents' rules. What parents do – their supervision, monitoring, and rule enforcement – is important; but so are the adolescents' beliefs about their parents' authority. Adolescents have considerable agency in their socialization. They are more likely to disobey parents when they attempt to control issues that adolescents do not believe to be rightfully theirs to control.

Beliefs about parental authority and control have also been examined among individuals living in societies that are in the midst of great social and economic change. Studies of this sort are useful because they permit comparisons between adolescents who grow up in the same country (and therefore share the same language, history, political system, and often religion) but who live in very different circumstances. China is in the midst of a great economic change. Adolescents living in rural areas, however, have been largely untouched by these changes. As we saw in Chapter 7, urban Chinese adolescents believe that it is more acceptable to disagree with parents than rural adolescents do (Zhang & Fuligni, 2006). Zhang and Fuligni also found that rural and urban Chinese youths did not differ in their beliefs about their parents' authority to make rules about conventional, multifaceted, and personal issues: they largely rejected this authority. Domain differences were not assessed, but Chinese adolescents believed that parents could legitimately make rules about only 5 out of the 13 items they examined (the items were the same as in Fuligni's 1998 study of multi-ethnic youth in the United States). Regardless of their urban or rural status, youth were not very accepting of parents' authority to make rules. The more educated their parents were, the more the teenagers accepted their authority and the right to disagree openly with them.

Like China, Iran has recently gone through a great deal of modernization, but at an uneven pace. This has resulted in a dual society with two different, conflicting socioeconomic systems. Larger cities have modernized rapidly. But traditional neighborhoods persist, partly due to the migration of millions of peasants, who have moved to the cities looking for work. Smaller towns and rural areas still emphasize traditional values. Beliefs about parental authority have been examined in a very heterogeneous group of Iranian mothers of 14-year-olds (Assadi, Smetana, Shahmansouri, & Mohammadi, in press). The mothers were from three different cities, Tehran, Isfahan, and Khomeinishahr, which vary in size, modernity, and social class. Mothers ranged from being illiterate, traditional, and with lower socioeconomic status to being well educated, modernized, and from an upper socioeconomic status background.

Regardless of their demographic background, Iranian mothers believed that parents have greater authority to regulate conventional issues – like doing the chores, or the type of language and the manners the teen uses – than prudential and personal issues. This may seem surprising, especially as the prudential issues studied here included risky behaviors – for instance doing drugs, staying out late at night, and smoking cigarettes. But the prudential category also included friendship matters such as befriending unsuitable persons, going to places with friends, or spending various amounts of time with friends. These issues were treated as prudential because initial analyses showed that mothers generally focused on their prudential dimension (as was found in other research, too). Iranian mothers did cede some authority to teens over personal issues (for instance choice of clothes, music, hairstyles, and TV programs, or how they spent their money and free time). Mothers believed that adolescents should have more authority over personal than other issues. Differences in educational level or social class did not influence these evaluations. But more educated mothers believed that parents had greater authority to control prudential and conventional issues. (This may explain why Zhang and Fuligni found that Chinese adolescents with more educated parents endorsed parental authority more, as adolescents may have ceded more authority to parents over conventional issues.)

We saw in earlier chapters that disagreements are a persistent feature of parent–adolescent relationships. This was the case in Iranian families as well. Iranian mothers reported having conflicts with their middle adolescents over everyday issues of family life. Their disagreements were low in frequency, moderate in intensity, and very likely to be resolved. Regardless of the mothers' educational or socio-economic backgrounds, conflicts were linked with their beliefs about legitimate parental authority, but the effects varied depending on the issue. Mothers reported having more frequent conflicts with their teenagers when they themselves, the mothers, believed that parents had *less* authority to control prudential (and friendship) issues. When mothers give adolescents greater authority over these issues, adolescents may have more latitude to engage in behaviors that mothers view as undesirable. On the other hand, mothers reported more frequent conflicts when they believed that parents had *more* authority to regulate personal issues. Conflicts may erupt over these issues because mothers place more restrictions on personal activities, which adolescents may view as unjustified. It appears that the domain of parental authority beliefs moderated parent–adolescent conflict.

Individual differences in the patterning of beliefs about parental authority

The research just discussed demonstrates that adolescents' beliefs about parents' legitimate authority change with age in some domains, but not in others. These studies focused on normal, regular trends. But all adolescents do not evaluate parental authority in the same way. They may vary in their beliefs. Differences in life circumstances, in the adolescents' experiences of being parented, or even in their ordinal position in the family may lead some teens to be more (or less) accepting of their parents' authority to control different types of acts.

The various beliefs of adolescents who affiliate with different peer crowds or reference groups provide one example. As I described in Chapter 5, crowds provide distinctive norms, which locate adolescents in the peer world. The old but still popular American movie *The Breakfast Club* provides a vivid illustration of these different norms. The story follows a group of five teenagers, each one the representative of a different high school crowd ("jocks," "populars," "brains," "outcasts," and "toughs"), spending a Saturday at school in detention together. These teens dress and act very differently. As they interact together, they reveal their involvement in very different clubs, organizations, and out-of-school activities. And they clearly have different orientations towards school – from the "brain," who belongs to the Physics Club, to the "tough," who could care less about school. But the movie also demonstrates vividly that these teens have different attitudes towards adult authority and rules, ranging from flagrant disregard to slavish adherence.

Indeed, crowds have been characterized as varying in their orientation towards, and involvement in, adult institutions versus peer institutions. This observation led Christopher Daddis (in press, a) to examine the distinct patterns of beliefs regarding the boundaries of legitimate parental authority among adolescents in different peer reference groups. He identified eight peer crowds in a large sample of primarily European American lower- to middle-class students in middle school and high school. Daddis found several different patterns of beliefs about parental authority among youth who identified with different crowds.

Adolescents who identified with three of the largest teen crowds all adopted patterns of beliefs that reflect (or deviate only slightly from) the typical developmental pathway described in earlier sections. Relative to the other crowds, students who identified with the "normal" crowd (who were reputed to be casually dressed and nice, and who did reasonably well in school) ceded authority to parents over prudential, conventional, and moral issues, but rejected parental control over personal issues. This is much as we have seen in other samples. Students who identified with the "prep" crowd (seen as stylish, somewhat cliquish, and popular) believed that parents should retain control over most issues. Compared to other crowds, these students did not reject parental authority over personal issues. Students identifying with the "jock" crowd (who dress in athletic clothes and participate in athletic teams) did not differ from other crowds in their authority beliefs. They endorsed moderate amounts of parental authority for all types of issues. All of these reflect fairly typical patterns of beliefs, with some variation in how personal issues are treated.

Three of the crowds ("toughs," "skaters," and "goths") were characterized either by involvement in problem behavior or by adherence to an alternative life style. Students identifying with the "tough" crowd were reputed to get in trouble and into fights, and sometimes to smoke or to use drugs. "Skaters" were described as liking to skateboard, hang out at the skate park, wear baggy clothes, and listen to rock and alternative music. "Goths" wore mostly black clothes, stuck to themselves, shopped at Hot Topic, had piercings, and liked heavy metal music. Adolescents who identified with these crowds endorsed patterns of belief that reflected personal control over all issues (moral, conventional, prudential, and personal). Therefore their beliefs deviated from the norm and from those of adolescents who identified with the three largest peer crowds (the "normals," the "preps," and the "jocks").

Students in the remaining crowds were distinguished primarily by their claims of personal authority over moral and prudential issues. For instance, students in the "hip hop" crowd (who were reputed to have a tough image and were described as wearing baggy clothes and listening to rap music) asserted more personal control over prudential and moral issues by comparison with students in other crowds. Likewise, students who identified with the "outcast" crowd (including "nerds" and "loners," who were, both, rejected by the mainstream school peer culture) asserted that they should have control over moral issues and that parents should have authority over the remaining ones. However, more than the members of any other crowd, students in the "outcast" crowd believed that parents had legitimate authority to control personal issues. Therefore the "hip hop" and the "outcast" crowds' patterns of beliefs about authority appear to reflect identities that located them as distinct from their peers.

In Chapter 5 I discussed research showing that adolescents use their peer groups as points of reference for their emerging beliefs about personal control. Adolescents may initially affiliate with different crowds on the basis of their orientations towards school and preferences for different activities and appearance. But their affiliation with different crowds also may lead teens to adopt the different patterns of beliefs about parental authority found among the other youth who identify with that crowd. And these different patterns of beliefs may become accentuated over time.

Two large-scale investigations conducted in Chile also focused on individual differences in the patterning of beliefs about parental authority. One project included 3,000 early, middle, and late adolescents studied at a single point in time (Cumsille, Darling, Flaherty, & Martinez, 2006). The other investigation followed 2,600 Chilean 11- to 16-year-olds for 3 years (Cumsille, Darling, Flaherty, & Martinez, 2009). Much like many other studies, the researchers found that beliefs differed according to age and domain. Chilean youth viewed parents as having more authority to regulate prudential issues related to cigarette, alcohol, and drug use than either personal issues (examined here through the use of free time and the choice of TV programs, movies, and videos) or multifaceted issues (represented here by a single item, namely hanging around with friends whom parents might view as problematic). Compared to younger adolescents, older ones believed that parents had less authority to regulate all of these issues. But, in addition to these normal changes, the researchers identified three distinct and relatively stable patterns of belief across the domains.

One pattern was called the *parental control* profile. Youth fitting this profile ceded control to parents over their substance and alcohol use and their associations with potentially problematic peers. They were relatively likely to cede control over personal issues, too, although less than over the other issues. This was the most pervasive pattern when adolescents were studied at a single point in time – but not when they were followed longitudinally. There were age differences within this general pattern, and they accounted for some of the variations from the typical pattern. The belief that parents should control personal issues was more common among early adolescents than among middle and late adolescents. Indeed, one item, "choice of free time activities," only fit the parental control profile for the youngest adolescents. And only a third of the oldest teens viewed parents as having the authority to control the other personal item (which pertained to TV and video choices). These age differences in the treatment of personal issues are in accord with normal patterns of development.

In addition, there were social class differences that were very similar to what Nucci and his colleagues observed among youth in Brazil (Nucci, Camino, & Sapiro, 1996), as discussed in Chapter 7. The parental control pattern was most common among lower socioeconomic status youth and least common among middle-class participants. Lower socioeconomic status youths' greater willingness to cede to parents control over personal issues appeared to reflect their awareness of the higher safety risks in their environment, and hence of the prudential dimensions of personal issues.

A second pattern reflected *shared control*. Youth exhibiting this pattern supported their parents' authority to make rules regarding the prudential issues of cigarette, alcohol, and drug use, but not those of hanging around with problematic peers, nor personal issues involving free time use and recreational choices. This pattern was most similar to the typical one found in other studies. It also was similar to the responses observed among American teenagers who identified with the "normal," "prep," and "jock" peer crowds in Daddis's study. Shared control prevailed among middle-class youth in Chile. It was also the most frequent pattern observed when adolescents were followed over time. Again, there were age differences within this general pattern. For instance, late adolescents were much less likely than younger teens to cede control over smoking to their parents. This is consistent with the notion that, as teens grow older, parental authority over prudential issues such as smoking transfers from parents to adolescents. And the number of youth who fit the shared control profile increased over time.

The smallest group, which was very low in frequency in both studies, reflected a pattern of high risk. Adolescents fitting this profile, referred to as the *personal control* group, believed that they should control all their acts. They did not cede authority to parents over any of the issues. The pattern was more prevalent among late adolescents than among younger ones. It was also characteristic of youth who were more involved in deviant behavior; and these were more likely to remain in the personal control group over time. This profile is reminiscent of the youth classified as high drug users in Nucci and his colleagues' (1991) study. Recall that they were distinguished by their view that drug use was a personal rather than a prudential issue. The same profile also resembles the patterning of beliefs found among "toughs," "skaters," and "goths" in Daddis's study of peer crowds.

In consonance with what is known about adolescent risk behavior, parents of teenagers in the personal control group provided less monitoring and support than parents of other adolescents did (at least according to adolescents' reports). Adolescents who had a greater sense of self-efficacy and whose parents had more rules were less likely to belong in the personal control group. Overall, then, these studies suggest that, with age, adolescents move towards a view of parental authority that becomes more balanced and differentiated by domain. Nevertheless, the timing of the adolescents' transitions from viewing parents as legitimately controlling some issues towards desiring and acquiring greater autonomy varies across adolescents and reflects differences in parenting and in life circumstances.

Summary and Conclusions

To summarize, adolescents and parents differ in their beliefs about the parents' legitimate authority to regulate different types of acts. Adolescents and parents alike overwhelmingly affirm that parents should be able to make rules about moral and conventional issues, even in late adolescence. However, there are limits to what parents can legitimately control. They do not have the authority to ask their children to behave immorally. As adolescents grow older, they are somewhat less accepting of parental authority over conventional issues. Also, adolescents and parents strongly endorse the parents' legitimate authority to make rules about prudential issues involving risk, like smoking cigarettes and using alcohol and illegal drugs. There is some evidence, though, that, with age, adolescents increasingly see these issues as personal choices – "personal but foolish."

In contrast, adolescents strongly believe that parents do not have the authority to regulate over the domain of personal issues. Parents agree to some extent, but still view themselves as having more authority than their children would like. As adolescents grow older, parents shift towards granting their children more control over personal matters and, to a lesser extent, over multifaceted and friendship ones (which involve overlaps between conventional or prudential matters and personal concerns). Multifaceted issues often are the source of conflict in adolescent–parent relationships. They represent the contested and shifting boundary between the parents' legitimate authority and the adolescents' personal jurisdiction. Parents' authority to control multifaceted issues declines during adolescence, but adolescents consistently claim more personal jurisdiction than parents are willing to grant.

The scope of what adolescents can control broadens during adolescence. The large discrepancies in parents' and adolescents' views of multifaceted, friendship, and personal issues are consistent with the notion that battles over autonomy are fought over them. Changes over time reflect the shifting boundaries of parental authority and the expansion of the children's personal domain during adolescence.

Studies of youth in several different cultures, including China, Chile, and the Philippines, reveal similar age and domain differences in beliefs regarding legitimate parental authority. Iranian mothers, too – both traditional and modernized – revealed differentiated beliefs about the parents' authority to make rules about their teenagers' behavior. However, research conducted with American youth identifying with different peer crowds, and various samples of Chilean youth, also demonstrate that there are individual differences in the patterning of beliefs about parental authority. These include deviations from the characteristic patterns; and the clearest example is furnished by the identification of a group of at-risk youth, who reject adult authority on all issues. Among Chilean youth, these different patterns were associated with different patterns of parental discipline.

The research discussed in this chapter raises an important methodological issue. In studying parenting, researchers often rely on a single reporter's perspective. Sometimes observers are trained to evaluate parents on different dimensions. But, more often, researchers rely on parents' or adolescents' perceptions of parenting. When researchers obtain both the adolescents' and the parents' evaluations, the two sets are usually discordant; the correlations between ratings or evaluations are typically low. This lack of agreement among parents' and adolescents' reports is often attributed to bothersome methodological problems, such as measurement error or informant bias. Others assert that a lack of agreement between parents' and adolescents' reports is not problematic. Whether their perceptions are veridical or not, adolescents may act on their own perceptions. Therefore, the argument goes, researchers should focus exclusively on adolescents' perceptions, because these are more likely to be associated with the way adolescents act and feel.

But the analyses presented here of the adolescents' and the parents' interpretations of conflicts, and of their beliefs about the parents' legitimate authority to control different types of act, demonstrate that there are multiple realities within the family. Parents and adolescents often agree, but sometimes they do not. Ratings are stable over time for some types of issues, but they change for others. The research discussed here and in earlier chapters suggests that, rather than reflecting methodological problems, discrepancies between adolescents' and parents' perspectives may be important and meaningful by mapping areas that deserve further study. Discrepancies can illuminate areas of tension and change in family processes and in adolescent development.

We have seen that adolescents gain increasing control over personal areas of their lives as they grow older. In addition, adolescents vary in their desires to control personal issues. This raises an important question of practical significance. How do parents help to support their adolescents' healthy psychosocial development? How much autonomy – at what ages and over what types of issues – promotes optimal adjustment? These questions will be discussed in the following chapter.

10

Parenting Styles and Practices

In the last chapter I discussed variations in beliefs about parental authority. My claim was that these beliefs are central to understanding different parenting styles and disciplinary practices. We are now ready to take up that claim. We begin by considering one of the most prominent psychological approaches to understanding parenting.

The Influence of Parenting Styles

Researchers studying human development have assumed that variations in parents' disciplining style, warmth, attention to the needs of the child, and parenting attitudes and beliefs can all be characterized in terms of consistent patterns of child rearing, or parenting styles. The assumption is that these parenting styles are systematically related to children's competence and development. Diana Baumrind's model provided perhaps the most influential and widely used scheme for describing parenting styles. She began her investigation by identifying a set of characteristics that, she believed, defined competence among North American children. Then she examined parents' child-rearing beliefs and practices, in order to identify the parenting styles that were associated with those positive outcomes (Baumrind, 1971). In a longitudinal study that has extended over 30 years, Baumrind followed a small group of primarily European American middle-class families from Berkeley, California. (Baumrind was attuned to the cultural contexts of development, and the original sample also included a small group of African American children. But, because of its small size, she did not follow this group over time.) Baumrind initially developed a typology of three distinct parenting styles, which were related to children's outcomes. Later, when the children in her

Adolescents, Families, and Social Development: How Teens Construct Their Worlds. Judith G. Smetana
© 2011 Judith G. Smetana

longitudinal study were 15 years old, she expanded the typology to four parenting styles.

According to Baumrind's widely used typology, parenting varies along two distinct dimensions: demandingness and responsiveness. Authoritative parents are both responsive and demanding. They set clear, reasonable standards for responsible behavior, which are consistent with their children's developing abilities. They are firm in their enforcement and provide explanations for their positions. They promote mature behavior through supportive rather than punitive methods, warmth, and responsiveness to children's needs.

In contrast, authoritarian parents are strict and highly demanding, but they are not responsive. These parents place a high value on obedience to rules. They discourage give-and-take between parents and children and do not take their child's needs into consideration. They also offer little explanation for their decisions.

Baumrind's third parenting style is described as permissive or indulgent. Parents in this category are responsive but not demanding. They make few demands for mature behavior on their children. They do not punish them for misbehavior. Whenever possible, they avoid asserting their authority. In addition, indulgent or permissive parents are warm, accepting, and tolerant of the child's impulses.

In later work, and partly on the basis of Maccoby and Martin's (1983) influential treatise, Baumrind distinguished permissive from uninvolved parents. The latter do not make many demands on their children either, primarily because they are disengaged from the needs of the child. Therefore parents of this fourth kind are neither demanding nor responsive (Baumrind, 1989). Baumrind viewed most uninvolved parents as falling within the normal range of parenting, although this style also includes more pathological forms, such as neglectful and rejecting–neglecting parenting.

From Baumrind's perspective, there is a clear and simple answer to the question of how parents can help to support their adolescents' healthy psychosocial development. Because authoritative parents set high expectations and support mature behavior, this parenting style is optimal for children's development and adjustment. Indeed, authoritative parenting has been associated with a wide range of positive outcomes in adolescence, including better academic performance, increased competence, autonomy, and self-esteem, more advanced moral development, less deviance, anxiety, and depression, and a more well-rounded orientation to peers (Baumrind, 1991a, b; Maccoby & Martin, 1983; Steinberg, 2001).

Parenting styles can be seen as reflecting the different beliefs about parental authority outlined in the previous chapter. Baumrind's typological perspective suggests that authoritative and authoritarian parents, who are, both, highly demanding, would consider themselves to have more of a legitimate right to regulate their teens' behavior than would permissive or indulgent parents, who allow considerable self-regulation of behavior and activities. Furthermore, authoritative parents encourage individuality and independence. They are highly responsive to their children's needs. Therefore, more than other types, authoritative parents may recognize that adolescents legitimately have the right to control some issues.

This is indeed the case. In a study investigating beliefs about parental authority among parents endorsing different parenting styles (Smetana, 1995a), I found that European American middle-class mothers and fathers who endorse different parenting styles differ in how much autonomy over personal issues they believe teenagers should have. (Uninvolved parenting was not examined in this study.) They also differ in how broadly or narrowly they draw the boundaries around moral and conventional issues (Smetana, 1995a). When making judgments about multifaceted issues, permissive parents ignore the conventional components and treat the issues as up to teenagers to control. In addition to constructing relatively broad boundaries around what constitutes a personal issue, permissive parents also "conventionalize" moral issues related to the family (like taking money from parents without permission, or breaking a promise made to one's parents) and treat them as conventional in some of their judgments. Therefore they are lax in asserting their authority on moral issues. At the same time, permissive parents treat potentially risky activities with friends (like going to a movie alone with a boyfriend or girlfriend, seeing a friend whom parents do not like, having a party when parents are away, or inviting a boyfriend or girlfriend over when parents are away) as if they were moral violations. Baumrind (1978) has claimed that, although permissive parents often are extremely lenient, they try to watch out for their children's safety. In validation of this assertion, permissive parents were *not* more lenient than other parents in their judgments of prudential issues.

Authoritarian parents do not differentiate between moral and conventional issues in their judgments. Rather, they over-extend the moral domain. They "moralize" social conventions by treating them as morally obligatory. Compared to other parents, they also view parents as having more of a moral obligation to make rules regarding multifaceted and friendship issues than other parents think. Therefore, in comparison with the authoritative type, authoritarian parents restrict adolescents' jurisdiction over issues that overlap the personal and the conventional (or prudential) domain, and they cast a wide net – inappropriately so – as to what they consider to be moral.

Only authoritative parents maintain clear boundaries among moral matters, conventional standards, and personal concerns. They grant teenagers autonomy over a limited range of personal issues, but not over multifaceted and prudential issues, nor over some matters of friendship. Their reasoning reflects a concern with the conventional, psychological, or prudential aspects of these matters. Their focus on the societal, health-related, or psychological concerns that complex issues raise may help teenagers to understand why limits are imposed in these areas. Defining the boundaries between these domains either too permissively or too rigidly may deprive adolescents and parents of the opportunity to negotiate appropriate boundaries, which in turn may undermine adolescent development.

Baumrind's approach to parenting styles clearly taps into other important components of parenting, such as warmth, coerciveness, and communicative style. This goes to show that parenting styles are not reducible to beliefs about parental authority. But considering these beliefs adds some specificity to our understanding of parental demandingness and responsiveness. It provides some insights into the specific areas where parents believe they ought to exert control or where they are willing to relinquish it in order to grant the child greater autonomy.

Parenting styles, parental authority, and adolescent–parent conflict

Different parenting styles are associated with how families handle and resolve conflict, although they do not fully account for these variations. Rather, family differences in adolescent–parent conflict reflect many other factors, including conceptions of parental authority and modes of reasoning about conflict. This conclusion is drawn from person-centered analyses (described in Smetana, 1996), which were conducted in order to distinguish various family profiles of adolescent–parent conflict. Ratings of conflict frequency and severity, as well as the variance in those ratings, were used in identifying different profiles among the (mainly) European American families described in Chapters 5 and 9 and in the sample of Hong Kong Chinese adolescents described in Chapter 7. A similar set of three profiles emerged in each analysis. Although the numbers of families fitting each profile varied somewhat from sample to sample, the similarity in the patterns provides some evidence that the latter are generalizable.

The largest number of families (about half or more in each sample) fit a profile that I labeled *frequent squabblers*. Their members reported having very frequent conflicts, but these were generally low in intensity. Thus, although they bickered a great deal, the families in question did not appear to have particularly angry or hostile conflicts.

I will refer to the second largest group as *easy-going* families. (In previous writings I have described this group as *placid*, but this term is a bit misleading, as it implies – incorrectly – that the families so characterized do not have conflicts.) Conflicts in these families were low in frequency and moderate in intensity. Thus easy-going families appeared to have few conflicts; but, when they did disagree, their disputes were angrier than those among the frequent squabblers.

In each sample we also identified a third profile, labeled *tumultuous*, which included only a small number of families. These families were characterized by frequent conflicts – although less frequent than among the frequent squabblers. But, unlike in the other two groups, conflict in tumultuous families was intense; it was also quite variable. And, although all of the families were drawn from community samples that did not specifically target high-risk youth, teens from tumultuous families appeared to be more at risk for problem behavior and maladjustment than teens from the other two groups.

Divorced, single-parent, and step-parent families were over-represented in the tumultuous group. Tumultuous parents were also less likely to be professionally employed, and they had lower incomes and socioeconomic status than other families. Tumultuous families were less likely than the others to resolve their disagreements, to compromise, or to resolve conflicts jointly – although, as we saw previously, compromise was generally infrequent among all families. Tumultuous families also endorsed authoritative parenting less than the other two groups, and they endorsed authoritarian parenting more than easy-going families.

Therefore both tumultuous and frequently squabbling families had relatively frequent conflicts, but those occurring in tumultuous families were distinguished by their intensity. And, when faced with conflict, these families were less likely than others to resolve them. Several lines of research suggest that adolescents who experience very angry, hostile, or intense conflict are at greater risk of dysfunction over time. Negative affect also is one of the most salient characteristics of adolescents' reports of "important" conflicts from the previous day, and it is associated with disengagement and lack of conflict resolution (Laursen & Koplas, 1995). Likewise, research on interparental conflict has shown the deleterious effects for children's adjustment of the parents' more open, hostile conflict among themselves. Our findings further suggest that tumultuous families' judgments of legitimate parental authority are part of their profile of risk.

Tumultuous parents were more restrictive than the others in drawing the boundaries of adolescents' personal jurisdiction. They viewed parents as obligated to regulate their children's personal issues. Tumultuous parents' greater intrusion into adolescents' personal domain was met with greater adolescent detachment, as was evidenced by tumultuous adolescents' higher ratings of emotional autonomy. They had higher scores on a measure that is generally seen to measure unhealthy detachment rather than healthy emotional autonomy. Furthermore, adolescents characterized as tumultuous generally had lower academic achievement than other teens and were more oriented towards friends as legitimate sources of authority for multifaceted issues. This is only an indirect measure of peer influence; but it is important to bear in mind that susceptibility to peer influence has been consistently found to be an important predictor of teenage problem behavior. In addition, tumultuous families tended to have more frequent and more intense conflicts over prudential matters related to drug, alcohol, and cigarette use than easy-going families did. Tumultuous adolescents also engaged in more youth-alone decision-making than youth in easy-going families. As will be discussed in greater detail in a later section, this form of decision-making, whereby adolescents make decisions without any input from their parents, is associated with greater deviance and conduct problems. Such a situation suggests that parents may be relatively uninvolved in teenagers' lives, despite their belief that they have the legitimate authority to control a broad swath of their children's activities. Teenagers from tumultuous families appealed to personal jurisdiction in their reasoning about family conflicts less than other teenagers did.

Frequent squabblers and easy-going families did not differ in their strong endorsement of authoritative parenting. However, easy-going families were more approving than frequent squabblers of permissive parenting, and they also differed from them in some of their beliefs about parental authority. Compared to easy-going parents, frequent squabblers regulated multifaceted and personal issues more and invoked social conventions more in their reasoning about adolescent–parent conflict. Easy-going parents resolved disagreements with their offspring more than did frequent squabblers, perhaps because they regulated their childrens' behavior less and employed less conflictive modes of reasoning when they disagreed. In reasoning about conflicts, easy-going parents focused more on the prudential and pragmatic aspects of their disputes. Frequently squabbling families may bicker more than others because parents and adolescents have these contradictory and difficult to resolve interpretations of their conflicts.

Parental psychological control

In research on parenting styles, parental control is seen as a single dimension, which ranges from excessive control to insufficient control. Over the past 20 years, though, researchers have stressed the need to differentiate this view of control further. High levels of control can refer to parents who supervise and have firm rules for their children and provide a great deal of structure and guidance. This notion can also include parents who are overly intrusive, use guilt, or threaten to withdraw their love if teens do not comply with their wishes. In Baumrind's model of parenting styles, authoritative parents have firm rules and use structure and guidance, but they are not overly intrusive. In contrast, authoritarian parents have firm rules, but they also use more intrusive forms of control, as we just saw in the description of tumultuous families and in the descriptions of some patterns of authority beliefs. These are different forms of control, rather than two ends of the same continuum.

Behavioral control refers to the rules, regulations, and restrictions that parents impose on their children. It also extends to their supervision and management of their activities. Behavioral control, which is associated with authoritative parenting, is considered to be a "good" form of control. It provides adequate structure, firm guidance for children, and monitoring of their activities. Indeed, too little behavioral control has been associated with externalizing problems, such as acting out, drug use, truancy, and antisocial behavior.

Recently, Wendy Grolnick and Eva Pomerantz (2009) have suggested that we abandon the construct of "control" altogether, with its positive and negative dimensions, and describe behavioral control in terms of "structuring." In these researchers' view, behavioral control and related constructs – such as firm (versus lax) enforcement, firm control, and strictness-supervision – should be seen as a dimension that is distinct from forms of control. As they define it, structure refers to parents' organization of children's environment, which is designed to facilitate children's competence. Structure is orthogonal to control, which is in turn related to autonomy. Although I will continue to refer to "control" in the following discussion in order to be consistent with the research literature, their distinction is worth bearing in mind.

The dimension of psychological control versus autonomy-granting was first identified by Schaefer (1965) as one of three central dimensions of parenting. As described by Laurence Steinberg (1990) and elaborated upon by Brian Barber and others (Barber, 1996, 2002; Barber, Olsen, & Shagle, 1994; Barber, Stolz, & Olsen, 2005; Soenens & Vansteenkiste, 2010), the more intrusive form of control is called psychological control. This form refers to parents' attempts to control children's activities in ways that affect their psychological world negatively. Psychological control, which includes parental intrusiveness, guilt induction, lack of respect for the child, and love withdrawal, undermines children's psychosocial development by interfering with their ability to become independent. It impedes the development of a healthy sense of self and personal identity. Parental psychological control has been linked to internalizing problems under forms such as anxiety, depression, loneliness, and confusion. It is also associated with higher levels of externalizing problems, with results such as conduct problems and substance use.

Barber (2002; Barber et al., 2005) has examined parents' use of psychological control (as well as their use of behavioral control and of a third dimension, involving support and acceptance) in different cultures. His research demonstrates that psychological control is evident in a range of nations and ethnic groups from all over the world, including North and South America, Africa, Asia, Europe, and the Middle East. Barber and his colleagues (2005) sampled youth from nations in all of these various geographical areas. The different groups varied on a number of dimensions, such as degree of industrialization, religion, and exposure to political violence. The results suggest that psychological control is pervasive, as are its negative effects for children's well-being. Psychological control is consistently associated with internalizing and externalizing problems, much as has been found in the United States. Summarizing the available research, Barber (2002) found that higher levels of psychological control are typically reported by boys rather than by girls; by younger rather than by older children; by ethnic minority rather than by majority (European American) families in the United States; and by lower rather than by upper socioeconomic status families.

A vivid example of the potentially deleterious effects of psychological control for well-being comes from recent research on children's evaluations of their parents' deployment of shaming. As noted in Chapter 9, shaming is a commonly employed discipline method in Asian cultures, and its use in the process of socialization is seen to be consistent with the priority placed on groups over the individual and with the emphasis on obedience and conformity in Asian culture. However, as Helwig (2010, June) has noted, the available research has focused on Asian parents' endorsement of this practice or on observations of its use in Asian child socialization. Helwig, To, Wang, Liu, and Yang (2010) sought to obtain children's perspectives on it.

These researchers compared rural and urban Chinese children's and urban Canadian children's judgments and reasoning about shaming, considered among other parental discipline practices. In response to a hypothetical moral transgression (a child knocks down another child on the playground and takes her ball), a parent was described, variously, as reasoning to the child (highlighting the consequences of the child's actions for the playmate); shaming the child (either by describing how the child's behavior would bring shame upon the mother and the family or by comparing the child unfavorably with a friend); or engaging in love withdrawal. Chinese children (both rural and urban) confirmed that shaming, particularly where the child's behavior was compared to other children's behavior, was the most common practice parents used in disciplining them. As expected, this was not the case with Canadian children, who reported that reasoning was much more common than the other parenting practices.

Despite these differences in frequency of use, all teenagers alike believed that shaming resulted in negative psychological consequences. Traditional, rural Chinese children below the age of 10 did not differentiate between reasoning and either form of shame; these discipline practices were all seen in a positive light. At about 10 years of age, however, rural Chinese children began to evaluate parents' use of shame critically. By adolescence, there was a clear preference for reasoning as the most positive form of discipline. A similar pattern was observed among both urban Chinese and Canadian children; their preference for reasoning was greater as children grew older. In their justifications, older children and adolescents from all settings criticized shaming as leading to greater psychological harm or feelings of low self-esteem for the recipient. Therefore Chinese children perceived harmful effects resulting from parental practices that are widely employed, culturally sanctioned, but psychologically controlling.

As this example suggests, the measurement of parental psychological control typically focuses primarily on the style of social interaction that undermines adolescent development. For example, Barber's measure asks whether the parent changes the subject when the teen has something to say; whether the parent tells the teen all of the things the parent has done for the child; and whether the parent would like to be able to tell the teen how to feel or think about things. Barber's claims regarding the negative effects of psychological control on adolescent development, as well as his claims about the need for psychological autonomy for the development of competence, are strikingly consistent with the way in which the personal domain has been described. In turn, this suggests that psychological control may pertain not just to style, that is, to *how* parents exert their control (for instance, by using shaming in response to a moral transgression), but also to *what* parents control. More specifically, teenagers may also feel psychologically more controlled when they view their parents as overly restrictive of their personal domains. Perceptions of psychological control may arise, or may be amplified, when parents exercise too much control over personal issues. This is because teens may disagree both with the fact that certain types of behaviors are being control-led – and hence with the resulting infringement on what is perceived as an arena of personal freedom – and with the style of control, or with how parents are managing their behavior. There is support for this claim.

Christopher Daddis and I (Smetana & Daddis, 2002) examined associations between psychological control (measured by using a standard scale) and teenag-ers' beliefs about legitimate parental authority to control acts in different domains. We also examined parents' restrictive control over different types of issues. Authority beliefs and restrictive parental control influenced teenagers' perceptions of parental psychological control, but only when the adolescents' authority beliefs and perceptions of restrictive control pertained to personal and multifaceted issues. That is, adolescents perceived their parents as psychologically more con-trolling when parents wielded more control over personal and multifaceted issues (but not when they restricted moral and conventional issues) and when teenagers believed that their parents should have less authority over these issues. We found this association in early adolescence and, even more convincingly, it was main-tained over time. Parents' more restrictive control of personal and multifaceted issues, combined with adolescents' rejection of this control, predicted higher per-ceptions of psychological control 2 years later. But parental psychological control was only associated with teenagers' perceptions of how much authority and control parents had, or should have, over personal areas of their lives.

This state of things highlights the importance of considering parental psycho-logical control in a developmental framework. The results of our study (Smetana & Daddis, 2002) provide a developmentally sensitive and domain-specific analysis of situations where adolescents might perceive their parents as employing psycho-logical control. We have seen that the teenagers' notion of what should be per-sonal expands with age. Likewise, there are corresponding age-related changes in adolescents' perceptions of appropriate parenting versus overcontrol of their behavior. What adolescents perceive as psychologically controlling behavior – the specific issues that parents regulate – changes during adolescence, as the personal domain expands.

Part of the challenge of parenting early adolescents is that parents must strike a delicate balance between exercising sufficient guidance and structuring to keep their children safe and imposing what teenagers perceive as too much control over personal issues. We have just seen that adolescents view the latter as psychologi-cally intrusive and coercive. Adding to this difficulty is the fact that teenagers and parents do not necessarily agree in their views of what constitutes psychological control and of when it is being employed.

Adolescents' perceptions of parental control and overcontrol have implica-tions for these teens' psychosocial adjustment. Perceived parental intrusion into the adolescents' personal freedom has potentially deleterious effects on their mental health. That is, teenagers who view their parents as more restrictive of their personal domains report more severe depression and anxiety. But psychiatric symptoms are not associated with greater parental rules and restrictions over prudential and conventional issues (Hasebe, Nucci, & Nucci, 2004). Adding further weight to these findings, the association between parental overcontrol and depressive symptoms has been observed among adolescents from both the United States and Japan. Therefore, as Barber has found in his cross-cultural investigation of psychological control, these effects appear to transcend the specific cultural context. At the same time, there may be some minor cultural variations in the ways in which particular items are viewed, as well as in associations between internalizing symptoms and parental control.

Hasebe and her colleagues validated their measures before employing them in the two countries. They only included items that were valid in both cultural contexts. As a reflection of cultural differences, one item, "who my boyfriend or girlfriend is," was treated as personal by American middle-class youth, but as multifaceted by Japanese youth. American teenagers progress rather seamlessly from same-sex friendships to opposite-sex friendships and to dating. They are typically involved in romantic relationships by middle adolescence. Although these romantic relationships are not as fleeting in middle adolescence as is often assumed, they are not seen as leading to serious commitments either. American adolescents therefore treat dating as a natural extension of friendship. In Japan, however, dating is a more serious affair, which signals the entry into a more committed relationship. Japanese youth evaluated this item differently because they were aware of the psychological risks of entering too casually or carelessly into such relationships. In addition, greater perceived parental control over overlapping (multifaceted) issues was also associated with psychiatric symptoms for Japanese adolescents, but not for American adolescents – which reflects perhaps the more encompassing reach of parental regulation and control in Japan (Rothbaum, Pott, Azuma, Miyake, & Weisz, 2000).

When does appropriate control become overcontrol? The foregoing discussion suggests that what is perceived as reasonable limits at one age might be seen as being too restrictive as the adolescent matures.

Ethnic and cultural variations in parenting styles and parental control

The question about the balance between appropriate regulation and overcontrol is pertinent in the context of an ongoing debate about parenting and parental control among American ethnic minority youth. The debate has been framed in terms of whether Baumrind's model of parenting styles is broadly applicable to youth of different cultures and ethnicities and whether authoritative parenting confers the same advantages among diverse groups of youth. Laurence Steinberg (2001) asserts that research from around the world demonstrates the beneficial effects of authoritative parenting for all youth. After examining the available research, he concluded that authoritative parenting is particularly effective in facilitating healthy adjustment in some areas (for instance, it protects youth from engaging in deviant behavior and it promotes psychosocial development and mental health) – but not in others. Thus, among diverse youth, authoritative parenting does not have consistently positive effects on academic achievement.

Authoritative parenting is more prevalent among European American parents than among ethnic minority parents in the United States – or among parents in many other cultures. Nevertheless, American youth from African, Asian, and Latino backgrounds all perceive their parents as being more authoritarian than European American adolescents do. The greater reliance on psychological control is part of what distinguishes authoritarian from authoritative parenting. But the negative consequences of authoritarian parenting do not appear to be as great for African American and Asian American youth as they are for youth from other ethnic groups (although such parenting does not positively impact on their adjustment).

Some researchers have claimed that Baumrind's parenting styles are derived from a culturally specific model of beliefs and that, in consequence, the model may not generalize well beyond European American youth. Ruth Chao (1994, 1995) argues that authoritarian parenting does not capture the essence of Chinese parenting or, more broadly, the values of Asian parenting. She asserts that control and restrictiveness are characteristic of Chinese families. This reflects a different set of underlying beliefs from those that hold among European American families. Chinese parenting reflects, namely, beliefs about role relationships as defined by Confucianism. For Chinese parents, strictness is rooted in the notion of training (*chiao shun* and *guan*) and with concerns about educating children in the appropriate behavior. This involves devotion and sacrifice on the part of the mother, so that the child may learn to meet societal expectations. Chinese parents are highly involved in child rearing, and they love and care for their children.

For European American families, however, strictness is located in Protestant Christian beliefs and takes a more punitive turn. Authoritarian parenting originating in Christian ideology aims to dominate or control the child, whereas Chao suggests that, for Chinese parents, strictness is in the service of training the child and of assuring harmonious relationships with others. Therefore Chao argues that parenting styles arrived at by studying North American parents cannot be simply translated into other cultures. Instead, parenting styles must reflect their sociocultural contexts.

Similar concerns can be raised about the nature of African American parenting. As discussed in Chapter 8, African American parenting is typically described as authoritarian, based as it is on the use of strict, parent-centered, and sometimes harsh discipline. Families are described as making decisions without any input from adolescents (although my research shows that, in African American middle-class families, parent decision-making is the norm only for conventional and prudential issues, and only as reported by mothers: Smetana, Campione-Barr, &

Daddis, 2004). Parent decision-making may be an adaptive response to the threatening environments that African American families often face. Living in unsafe environments may pose particular threats for families who also live in poverty. But having higher incomes, more prestigious jobs, or living in safer neighborhoods does not protect African American adolescents from the pervasive risks of racism and prejudice. These are threats that all African Americans face (recall the example in Chapter 8 of DWB – "driving while black"). Therefore the parents' greater strictness and behavioral regulation may protect children from harm. Indeed, parent-unilateral decision-making – that is, situations where parents make decisions without any input from the child – has positive effects in African American families regardless of their socioeconomic status (Lamborn, Dornbusch, & Steinberg, 1996).

As discussed in Chapter 8, middle-class African American parents use strict discipline. They exact respect and obedience from their children, as one might expect from authoritarian parents, and they set firm guidelines. But they encourage their teenagers' self-reliance and independence about many things, as one might expect from authoritative parents. African American teenagers perceive their parents as supportive, loving, and warm, which is also consistent with authoritative parenting. Strictness is in the service of the children's needs and corresponds to the parents' perceptions of the risks to their children from the larger social world. As the examples in Chapter 8 illustrate, African American parents are clearly concerned with their teenagers' well-being and future success. Therefore describing African American parents as authoritarian provides a limited and incomplete picture. In many ways, their parenting entails a mixture of authoritative and authoritarian elements.

Indeed, this is what I found when I tried to categorize African American parents according to their dominant parenting style. I used responses to the same questionnaire measure I had used successfully when studying European American families (Smetana, 1995a). This survey includes separate scales of authoritarian, authoritative, and permissive parenting (Buri, 1989, 1991). When I applied these scales to the responses received from European American parents and adolescents, the items cohered in the expected way, the scales were highly reliable, and parents could be categorized as having a dominant parenting style. But this did not work with the African American parents' responses to the same survey. The items did not cohere into the same scales, and the scales that emerged empirically from the analyses – particularly for permissive parenting – were not statistically reliable. The majority of African American families could not be categorized as endorsing a single parenting style. Most parents received high scores on both authoritarian and authoritative parenting. Thus, when examined both quantitatively and qualitatively, these parents' responses defied easy categorization.

As I described earlier, African American parents acknowledge the need for firm limits around some issues and the need for children to comply with parents' wishes. At the same time, they recognize children's developing desires for independence and their need to develop self-reliance. Gene Brody and Douglas Flor (1998) describe poor, rural African American parents as employing "no-nonsense parenting." In their view, this refers to parenting that is nonpunitive, demanding, and warm, but where parents have considerable authority and do not negotiate or solicit input from the child. This model comes much closer to the mixed kind of parenting we observed in African American middle-class parents than the description of parents as authoritarian does, although it does not adequately recognize the parents' concerns with the adolescents' developing independence.

This discussion of Asian and African American parenting highlights the different meaning that particular parenting practices may have in different contexts. Practices that appear strict or even harsh to an outside observer or on an objective measure may not be perceived as such from within the family or social group. Of course, this underscores the fact that the meaning of particular social acts is not given in the act itself. Meaning is constructed in different social contexts. Individuals actively interpret their social experiences and make sense of them in light of their past experiences and beliefs about the social world.

One approach to these concerns is to re-conceptualize parenting styles as broad contexts that foster different emotional climates in the family. This is the approach that Nancy Darling and Laurence Steinberg (1993) adopt. They propose that parenting styles create different psychological environments, which change the meaning of particular, isolated parenting practices. In their view, the same parenting practice could have different effects if parents endorsing a different parenting style deployed it. For instance, the same parenting practices in the emotional climate of authoritarian or of indulgent parenting may have different meanings for the child, and therefore have different consequences for adjustment. In a technical sense, then, Darling and Steinberg elaborate on Baumrind's model so as to view parenting styles as changing (or moderating) the effects of different parenting practices on children's adjustment. Their new model still embraces the notion of parenting styles, but also underscores the need to take into the picture the child's interpretations of parents' actions.

Many scholars have expressed concerns about the usefulness of broad parenting styles, or parenting "traits." Along with others (Grusec, Goodnow, & Kuczynski, 2000; Grusec & Goodnow, 1994; Turiel, 2005), Eleanor Maccoby (2007), one of the pioneers of psychological research on parenting and socialization, notes that the model does not take into consideration a myriad of factors, such as the characteristics of the child, the situation, the parents' varying goals in different situations, and the children's interpretations of their parents' actions. Parenting styles capture a great deal of information about parenting in a parsimonious and easily comprehensible way. Yet, as with the categories of individualism and collectivism, this parsimony may be achieved at the expense of specificity. We saw in Chapter 4 that children, adolescents, and adults have qualitatively different responses to different types of situations, including moral, conventional, personal, and prudential ones. The contexts in which these responses occur, the type of response, and who responds vary for different types of transgressions. In a similar vein, we can question whether parents have a consistent style of interaction across all situations. They may behave strictly, even harshly and angrily, when prudential concerns are at stake and they fear for their child's safety. However, they may take time to reason and negotiate in a warm and responsive manner about other issues. In other words, parents respond differently to different types of acts. They take into account the domain of the situation.

In addition, as Joan Grusec and her colleagues (Grusec et al., 2000; Grusec & Davidov, 2007; Grusec & Goodnow, 1994) have argued, it is essential that children perceive accurately what parents are saying. This depends on the parents' ability to communicate in a way that is comprehensible and appropriate for the child's level of understanding. Parents must also consider children's cognitive abilities, their ability to interpret and read emotional cues, and their psychological understanding – for instance whether they can understand others' intentions. Reciprocally, children respond differently to parents' actions depending on their interpretation of situations – for instance whether they view them as entailing moral, conventional, or psychological concerns. Factors such as cognitive abilities, temperament, and mood also come into play. We saw earlier that children respond to the domain-appropriateness of adult messages. And, as we shall see, individuals' interpretations of situations are complex. They rest to some extent on their factual beliefs and informational assumptions.

Contextual variations and informational assumptions

Another way to conceptualize ethnic, cultural, and other group variations in parenting is to consider them in light of these groups' different beliefs about the nature of the child, the efficacy of different child-rearing practices, and the social world more generally. Varying beliefs and informational assumptions about children, development, and the best way to achieve desired child-rearing goals may change the meaning of child-rearing practices, or may even lead to different practices. For instance, to use the example offered in Chapter 4, if one were to believe that spanking is beneficial for child development, spanking might become the preferred way to gain compliance with parental rules and prohibitions. In this case spanking would be an intentional act, but it would not necessarily be morally wrong. Others, however, may view spanking, or corporal punishment more generally, as ineffective. Indeed, it may be seen as psychologically and physically damaging to the child. In this case spanking would be seen as a moral violation and as a practice to be shunned. Whether one considers corporal punishment to be morally reprehensible or not depends in part on whether one believes that it is an efficacious or necessary way to teach children about societal expectations. Different groups vary in these beliefs, which sometimes leads to deeply contested arguments about best practices for child rearing.

Individuals may have similar moral beliefs about the permissibility (or lack of permissibility) of inflicting harm on others. But they may vary in their informational assumptions about child rearing and about the efficacy of spanking (or, for that matter, shaming) as a teaching method. Research has shown that manipulating these informational assumptions changes the meaning of the acts, and hence the individuals' moral evaluations of them (Wainryb, 1991). It follows that different factual beliefs may inform parenting practices. For instance, we saw that the greater use of spanking among African American than among European American families reflects beliefs about the efficacy and acceptance of this practice.

A study by Jennifer Lansford and her colleagues (Lansford et al., 2005) sheds light on this issue. These researchers demonstrated that cultural differences in what is considered fair, reasonable, and appropriate parental discipline can be understood in terms of differences in informational assumptions. The team examined how the cultural normativeness of different disciplinary practices changed the influence of physical discipline on children's adjustment. The researchers conducted interviews with mothers and their 6- to 17-year-old children in China, India, Italy, Kenya, the Philippines, and Thailand. These countries vary widely in their use of physical discipline as a matter of norm. The interviews focused on mothers' disciplinary practices, including physical discipline (spanking or slapping, grabbing or shaking, and beating), and also on how typical these practices were in the culture.

When children were exposed to frequent acts of physical correction and disciplining, they were more anxious regardless of the cultural context. Moreover, in countries where physical discipline was very much the norm, children were more aggressive regardless of their own personal experiences of receiving physical discipline. This demonstrates clearly that physical discipline, particularly in its more extreme forms, has adverse effects on children's development. But, as expected, children's perception of how normative physical discipline was altered its effects on their adjustment. When physical discipline was more frequently employed and a characteristic form of discipline in a particular country, the adverse effects, including aggression and anxiety, were less extreme. Informational assumptions changed the meaning of the practice, at least to some extent. Children were more likely to attribute physical discipline to good and caring parenting. When the practice was seen as normative, its negative effects on adjustment were lessened, although they still existed. (Note that much of the current debate about corporal punishment focuses on spanking on the buttocks, not on more extreme forms, like shaking and beating.)

As Lansford and her colleagues note, there are many parental practices and behaviors that do not appear to have detrimental effects on children's adjustment, even though observers from other cultural contexts might consider them to be harmful. For instance, as these researchers describe, initiation rites performed at puberty in traditional cultures may involve cutting and scarring. There are folk remedies for illness that may leave burns. In American culture, practices like ear and body piercing, tattooing, and male circumcision all physically hurt children and adolescents in the short-term and have long-term consequences for one's appearance. However, they are not considered to have detrimental effects on adjustment. (Indeed, cosmetic practices like piercings and tattooing are meant to enhance physical attractiveness, and hence to facilitate positive adjustment.) When we evaluate practices in other cultures, we often struggle to coordinate our moral judgments about harm with the need to respect alien cultural traditions and beliefs.

These studies show that, in addition to considering overcontrol in a developmental context, we must also consider the cultural context of beliefs and behaviors. We now turn to a consideration of how much regulation – over what types of issues and at what ages – is healthy for adolescent development.

Parental Undercontrol

Lack of parental involvement in adolescents' decision-making is deleterious for adolescent development. Researchers studying adolescents' participation in family decision-making have distinguished between "youth-alone" decision-making (where adolescents make decisions without any parental input), and "parent-unilateral" decision-making, where parents make decisions without any adolescent input. These are two extremes on a continuum. Joint decision-making, where teens or parents jointly decide, falls in-between (Dornbusch, Ritter, Mont-Reynaud, & Chen, 1990; Fuligni & Eccles, 1993; Gutman & Eccles, 2007; Lamborn et al., 1996). Modes of decision-making have been further differentiated to include situations where decisions are made either with parental or with adolescent guidance. (Some studies have treated these modes as part of joint decision-making; others have treated them as steps along the continuum.)

There is conclusive evidence, from diverse samples, that youth-alone decision-making, particularly during early adolescence, has negative consequences for adolescents' adjustment and development.[1] These negative effects are wide-ranging. They include low levels of self-reliance, of self-esteem, and of work orientation, and greater levels of deviance, for instance drug and alcohol use, school misconduct, and antisocial behavior. They also include poorer performance in the academic arena, including lower grades, lower academic expectations, and less time spent on homework.

Nevertheless, the negative effects of youth-alone decision-making depend on the ethnic and racial composition of the community. For instance, youth-alone decision-making has more negative consequences for Latino youth growing up in ethnically mixed communities than for those growing up in predominantly White communities. For African American teenagers, instead, the opposite is true: youth-alone decision-making has a more negative impact on African American adolescents living in White communities than on those living in ethnically mixed communities. We can speculate that there may be more of a safety net, in terms of community involvement in child rearing, for African American adolescents who live in neighborhoods that are more heavily African American.

Family decision-making varies, depending on the domain of the issue involved (Hasebe et al., 2004; Smetana, Campione-Barr et al., 2004). In general, teenagers' role in family decision-making increases as they grow older. But teenagers' independent decision-making also proceeds at different rates for different types of issues. Typically, parents have more input into decisions regarding conventional and prudential issues than in decisions about personal and multifaceted issues. This is especially the case in early adolescence. The greatest tilt towards adolescent autonomy is over personal issues. This pattern of development is similar to the one we found in beliefs about legitimate parental authority.

My study of African American families, discussed at length in Chapter 8, shows that the negative effects of youth-alone decision-making may be domain-specific. For middle-class African American youth there were wide-ranging negative consequences of making completely independent decisions over multifaceted issues in early adolescence. Early adolescents who constructed the boundaries of their authority more broadly and reported great or total autonomy in making decisions about multifaceted issues also reported lower self-worth, poorer academic performance, and greater deviance. In addition, greater decision-making power over conventional standards and safety (prudential) issues in early adolescence was linked with lower self-worth. When early adolescents have greater independence from parents in making decisions over issues like staying out late, going to places without their parents' knowledge, and spending time with romantic partners, they may take advantage of their freedom and engage in behaviors that could get them in trouble. Moreover, community context (specifically, the racial composition of the neighborhood) influenced outcomes in much the same way as Lamborn and her colleagues found. More youth-alone decision-making over multifaceted and personal issues in early adolescence had more negative effects for African American youth living in more homogeneously White communities (as measured by the racial composition of their census tract) than for African American youth living in more racially mixed communities. This may reflect the potentially greater risks of racism and prejudice for African Americans living in more integrated communities. There are fewer risks of "driving while black" incidents if almost everyone in the neighborhood is black.

Greater teen-alone decision-making in the early adolescent years influenced middle-class African American teenagers' adjustment 5 years later, at least for personal issues. According to both adolescents' and mothers' reports, adolescents who had greater decision-making autonomy over personal issues in early adolescence reported higher levels of depressed mood 5 years later. However, it is interesting to note that the negative effects of early adolescent autonomy over multifaceted issues did not persist into late adolescence. I will discuss long-term influences on healthy adjustment in the following section.

Healthy adjustment

In the much-loved fairy tale of Goldilocks and the Three Bears, Goldilocks wanders into the three bears' empty house and sees three bowls of porridge. Deciding that she is hungry, she tastes the porridge from all three bowls. The porridge in the first bowl is too hot, the porridge in the second bowl is too cold, but the third is just right. Likewise, we have seen that too much parental control of personal issues may be perceived as too intrusive. On the other hand, too little parental regulation and involvement leads to deviance and depression. How much is just right? The answer is complex because, as the foregoing discussion suggests, it varies according to age (which is a marker of developmental maturity) and according to the type of act for which control is asserted or autonomy is sought. Within general normal patterns, it also varies according to the social context, including the cultural, ethnic and racial, and socioeconomic niche.

One clue about healthy autonomy-granting comes from my study of African American families. As discussed before, too much independent decision-making over personal issues in early adolescence has deleterious long-term effects on the adolescents' adjustment. But, both for this set of issues and for multifaceted ones, increases in autonomous decision-making from middle to late adolescence lead to better self-worth and less depression. Overall, "holding the brakes" in autonomy-granting over personal and multifaceted issues in early adolescence and then allowing gradually more decision-making input in middle to late adolescence turned out to be maximally adaptive for middle-class African American adolescents' psychosocial adjustment.

Do these findings generalize to youth of different cultures or ethnicities? There is evidence to suggest that this general developmental pattern can be applied more broadly. However, there are some slight variations in the timing of autonomy and in the relationships between autonomy and adjustment in different cultural and ethnic contexts.

This assertion is based on several sources. One source is the studies of the desired pacing of behavioral autonomy discussed in an earlier chapter. These studies show that adolescents from different cultural and ethnic groups follow a similar pattern of age-related changes in their expectations for autonomy. Autonomy proceeds by being gained first over personal issues, then over multifaceted issues, and later over prudential issues. However, the time when autonomy is expected to settle over each of these kinds of matter varies both within and across cultures (Feldman & Rosenthal, 1990; Fuligni, 1998; Zhang & Fuligni, 2006). For example, in studying different ethnic groups in the United States, one finds that European American adolescents generally expect autonomy at earlier ages than Chinese American youth do (Fuligni, 1998). However, this difference disappears with acculturation (that is, with the increasing number of generations in which adolescents or their parents were born in the United States). As successive generations of Chinese families grow up in the United States, they begin to resemble European American families more and more.

Recently there have been several research studies employing sophisticated longitudinal designs to compare the developmental pathways of family decision-making among youth from different ethnic, racial, or cultural groups. For instance, Leslie Gutman and Jacquelynne Eccles (2007) compared growth in family decision-making opportunities (unfortunately assessed by the criterion of only one general item) among African American and European American early adolescent boys and girls. They tracked adolescents over 5 years, from when they were 13 years old until they reached 19 years of age. They found that African American and European American boys and girls followed similar developmental paths. Regardless of ethnicity or gender, the average teenager experienced increased opportunities to make independent decisions from the age of 13 up until the age of 19. For all youth, decision-making typically involved input from parents rather than complete independence. However, there were group differences in the developmental norms. European American middle adolescents (15-year-olds) had greater opportunities to participate in decision-making than African American teens had at the same age. The greatest gains in decision-making opportunities occurred at later ages for girls than for boys, which perhaps reflected parents' concerns about the particular risks that girls face.

Like myself, Gutman and Eccles found in their study that African American youth who were given increased decision-making opportunities from middle to late adolescence showed better adjustment. More specifically, they reported less depression. For European American youth, however, the opposite was true. Increased decision-making opportunities from middle to late adolescence led to more depression. The European American middle adolescents already had higher average levels of decision-making opportunities compared to African Americans at that age. The researchers speculated that gaining more autonomy on top of the already high levels that European American middle adolescents enjoyed may have had negative consequences for their adjustment. This appeared to be the case even when the pacing of this process was the same as for African Americans. When autonomy is already high, increasing the opportunities for independent decision-making may result in developmentally inappropriate levels of autonomy. Unfortunately, because this study did not sample different domains, we cannot pinpoint the types of issues where "too much" autonomy has deleterious effects. We can speculate, though, that this pertains to prudential and conventional rather than personal issues.

Gutman and Eccles's study offers a useful comparison between African American and European American boys and girls around the changes that occur over time in family decision-making. But these researchers did not explore the very different types of decisions that adolescents may make. We must turn elsewhere to understand how decision-making differs across domains. Researchers Laura Wray-Lake, Susan McHale, and Nan Crouter (2010) provide such an analysis, although only for European American youth. They examined the growth of autonomy in family decision-making for different types of issues. They followed children longitudinally from age 9 to age 20. Overall, the normal trend was that, from late childhood (ages 9 to 11) on, teenagers gradually had more input into family decision-making. Increases stayed relatively flat during early adolescence (ages 11 to 13), then went up steadily from the age of 13 to the age of 15. Adolescents' input into family decisions increased rapidly in middle to late adolescence. Therefore it appears that, at least among European American middle-class youth, greater autonomy in decision-making is achieved in middle to late adolescence. The norm in this sample was that families engaged in joint decision-making until their offspring were aged 18. Then there was a shift towards more self-governed decision-making on the part of the teens.

However, these researchers only examined the parents' reports on family decision-making. Parents generally provide more conservative estimates of adolescents' autonomy than adolescents themselves do. For instance, when parents report that decisions are made jointly, teenagers are likely to say that they made these decisions with some parental input. When parents report that teens make decisions with their input, adolescents view those decisions as made by themselves alone; and so on. Hence it is likely that Wray-Lake and her colleagues' study overestimates the parents' involvement in family decision-making, as compared to what their adolescent offspring may report.

The age-related trajectories were relatively similar across different issues. However, the amount of autonomy adolescents achieved at each age varied for different types of issues. As we might expect on the basis of the earlier discussion, parents perceived teenagers as having the greatest autonomy over personal issues and the least autonomy over conventional and prudential issues. Multifaceted issues fell in-between. Children who were more open to supervision in middle childhood were granted more autonomy as they grew up. This is because parents who perceive their adolescent children as being easier to supervise may believe that they are ready to assume more autonomy.

Lili Qin, Eva Pomerantz, and Qian Wang (2009) provide further elaboration on these themes. The three researchers followed Chinese early adolescents in Beijing and (primarily) European American early adolescents in Chicago every 6th month for 2 years. They examined the influence on emotional functioning of the early adolescents' autonomy to make decisions about personal and multifaceted issues. Emotional functioning was defined broadly, so as to include life satisfaction, self-esteem, and positive emotions, as well as negative emotions and anxiety.

Like others, Qin and her colleagues found that, with age, both American and Chinese urban adolescents reported increases in their decision-making autonomy. Parent decision-making declined across early adolescence, both for American and for Chinese children. However, the two cultures differed with respect to the type of decision-making that was developmentally expected. Both American and Chinese children made decisions mostly on their own or with some parental input. (This seems to contradict what Wray-Lake and her colleagues reported, but remember that the latter examined parent reports only.) However, this was true to a greater extent among American than among Chinese children. American early adolescents shifted away from greater parental input towards making more decisions on their own (or with reduced parental input). Chinese early adolescents replaced parental control over decision-making with more jointly made decisions. The differences between American and Chinese children's autonomous decision-making became accentuated as they moved through 7th and 8th grade and American children increasingly made decisions on their own.

For both Chinese and American youth, gains in decision-making autonomy in early adolescence had a similar, positive influence on emotional adjustment. The more the parent decision-making decreased over time, the better the children's emotional functioning was. More specifically, as we might expect at these ages, joint decision-making led to better emotional functioning, whereas parent decision-making led to worse emotional functioning over time. However, increases in child decision-making (either by the child alone or with parental input) during early adolescence enhanced emotional functioning more for American than for Chinese children. This is because American children typically experience relatively large increases in autonomy, whereas, for urban Chinese children, such increases are typically relatively small. Nevertheless, Chinese children's emotional functioning suffered if Chinese parents did not loosen up. If Chinese parents continued to make decisions for their offspring, there were negative consequences for the Chinese adolescents' psychosocial health.

Summary and Conclusions

Diana Baumrind's influential research on parenting styles can be revisited in terms of different domains of parental authority. But research reviewed previously on adults' and children's responses to different types of transgressions raises concerns about whether parents are consistent in their style of parenting. Parents respond with differently strategies depending on the situation; they not consistent in their parenting style. Questions have also been raised about whether parenting styles have the same meaning across cultures and ethnic groups. Furthermore, recent research has focused on differentiating forms of control. Psychological control can be defined as overcontrol of the personal domain, which has been linked to internalizing distress.

This chapter also considered the question of how much autonomy is appropriate during adolescence. The definitive answer appears to be: it depends. That is, it depends on the age of the child, the domain of the issue, and the sociocultural context. The context may change the meaning of behaviors, due to cultural variations in beliefs. It may also alter the risks or the opportunities and affordances of the environment. Behaviors that reflect simple personal choices in one environment may be fraught with danger in another.

Despite all of these qualifiers, there are some unambiguous trends. The evidence indicates that making decisions without any input from parents in early and middle adolescence has clear negative consequences for teenagers' psychosocial adjustment. This is the case even when decisions pertain to personal issues. Early and middle adolescents who are allowed to make decisions about personal as well as multifaceted issues on their own, without any parental guidance or input, report lower self-worth and more deviance. Continued parental involvement in these decisions, in the form of joint decision-making or parental guidance and input, is important for healthy adjustment, at least through middle adolescence.

This may seem to contradict much of what has been said in the previous chapters about the importance of personal choice. But in my view it is not. Adolescents' appeals to personal preferences and choice have an important developmental function. But we have also seen that, although adolescents push for more autonomy in situations of conflict or negotiation, parents typically decide how much, and what types of, autonomy to grant to their children (Daddis & Smetana, 2005). Parents are ultimately "the deciders." Effective parenting does not mean that younger adolescents should make all of their decisions, even about personal issues, without some parental knowledge or input. Nor does it mean, on the other hand, that adolescents must seek parental approval each time they choose which sweater to wear, what book to read, or how to comb their hair. Effective parenting implies that parents are available, knowledgeable, and generally informed as to adolescents' choices and that they help to structure and guide their offspring appropriately. They need to be supportive of adolescents' needs for autonomy, even if they somewhat limit adolescents' options. When an adolescent makes decisions alone, without any overall parental involvement, knowledge, or guidance, this may reflect unhealthy detachment on the teen's part. It could also reflect overly permissive, or even neglectful parenting. In any case, the results demonstrate that is important for adolescents to enjoy autonomy over personal issues, but to have it in the context of support and guidance – until later on in adolescence, when they are competent to make decisions completely on their own. Wray-Lake and her colleagues' (2010) study suggests that this moment may occur in late adolescence.

This is in keeping with recent theorizing about autonomy, which has focused on the self-governance of behavior in the context of supportive guidance, relational ties, and social commitments (Collins, Gleason, & Sesma, 1997; Zimmer-Gembeck & Collins, 2003). The claim is that behavioral autonomy "pertains not to freedom *from* others (e.g., parents), but freedom *to* carry out actions on one's own behalf while maintaining appropriate connections to others" (Collins et al.,

1997, p. 78). Adolescent development appears to be facilitated when adolescents are allowed to express and make their own choices with some parental awareness and communication. This may be particularly important in areas or about issues where the boundaries of personal jurisdiction are shifting, hence in flux, and where new freedoms are being granted or mastered. However, the timing and level of autonomy-granting varies somewhat for different ethnic and cultural groups.

At the same time, too much parental involvement in decision-making, particularly in later adolescence and over decisions in the personal domain, has its own set of risks. It denies adolescents the opportunity to learn new skills, make choices, develop competence, and act independently. And research clearly shows that too much parental involvement is associated with psychosocial maladjustment, particularly reflected in internalizing problems. There are also individual variations within families (as a consequence of siblings' ordinal position in the family) and across families (as a consequence of parenting and peer relationships).

In this chapter I have shown that, with age, adolescents become more involved and have more of a "say" in family decision-making. Nevertheless, these changes do not occur as rapidly as adolescents would like; teenagers typically desire more autonomy than they are granted. But it is not always the case that autonomy comes from the parents' bestowing or allowing it. In the next chapter we shall consider some ways in which adolescents may take things into their own hands and use more subversive tactics to gain more autonomy.

Note

1   It is worth noting that youth-alone decision-making differs from premature adolescent autonomy, which also has negative effects. Premature adolescent autonomy refers to a process whereby adolescents' increasing involvement with deviant peers, accompanied by parents' disengagement from family management and guidance, leads to increased problem behavior (Dishion, Nelson, & Bullock, 2004).

11

Disclosure and Secrecy in Adolescent–Parent Relationships

Movies depicting American popular culture frequently focus on the lives of teenagers as they interact with their peers. Parents are typically absent. When they do figure in the plot, they are often portrayed as clueless or incompetent. For instance, like many other movies of this genre, the 2004 hit movie *Mean Girls* focuses on one adolescent's relationships with different peer groups, in the context of an American high school. The main character, Cady, moves to the United States after spending her childhood – and being schooled at home – in Africa. This device in the plot gives her an outsider's view of American teen culture. Cady becomes part of an exclusive group of girls, called the "plastics." Unbeknownst to her parents, she hosts a party at her parents' house while they are away. When her mother finds some of her favorite objects tucked away under the kitchen sink (hidden so that they would not get harmed during the party), Cady lies about why they are there. Her parents also do not know that Cady, who normally excels at math, is deliberately failing her math class that semester. This portrayal of Cady's experiences, rife as it is with nondisclosure, deception, and lying, is typical of the plot of many popular teen movies. But does it accurately reflect the reality of Western (or even just American) teenagers' lives?

Deception and Lying

Until recently, the research relevant to this issue focused narrowly on lying. According to some sources, lying to parents is relatively common during adolescence. The Josephson Institute administered a survey about honesty and integrity to nearly 30,000 students in high schools across the United States. The results were discussed in a recently issued Report Card on the Ethics of American Youth

Adolescents, Families, and Social Development: How Teens Construct Their Worlds. Judith G. Smetana
© 2011 Judith G. Smetana

(Josephson Institute, 2008). In their overview of the results, the authors stated that the findings show "entrenched habits of dishonesty" that are at alarmingly high rates. Nearly 80% of the sample reported lying to parents about "something significant" at least once in the past year. More than half of the students reported lying to parents two or more times a year. Similar results have been obtained in studies of smaller, less representative samples of adolescents. For instance, Lene Jensen and her colleagues (Jensen, Arnett, Feldman, & Cauffman, 2004) found that nearly all high school students in their European American middle-class convenience sample reported lying to parents at least once during the past year, about one out of the following seven issues: money, friends, sexual behavior, friends, parties, dating, and alcohol and illegal drug use. High school students viewed lying to parents as more acceptable than college students did. Boys viewed lying to parents as more acceptable than girls did.

Does this represent an "alarming trend," as the team from the Josephson Institute claims? In fact, the Josephson report also showed that the overwhelming majority of the adolescents surveyed were of the view that it does not pay to lie or cheat, because doing so hurts one's character. And nearly all adolescents agreed that it is important to have people who trust you. Adolescents, both in the Josephson Institute survey and in Jensen and her colleagues' study, reported lying on average once or twice a year. So one might very well ask: Why was the rate of lying so low? After all, survey research and more intensive research studies have shown that adults lie a great deal, and in a variety of circumstances. In a daily diary study of lying in everyday life, social psychologist Bella DePaulo and her colleagues (DePaulo, Kashy, Kirkendol, Wyer, & Epstein, 1996) found that adults reported telling anywhere between zero and 46 lies a week. And a recent survey of the readers of *Redbook* magazine showed that 84% of those surveyed admitted to lying to their children at least once a month (Scher, 2009). The lies ranged from innocuous ("the tooth fairy was too busy to come last night," or "we're out of Twinkies") to more serious ones ("Fluffy went to live on a farm"). The author of the article condemned lying (and indeed quoted developmental psychologist Nancy Darling on its potentially deleterious effects on trust in parent–adolescent relationships). But the author also noted that "a judiciously deployed lie is as much a part of a mother's arsenal as hand sanitizer and string cheese." In discussing these survey results, *New York Times* columnist and parenting blogger Lisa Belkin (2009, February 24) noted that most of the time, when parents lie to children, they are not really "flat-out" lying; rather they are being kind, protective, or simplifying the truth until the child is developmentally mature enough to grasp it.

But these examples underscore the moral ambiguity of lying. Moral philosopher Sissela Bok (1989) asserts that there is a very strong moral presumption against lying, because lying undermines social trust. It would be difficult to live in a society where one could never trust the information one reads or receives. Yet, observes Bok, very few philosophers have taken an absolutist position on truth telling. Most have acknowledged that there are cases – such as when innocent lives are at stake – where lying is morally justified. For instance, if a murderer is running past, is one morally obligated to tell him (or her) which way the intended victim ran? One criterion for evaluating whether deception or lying is acceptable is to consider instances where other reasonable people in different roles and circumstances would endorse the lie if they knew about it.

This notion of role switch, or reversal, is particularly difficult to put to work in parent–child relationships, because the power balance is unequal. Annette Baier (1986), another moral philosopher, claims that, in hierarchical relationships, individuals of lower status (and hence with less power) are much more restricted than individuals of higher status in their ability to enter freely into voluntary agreements and to trust that the other will keep an agreement. These situations entail a reliance on others' good will. In an interview with *Washington Post* writer Shankar Verdantam (Vendantam, 2007, February 19), psychologist Bella DePaulo described a study in which she asked people to recall the worst lie they had ever told and the worst lie ever told them. She noted that perceptions of lying relied heavily on individuals' particular point of view. Many young people reported that the worst lie ever told them came from a parent who was concealing news that someone they loved was sick or dying. Parents, however, rarely saw these types of instances as serious ethical breaches. Rather, they saw them as acts of love and compassion.

Although parents may lie to children for other-oriented reasons, as DePaulo's example suggests, children's lies to parents typically are self-serving. When individuals have been asked to report on a daily basis about their relationships, research has found that, in general, people lie much less often in emotionally close relationships (for instance with close friends or romantic partners) than in more distant social relationships (such as acquaintances or strangers). Lying to mothers, however, was the exception. College students reported lying to mothers in one out of every two social interactions, a rate that was considerably higher than the frequency of lies told to close friends and romantic partners (DePaulo & Kashy, 1998; Kashy & DePaulo, 1996). Lies told to mothers were twice as likely to be self-centered ("she'd kill me if she thought I wasn't studying") than other-oriented ("I didn't want her to feel bad"). Like Baier, the researchers attributed this phenomenon to the asymmetrical nature of parent–child relationships. When individuals have less power in the relationship, they may resort to deception and lying to get what they want. Recall that this was also what Perkins and Turiel (2007) found in their study of lying, discussed in the previous chapter. They found that adolescents reported a greater willingness to lie to parents than to friends, particularly when they felt their personal choices were restricted.

In fact, outright lying has been associated with tolerance of deviance, association with deviant peers, and actual deviance. Frequent lying is considered a symptom of conduct disorder. But lying is not the only form of deception. Although research shows that there is a strong statistical association between lying and secrecy, these two forms of behavior are clearly not identical. In the movie

Mean Girls, the protagonist, Cady, engages in several forms of deception. She lies to her parents, but she also simply does not tell them about some of her behavior, like failing math or hosting a party. As this example suggests, lying may be the most egregious form, but it is not the only way in which adolescents can get what they want in their relationships with parents. There are other strategies adolescents use in order to "manage" information about who their companions are, what they are doing, and where they are going when they are away from home.

Strategies can range from simple acts of omission, such as Cady not telling her parents about her activities, to more active attempts at deception. Adolescents can avoid discussing the issue entirely by switching the topic of conversation when a sensitive issue comes up, or they can simply fail to mention information. They also can provide partial information. For instance, they can mention that they are going to a friend's house for the evening and not mention that the friend's parents are not going to be home. Or they can tell their parents that other adolescents at a party were drinking but "forget" to tell them that they were drinking as well. They can share information only when they are asked for more details. Both avoidance and partial disclosure are ways of concealing information, but neither is as deceptive as lying. Indeed, if adolescents are willing to disclose more when their parents ask for information, this raises the possibility that they will "come clean" and tell parents everything they need to know. In this way, adolescents who are initially reluctant to share information may fill in the details when parents ask for them. Communications researchers have viewed avoidance and partial disclosure as the most effective means of nondisclosure. Because they do not require adolescents to falsify information, they may be morally less problematic (Buller & Burgoon, 1994).

When lying is examined in the context of other strategies for managing information, it reveals itself to be actually quite infrequent and far from the norm (Darling, Cumsille, Caldwell, & Dowdy, 2006; Villalobos & Smetana, 2009). In one of their studies, Nancy Darling and her colleagues found that (mostly European American) adolescents lied in nearly a third (27%) of the instances where they disagreed with their parents and chose not to make disclosures (Darling et al., 2006). But when the broad spectrum from lying to full disclosure was considered, the frequency of lying was much lower. In one of my recent studies, less than 10% of the strategies used by adolescents for different types of issues involved lying – and this result takes into account all cases, including those when adolescents made full disclosure to parents, and all the various ways in which they evaded the issue when they did not (Smetana, Villalobos, Tasopoulos-Chan, Gettman, & Campione-Barr, 2009). In one of the few studies designed to assess adolescents' lying about different types of activities, Myriam Villalobos and I (Villalobos & Smetana, 2009) found that Puerto Rican middle adolescents residing in the United States reported that they did not lie often to parents. They lied mostly about their risky behavior, like whether or when they were drinking beer. (These issues were considered to be prudential matters.) They lied somewhat less about peer activities, and least of all about their personal activities. Other forms of information management are more common. Although adolescents may view lying as justified in some instances, they do not need to resort to it. They can simply not bring up the issues involved, or avoid those topics. Adolescents do not interpret as lying forms of information management such as avoidance or providing partial information, because they do not give their parents untrue statements, which they intend their parents to believe (Marshall, Tilton-Weaver, & Bosdet, 2005).

Communications researchers Tamara Afifi and her colleagues (Afifi, Caughlin, & Afifi, 2007) have asserted that secrecy and deception need to be distinguished. In their view, secrecy can involve outright lying as well as acts of omission, such as leaving out important information that parents might want to know. Deception can involve expressing oneself in a vague or ambiguous way, or exaggerating or minimizing information (Buller & Burgoon, 1994). These procedures are all deceptive inasmuch as the person keeping the secret intends to hide information from someone else and therefore to induce false beliefs. But Afifi and her colleagues claim that secrecy is broader than deception. It includes instances where the secret keeper's intention is not to induce false impressions but to make no impression at all – that is, to keep information private. Adolescents may keep secrets both because they believe that parents will not approve of their behavior and because they believe that their behavior is none of their parents' business. As we shall see, both these types of reasons are important in considering secrecy and nondisclosure during adolescence.

Adolescents' Secrecy with Parents

Secrecy has been distinguished also from lying. When studied empirically, lying and secrecy overlap to some extent, but not completely (Engels, Finkenauer, & van Kooten, 2006). Lying is just one of several ways of keeping things secret. Likewise, secrecy and disclosure have been described as opposite ends of the same continuum, but they are not. They are only moderately (and negatively) associated (Finkenauer, Engels, & Meeus, 2002; Finkenauer, Frijns, Engels, & Kerkhof, 2005; Frijns, Keijsers, Branje, & Meeus, 2010; Smetana, Metzger, Gettman, & Campione-Barr, 2006).

Researcher Tom Frijns and his colleagues maintain that, whereas not disclosing something to parents might be effortless, keeping a secret requires a conscious decision. It can be hard work. Adolescents who are keeping a secret need to monitor their conversation carefully, and perhaps even to suppress thoughts of the secret. As this description suggests, adolescents who keep more secrets from their parents show poorer psychosocial adjustment, which can take the form of greater loneliness, more depressed mood, poorer self-esteem, more physical complaints, more problem behavior, and more intense conflicts with parents

(Finkenauer et al., 2002; Laird & Marrero, 2010; Smetana, Metzger et al., 2006). They also show greater emotional autonomy (Finkenauer et al., 2002). While this seems to suggest that secrecy also has positive consequences for adjustment, the measure of emotional autonomy used here assessed detachment from parents rather than healthy emotional autonomy. Thus the consequences of secrecy appear to be uniformly negative. Following nearly 1,000 Dutch adolescents annually over 4 years, Frijns and his colleagues (Frijns et al., 2010) found that, over time, secrecy was linked to delinquency. In turn, delinquency contributed to greater secrecy towards parents. Secrecy also led to greater depressed mood, although the effects were not long-lasting and only extended to early adolescence. But it is also important to note that there are normative, developmental changes in levels of secrecy. Recent longitudinal research on the same sample of Dutch teens, which followed them from 13 to 17, showed that there was a linear decline in secrecy with age and that the decline was faster for boys than for girls (Keijsers, Branje, VanderValk, & Meeus, 2010).

My students, together with myself and a colleague, have studied adolescents' daily secret keeping from mothers and fathers, sampling a group of inner city, ethnically diverse middle adolescents. Every day for 14 days, these adolescents completed diaries online (on the Internet), reporting whether, how much, and on what issues they kept secrets from their mothers and fathers that day. We examined four categories of issues: school and schoolwork, personal issues, multifaceted issues, and bad behavior (Smetana, Villalobos, Rogge, & Tasopoulos-Chan, 2010). Keeping secrets from mothers fluctuated from day to day. Adolescents who had poorer relationships with their parents overall kept more secrets from them on a daily basis. They also kept from mothers more secrets about personal issues than about either their bad behavior or school. This indicates that, as Afifi and her colleagues (Afifi et al., 2007) suggested, maintaining privacy is an important motivation for secrecy. Like Frijns and his colleagues, we found that adolescents who kept more secrets from mothers reported greater involvement in problem behavior. But, surprisingly, adolescents who were more involved in problem behavior also reported keeping fewer secrets about their personal activities. This may have been a deliberate strategy, designed to deflect attention from their problem behavior. For instance, if teenagers are more open about personal issues – like how they are feeling that day or how they spent their free time – parents may believe that their teenagers are sharing information about other issues too – for instance whether they are drinking beer or wine, or smoking marijuana. But, as we just noted, keeping secrets is stressful. It takes psychological effort. Therefore another explanation for this finding is that details about personal activities may "leak out" because of the effort involved in keeping other, more dangerous activities secret.

Finally, communications researchers have distinguished between secrecy and topic avoidance. Secrecy involves hiding information from another person, but topic avoidance may not. Topics that are fully known to others can be avoided and not discussed (Guerrero & Afifi, 1995). For instance, adolescents may avoid discussing their political beliefs with their parents precisely because they have well-known but different beliefs, and expressing those beliefs may lead to family conflict. Therefore secrecy can be seen as a subset of topic avoidance.

What Do Adolescents Choose to Conceal from or Reveal to Parents?

Trends in disclosure and topic avoidance with parents

Topic avoidance peaks in adolescence. Pre-teens (11-year-olds), teenagers (16-year-olds), and young adults (23-year-olds) have been surveyed about how much they avoid telling their mothers and fathers things about various topics (Guerrero & Afifi, 1995). Such topics included talking about negative experiences; about friendships, feelings for friends and activities with friends; about feelings for potential or actual romantic interests; and about dangerous behavior. Teenagers avoided discussing these topics more than pre-teens or young adults did. The specific topics discussed or avoided were consistent with James Youniss and Jacqueline Smollar's (1985) conclusions. These researchers found that American, primarily White, middle and late adolescent boys and girls did not communicate much with their parents on issues like dating, although they disclosed more to mothers than to fathers. Adolescents did talk to both parents, instead, about schoolwork, future plans, and social issues.

What adolescents choose to tell or not to tell their parents also changes with age. On the basis of a review of 50 studies, Duane Buhrmester and Karen Prager (1995) found that, with age, adolescents revealed more about their private thoughts and feelings towards same-sex friends and, later, towards romantic partners. Self-disclosure to parents declined across adolescence. Recent studies have confirmed these age trends: 16–18-year-olds disclosed less to parents about their private thoughts and feelings and spent more time alone than 12–13-year-old early adolescents did (Finkenauer et al., 2002). There has been a change of emphasis in current research, however. Researchers are now focusing on disclosure regarding activities rather than self-disclosure of feelings or thoughts. When adolescents have been followed longitudinally over several years, adolescents' disclosure about their activities also has been found to decline during adolescence (Keijsers, Frijns, Branje, & Meeus, 2009; Laird & Marrero, 2010).

When one considers the specific activities that adolescents disclose or conceal, the picture is somewhat more complex. Overall, it appears that, at least for European American and European youth (who have been the focus of most of the research), willingness to share information with parents about one's activities decreases around middle adolescence (Finkenauer et al., 2002; Keijsers et al., 2009;

Laird & Marrero, 2010; Smetana, Villalobos, Tasopoulos-Chan et al., 2009). Adolescents also become less willing, with age, to tell parents about their involvement in risky activities (which we have characterized as prudential matters). This appears to coincide with an increasing involvement in such activities (Smetana, Villalobos, Tasopoulos-Chan et al., 2009). But there is some good news. Late adolescents seem to be more willing than middle adolescents to tell parents about what they are doing with friends and peers (Smetana, Metzger et al., 2006). This may be because crowd activity and conformity to peers are at their peak during middle adolescence. As adolescents become more comfortable in their emerging identity and as their involvement in peer crowds wanes, they may be more willing to share with their parents information about their peers.

There are also pervasive gender differences in the degrees of willingness to divulge information to parents. Across adolescence, both boys and girls share with mothers more confidences than with fathers about their everyday activities, and especially about personal matters. And, not surprisingly, girls share more with mothers than boys do. Girls' greater disclosure, especially towards their mothers, may be due to the fact that girls are socialized so as to be more expressive and to value intimacy in interpersonal relationships. But, in addition, mothers and fathers have different ways of communicating with their adolescents. For instance, Youniss and Smollar (1985) report that both boys and girls view fathers as employing more guarded forms of communication and as relying more on authority in resolving disputes than either mothers or close friends of either gender do. Compared to others, fathers also demonstrate less mutual openness and are more likely to reject their offspring's point of view. It is not surprising that individuals disclose less in a context where their point of view is likely to be rejected! In contrast, teenagers, and particularly girls, view communication with their mothers (as compared to other interaction partners) as more open, cooperative, and accepting. Such communication is more likely to be seen as reflecting a symmetrical understanding.

In contrast to Youniss and Smollar (1985), some researchers suggest that fathers know more about the daily experiences of their sons than about those of their daughters, and that adolescent boys selectively disclose more about personal topics to fathers than to mothers (Bumpus, Crouter, & McHale, 2001; Noller & Callan, 1990). In reviewing the different gender configurations, Buhrmester and Prager (1995) concluded that the lowest amount of disclosure is between fathers and daughters and the greatest is between mothers and daughters. Disclosure between both parents and their sons falls in-between. Recall that mothers and daughters also experience the greatest amount of conflict of any parent–child dyad. Taken together, such closeness and conflict most likely reflect the intense nature of mother–daughter relationships.

Why does topic avoidance increase, whereas disclosure declines during adolescence? In earlier chapters we saw that disagreements with parents during this period are a fact of life. In the context of warm and supportive parent–adolescent relationships, moderate amounts of conflict about everyday issues provide an opportunity for parents and children to articulate, challenge, and negotiate their divergent perspectives. In turn, these negotiations lead to changes in the boundaries of parental authority and to increases in adolescents' autonomy. Many of the issues that cause conflict – like chores, curfews, and choice of activities – pertain to matters that occur at home. Therefore they are easily observed and supervised by parents. But, as they grow older, American adolescents spend more time out of the house and in the company of peers. (Others have noted that this is not as typical for teenagers worldwide. For instance, Japanese teens spend much less time with peers than American youth do: see Rothbaum, Pott, Azuma, Miyake, & Weisz, 2000. And teenagers in many societies have longer school days and more homework to do than American children, which limits their opportunities to spend time with peers.)

As adolescents mature and spend more time away from home, it becomes more difficult for parents to supervise their children's activities directly. They must monitor behaviors at a distance and in more indirect ways. Instead of directly observing their children's activities, or even participating in them, parents must use other means to keep in touch. For instance they may resort to cell phones or text messaging as a way of maintaining contact. This increases the opportunities for adolescents to withhold information from parents, if they choose to do so. Also, adolescents' ability to communicate with peers by using new social media like Facebook, MySpace, and twittering also provides contexts where they may share information about their behavior to a wide circle of acquaintances and friends – but, typically, not with their parents. (Having to be "friended" on Facebook is one mechanism for keeping parents in the dark!)

Adolescents may decide not to share with parents information about their activities or their feelings because they believe that their feelings or activities are private, personal, and none of their parents' business. And, as we have seen, the personal domain increases in scope during adolescence. Adolescents may also engage in activities that would elicit parental disapproval or punishment, like failing a subject in school or giving a party, as Cady did in *Mean Girls*. Experimentation with risky behaviors also increases during adolescence. In these cases teenagers may withhold information, or they may keep secret their personal and prudential activities rather than risk overt conflict with their parents. In Chapter 7 we saw that, when teenagers air disagreements with their parents, they typically do not get their way. Most conflicts are resolved by teens having to comply with their parents' wishes. Therefore nondisclosure to parents is another way for adolescents to get what they want. It is an easy way of short-circuiting the negotiation process and of taking an alternate route to autonomy. It is interesting to note that nondisclosure and topic avoidance appear to increase in middle adolescence, just as conflicts with parents decline in frequency and as their intensity peaks. Given this correspondence, it is worthwhile to consider why adolescents may choose to disclose or to conceal information from parents.

Adolescents may disclose things to parents either because they agree with them or because they disagree with them but choose to make a clean breast of it. Nancy Darling and her colleagues (Darling et al., 2006) queried middle-class European American high school students about 36 potential issues of disagreement. They found that students rarely disclosed matters fully to parents in situations where they disagreed with them. Adolescents disagreed with their parents about an average of 16 issues, and made full disclosure, on average, about only 4 of these issues. Teenagers who "told all" about their activities when they disagreed with their parents did so primarily because they felt obligated. Less frequently, they disclosed matters fully because they hoped to change their parents' minds, or they figured that they could not get away with not disclosing (no moral high ground here!). Girls disclosed matters fully more than boys did. Teenagers who viewed their parents as authoritative were more likely to keep their parents fully informed. This is consistent with the notion that more authoritative parents are more supportive and responsive, and also more willing to negotiate with the teen. But even with authoritative parents, the rate of full disclosure was still very low. Teenagers who engaged more in parentally approved leisure activities were also more willing to disclose. (Teenagers who are busy with sports and after-school activities are probably not the kind to hang out in malls or with deviant friends and to get into trouble.)

On the other hand, adolescents did not make full disclosures for the vast majority of the issues where they disagreed with parents. The more the adolescents disagreed, the less their parents knew about their activities. When adolescents actively withheld information, they believed that their parents had little knowledge of their day-to-day activities. Therefore it appears that, in situations of disagreement, adolescents rarely tell their parents the full story.

But what does telling the full story (that is, full disclosure) mean to adolescents? Researchers have assessed full disclosure by asking whether adolescents "tell parents all the important details" (Darling et al., 2006; Smetana, Villalobos, Tasopoulos-Chan et al., 2009; Yau, Tasopoulos-Chan, & Smetana, 2009). But in a qualitative study focusing on disclosure to parents about peers (which will be discussed in more detail below), Jeremy Bakken and Bradford Brown (2010) make two interesting points about full disclosure. The first point is that, even when the adolescents in their study indicated that they fully disclosed matters, further probing in the context of qualitative interviews revealed that the majority contradicted themselves. Their detailed responses suggested that what they initially described as full disclosure was not such. And the second point that Bakken and Brown make is that, to the adolescents in their study, full disclosure meant telling parents all the basic details – the who, what, where, and when of their activities. This is often what parents really want to know. But this did not imply telling parents *everything*. Indeed, in their study, many parents indicated that full disclosure does not require knowing all the minor details. This point is well taken. Most researchers (myself included) have taken at face value adolescents' responses that they fully disclose matters to parents. But it appears that, when adolescents claim they fully disclose, this means that they share most but not all of the details. They may keep minor (or more sensitive) details to themselves. Indeed, when interviewed about conflicts, one of my study participants, 14-year-old Jessica, elaborated on why she did not fully disclose information to her parents:

> Because it's none of their business, and they don't understand and they'll just get mad, so I just save a lot of trouble. My Mom and Dad, when they say, "How was school?," they don't mean to say minute by minute, in detail, everything that happened. And maybe some things are private that I don't want to say, and maybe if I had a bad day on my test, I feel bad about it, and don't really want to talk about it then. Maybe I can talk later.

As this suggests, adolescents may keep details of prudential and personal matters to themselves, for different reasons.

Disclosure also varies depending on the "who," "what," "when," and "why" details. Consider the following example, taken from Smetana and Metzger (2008). Adolescents may have different feelings about voluntarily disclosing to their parents (and parents might respond differently to hearing) that they were drinking alcohol at a party from the feelings they may have about disclosing (or parents may have about learning) that they have a new romantic interest, in someone to whom they have recently sent a love note. Adolescents may choose not to tell their parents about either of these events. And just because adolescents feel obligated to disclose to their parents, it does not follow that they will necessarily do so. Additionally, adolescents (and their parents) may differ in their beliefs about teenagers' obligations to share this kind of information.

Adolescents' decisions about whether or not to share information with their parents may be motivated by different reasons, and their disclosure might elicit different parental responses. In the example of a teen drinking alcohol at a party, adolescents may believe that they are obligated to tell their parents such things, but they may still conceal their behavior because they fear parental disapproval or punishment. Once informed, parents may react with alarm or anger. When considering whether to share information about sending a love note to the object of a new romantic interest, adolescents may feel that they do not have an obligation to disclose this information to parents. They may choose not to tell out of embarrassment, or from a belief that these "matters of the heart" are private. But, in either case, deciding to reveal one's feelings and actions to parents could potentially lead to greater closeness, attachment, and intimacy. This example suggests that we need to consider the types of activities adolescents disclose or conceal and their beliefs about whether they are obligated to tell their parents about those activities. We also need to consider their reasons for disclosing or concealing their activities from parents.

Adolescents' obligations to tell their parents about their activities

The more the parents are seen as having the legitimate authority to regulate an issue, the more the adolescents see themselves as obligated to tell their parents about it. We learned in Chapter 9 that adolescents believe that parents have the legitimate authority to regulate moral, conventional, and – to a great extent – prudential issues, but that they reject parents' authority to control personal issues. Adolescents believe that they, and only they, should be able to make decisions about, and control, personal issues. Because personal matters are, by definition, private, adolescents and parents may not view adolescents as obligated to share information about activities in this arena. Disclosure to parents may enhance parents' and adolescents' sense of closeness and intimacy, but sharing information is at the teenagers' discretion, and it is not required. However, because parents consistently grant adolescents less autonomy over personal issues than adolescents feel they are due, the two parties are likely to disagree over the adolescents' obligations to disclose personal matters. Parents view teenagers as more obligated to reveal information about personal issues than teenagers view themselves to be.

This is precisely what we have found. Beliefs about legitimate parental authority are very highly associated with beliefs about teenagers' obligations to disclose to parents ("*Should* teens tell parents what they are doing, that is do they have a duty or obligation to tell parents about their behavior?" Smetana, Metzger et al., 2006). Domain differences in the adolescents' obligations to disclose various matters to parents mirror those found in relation to beliefs about parental authority: the two types of judgment are strongly related. Both parents and adolescents view teenagers as very highly obligated to tell parents about their behavior in areas of prudential concern, such as drinking alcohol or smoking marijuana. Teenagers are not seen as having an obligation to disclose to parents details about personal issues, like how they spend their earnings or allowance money, or what they do with their free time. Obligations to share information about moral and conventional issues, as well as about peer issues, fall in-between. Reflecting parents' recognition of their increased autonomy, late adolescents are seen as having less of an obligation to disclose to parents than middle adolescents are. However, parents consistently view teenagers as more obligated to tell parents about their activities than adolescents view themselves.

This is also what Bradford Brown and his team of researchers at the University of Wisconsin found in a small study of American families from Hmong (Laotian) and African backgrounds (Brown, Bakken, Nguyen, & Von Bank, 2007). They examined beliefs about the parents' right to know about four different aspects of teenagers' peer relationships. They distinguished among the "who," the "what," and the "when" of peer relationships – for instance where teens are going with their friends, what they are doing, and with whom. They also considered the positive and negative features of peer relationships – for instance how well teens are getting along. As I found in my research, Hmong and African American parents believed that they had more of a right to know about these different aspects of peer relationships than their adolescent offspring granted them. Hmong and African Americans did not differ in their beliefs about the parents' right to know about different aspects of teenagers' peer relationships. Their evaluations of the different aspects of these relationships did not differ either.

More generally, though, this study does raise questions about whether youth from different ethnic groups differ in their willingness to share information with parents. Much of the research on adolescents' disclosures to parents discussed thus far has focused on European American or European youth. In an earlier chapter we saw that, even when adolescents from diverse cultural, racial, and ethnic backgrounds comply with their parents' wishes, they still want more autonomy than their parents would typically grant. Most ethnic minority youth in the United States, as well as youth in other cultures, may face strict parental control, cultural values emphasizing respect for parents, and strong expectations for obedience. Under these conditions, adolescents who desire greater autonomy may strategically manipulate information to get their way (remember that a similar point was made about individuals – usually women – in subordinate positions in hierarchical societies).

Feelings of interdependence and loyalty to the family are important cultural values for both Asian and Latino families. Both Asian and Latino cultures also emphasize children's obligations to aid and assist the family in the present and in the future. These obligations could include sharing information, particularly about issues of potential impact on the family. At the same time, the more hierarchical structure of the family may make it more difficult for youth from some ethnic minorities to raise certain topics with their parents. This state of things may be complicated even further by the effects of acculturation among immigrant families. In the following sections we consider disclosure and nondisclosure among European American families, as well as among families from more diverse backgrounds.

Disclosing and concealing information from parents about different types of activities

Adolescents' willingness to disclose to parents their moral, conventional, prudential, or personal activities does not mirror their beliefs about the obligation to make these different disclosures. Despite their feelings of obligation, adolescents are typically not willing; nor do they actually tell their parents much about their activities. On average, they "sometimes" tell their parents what they are doing and with whom they are doing it. And mothers overestimate their teenagers' – especially their daughters' – voluntary disclosure regarding their personal activities (Smetana, Metzger et al., 2006). Mothers believe that their daughters tell them much more about their personal lives than daughters actually do. Parents know less than they think they do!

Disclosing and concealing about school and schoolwork

Adolescents disclose more to parents (and keep fewer secrets) about schoolwork – for instance getting a bad grade, not doing well on an assignment, or not completing homework or assignments – than about other activities – for instance personal ones, or behaviors related to their peer relationships (Smetana, Metzger et al., 2006). In their classic book on adolescent–parent relationships, Youniss and Smollar (1985) similarly found that school was one of the topics that adolescents discussed with their parents. Often, school and what happened during the day can be a fairly neutral topic to talk about, especially among youth who are not at high risk of school failure. Academic performance is of concern to parents; school and future careers are areas where adolescents seek parental advice. Indeed, my studies have shown associations between adolescents' academic performance (as indicated by their grade point average) and their willingness to share information with parents about school, schoolwork, and homework. Students with better grades reported telling both their mothers and their fathers a fair amount. Adolescents who do better at school are also more willing to share information about personal and other activities, but the association between grade point average and disclosure was stronger for schoolwork than for other issues.

Disclosure to mothers and fathers about schoolwork was examined in the daily diary study discussed earlier. In addition to reporting on a daily basis about their secrecy towards parents, students completed daily diaries regarding their disclosure to parents about different types of activities, including school (Smetana, Villalobos, Rogge, Tasopoulos-Chan, & Gettman, 2009). Not surprisingly, during weekends, African American, Latino, and European American middle adolescents disclosed less to parents about school – their grades on tests and assignments, or their homework – than on weekdays. Overall, they did not share with parents more information about school and homework than about other activities. However, they shared more about school-related activities and issues on days when they also reported better relationships with mothers, and this was not simply a function of how much time they spent together that day. Daily variations in the quality of their relationships influenced how much they were willing to share information about what happened at school on that day.

Disclosing and concealing facts about risky behavior

Both adolescents and parents believe that the former are highly obligated to tell the latter about their risky behavior. These are the activities that parents are often most concerned about – and also the activities that adolescents are most likely to conceal from them. Very little of the recent research has concerned itself with these types of issues. Teenagers have not been asked how much they voluntarily tell their parents about these things. Most of the measures used to study adolescents' willing disclosure to parents include just a few items, such as how adolescents spend their free time and where they go when they are not in school. In a recent study, however, we asked adolescents explicitly how much information they share with their parents willingly (without being asked) about different risky behaviors (Smetana, Villalobos, Tasopoulos-Chan et al., 2009). To ensure that adolescents were describing activities relevant to their lives, we first asked them whether they had actually engaged in each of the different behaviors. We assessed their voluntary disclosure to parents about that issue when they reported at least one instance of involvement in the behavior.

Thirteen-year-olds reported that they had very little involvement in risky behaviors (like smoking cigarettes, drinking beer or wine, or going to a party where teens were drinking). Indeed, the only behavior in the prudential category that younger adolescents engaged in with any frequency was driving with teen drivers. This activity may not seem as risky as experimentation with illegal substances and alcohol. However, it is in fact, along with night driving, one of the two highest risks for fatal car accidents for middle adolescents (Chen, Baker, Braver, & Li, 2000). Not surprisingly, middle adolescents reported more involvement in risky behaviors – and they also told their parents much less about them – than younger teens did. They did not tell their parents about these activities primarily because they wanted to stay out of trouble, avoid punishment, and stay in their parents' good graces. In other words, they used self-serving reasons rather than other-centered reasons – hardly the type of motivation that makes deception justified, according to ethicist Sissela Bok.

Adolescents' reasons for not disclosing their activities to their parents were also linked to different strategies for managing this information. When adolescents believed that their parents would disapprove of their behavior, or that they themselves would get in trouble, they either avoided discussing the issue or they lied. As I noted earlier, lying was infrequent compared to other strategies for managing information. Adolescents who lie more often are more involved in substance use and antisocial behavior (Marshall et al., 2005). And in our study, by comparison to early adolescents, older ones reported more problem behavior, like drinking alcohol and experimenting with drugs. They also lied somewhat more than early adolescents. Nearly a third of the 10th graders who feared parental disapproval for their actions reported lying as their predominant strategy for managing information about risky activities.

We found in another study that American middle adolescents (averaging 16 years of age) of lower socioeconomic status did not tell their parents about their involvement in risky behavior mostly for fear of parental disapproval (Yau, Tasopoulos-Chan et al., 2009). The nearly 500 youth in this study were from Mexican, Chinese, and European American backgrounds. Youth from varying backgrounds chose not to disclose to parents their risky behavior primarily because they were concerned with parental disapproval and punishment. (We took into account ethnic group differences in parents' education and in whether the teens were immigrants of the first, second or third generation to reside in the United States.)

Latino youth generally have been found to be more involved in problem behavior than youth of other ethnicities (Gonzales et al., 2008). This was also the case in our study. Mexican American adolescents, who were primarily second and third generation in terms of their residence in the United States, engaged more in risky behavior (including drinking alcohol, experimenting with illegal drugs, and having unprotected sex) than either European or Asian American youth. They also disclosed less about it to their parents than European American adolescents did. One explanation for the higher rates of problem behavior among Latino teens is that they are more likely to live in poverty and to have less educated parents, particularly as compared to Asian American adolescents. These educational differences were apparent in our sample as well. Parents of the Mexican American teens had less formal education than the parents of Chinese American adolescents. But this did not account either for the ethnic difference in problem behavior or for Mexican American teens' lower levels of disclosure about these activities as compared to those of European American youth. Mexican culture emphasizes conformity to external standards. Therefore Mexican American adolescents who were engaging in problem behaviors may have felt that there was more at stake for them when they violated parental standards than other youth did.

This is consistent with what researcher Elena Jeffries (2004) found in a small qualitative study. She examined trust in low-income African American, Latino, and Asian adolescent boys' relationships with parents. In contrast to Asian boys, half of the Latino and African American boys reported sharing "everything" with at least one of their parents (and typically more with fathers than with mothers), or sharing only partial information. Boys reported drawing the line, though, at disclosure about certain issues, which included poor school performance, disobedience, sexual activity, and crushes. Except for the latter, these are issues that we have treated as prudential or multifaceted (and as having prudential components) in our research. Jeffries found that boys generally did not disclose facts about these things to their parents.

In our study, youth of different ethnicities managed information about their risky activities mainly by not discussing them with parents. Nearly half of all teens reported that they avoided discussing such issues either with mothers or with fathers. Less commonly, they reported that they told their parents about their behavior, but only when they were asked. But avoidance around prudential activities was more common for Mexican and European American adolescents than for Chinese American adolescents. Chinese American teens were more likely to tell their parents about their behavior – but, again, only when asked (Tasopoulos-Chan, Smetana, & Yau, 2009).

Chinese American teens' strategies for managing information about their prudential activities varied according to their family histories of immigration. Second-generation youth (who were born in the United States, but whose parents were not) were more likely than immigrants to avoid discussing their prudential behavior with parents. Instead of avoiding the topic completely, Chinese immigrant youth were more likely to disclose facts only when asked, or to tell their parents about their prudential activities but omit important details which their parents would want to know. In conclusion, immigrant youth were more willing than American-acculturated teens to keep the lines of communication at least partially open. As they became more acculturated to the American way of life, those lines of communication shut down.

Disclosing and concealing facts about peers and romantic relationships

Peer issues (like whether adolescents are dating, whether they are spending time with friends whom parents don't like, or whether they are spending time alone with a boyfriend or girlfriend) may also be sensitive topics, off-limits for parents to discuss. In general, disclosure about these issues is moderate. In one study, we found that middle and late adolescents kept more secrets about peers than about personal and school activities (Smetana, Metzger et al., 2006). Early and middle adolescents do not appear to differ in their willingness to tell parents about their peer activities (Smetana, Villalobos, Tasopoulos-Chan et al., 2009). In another study, however, late adolescents were more willing than middle adolescents to tell their parents about these activities (Smetana, Metzger et al., 2006). Adolescents' reason for not sharing information about their peer relationships and about activities with peers is primarily that they view these matters as private and as not involving harm. To a lesser extent, they are also concerned about potential parental disapproval and punishment (Smetana, Villalobos, Tasopoulos-Chan et al., 2009). As teenagers embark on romantic and sexual relationships, they may feel squeamish about too much disclosure. Indeed, we have found that adolescents' main strategy for managing information about peers was to avoid discussing the topic (Smetana, Villalobos, Tasopoulos-Chan et al., 2009). In Elena Jeffries's qualitative study, discussed in the previous section, she quotes one African American boy, Devon, as responding in the following way to the interviewer's query about examples of issues that he would not tell his mother:

DEVON: Sex and stuff like that. We don't talk about that.
INTERVIEWER: And what about sex do you think prevents you from talking about it?
DEVON: My parents think I'm still a kid, so they don't want me to grow up most of the time.
INTERVIEWER: How would they react if you talked to them about sex?

DEVON:	They really wouldn't care. They're like, "Do what you want, just make the right decisions. Don't get anyone pregnant, use condoms."
INTERVIEWER:	And did that ever happen? Did they talk to you?
DEVON:	Every once in a while.
INTERVIEWER:	And would that be you kind of initiating or ...?
DEVON:	It's like, it's most of the times they start talking about things like that and I tell them, "Why am I talking to you about it? Now all of a sudden you want to hear about it?" (Jeffries, 2004, p. 116)

In addition to studying parents' and adolescents' beliefs about parents' right to know about peer relationships, Brown and his colleagues also examined what Hmong and African American parents know and what their adolescents tell them about those relationships (Bakken & Brown, 2010; Brown et al., 2007; Nguyen, Brown, Von Bank, & Bakken, 2007). The central themes that Hmong parents emphasized in their interviews were respect for authority and for Hmong cultural traditions. Hmong adolescents endorsed these values, but they also wanted to engage in American culture. The severe restrictions their parents placed on their peer interactions prompted them to be "selective and strategic" in the information they shared with their parents. Hmong youth reported less full disclosure of information about peers, more topic avoidance, and twice as much deception in comparison with African American adolescents. Jacqueline Nguyen and her colleagues (Nguyen et al., 2007) provide the following example, in which Jenny, a 15-year-old girl, was discussing informal rules regarding dating:

> In Hmong culture, you could not [go to your boyfriend's house], it's embarrassing to do that. Like, "Oh, she's not even the daughter-in-law yet and she's all around our house and hanging all over our son," you know. "We don't want that kind of wife, that kind of daughter-in-law, 'cuz that's slutty," you know.

Much like what we found among primarily European American teenagers, Hmong and African American teenagers justified not telling their parents about their peer relationships with the excuse that they wanted to avoid punishment. They also believed that their parents would not grant them permission, and they viewed their activities as private (Bakken & Brown, 2010). But there were also culturally distinctive reasons for not sharing with parents information about their peer relationships. African American adolescents expressed relational concerns. They attempted to balance respect for their parents' authority and willingness to maintain trusting relationships with them with a desire for greater autonomy. Hmong teenagers described how their parents did not understand what it is like to be a Hmong teenager in American society. They thought that Hmong parents ought to be more trusting. They managed information so that they could do what they wanted and still earn their parents' trust.

Disclosure to parents also varies for different types of peer and romantic issues. In studying primarily European American middle and late adolescents, Christopher

Daddis and Danielle Randolph (2010) found that adolescents disclosed more to parents about issues related to the identity and choice of a romantic partner (such as what kind of person the boyfriend or girlfriend is, and where they go on dates) and about their everyday expression of romantic relationships (like what activities the couple chooses to do together) than about sex and unsupervised activities. The latter included being at the boyfriend or girlfriend's house when their parents are not at home; being alone with, or in a bedroom with, the boyfriend or girlfriend; and whether they are having sex. This suggests that adolescents were more willing to share information about publicly observable and verifiable aspects of their romantic relationships than about the more private ones. Adolescents who had had more dating experience disclosed more to parents about the everyday expression of their romantic relationships. Regardless of age, adolescents may come to share more information with their parents about how they express their romantic lives as they gain more romantic experience, and perhaps become more comfortable and confident about it. Moreover, middle – but not older – adolescents disclosed more about the way they expressed their romantic relationships, about their choice, and about the identity of their romantic partners if they believed that these things had consequences for others.

Not surprisingly, late adolescents were less likely than middle adolescents to disclose facts about supervision and sexual experience. Of course, as teens grow older, they may have more sexual experience and more opportunities to engage in unsupervised activities with romantic partners. But this age difference was evident even when adolescents' prior history of sexual and romantic experience was considered. Girls also disclosed more to parents about the identity and choice of their romantic partner and about the everyday expression of their romantic relationships than boys did. Except for sex and supervision issues, both girls and boys disclosed more about their romantic relationships to mothers than to fathers. Furthermore, boys and girls did not differ in their disclosures about sex and supervision; but they disclosed more to parents if they believed that these issues had harmful consequences. In other words, adolescents appeared to be more willing to disclose to parents facts about sex and supervision when they viewed these issues as prudential or moral matters (and therefore legitimately regulated by parents) rather than as purely personal concerns. This is consistent with what we have learned about adolescents' perceptions of their obligations to disclose matters to parents. Beyond the prudential issues involved in sexual activity, going on dates was seen by some of these teens as having consequences for parents. Not all teens had drivers' licenses, and therefore they depended on parents for transportation and the like.

Disclosing and concealing personal activities and feelings

There is some evidence, although limited and inconsistent, to suggest that adolescents share with parents less information about personal matters than about other everyday issues, such as homework and peer relationships. In one of my studies, we found that diverse, lower middle-class American 12th graders were less willing to make voluntary disclosures about personal activities than about these others (Smetana, Metzger et al., 2006), although 9th graders did not differ in this respect. European American lower middle-class boys, in particular, avoided discussing personal issues with parents rather than disclosing them fully or partially (Smetana, Villalobos, Tasopoulos-Chan et al., 2009). Furthermore, the daily diary study of poor urban teenagers discussed earlier revealed that these teenagers disclosed less to mothers about their personal activities than about either school or their bad behavior. The primary reason why adolescents do not disclose personal issues is that they believe that these are private and harmless matters (Smetana, Villalobos, Tasopoulos-Chan et al., 2009; Yau, Tasopoulos-Chan et al., 2009). Much less frequently, adolescents believe that telling their parents would make them feel bad, embarrassed, or ashamed. They also indicated, occasionally, that parents would not listen or understand, or that parents would think less of them if they knew about their thoughts, feelings, or behaviors.

We also saw earlier that adolescents may view lying to parents about personal issues as justified in some instances. But in reality they rarely lie about personal activities. And teens who did reported feeling more depressed. Lying about prudential or peer activities did not have the same negative consequences for adjustment (Smetana, Villalobos, Tasopoulos-Chan et al., 2009; Tasopoulos-Chan et al., 2009). As we have seen, parental overcontrol of the personal domain is associated with depression and anxiety. Therefore a question to be explored in future research is whether adolescents feel more motivated to lie about personal matters when they feel that parents intrude too deeply into their personal domains.

For personal issues, adolescents rarely use partial disclosure strategies, such as omitting important details that parents would want to know (Smetana, Villalobos, Tasopoulos-Chan et al., 2009; Tasopoulos-Chan et al., 2009). It is likely that they do not rely much on these strategies because they do not feel obligated to tell their parents about personal issues in the first place. In our study of Chinese, Mexican, and European American youth, information about personal activities was managed primarily by telling parents only when they asked. This strategy was particularly favored in interactions with fathers.

In her qualitative study, Jeffries (2004) found that Asian boys did not communicate much with their parents about a variety of topics. They believed that parents would not approve, understand, or care. These concerns were not evident among Latino and African American boys in her sample, but the Hmong informants studied by Bakken and Brown (2010) expressed similar sentiments. Asian boys viewed their reluctance to disclose as an aspect of their cultural background. Jeffries (2004, p. 1170) described Daniel, a Chinese American boy, as stating: "Asian people, right, the kids, right, they don't talk to you, their parents, about personal stuff that much. Especially girls and stuff … You just don't [talk to them]."

As this suggests, there are cultural differences in adolescents' willingness to disclose to parents details about personal issues. In studying American adolescents from Mexican, Chinese, and European backgrounds (Yau, Tasopoulos-Chan et al., 2009), we distinguished between two types of personal issues. We examined personal activities, such as how adolescents spend their time or their money. We also examined a closely related aspect of the personal domain: adolescents' willingness to disclose to parents their personal feelings. These included how they felt about their hair, skin, height, and weight, whether they felt anxious and depressed during the day (or happy, excited, or enthusiastic), and their feelings towards their boyfriend or girlfriend. Other research has treated these types of items as being within the realm of self-disclosure, or of individuals' disclosure of private thoughts and feelings. Self-disclosure was a topic of much interest in the 1980s and it was extensively studied among adolescents as well as among young adults. Self-disclosure is thought to be important for the development of relationship intimacy. In contrast, as I have suggested, the adolescents' disclosure of activities is linked to the development of their autonomy. Conceptually, though, both the disclosure of personal activities and the disclosure of private thoughts and feelings can be seen as aspects of the personal domain.

In general, Chinese American (primarily immigrant) adolescents told their parents less about their personal feelings than European and Mexican American youth did. They also divulged less about personal activities than European American youth did (Yau, Tasopoulos-Chan et al., 2009). Instead they relied more on partial disclosure, telling their parents only when asked. This is strikingly consistent with what both Jeffries (2004) and Bakken and Brown (2010) found in their qualitative interview studies. To repeat the words of Daniel, quoted earlier, "Asian [...] kids don't talk to [...] their parents about personal stuff that much." Regardless of their ethnic background, the primary reason why adolescents did not share with parents information about personal activities and feelings was that they believed these to be personal and harmless matters.

But youth in each ethnic group also had distinctive reasons for not talking to parents about personal matters. Chinese families believe in moderating or suppressing emotions (Eid & Diener, 2001). Reflecting this and echoing the comments made in Jeffries's interviews, Chinese American adolescents also withheld information about personal issues because they believed that their parents would not listen, care, or understand. (Recall that we obtained similar responses in our interviews with Chinese adolescents in Hong Kong and Shenzen when discussing the topic of issues they would not raise with their parents.) In contrast, and especially regarding disclosure to fathers, European American adolescents emphasized that personal activities are not harmful. And, compared to Chinese American youth, Mexican American adolescents focused more on worries about parental disapproval. More specifically, disapproval was of greater concern to Mexican American adolescents whose parents had immigrated to the United States (that is, to second-generation youth) than to youth whose parents had been born in the United States (that is, to third-generation youth). But, as successive generations of Mexican American adolescents acculturate to American society, they appear to construct broader boundaries of the personal domain. More than teens of the second generation, those of the third believed that their activities were personal matters.

In her qualitative study, Jeffries (2004) noted that all of the African American and Latino boys she interviewed (but never the Asian boys) shared confidences with at least one parent. The more secure they felt in their relationships, the more likely it was that they shared private thoughts and feelings. With them just as with the African American boys interviewed by Bakken and Brown (2010), trust was important and connected to the belief that their parents were always going to be there for them. There is a great deal of evidence supporting the notion that adolescents' willingness to tell parents about their activities is associated with more trusting relationships. The effects of trust appear to go both ways; greater trust may lead to greater disclosure, and vice versa. Furthermore, parents' trust in their teen is distinct from adolescents' trust in their parents. Effective parental monitoring is built on a foundation of trust and on the parents' beliefs in the trustworthiness of their teen. Parents must trust their offspring to be responsible, follow their rules, and share information about their plans, activities, companions, and whereabouts. And greater parental trust is associated with greater disclosure (Kerr & Stattin, 2000; Kerr, Stattin, & Trost, 1999; Stattin & Kerr, 2000).

Adolescents who believe that their parents are emotionally trustworthy and who expect them to act accordingly will be more willing to make disclosures about their activities. When adolescents do not feel obligated to report their activities to parents, as is the case for personal matters, trust becomes especially important. And the evidence is clear that teenagers are more willing to share with parents information about their activities when they have more emotionally close and trusting relationships and when parents are more authoritative, responsive, and accepting (Darling et al., 2006; Smetana, Metzger et al., 2006; Smetana, Villalobos, Tasoploulos-Chan et al., 2009; Soenens, Vansteenkiste, Luyckx, & Goossens, 2006). This is particularly true for disclosure about personal issues (Smetana, Metzger et al., 2006).

In our daily dairy study, adolescents who reported more trusting relationships with each parent also reported disclosing more to that parent. But beyond the effects on disclosure of overall levels of trust, adolescents also revealed more to mothers about their personal activities on days when they spent more time together and reported a better relationship with them (Smetana, Villalobos, Tasopoulos-Chan et al., 2009). When relationships are generally positive, something as simple as spending more time together may contribute to a climate of trust, where personal matters can be divulged (as well as potentially providing more opportunities for disclosure to occur). Adolescents also disclosed more to fathers when they had better overall relationships with them. But the way they felt about their fathers each day did not influence daily fluctuations in disclosure. African American boys were more likely than all other boys to disclose personal issues to their mothers, whereas African American girls were less likely than other girls to tell their mothers about these issues. As I noted in an earlier chapter, this may reflect the gendered nature of African American parent–child relationships. But it also suggests that the meaning of trust and emotional closeness may differ for youth of different ethnicities.

Indeed, family closeness is expressed in different ways in families of different ethnicities. Catherine Hardway and Andrew Fuligni (2006) found that family connectedness had a somewhat different meaning among Mexican, Chinese, and European American adolescents. In European American families, connectedness is based primarily on the emotional quality of the dyadic relationship. It has a more voluntary flavor. However, in Chinese and Mexican American families, connectedness is based more on feelings of obligation to assist, respect, and support the family. Chinese American youth in our multi-ethnic study felt less emotional closeness to parents than European and Mexican American adolescents did. However, the processes were the same. Trust and closeness had similar effects on disclosure to parents for youth of different ethnicities. Disclosure was enhanced for diverse youth when they felt emotionally closer to their parents.

What Do Parents (Think They) Know about Adolescents' Activities?

Thus far, the focus has been on the adolescents' management of information about their activities and friends. But we can also ask what parents think they know about their adolescent children's activities. And if adolescents are not willing to tell them what they are doing, how (else) do they find out? We saw that, on average, adolescents disclose more to their mothers than to their fathers. Correspondingly, a well-established finding is that mothers know more about their children's lives than fathers do (Bumpus et al., 2001; Crouter, Helms-Erikson, Updegraff, & McHale, 1999; Crouter & McHale, 1993; Crouter, McHale, & Bartko, 1993; Waizenhofer, Buchanan, & Jackson-Newsom, 2004). Mothers are more involved in the everyday details and responsibilities of the family and provide more emotional support to adolescents than fathers do. This is reflected in the fact that mothers and fathers obtain information about their offspring's behavior in different ways. Mothers generally use more active methods than fathers do. They rely more on asking their adolescents directly, on asking informed others (like teachers or one's spouses) about what teens are doing, and on participating in activities with their children (and driving them to activities). Fathers rely more on obtaining information from their wives, particularly about their daughters (Crouter, Bumpus, Davis, & McHale, 2005; Waizenhofer et al., 2004).

An analysis of how parents obtain their information, gleaned from European American mothers and fathers of 16-year-olds, further reveals that the parents' information gathering falls into three distinct profiles, which differ somewhat for mothers and fathers (Crouter et al., 2005). Some fathers rely primarily on their spouses for information. Some rely on other members of the family (such as siblings) or on outsiders. Some use relational methods, such as listening and observing, learning from their offspring's self-disclosure, or soliciting information directly. Mothers, too, use relational methods, but they also question their teens or they rely for information on others, including their spouses. Using relational methods with early adolescents appears to be most effective method over time. It leads to gaining greater parental knowledge of middle adolescents' behavior. These methods were also associated with less risky behavior (such as alcohol, substance, and cigarette use, or skipping school) 1 year later.

The monitoring debate

For many years, both developmental scientists and the general public have assumed that it is important for parents to monitor and supervise adolescents. The prevailing wisdom is that the more parents keep track of their adolescents' activities, the less likely it is that adolescents will associate with deviant peers or engage in juvenile delinquency, illegal substance, alcohol use, or risky sexual behavior. Indeed, the well-disseminated public service announcement – "It's 10 o'clock: Do you know where your children are?" – has been used for years to alert parents to the importance of parental monitoring.

But more recent research has challenged this assumption. It is true that teenagers whose parents know more about their activities engage in lower levels of risky behavior. But the links between what parents are doing – their active attempts to monitor and keep track of their adolescents – and what they actually know are much less robust than researchers and the general public have assumed. And the associations between what parents do to keep track of their teenagers, what adolescents willingly disclose, and the risky and problematic behaviors of adolescents also turned out to be much more complex than the public service announcement has led us to believe.

Several groundbreaking studies by Swedish researchers Hakan Stattin and Margaret Kerr (Kerr & Stattin, 2000; Kerr, Stattin, & Burk, 2010; and see also Crouter & Head, 2002) have called attention to the fact that, in most research, monitoring has been assessed in terms of what parents *know* about children's activities rather than in terms of what parents are actually *doing* to keep track of them. The classic measure of parental monitoring asks how much parents *really know* about where the teen goes at night, where the teen is most afternoons after school, how money is spent, what the teen does with the available free time, and who the teen's friends are. These questions refer to the parents' mental state (their state of knowledge), not to their parenting behavior or to how they go about finding out the answers to these questions.

The surprising finding from Stattin and Kerr's research is that only adolescents' voluntary disclosure to parents was associated with how much parents knew about their children's activities. Parents' monitoring and tracking (referred to as behavioral control) and parents' asking, or their attempts to solicit information from their teens, did not lead to greater parental knowledge. This was the case even when the researchers took into account the level of trust in the parent–adolescent relationship. (Kerr and Stattin did not, however, distinguish between disclosure and secrecy in their measure of disclosure. We saw earlier in this chapter that this is an important distinction.) In turn, parents who knew more about their adolescent children's activities had offspring who engaged in lower levels of norm-breaking and delinquency. In fact, Kerr and Stattin's study showed just the opposite of what might be expected. Adolescents whose parents asked more questions – who actively solicited more information about their activities – engaged in more, not in less, norm-breaking and delinquency.

The study discussed earlier, which examined the different profiles of parents' information-seeking, showed similar results (Crouter et al., 2005). These researchers found that mothers and fathers with a relational style that entails high levels of child disclosure, as well as parental listening and observation, knew more about their middle adolescents' activities – which, in turn, led to lower levels of risky behavior over time. For fathers, obtaining information from one's spouse also showed significant over-time associations with parental knowledge and subsequent reductions in risk. This research is especially noteworthy, as it entailed longitudinal analyses carried out over 4 years, and it controlled for initial levels of risky behavior.

Therefore the evidence shows that parents' knowledge comes primarily from adolescents' willingness to divulge details of their lives, and not from parents' attempts to control and keep track of their teenagers' activities. This contradicts the prevailing assumptions about the role of parents in keeping teenagers out of trouble. It puts the onus on the adolescents' willingness to disclose rather than on the parents' tracking and surveillance. Adolescents can decide whether to keep their parents informed about their activities or to conceal them and withdraw information from their parents. This shifts the focus from what parents are doing (that is, their parenting practices) to adolescents' active management of information about their lives. It suggests that the slogan "It's 10 o'clock: Do you know where your children are?" should be changed to: "It's 10 o'clock: Have your children told you where they are?"

From the parents' perspective, child disclosure has been labeled a passive method of obtaining information, because it relies on the child's and not the parents' actions. More active means for keeping track of adolescents' behavior include asking for information. But, particularly in families with only one wage earner, mothers who used more active methods had adolescent children engaged in greater deviance (Waizenhofer et al., 2004). The speculation was that this situation might be due to the fact that more active attempts at supervision feel intrusive. However, other researchers have found that mothers use more active methods when they suspect that their teenage child is involved in misconduct (Tilton-Weaver & Galambos, 2003). As Kerr and her colleagues found, parents may resort to direct questioning about their teenager children's activities and whereabouts when these children are already engaged in risky behavior.

Kerr and Stattin strongly believe that their research demonstrates the importance of good parent–child relationships in preventing youth antisocial behavior (Kerr & Stattin 2003; Stattin & Kerr, 2000). That is, although their research highlights the importance of adolescents' willingness to share with parents information about their behavior, they believe that disclosure reflects the climate of the parent–adolescent relationship. Therefore they do not regard the results of their research as challenging the view that parents are important in facilitating adolescents' healthy psychosocial development. Nevertheless, their findings have been controversial. Some researchers claim that they have underestimated – and undermined – the role of parenting in preventing problem behavior. Therefore researchers have sought to clarify the influence of parenting on disclosure and problem behavior.

Anne Fletcher and her colleagues (Fletcher, Steinberg, & Williams-Wheeler, 2004) re-analyzed data from a large longitudinal study, to examine the long-term influence of parenting on parental knowledge and on adolescent problem behavior (they did not consider the influence of adolescent behavior on parenting). They found that, when examined at the same point in time, American youth of high school age who had warmer relationships with their parents and who were monitored more at home had parents who knew more about their activities. Parental knowledge, in turn, was associated with less problem behavior. Fletcher and her colleagues' over-time analyses, unlike those of Stattin and Kerr (2000), revealed that parental control had direct effects on adolescents' problem behavior and substance use, as well as indirect effects through their influence on parental knowledge. (It is worth noting that the team's measure of parental knowledge came only from adolescents' reports; the parents' perceptions were not obtained.) In consequence, these researchers claimed that Stattin and Kerr had underestimated the role of parenting in preventing problem behavior.

Other studies have also examined parenting in relation to substance use, delinquency, and affiliation with substance-using and delinquent peers in middle to late adolescents. A study of Belgian families (Soenens et al., 2006) showed that teenagers who were more willing to share information with their parents had mothers and fathers who were more responsive, relied more on behavioral control, and also employed less intrusive parenting (that is, less psychological control). Therefore these researchers concluded that both parenting and self-disclosure on the part of youth influence parents' knowledge of teens' activities. This, in turn, influences adjustment. The researchers obtained different informants' ratings of disclosure and parental knowledge. But, because the variables were all measured at a single point in time, the causal pathways are unclear. Nevertheless, these studies suggest that adolescents' willingness to disclose matters to parents is part of a reciprocal process rooted in warm and responsive parent–adolescent relationships.

The importance of reciprocal parent–child processes

This conclusion, and the importance of reciprocal processes, are well established in longitudinal studies of problem behavior. Numerous studies have shown that conduct problems during childhood and adolescence and problematic adolescent–parent relationships co-evolve and mutually influence each other. A very well known example is supplied by research from the Oregon Social Learning Research Group. In carefully conducted studies, these researchers have shown that parents react to increases in adolescents' problem behaviors and deviant conduct with greater hostility and less responsive, engaged parenting. In turn, parents' maladaptive responses lead to more problem behavior. Thus parenting and adolescent behaviors involve transactive processes (Dishion, Nelson, & Bullock, 2004).

Transactive processes are also at play in adolescents' involvement in risky sexual behavior, which includes greater numbers of sexual partners, more frequent sexual intercourse, and more unprotected sex. Analyses of a large sample drawn from a nationally representative survey of youth show that adolescents who more regularly engage in activities such as eating dinner together with their families or having fun together, and whose fathers know more about their activities, are less likely than youth with less engaged parents to be involved in risky sexual behavior. But the reverse direction of causation is also true: adolescents who engage in more risky sexual behavior report lower subsequent levels of parental knowledge about their friends and activities and less engagement in family activities (Coley, Votruba-Drzal, & Schindler, 2009). It is not possible to specify a single causal chain; rather, these behaviors interact.

Similarly, in examining adolescents and parents every year for 4 years, researchers found that parents' knowledge and better parent–adolescent relationships led to less antisocial behavior, and vice versa (Laird, Pettit, Bates, & Dodge, 2003). And youth who engaged in more substance use or antisocial behavior lied more and disclosed less to parents, which resulted in lower parental knowledge. This, in turn, predicted more substance use and antisocial behavior in the following year (Marshall et al., 2005). All these studies demonstrate that there is a complex interplay and reciprocal associations between parent–adolescent relationships and adolescents' behavior. They confirm the importance of engaged, responsive parenting in protecting adolescents from involvement in risky behavior. But they also show that parents back off and become less engaged and responsive when their teenagers get into trouble.

Recently, Margaret Kerr and her colleagues in Sweden (Kerr et al., 2010) sought support for their original hypothesis about the unique role in predicting parental knowledge of the adolescents' willingness to make disclosures to parents. They followed a large sample of Swedish 12–15-year-olds for 2 years, in order to untangle the complex interrelationships among adolescents' disclosure, parental monitoring, and juvenile delinquency. They tested several different models. The *parent-driven* model examined whether parental monitoring elicits greater disclosure and discourages delinquency, either directly or with one as a consequence of the other. This is the "It is 10 o'clock: Do you know where your children are?" model. It tests the assumption guiding earlier research, which demonstrated the importance of parental monitoring. They also examined a model that treats *teen disclosure* as the causal factor. Here adolescents' willingness to disclose matters to their parents was seen as enhancing the likelihood that parents would ask questions about their children's activities and would enforce more rules. These increased monitoring processes might then lead to lower levels of delinquency. Therefore, in this model, teenagers' telling results in greater parental asking, which, in turn, lowers the level of risk of misconduct. The third alternative was that *delinquency* itself drives the process. Adolescents who engage in delinquency have more to hide from their parents. Therefore they disclose less. And, as a result of adolescents' delinquency, parents may become disengaged and therefore monitor their adolescents' behavior less. The fourth model, referred to as *youth-driven*, combined elements of the delinquency and disclosure models. In this model, delinquency and disclosure are not causally related, but both of these youth-driven behaviors might influence parental monitoring in the ways just described.

Kerr and her colleagues examined these different models in two steps. One step looked at long-term associations between parental knowledge and how it was obtained; the second step examined over-time links between knowledge and delinquency. The first step replicated the researchers' earlier cross-sectional work. Their longitudinal analyses demonstrated that only adolescents' voluntary disclosure of information led to increased parental knowledge over time. Parents' efforts to monitor their children's activities did not yield benefits in terms of increased knowledge, nor did they elicit more disclosure from the teens over time. However, there was evidence (if somewhat less robust) that adolescents' willingness to share information with their parents led to increased parental solicitation of information in the long run.

For the second step – examining links between parental knowledge and delinquency – the results supported the delinquency-driven process. The less adolescents disclose to parents about their activities, whereabouts, and companions, the more they engage in delinquent behaviors. And, as parents ask more questions, teenagers engage in more delinquency. Therefore Kerr and her colleagues concluded that parents' attempts to monitor their offspring's behavior had little effect on their knowledge, or did little to protect youth from delinquency.

Two other recent studies contribute to our understanding of these processes. In one, European and African American families were followed yearly from the age of 11 to the age of 13 (Laird & Marrero, 2010). In the other, Dutch families were followed yearly from 13 to 16 (Keijsers et al., 2009). Both studies showed clearly that adolescents disclosed less to parents about their activities as they grew older. And the parents' use of control and solicitation of information also declined over time.

Like other researchers, Laird and Marrero (2010) found that greater parental knowledge both influenced and was influenced by greater delinquency over time; the links went both ways. Adolescents' willingness to share information, as well as parents' solicitation of information, led to increased parental knowledge and to smaller increases in delinquent behavior over time. However, this is one of very few studies to examine the effects of more specific forms of information management, like full disclosure, partial disclosure, or lying, on reductions in juvenile delinquency. And the authors found that the specific forms of information management mattered in terms of decreasing the likelihood of juvenile delinquency. Full disclosure, or telling parents all the important details without being asked, had protective effects. In contrast, partial disclosure (leaving out important information that parents would want to know) led to increases in delinquent behavior over time. However, partial disclosure had fewer negative effects when parents used more control. (These researchers did not, however, assess the different types of activities that adolescents disclose or conceal.)

In Kerr and Stattin's (2000; Kerr et al., 2010) research, adolescents' voluntary disclosure to parents was treated as diametrically opposed to parents' information-seeking (solicitation). Kerr and Stattin tested models suggesting that either adolescents share information willingly with parents or parents ask questions to gain more information. But these two processes may also occur as a single bi-directional one. After all, parents can ask questions because they are suspicious and worried that their offspring are involved in forbidden activities. Parents can also ask questions and inquire about adolescents' activities because they are genuinely interested and involved. Parents who suspect their children of being involved in delinquent activities may also have a poorer relationship with them and may spend less leisure time with them. Generally, when adolescents disclose more to their parents, the latter express more satisfaction with the relationship (Finkenauer, Engels, Branje, & Meeus, 2004). This, in turn, may lead to more parental interest and questioning about adolescents' activities and companions, and also to more adolescent disclosure.

Dutch researcher Loes Keijsers and her colleagues (Keijsers, Branje, VanderValk et al., 2010) tested these associations in a longitudinal study. Both according to mothers' and to adolescents' reports, parents who asked more questions had children who disclosed more over time. Youth who were more willing to disclose to parents engaged in less juvenile delinquency 1 year later. When adolescents' disclosure was taken into account, parents' attempts to solicit more information did not influence later levels of juvenile delinquency. Therefore adolescent disclosure appears to be more important than parental solicitation in predicting lower

levels of later juvenile delinquency. Nevertheless, adolescent disclosure and parental solicitation are very strongly intertwined. Parents can ask questions to elicit
disclosure, at least to some extent. In later sections we will see that asking questions and using control can also be seen as intrusive, so what parents ask about
and how they do it are important. Parenting appears to be one way of facilitating
adolescent disclosure, but it does not directly protect against delinquency and
problem behavior. As we have seen, adolescents manage the amount of information they provide to their parents, and therefore the amount of autonomy they
have.

Keijsers and her colleagues (Keijsers et al., 2009) likewise found that more disclosure led to less delinquency over time, although they did not distinguish
between full disclosure and other strategies for managing information. But they
found that the positive effects of greater disclosure were accentuated in highly
supportive families. Adolescents' greater willingness to share information with
parents protects youth against involvement in delinquent behavior. However, the
benefits of disclosure are greater when parents supervise and regulate their teenagers' behavior (that is, use more behavioral control) and are more responsive to
adolescents' developmental needs.

The first generation of research in the monitoring debate provided a useful
corrective to the long-standing assumption that these processes are simple and
"top down." That is, the assumption has been that, if parents monitor their adolescents, they will be able to keep them out of trouble. But it is clear now that the
story is not so simple or straightforward. And this is because the effects do not go
simply from parents to children. Children have more agency than they have been
credited with, and there are reciprocal processes at play. New research has demonstrated that parents learn about their adolescent offspring's activities from what
teens are willing to tell them. Current research still supports the notion that
parents who know more about what their teens are doing, where they are going,
and who their companions have teens who show better psychosocial adjustment.
But adolescents have a more active role in these processes than was initially
assumed. They decide how much to disclose or conceal. Parental control and
monitoring do have beneficial effects, although the overall effects are more
complex than originally envisioned: they depend on the specific behaviors parents
are trying to control.

Domain-specific effects of behavioral control

In considering the effects of parenting and behavioral control, it is important
to pay heed to the types of activities parents wish to control. As we might
expect, adolescents who perceive their parents as using more behavioral control
disclose their multifaceted and risky prudential activities more fully. They
also disclose marginally more about their peer activities (Smetana, Villalobos,

Tasopoulos-Chan et al., 2009). In addition, when parents are perceived as (behaviorally) more controlling, adolescents are less likely to avoid talking to them about their multifaceted activities. These findings are all consistent with the notion that parents who use more behavioral control may protect their teenagers from adverse outcomes.

But we have found that teenagers who view their parents as using more behavioral control also lie more about their personal activities (Smetana, Villalobos, Tasopoulos-Chan et al., 2009). This is similar to what Christopher Daddis and myself found in our study of the antecedents of psychological control (Smetana & Daddis, 2002), discussed in Chapter 10. Teenagers who believed that their parents ought to have less authority over personal issues and who viewed their parents as more restrictively controlling their personal domain rated their parents as higher in psychological control 2 years later. Furthermore, teenagers who perceived their mothers as psychologically more controlling in early adolescence reported that their parents monitored them more 2 years later, in middle adolescence. In other words, at high levels, the difference between psychological and behavioral control becomes blurred. The two categories become difficult to distinguish, because behavioral control begins to feel more like intrusive psychological control to adolescents. In keeping with this claim, Gregory Pettit and Robert Laird (2002) speculated that mothers who are overly attentive to their child's behavior in earlier developmental periods may have difficulty with the autonomy issues of adolescence. Adolescents may find parental monitoring and supervision – particularly over personal issues – to be psychologically intrusive and too controlling as they grow older.

Fumiko Kakihara and Lauree Tilton-Weaver (2009) tested this notion explicitly in an experimental study. They examined whether middle adolescents interpret parental behavioral and psychological control differently. They asked adolescents to evaluate different parental responses representing moderate or high levels of behavioral and psychological control. They also considered whether control pertained to a personal issue (friendship choices) or to a prudential issue (alcohol use). For each situation, they evaluated adolescents' competence, mattering to parents, and parental intrusiveness. Contrary to the conventional wisdom about the positive effects of behavioral control, adolescents interpreted high levels of behavioral control more negatively than moderate levels. They also did not differentiate between high level of behavioral control and psychological control. They interpreted them both as indicating less mattering and more intrusiveness. And, regardless of the type of control, high levels of control over personal issues were interpreted most negatively. This suggests that, when parents employ high levels of psychological and behavioral control, particularly regarding personal issues, these two forms of control are not perceived as distinct.

Others have also found that the effects of behavioral control depend on the specific behaviors that are controlled. Studying middle and upper middle-class, primarily White, groups of Canadian teenagers, a team of researchers found that adolescents who perceived their fathers as lower in behavioral control regarding prudential and other multifaceted issues also reported more externalizing problems (Arim, Marshall, & Shapka, 2010). This is consistent with other findings. On the other hand, high levels of perceived parental behavioral control over friendship issues were also associated with more externalizing problems – for instance aggressive behavior and rule breaking.

Summary and Conclusions

As they grow older, adolescents become less likely to share with their parents information about their activities. Despite research suggesting that adolescents lie all the time, lying appears to be relatively infrequent when examined in the context of other strategies for managing information. Instead, adolescents may avoid discussing topics, or they may disclose facts about their lives only partially. Adolescents are more likely to manipulate information when they disagree with parents. Nondisclosure, topic avoidance, and secrecy are conceptually distinct, but they are all strategies that adolescents may adopt for the sake of avoiding overt conflict with parents. Therefore, for better or worse, they may provide alternate ways of obtaining autonomy. As adolescents grow older, it becomes more difficult for parents to monitor their activities, and this provides more opportunities for adolescents simply to do what they want without telling their parents.

Adolescents divulge information about homework and school more than other issues. Adolescents do not tell parents about their involvement in risky behaviors primarily because they worry about parental disapproval and about getting in trouble. They are also more likely to lie about these activities than about others. Likewise, adolescents withhold information about peer and romantic issues because they fear parental disapproval, but also because they view these matters as personal and not harmful. There are ethnic differences as well as acculturation differences in adolescents' willingness to talk to parents about friends, romantic relationships, and personal issues. When adolescents withhold information about their personal activities, it is primarily because they view them as personal matters and not their parents' business. Chinese American adolescents are more likely to conceal information about personal activities and feelings than Mexican and European American youth are, based on personal reasons. They also believe that their parents will not listen or understand. Different ethnic groups in the United States vary in their feelings of closeness to parents and in how closeness is expressed. But, across groups, the processes are the same. Close, trusting relationships and more responsive, accepting parenting are associated with more disclosure to parents.

Parents know far less about adolescents' activities, whereabouts, and companions than they think they do. Parents have various strategies for keeping track of teens, and mothers and fathers typically differ in the strategies they use. A long-standing assumption has been that more parental monitoring helps to keep adolescents out of trouble. However, monitoring has been examined, typically, in terms of parental knowledge rather than in terms of actual surveillance and tracking. Current research shows that adolescents' willingness to make disclosures is a more important source of parental knowledge than parents' control or solicitation of information. In turn, parents who know more have teenagers less likely to be involved in juvenile delinquency. But these relationships are complex and bi-directional. Greater parental knowledge is linked with fewer conduct problems on the teenagers' part; but the more adolescents are engaged in delinquency and problem behavior, the more their parents disengage and stop asking questions. Moreover, asking questions can be perceived as intrusive, but it also can indicate interest and involvement, which leads to more disclosure. The effects of greater (full) disclosure are accentuated in highly supportive families. In addition to out-right lying, partial disclosure – and especially leaving out important information that parents would want to know – has been found to lead to increased delinquency in the long run.

Finally, researchers have assumed that behavioral control has positive effects by keeping youth out of trouble. But if behavioral control is good for teenagers' psychosocial development, is using more of it even better? Apparently not. Recently, researchers have found that high levels of parental behavioral control, particularly when applied to personal issues, is considered intrusive. The differences between behavioral control and psychological control become blurred. This points to the importance of considering the domain of the issue being controlled and the types of issues that adolescents tend to disclose or to keep secret.

12

Coordinations and Change in Social Development

In previous chapters I have considered how adolescents' and parents' different perspectives on their relationships and on their worlds potentially lead to disruptions and conflicts in their relationships. I also considered teenagers' different strategies for managing information about their activities. I claimed that strategic management of information provides a more subversive, alternate route to autonomy. My focus in this book has been on the diverse types of social knowledge that individuals bring to bear on family situations. We saw that the different strands of social knowledge do not exist in isolation from each other. They may interact, conflict, and be coordinated in adolescents' and parents' social reasoning and behavior. In this chapter we shall consider how these different threads of social understanding develop and become coordinated in adolescence. We begin by considering age-related changes in the adolescents' concepts of self and personal choice.

Developmental Changes in Adolescents' Thinking about Self and Personal Issues

In Chapter 5 I treated adolescents' appeals to personal choice as part of a broader psychological system of social knowledge, which emerges in early childhood. Thus far, I have focused on children's and adolescents' ability to differentiate personal from moral and conventional concepts. It should come as no surprise, however, that these concepts also become more sophisticated as adolescents grow older. More specifically, research conducted with primarily North American middle-class youth shows that an understanding of mind, self, and personal choices

Adolescents, Families, and Social Development: How Teens Construct Their Worlds.   Judith G. Smetana
© 2011 Judith G. Smetana

becomes elaborated through social interaction with parents, siblings, and peers during childhood and adolescence.

Early adolescence

During middle and late childhood, children's understanding of the self is trait-like. As Susan Harter (2006) has explained, children describe themselves in terms of traits and competencies, such as *smart* and *dumb*. They start to use these characteristics to compare themselves to others (Harter, 2006). Their understanding is transformed during early adolescence and gives rise to more abstract, integrated, and psychological notions (Broughton, 1978; Damon & Hart, 1988; Harter, 1999, 2006; Harter, Bresnick, Bouchey, & Whitesell, 1997; Nucci, 2001). Detailed semi-structured interviews with American children about their conceptions of mind, self, and reality show that early adolescents begin to distinguish between mental and physical reality. They view mind and self as independent of physical activity. In response to questions about the nature of the self, Colin, an early adolescent boy, responds:

> I think it means not just the person, but the inside of the person. Each person is the self, different from another person. Because each person is different in the way their mind works. It is not physical. It is an emotional or mental thing like that. (Broughton, 1978, p. 87)

Susan Harter and Ann Monsour at the University of Denver (1992) report that early adolescents' self-descriptions start to become increasingly abstract and integrated into higher-level abstractions. For example, early adolescents who at younger ages might have described themselves as smart, creative, and curious may combine these characterizations into the notion that they are intelligent. Also, they may come to see that they exhibit different characteristics in different situations and in different roles (for instance, they are industrious at school but whimsical with friends, lazy with parents but energetic at school, cool with friends but geeky with strangers). These multiple role-related selves first emerge in early adolescence. As these examples suggest, self-descriptions in early adolescence may be contradictory, but they remain compartmentalized. Young adolescents are unable to see the contradictions and fully to integrate all of these diverse aspects of their selves. But because they are not aware of these contradictions, they do not experience any psychological turmoil about expressing them.

Using somewhat different methods, Travis Proulx and Michael Chandler (2009) found a similar trend. They asked a small sample of teenagers to describe instances where they engaged in good and bad behavior and then asked them to explain how they can behave in such different ways and still be considered the same person. The youngest teenagers in this study described their behavior in a seamless way. They viewed themselves as fully autonomous and responsible agents, in charge of their behavior under every circumstance. In the researchers' words,

> Rather, by this reckoning, the appearance of seemingly contradictory intentions constitutes nothing more than mere appearance. Like the Mafia don who both cuts throats and cuddles his grandchildren, all to bring about "what's best for the family," [these] participants [...] claimed that all of their actions were owed to one and the same self-chosen volition that, while differently manifesting itself in different contexts, does not *itself* change from situation to situation. (Proulx & Chandler, 2009, p. 270)

They had what the researchers described as a "singular self."

The transition from more physical to psychological notions of self is also evident in early adolescents' thinking about personal issues. Using hypothetical scenarios, Larry Nucci (1996, 2008) has found that, in middle childhood, European American children view the personal domain in terms of maintaining control over personal activities. Children believe that individuals have different personalities because they like to do different things; their self is expressed behaviorally, through their choice of activities. Control over personal issues takes on new dimensions during early adolescence. Whereas at earlier ages children emphasized behavioral choice, now adolescents emphasize maintaining privacy. In Chapter 5 we saw that concerns with privacy are evident in early adolescents' reasoning about conflicts. Recall 13-year-old Roberta's remark: "I want to talk [on the phone] longer, and usually I want it in private, too ... I like talking on the phone, and I don't like them to hear what I'm talking about."

But, in early adolescence, what is to become the basis for (American) teens' autonomy is formulated reactively, in terms of differentiating the self from others. (Some have claimed that this process is less likely to occur among non-Western youth, but this objection has not been tested by using the types of interviews that Nucci conducted.) This first differentiation of the self is articulated through the need for freedom of choice and through the ability to be different from others; and it results in the attitudes to peer groups and peer group conformity also described in Chapter 5. Early adolescents worry about loss of self and identity through too much conformity to the crowd. As one 13-year-old girl cited by Nucci states:

> I mean everybody's got to be free you know, and growing your hair different is a way of being you know free, making a decision. I hate to be like everybody else. Because you know, I just like to look like myself, not like what somebody wanted me to look like, or you know, what my friends look like. (Nucci, 2008, p. 31)

At the same time, as I discussed in some detail in Chapter 5, adolescents often express their need for a unique identity by affiliating with a crowd and conforming to peer group conventions. Therefore the emphasis on desires for freedom and choice in early adolescence may be expressed somewhat paradoxically, in terms of the need to belong to peer groups. This may reflect flux and lack of stability in early adolescents' personal concepts.

This is consistent with Susan Harter's research. She demonstrates that multiple selves flourish across multiple roles in early adolescence. Harter further claims that this proliferation of multiple selves leads to increased sensitivity to the potentially different opinions and norms of individuals who matter to the teen in each context. In turn, this increased sensitivity to the opinions of others can sometimes promote the construction of a false self. A false self is one that does not mirror the individual's authentic experience. Being hypocritical, "acting phony," or "putting on an act" are all ways in which adolescents describe their false selves. A false self contrasts with the true self, or "the real me inside." According to Harter, false selves do not become salient until early adolescence (Harter, 2006; Harter, Marold, Whitesell, & Cobbs, 1996). Not surprisingly, adolescents who engage in more false-self behavior show less awareness and knowledge of their true self and tend to devalue it more. They also show poorer adjustment, including more depressed affect, poorer self-concept, and increased hopelessness about the future (Harter et al., 1996). The most frequent reason adolescents give for engaging in false self-behavior is to win the approval of others, such as parents or peers. Teens who engage in false-self behavior for this reason are psychologically better adjusted than adolescents who engage in false-self behavior in order to devalue their true self or to experiment with different roles.

Middle adolescence

Middle adolescence brings an increased focus on introspection and a further proliferation – but also some integration – of multiple selves (Damon & Hart, 1988; Harter, 2006; Harter & Monsour, 1992; Proulx & Chandler, 2009). The self becomes more differentiated as individuals make finer distinctions and discriminations. For instance, adolescents may come to view themselves as really close to their mothers but distant from their fathers. Whereas contradictions went unnoticed in early adolescence, Harter and Monsour (1992) claim that middle adolescents increasingly detect these contradictions in their self-descriptions. They experience them, subjectively, as conflicts and confusions (Harter & Monsour, 1992). Girls perceive contradictions in their self-attributes more than boys do, and also find them more upsetting. And the more girls endorse a feminine role orientation, the more upsetting they find these contradictions (Harter, 2006). Although middle adolescents are able to perceive these multiple selves, their conceptions are limited. They are not yet able to integrate them into a cohesive whole, which encompasses contradictions.

Proulx and Chandler (2009), too, find that middle adolescence is characterized by what they refer to as a hierarchical self. Here there may be many different desires, but "one of these desires rises above the others and speaks louder than its fellow self-inhibitors" (p. 270). That is, adolescents describe their good behavior as actively, consciously, and willfully controlled by their selves most of the time, but occasionally bad behavior "sneaks out."

As this suggests, by comparison with early adolescence, there is now also a greater integration of the different aspects of the self into a core inner true self, or essence. Nucci (2008) claims that middle adolescents are more aware of their true selves, or "the real me." They attempt to align the "outside self" of activities and public appearance with their true self. Control over the personal domain becomes one way of discovering, maintaining, and asserting this inner core. Discussing why the boy in a hypothetical scenario should be able to make his own choices about his hair length, a 17-year-old girl in Nucci's research expresses this idea in the following way:

> That's the way he thinks, and the way he acts, and the way he wants to be, and the way he wants others to see him, and the way he sees himself. It seems that you should be able to be a whole person and have your outside look like your inside looks, and people can't determine what your inside looks like, the only person who can decide is you. So it seems that those should go together and that would be why people should determine their own appearance. (Nucci, 2008, p. 32)

Controlling one's appearance is one way of giving others an accurate representation of one's self; it allows one to represent the self in a public way (Nucci, 2008). But it also allows adolescents to construct a concrete representation of the self, and thus to come to know themselves better. Many American teens' bedrooms become extensions of their personal style and appearance. Adolescents may add decorations and flourishes to reflect their interests and to declare who they are and who they would like to be. This may be why conflicts over the condition or appearance of the bedroom are so heated during middle adolescence. The bedroom becomes an extension of the self and an important vehicle for expressing one's identity. Of course, many youth (in the United States and elsewhere) do not have their own bedrooms or private areas in the house, but they may express these same concerns in other contexts and over other issues. Recall Anchee Min's description of Little Green's attempts to assert her identity through her appearance.

Violations of privacy may be more disturbing during middle adolescence than at earlier ages. Once adolescents begin to view the self as having an inner core or essence, invasions of privacy potentially become more serious. They may expose aspects of the self that adolescents do not want to reveal. Again, this is of relevance for adolescent–parent relationships. Adolescents may react strongly to parental behaviors that are perceived as attempts to violate their privacy, and this leads both to increases in conflict and to a greater emphasis on managing information. Therefore managing information about personal issues, friendships, and romantic interests may have a developmental component. With age, these issues are increasingly viewed as private matters.

Indeed, associations between adolescents' perceptions of privacy invasion and adolescent–parent conflict were examined longitudinally in a recent study (Hawk, Keijsers, Hale, & Meeus, 2009). Dutch adolescents' perceptions of parental privacy invasion were associated with their conflicts with parents 1 year later, but only when privacy invasion was measured in middle adolescence (at age 15). In keeping with the description of privacy as an emerging concern of middle adolescence, associations were not observed when privacy invasion was measured in early adolescence, at age 13.

Late adolescence and emerging adulthood

During late adolescence and emerging adulthood, the contradictory aspects of adolescents' self-portraits are no longer seen as being in opposition to each other (Harter & Monsour, 1992). They become integrated into a more abstract, higher-order construction. Harter (2006) notes that late adolescents no longer view contradictory attributes as reflecting conflicting characteristics. For instance, an adolescent who perceives herself as a diligent student but lackadaisical towards schoolwork is quoted by Harter (2006) as stating: "That's normal, I mean you can't just be a total 'grind.' You'd be pretty boring if you were. You have to be flexible" (p. 546). The notion of being flexible allows adolescents to coordinate the perception that one is diligent with the perception of being a slacker when it come to doing homework, just as the description of oneself as moody allows both for the possibility of being depressed sometimes and cheerful other times.

Proulx and Chandler (2009) also find that late adolescents describe the self as unified (or "multiplicitous"). Individuals have different desires and beliefs that arise in different circumstances, and these circumstances elicit good or bad behavior. Yet, much as Harter and Monsour (1992) have found, late adolescents believe that individuals remain the same person regardless of their behavior. But there is an additional wrinkle. Proulx and Chandler also found that, by late adolescence, adolescents attribute their good behavior to internal causes; they view the self as volitional and active, and they take full responsibility for their good behavior. When making attributions about their bad behavior, however, late adolescents tended to blame their moral failings on external circumstances. Therefore, although they describe themselves as having a unified self, their bad behavior stands outside of it and is seen as due to situational causes.

Nucci (1996) claims that the result of more integrated notions of the person is a view of the self as labile. The self constantly evolves as one makes personal decisions. Because the self changes through decision-making, adolescents no longer rely on a notion of a true self or essence. Instead, the self is constantly being transformed in the process of making personal choices. One 19-year-old elaborates:

> It [the self] is a process, it's not static. It's dynamic. It's always changing. You make yourself as you're going along by choosing to do those things that are coherent with what you think you are at that time or want to become. (Quoted in Nucci, 1977, p. 158)

American late adolescents come to view decisions regarding controlling one's appearances as personal matters that are essential to the self. Adolescents also become concerned with impression management – with presenting a self that will generate the type of public responses they desire. Similar concerns with the presentation of self also arise in relation to the importance of privacy. In keeping some things private, adolescents must consider the social effects of what they reveal to others. As Nucci notes, society cannot dictate one's personal choices. This is clearly a subjective assessment. But, in considering the effects of personal choices on others and what one should divulge, late adolescents increasingly coordinate their notions of what is personal with conventional and moral issues. Thus development appears to resolve earlier incongruities and contradictions in reasoning and to lead to increased integration and coordination of social concepts. Control over personal issues becomes important to coordinating the self-system and constructing an internally consistent whole.

To summarize thus far, more abstract notions of the personal domain emerge across the second decade of life. Over time, these notions become increasingly integrated into a coherent self-system. (Although there is some preliminary evidence from Proulx and Chandler that this integration may be achieved by sometimes disavowing one's bad behavior, these researchers did not define or investigate what "bad behavior" meant to their participants). We saw in earlier chapters that social interactions with parents, siblings, and friends facilitate the development of personal concepts. For instance, as described in Chapter 5, the parents' provision of choices in childhood sends tacit messages about what is personal and what is not. Interactions with parents and peers during adolescence similarly provide opportunities for adolescents to consider and negotiate the boundaries and the content of the personal domain – and these interactions also facilitate the emergence of more mature concepts. It is important to remember that, although parents tacitly communicate about what they believe to be personal, children, adolescents, and adults also make claims, in an active manner, about what they believe should be personal. Desires for increased personal jurisdiction lead to increased conflict with parents, particularly during the first part of adolescence, and to efforts to manage information in the second. In the next chapter we shall consider how relationships with parents change in emerging adulthood. But first we consider how recent changes in adolescents' modes of communication and, specifically, how the dramatic increase in the use of social media may reflect alterations in autonomy.

Personal Expression, Privacy, and Social Media

New technology has dramatically altered adolescents' social interactions. There has been an explosion in adolescents' use of social media, including blogging, frequenting online chat rooms, and online social networking (for instance through sites such as MySpace, Facebook, Friendster, and Bebo). The Pew Internet and American Life Project is tracking American adolescents' and adults' use of social media in order to understand this emerging phenomenon better (Lenhart, 2009, May 23). They have found that nearly all American adolescents aged 12 to 17 spend time with their friends in face-to-face interaction. Two thirds also use cell phones, mostly to talk to friends on a daily basis. But almost two thirds of those surveyed also send messages to friends by texting, sending emails, or using social networking sites. And, among the last ones, nearly half use this medium to communicate daily with friends. Most American 15- to 17-year-olds have online profiles on social networking sites (Lenhart, 2009, May 23). Indeed, proportionally more middle adolescents maintain online profiles than either younger adolescents or adults over 24 years of age, although the biggest users are late adolescents and emerging adults (18- to 24-year-olds).

There has been widespread public anxiety about the types of personal information that teenagers make available online (Livingstone, 2008). And adolescents' extensive use of social media suggests an interesting paradox. Throughout this book, I have described adolescents as being concerned with expanding and controlling their personal domains. Yet adolescents appear to be sharing personal, even intimate information with ever-widening circles of friends and casual acquaintances. For instance, researchers Kaveri Subrahmanyam, David Smahel, and Patricia Greenfield (2006) from the University of California, Los Angeles found that, in using online chat rooms (both monitored and unmonitored), younger teens provide more identity information – such as age, gender, and location – in their chats than older adolescents do. In contrast, 18- to 24-year-olds are more likely than younger teens to include sexual content. Adolescents appear to provide very personal information in contexts that are easily accessible to friends and strangers alike.

But emerging scholarship suggests that privacy concerns do loom large for teenagers when they use social media. As I mentioned in Chapter 11, social networks offer a context for managing social relationships. Nearly all adolescents (as well as adults) use online networks to stay in touch with pre-existing friends. Far fewer adolescents and adults, although still a considerable percentage (49% of each), use online social networking to make friends (Lenhart, Madden, Smith, &

Macgill, 2007). Livingstone (2008) claims that adolescents view online social networking mostly as a peer context that is safe from parents' surveillance. In other words, it provides a milieu for information management. Adolescents have the option to keep information private by choosing whom to "befriend" and whether to keep their profiles private. They use social media as a tool for creating and managing their identity. Their profiles afford an opportunity to construct and present their self and to experiment with their identity in a social environment. Whereas adults may view it as risky to make information available on these sites, adolescents do not.

Indeed, a daily diary study of college students' use of Facebook (one of the most popular social networking sites in the United States) showed that much of the information adolescents presented on their profile page was relatively innocuous (Pempek, Yermolayeva, & Calvert, 2009). They expressed their identity mainly by posting information about their interests and media preferences, like their favorite music, movies, and books. These are primarily personal issues. Therefore it appears that only the medium is novel. The developmental processes at work are the same; they are merely expressed in a new context. Adolescents are constructing their identity through exercising personal choices.

According to Pempek and colleagues (2009), teenagers post pictures of themselves as a way of expressing their identity. In their study, girls posted photos more often than boys did. They also frequently untagged (deleted) photos that others posted of them, mainly because they did not like the way they looked. Boys also deleted photos of themselves, but they were more likely than girls to do this because the photos depicted behaviors (like drinking) that they did not want others to see. It may be that the ability to change rapidly the information posted on one's social networking profile gives adolescents an opportunity to construct and explore the multiple selves that emerge in middle adolescence. It may also allow them to experiment with reconciling the outside self of public appearance with their "true" or authentic self.

Blogging, too, appears to provide a context for identity construction and expression. According to the Pew Internet and American Life Project, the primary reasons for blogging are creative self-expression and the documenting and sharing of personal experiences – concerns that are particularly salient during adolescence (Lenhart & Fox, 2006, July 19). The use of sexual content in chat rooms has also been seen as reflecting adolescents' attempts to explore their sexual identity (Subrahmanyam et al., 2006).

Livingstone's (2008) conclusions about social networks as primarily a means of peer communication were based on qualitative interviews with a small group of adolescents. The discussions of privacy, she notes, were the liveliest part of her interviews. She proposes that privacy in the context of online social networking pertains to controlling *who* knows what about you, rather than to *what* they know. Livingstone states: "The point is that teenagers must and do disclose personal information in order to sustain intimacy, but they wish to be in control of how they manage this disclosure" (p. 405). Indeed, disclosure of some personal information online (for instance, descriptors such as age and gender) is merely a way of conveying information that is typically observed in face-to-face interaction (Subrahmanyam et al., 2006). As these researchers note, though, the pitfall of using social networking sites like Facebook is that these do not allow adolescents to make subtle discriminations among their social relationships. They fail to capture the varying levels of privacy that adolescents may wish to maintain in making information available. Nevertheless, these researchers believe that adults' concerns about privacy risks in adolescents' use of social media are somewhat overblown. Most adolescents do maintain some control over who can access their profiles.

Coordinations between Personal Concepts and Concepts of Morality

A central proposition of this book is that individuals distinguish among different types of social knowledge. Much of my focus has been on the personal domain and its relevance for adolescents' developing autonomy. But various theorists have noted the close relationship between psychological notions of self and individuals' understanding of moral issues. For instance, Piaget (1965) claimed that some individuality is necessary for the development of moral judgments. And as I noted in Chapter 4, philosophers also view claims about rights as having their basis in establishing and maintaining personal agency (Dworkin, 1978; Gewirth, 1978). In agreement with these notions, researchers from the social domain perspective, including Charles Helwig (2006) and Larry Nucci (1996, 2008), have asserted that personal concepts inform the construction of morality. The elements of the personal domain, such as control over one's body and claims regarding freedom of expression, communication, and association, provide the grounding for moral conceptions of rights.

In Chapter 4 we saw that, when harm is presented in a direct and unambiguous way, nearly all children and adolescents judge it to be wrong to harm another. The ability to make rudimentary moral judgments about hypothetical situations that are straightforward and familiar and involve physical harm and others' welfare emerges between 2 and 3 years of age (Smetana & Braeges, 1990). Numerous studies (reviewed in Smetana, 2006) have shown that these judgments become more stable and are reliably applied by age 4. But this does not mean that 4-year-olds make mature moral judgments! As they grow older, children are increasingly able to take into consideration diverse beliefs, motives, and intentions in making moral judgments.

The claim is that concepts of rights have their basis in children's developing notions of the personal domain. A general understanding of moral rights, at least among North American children, develops during childhood. Charles Helwig's careful studies demonstrate that Canadian children as young as 6 years of age view freedom of speech and religion as universal rights, which apply in all cultures. They also view restrictions placed on these rights by governments as wrong or illegitimate (Helwig, 1997, 1998). However, Helwig found age-related differences among young children's justifications for upholding freedom of speech and religion. At first, children (6-year-olds) link these rights to their developing notions of the personal domain. They support civil liberties by appealing to needs for personal choice and individual expression. Beginning around 8 years of age, however, children start to see the broader implications of these rights for society, culture, and democratic institutions. For instance, they view freedom of speech as a way to correct societal injustices by enabling individuals to voice their concerns in protests or petitions. They also regard these freedoms as facilitating the kind of communication among individuals that could potentially lead to societal change (Helwig, 1998).

And more: recall that, as we saw in Chapter 6, Helwig and his colleagues' studies have shown that children in China also apply concepts of rights. By middle childhood, children develop more mature notions of the political realm and rights. Their conceptions include an understanding of the value and function of civil liberties within a democratic political order. More sophisticated understandings of how rights are applied in different social contexts develop during adolescence. Adolescents become more able to understand how the features of situations influence rights. They also become more adept at considering the influence of psychological factors like their perceptions of the competence and maturity of agents to exercise their rights.

Therefore the basic features of civil liberties as moral rights develop in childhood. Except for the research in China, Helwig's approach and methods have not been used to study young children's conceptions of rights in other parts of the world. But in Chapter 6 I described other approaches to studying adolescents' conceptions of rights cross-culturally. For instance, Wainryb and Turiel's research on the Druze Arabs in Israel also included a study focusing on Druze Arab 13- and 17-year-olds' and adults' evaluation of freedom of speech, religion, and reproduction (Turiel & Wainryb, 1998). When these three rights were presented abstractly, Druze participants overwhelmingly endorsed them for individuals in their own country – although for freedom of speech and religion more than for reproduction. They also evaluated negatively laws that restricted these freedoms. Age differences reflected in their judgments paralleled what Helwig (1995) has found. Late adolescents and adults viewed it as more acceptable to violate unjust laws restricting civil liberties than early adolescents did. Also in harmony with Helwig's (1995) findings, when Druze participants applied the same rights in conflicting situations, they sometimes subordinated those rights to other social and moral concerns. In other words they believed that there are legitimate reasons to restrict rights in some circumstances; rights did not "override" all other considerations.

Their evaluations also reflected the hierarchical structure of their society. As we saw in the study of Druze Arabs described in Chapter 6, rights were applied differently to males and females. Druze participants viewed it as more of a wrong for husbands and fathers to restrict their sons' than their wives' and daughters' freedoms. But women also viewed the restriction of their rights as unfair. Therefore this study demonstrated a complex coordination of rights with other types of concerns. The social structure clearly influenced the way in which individuals thought about morality – and it was not a simple way.

Another line of research has been informed by policy concerns, as reflected in the United Nations' Convention on the Rights of the Child; and this line was developed to address the need to establish universal rights that can be used to guide policy in different countries. The focus of this research is on distinctions between children's nurturance and self-determination rights. Nurturance rights are defined broadly as society's obligation to consider the best interests of the child and, more narrowly, as the child's right to care and protection. Thus nurturance rights can be seen as similar or analogous to what I have referred to throughout this book as moral issues. In contrast, self-determination rights are defined as children's ability to exercise control over different areas of their own lives even when their views might conflict with those of the supervising adults, and as children's right to freedom of expression. Self-determination rights correspond to what I have referred to here as personal issues.

Several cross-cultural studies have examined whether children's reasoning reflects particular cultural orientations towards rights. For instance, in one study, rural and urban early and late adolescents from mainland China evaluated children's nurturance and self-determination rights (Lahat, Helwig, Yang, Tan, & Liu, 2009). Late adolescents (and urban youth) endorsed self-determination more than early adolescents (and rural youth) did. Adolescents prioritized self-determination rights both when these rights were in conflict with authority's desires and when they conflicted with nurturance rights. In these cases, adolescents reasoned about concerns for personal choice and autonomy. In contrast, adolescents' reasoning about nurturance rights focused on their own psychological and physical well-being. Thus this study, much like the study of Druze Arabs just described, demonstrates that the endorsement of rights and personal choice is not restricted to individuals in Western cultures.

Nurturance and self-determination right have also been compared among Malaysian ethnic Chinese, Canadian, American, and Swiss early adolescents (Cherney & Shing, 2008). Regardless of their country of origin, all early adolescents advocated rights on the basis of concerns with fairness, autonomy, and democratic decision-making. Under some circumstances, adolescents also rejected existing cultural practices. There were cross-cultural differences in whether individuals emphasized nurturance versus self-determination rights. The differences were based on how these individuals evaluated the features of the different situations. But children's developmental competence was an important concern in considering whether adolescents should be granted rights. As Helwig (1997) has claimed, as children grow older, they are better able to consider the influence of psychological factors when making judgments.

These studies compared adolescents' evaluations of rights as presented in straightforward situations with their evaluations of rights in situations where there were competing moral concerns, or where moral considerations were in conflict with conventional matters. But in some situations individuals must coordinate moral issues with personal choices in order to behave in their own self-interest. And there may be ambiguity about whether particular actions cause harm. In ongoing research, Larry Nucci and Elliot Turiel (2007, 2009) are investigating children's and adolescents' ability to weigh different types of concerns. They are in the course of examining children's and adolescents' moral evaluations about either helping someone in need or refraining from inflicting harm (either directly or indirectly) to the other person.

In one set of stories, both the moral situations of helping and those of harming were depicted in a straightforward way, without competing goals. Overall, Nucci and Turiel found that, in these situations, evaluations did not change with age. As we have found in studying very young children, there was near unanimous agreement that it is wrong to harm and good to help. As one 8-year-old participant stated: "He's stealing, and [...] it's not good to steal." Another 8-year-old said: "It's someone else's $10 bill, she shouldn't keep it because it's not hers."

Children and adolescents also evaluated situations where the moral choice was in conflict with the protagonist's personal goals (that is, with self-interest) or with the needs or desires of a third party. For instance, in one story, a child needs to earn money in order to participate in an activity with her friends. She is on an empty bus, when a second person unknowingly drops money while attempting to pay the bus fare. The child has to decide whether to alert the passenger or to keep the money for herself. In addition, Nucci and Turiel systematically varied the scenarios to describe the protagonist as a neutral other, as a sympathetic or needy other, or as an antagonistic other (as in situations where the transgression was provoked). For instance, in the story about the dropped money, the actor was variously described in a neutral way or as a vulnerable child.

These results were complex. Along with their understanding of fairness, adolescents showed a greater capacity to incorporate ambiguous aspects of moral situations as they got older. For example, in considering direct harm in conflict situations (such as hitting in response to provocation), many children thought that it was permissible to hit back and that one should be able to engage in "self-defense" in these situations. More 10- to 14-year-olds than 8- and 16-year-olds thought that they had the right to self-defense in response to hitting. But when the child who hit first was described as emotionally vulnerable, the moral acceptability of hitting in self-defense disappeared.

Moral thinking did not progress in a linear fashion. Rather, there was a U-shaped pattern of moral growth in children's and adolescents' judgments and in their ability to integrate divergent aspects of situations. There were periods of transition in teenagers' thinking. Adolescents (14-year-olds) were more able than younger children to consider aspects of moral situations, but they applied moral criteria unevenly and with uncertainty. During this transitional period, adolescents attended to new features of moral situations and groped towards more complex integrations of moral thought. In particular, in early to middle adolescence, their attempts to establish boundaries of personal jurisdiction resulted in an over-application of conceptions of rights in morally ambiguous contexts. They were "blinded" by the personal aspects of situations and gave more weight to personal prerogatives and personal goals in early to middle adolescence relative to pre-adolescence or late adolescence. As a 14-year-old in Nucci and Turiel's (2007, 2009) study stated, "I think she has a right to do what she wants to [about stealing]. Because it is once again his decision to do what he wants" (quoted in Nucci, 2008, p. 49). Another adolescent of the same age noted: "He's got every right to keep the ten dollars, like I said, because it's in nowhere land. And it's his; he found it. It's not in the kid's house or anything" (quoted in Nucci, 2008, p. 48).

Readers may have noticed that this description of uncertainty and instability in early to middle adolescents' ability to integrate different moral notions resembles the picture of conflicts, confusions, and contradictions emerging from the self-descriptions of middle adolescents in Susan Harter's analysis. Yet, although some interesting parallels indeed exist, there are also important differences. Harter presented contradictions in self-descriptions (and the resulting conflicts) as the defining characteristic of middle adolescents' thinking about the self. The over-extension of the personal domain, which Nucci and Turiel (2008) found in moral thinking at this age, was much more limited in its scope than Harter found in describing middle adolescents' self-conceptions. Instability in thinking was apparent only when adolescents attempted to coordinate reasoning about harm with the idea of helping in conditions that involved vulnerable individuals. Uncertainty and ambiguity in moral thinking was not evident in evaluations of straightforward, prototypical moral issues, or in judgments about neutral situations or provoked transgressions. In addition, Harter and Monsour (1992) found that contradictions in self-descriptions resulted in subjectively experienced conflicts and confusion. In contrast, Nucci and Turiel provide little evidence that teenagers' over-application of personal concepts in morally ambiguous contexts was psychologically troublesome or problematic. Adolescents did not subjectively experience such contradictions as conflictual. Rather, the latter appeared to represent adolescents' efforts to coordinate the boundaries of the personal and moral domains.

As adolescence progressed, teenagers were better able to distinguish personal choices from conceptions of rights. They became better able to coordinate the moral, conventional, and personal aspects of multifaceted moral situations. For instance, a 16-year-old responded: "Like I said before, you don't have a right to steal money, and this is still stealing because you know who dropped that money.

It's not like breaking into someone's house, but it's still stealing" (quoted in Nucci, 2008, p. 49). Developmental changes reflected shifts in understanding what it means to have a "right" to do something, as opposed to having the free will to determine one's actions. This change was combined with shifts in the conception of one's objective moral obligations to others. There was a greater tendency among older adolescents to evaluate moral actions independently of the relationship between protagonist and victim. They also appeared more inclined than early adolescents to express forgiveness and compassion. All this indicates that older adolescents were better able to coordinate the moral and the personal domain when these were in conflict.

Although the results of Nucci and Turiel's (2007) study are preliminary, several other studies have shown similar age trends. In Chapter 6, I discussed Helwig's research on adolescents' conceptions of rights in abstract, contextualized, and multifaceted situations (where the contextualized conflicts resulted in physical harm or inequality). As I noted earlier, the great majority of Helwig's adolescent participants viewed freedom of speech and religion as universally applicable rights, both when they were presented in abstract form and when they were presented in contextualized situations. In general, older adolescents gave priority to civil liberties across a broader range of situations than younger adolescents did. But the types of complex integrations of moral thought that Nucci and Turiel (2007) observed were also evident in older adolescents' evaluations of multifaceted situations. Older adolescents were better able to coordinate their notions of equality with psychological differences in individuals, much as Cherney and Shing (2008) reported in their cross-cultural studies of rights.

Similar results were found in the longitudinal study of adolescents' perceptions of the right to engage in potentially harmful risky behaviors (Flanagan, Stout, & Gallay, 2008), described in Chapter 9. Recall that this research examined 11- to 18-year-olds' beliefs in the government's right to intervene in, or regulate, potentially risky behaviors (referred to as public health beliefs), and the same teenagers' endorsement of individual rights. These beliefs followed different developmental trajectories over the 3 years of the study. Both when they were examined at a single point in time and when they were examined over an extended period, middle adolescents were less likely to believe that society had the right to control individuals' involvement in risky behaviors than early or late adolescents were. By late adolescence, teens appear to develop more sophisticated conceptions of health beliefs, which involve a coordination between individual rights (individuals' personal choice to experiment with substances) and "a recognition of the need for laws enacted by government that constrain individuals' rights in the interest of a larger public good" (Flanagan et al., 2008, p. 831). Thus, much as Nucci and Turiel (2007, 2009) found, middle adolescence involves an over-extension of the personal domain and what the authors refer to as "an ardent commitment to personal rights as a basis for making decisions" (Flanagan et al., 2008, p. 831). But by late adolescence youth are able to strike a better balance between the right to autonomy and their understanding of the need for society to protect the welfare of its citizens.

We also found evidence of similar age-related trends in a recent study of adolescents' and parents' evaluations of helping in hypothetical situations where the adolescent's or the parent's needs were in conflict with the other's personal desires (Smetana, Tasopoulos-Chan, Villalobos et al., 2009). Previous research has shown that children and adolescents overwhelmingly evaluate hypothetical actors as being obligated to help individuals when needs are great and individuals are in great distress. But here we examined competing desires manifest in the types of everyday situations that teenagers and parents often face. And a novel feature of this study was that we obtained parents' as well as their adolescent children's evaluations.

The interpersonal needs depicted in these stories were mundane, and they were systematically varied so as to reflect very minor or moderate needs. But in all cases they conflicted with competing and potentially legitimate personal desires. For instance, in one story, Mary and her friends want Mary's mother to help them with preparing an act for a school talent show. Mary's mother has a special expertise that could help them win, which the teens desperately want. However, Mary's mother is looking forward to attending her monthly book club meeting. Should Mary's mother help? In another story, Ellen's father has hired some waitresses for a big holiday party, but one of the waitresses has called in sick. Ellen's father cannot find a replacement. He asks Ellen, who has experience as a waitress, to help. But Ellen has been looking forward to a long-planned sledding party with a big group of friends. Should she help? As these examples illustrate, the stories swapped the character (parent or child) whose need conflicted with a personal desire.

Parents considered it more obligatory to help both the parents and the teens and less permissible for both to assert personal desires in the condition where needs were greater, even though the levels of needs depicted in all of these stories were quite minimal overall. Parents also allowed adolescents more autonomy. Compared to their children, parents viewed it as more permissible for hypothetical teens to satisfy their personal desires in situations where parents' needs were low. In sum, parents coordinated and balanced adolescents' desires for greater autonomy with obligations to assist other family members who asked for assistance.

As I noted in Chapter 1, a persistent theme emerging from public opinion polls and social science commentaries is that American youth are selfish, lacking in moral values, and in a state of moral decline. Furthermore, researchers comparing the responses of Americans to those of individuals from other, more collectivist cultures have asserted that Americans consider themselves to be morally obligated to help only in extreme circumstances and in cases where needs are pressing. But these claims were not born out in this study. European American adolescents viewed teens as relatively obligated to help their parents even when the needs were trivial. Their reasoning focused on concern for others ("she should stay home so she could please her parents") and role responsibilities ("'cause family matters more").

Adolescents did use personal reasons to justify ignoring parents' requests for help and satisfying personal desires ("'cause I just like going out with my friends and stuff like that, and it's probably just good for her to get out and have some fun"). In these situations, their reasons were based in equal measure on personal and on pragmatic reasons ("because he already had plans") and on prudential justifications ("he probably needed to study and getting good grades is more important"). In contrast, even when parents believed that it was permissible for adolescents to fulfill their personal desires, they rarely reasoned about adolescents' personal choices. Parents focused primarily on the pragmatic or prudential aspects of the situations. The prevalence of personal reasoning among adolescents and its absence among parents reflect the paradigmatic differences between parents' and adolescents' perspectives, which I have described as characterizing situations of adolescent–parent conflict.

To elucidate age trends further, we also compared 12- and 15-year-olds' responses with college students' judgments. There was no clear and linear age trend reflecting an increased awareness of the need to help parents. Indeed, when interpersonal needs were low, adolescents (7th and 10th graders) viewed hypothetical teen actors as having more of an obligation to help their parents and considered it less permissible to ignore parental requests and fulfill their personal desires than college students did! College students, who were living away from home for the first time, appeared to be less "tuned in" to hypothetical parents' desires in these low-need situations.

But, reflecting the U-shaped trend found in Nucci and Turiel's (2007) study, both early adolescents and college students viewed hypothetical teens as significantly more selfish than middle adolescents did when these teens would consider personal desires in situations where parents expressed greater interpersonal needs. Middle adolescents were aware of their obligations to help. However, they believed that they had more of a right to satisfy their personal desires than younger and older adolescents did, and they considered it less selfish when they satisfied them.

Development within and across Domains

So, what do these studies imply about development? What is development the development of? Let me start with what it is not. The research reviewed here and in earlier chapters differs from theoretical perspectives that argue that social and moral reasoning develops in broad orientations or global stages. For instance, the findings are not consistent with Laurence Kohlberg's (1984) well-known theory of moral judgment development. As noted earlier, in Kohlberg's moral-stage theory, moral concepts develop through a series of six universal, sequential, and hierarchical stages, in which concepts of justice and rights become progressively differentiated from nonmoral concepts like social conventions, personal preferences and entitlements, and concerns with prudence and pragmatics. According to Kohlberg, only individuals who are at the most advanced level of moral reasoning fully differentiate and prioritize justice and rights over nonmoral concerns. However, Kohlberg's own empirical research indicates that few, if any, individuals actually attain this advanced level of moral reasoning. His research reveals that most individuals are stuck at what he refers to as the "conventional" level, where moral reasoning is structured by interpersonal needs, role obligations, and respect for societal rules and authority.

As we have seen throughout this book, there is persuasive evidence that even young children treat moral issues pertaining to harm, welfare, and rights as qualitatively distinct – along a number of dimensions – from social conventional norms (including respect for societal rules and authority), from matters of prudence, and from personal preferences and choices. Kohlberg's claim that individuals are not attuned to distinctly moral concerns may be more of a reflection of the methods he used than of limitations in adolescents' moral reasoning. He derived his six-stage theory of moral judgment development from responses to complex, hypothetical dilemmas entailing conflicting moral and nonmoral concerns.

We have seen that the way individuals weigh and coordinate different features of situations varies depending on the parameters of these situations, as well as on individual circumstances. Research discussed here and in earlier chapters demonstrates that, when considering moral matters, adolescents coordinate moral with – and sometimes (but not always) prioritize moral over – conventional, personal, and pragmatic concerns. Therefore the age-related differences are not in whether children and adolescents view issues as moral and pertaining to justice, welfare, and rights. Rather, these differences are in how they weigh and coordinate conflicting moral concerns or moral, conventional, and personal features of situations. As adolescents mature, they conceive of moral concepts as more broadly applicable and generalizable. But at the same time they are better able to consider the context. This means that the way in which individuals coordinate moral, personal, and conventional concerns in particular situations depends in part on the features of different situations and on their salience. These features may be evaluated differently in different contexts. The salience of different features (for instance safety concerns, or autonomy) may be heightened in different cultural, ethnic, and socio-economic status contexts.

Furthermore, as we have seen repeatedly throughout this book, concerns with individual rights – with autonomy, personal freedoms, and personal choice – are all legitimate concerns, which are articulated by children, adolescents, and adults in different cultures – and not just in the West. They reflect central components of the self and, as various theorists have claimed, basic human needs. Therefore, on the basis of a great deal of empirical evidence, I have argued that these are concerns of individuals both in individualistic and in collectivistic cultures. Part of my argument has been that these broad cultural categories do not do justice to the variations in reasoning that are found within individuals across cultures. Concerns with autonomy, agency, and personal choice may, at times, conflict with, and be subordinated to, moral matters and conventional norms; but individuals are concerned with establishing the boundaries of the personal domain and the right to control certain issues. The evidence clearly points to the negative consequences for adjustment and mental health, for individuals worldwide, of situations where the personal domain is overly restricted (although what is perceived as over-control – and also as personal – varies in different cultural contexts).

Furthermore, it should be noted that this view also bears on socialization approaches to social development – which, in my view, place undue emphasis on compliance (committed or otherwise) as the focal measure of successful social development. Clearly, children need to learn the appropriate norms, rules, and conventions of their society. They also need to acquire moral values. But I have argued that children are actively engaged in interpreting and evaluating the different social conventional rules, norms, and standards they encounter. An understanding of cultural norms and expectations and of moral matters develops through reciprocal interactions. And as we have seen, healthy social development involves pulls towards acquiring culture-specific expectations and norms, pushes towards questioning them (especially when they involve violations of rights and harm to others), and needs to establish arenas of personal choice and decision-making.

Therefore there is no "one size fits all" answer to how adolescents at different ages reason in particular situations. As they grow older, adolescents are better able to take into consideration the psychological characteristics of the actors and the nature of the conventional concerns. At the same time, they view justice and rights as more broadly applicable, and as sometimes overriding other concerns. Thus there are universal features of moral judgments, but they are influenced by their social context, as well as by the relevant informational assumptions.

Moreover, along with others, I have claimed that different types of social interaction influence the development of different systems of social knowledge (moral, conventional, and psychological). But, in addition, children and adolescents grow up in very different circumstances, both within and between cultures. These different social experiences also produce individual differences in how concepts are applied in particular situations. For instance, in considering adolescents' judgments regarding legitimate parental authority, we saw that adolescents' experiences with parents and peers affect how broadly or narrowly they construct the boundaries of the personal (and other) domains. Parenting styles, parental discipline practices, and identification with particular peer crowds all may influence adolescents' social judgments. This means that, with age, adolescents' social reasoning is *both* more context-bound and more generalizable. Although this may seem paradoxical, it reflects the individuals' developing ability to coordinate different features of situations in an integrated way.

This focus on integration as a central feature of adolescent development is congruent with another body of research, which emerges from recent studies of adolescent brain development (see Steinberg, 2005, 2008 for reviews). This research has shown that normal development during adolescence can be understood in terms of the "coordination of emotional, intellectual, and behavioral proclivities and capabilities" (Steinberg, 2005, p. 69). The focus of this research is much different from what I have described in this book. It is on how different aspects of brain development become coordinated. It focuses in particular on the integration of brain regions and systems that regulate behavior and emotion (also on the development of response inhibition and on the calibration of risk and reward). Nevertheless, the argument is similar. Development during adolescence (and young adulthood) involves the coordination of different systems (here, of social knowledge) that may develop in different ways and at different rates. Their lack of coordination may lead to potential difficulties in development, and successful development is marked by their integration or coordination.

Recently, it has become popular, particularly in social psychology, to discount the view that individuals are rational beings. Instead, one prominent view is that individuals rely heavily on implicit knowledge, or nonconscious social cognition (Bargh & Chartrand, 1999). The proposition, as applied to moral and social reasoning, has been that individuals respond to social events in primarily affective, intuitive, and automated ways. Therefore it is claimed that, in everyday life, reasoning rarely results from a deliberative process. According to this view, most of the time we are sleepwalking. We are said to respond to situations in an emotional, nonreflective way; only very occasionally do we reason or deliberate. (One wonders whether the authors of these accounts view their own theoretical products in a similar way, or whether these views only apply when they think about others as mostly nonrational.) A further corollary of this proposition is that reasoning (cognition) is seen as distinct from affect. They are described as separate realms. In this view, affective reactions, not cognition, are seen as the norm in our everyday social lives.

In contrast to this view, I have presented evidence here to show that children, adolescents, and adults are active, volitional beings who seek to make sense of their social surroundings. They reflect and act on their moral, social, and personal understandings. As Turiel (2002) noted, "deliberation and reflection [...] should not be taken to mean only that we sit down, take time off, sip a cup of coffee, and ponder the universe" (p. 292). Once ideas have been formed, thinking and reasoning may seem to occur in an automatic way; but my claim here is that adolescents form their ideas through thought and reflection. Therefore, adolescents may contest their parents' conventions and challenge the status quo in terms of where the boundaries of personal issues should be drawn. They may incorporate these ideas into their responses to social events. But this does not mean that adolescents necessarily sit down and brood about these issues. They reflect and act in a seamless way.

My approach to analyzing adolescent–parent interactions focuses on social cognition, or the meaning that adolescents and parents make out of their social interactions. But it should be clear by now that these discussions – and adolescents' and parents' constructions of the social world more generally – involve feelings and emotional responses. Reasoning is not necessarily "cold-blooded" or devoid of emotion. As we saw in Chapter 4, emotions are deeply embedded in social reasoning. And, as the analyses of adolescent–parent conflict suggest, distinctions between reasoning and affect cannot always be easily drawn. The emotional force of adolescent–parent disagreements may lead to transformations both in the adolescents' and in the parents' reasoning.

Summary and Conclusions

For much of this book, I have focused on how children, adolescents, and adults in different contexts and cultures apply moral, conventional, and personal concepts to their thinking about different social situations. I have focused, in particular, on adolescents' thinking about adolescent–parent relationships and on how adolescents' perspectives sometimes clash with their parents' perspectives. In this chapter I have elaborated on the description of moral and personal concepts by discussing how concepts in each domain change with age and with increasing social experience. In Chapter 5 I have also described age-related changes in social conventional concepts; you may recall that adolescents' understanding of conventions moves through successive phases of affirmation, and then negation, of the importance of conventions in structuring social life. Therefore, during adolescence, concepts in each domain become more complex and differentiated. I have also described how age-related changes in thinking influence the coordination of concepts in different domains.

In this chapter we saw that there are some "bumps on the road" to these new advances in thinking. Middle adolescence (at least among the North American children who have been the focus of much of this research) appears to be a period of particular difficulty and vulnerability. Adolescents struggle to resolve problems in their understanding of both self and morality. They may experience increased conflict and confusion as they seek to reconcile divergent and sometimes contradictory aspects of the self, which were not evident to them at earlier ages. Thus advances in awareness bring new problems to be resolved. Furthermore, Harter (2006) has made connections between these intrapsychic conflicts of middle adolescence, to which girls are more prone, and girls' increased risks of depression, which also arise at this age. Adolescents also appear to over-extend the personal domain in their attempts to coordinate moral notions of rights with their developing notions of the personal. For a brief period of time they may be insensitive to the moral dimensions of some complex situations. These concerns with self, identity, and personal expression are evident in adolescents' interactions that use social media. But, while these emerging technologies represent new social contexts, the issue of establishing the self, identity, and control over personal issues is the same, whether it is expressed on social networking sites or in face-to-face peer interactions.

As all this suggest, social development during adolescence is complex and fraught with both challenges and opportunities. But by the end of the second decade of life most adolescents have more nuanced, contextually sensitive, and integrated social, moral, and personal understandings of their social world. Adolescents construct, elaborate, and negotiate their social worlds in their interactions with parents, siblings, and peers. We will conclude in the following chapter by considering transitions to adulthood and the changes they bring to parent–adolescent relationships.

13

Life Beyond Adolescence
Transitions to Adulthood

In Chapter 12 we saw that different strands in the social understanding of teenagers become elaborated upon and coordinated in adolescence. In this final chapter we consider changes in parent–child relationships as adolescence draws to a close. We also reflect on the implications of adolescent–parent relationships for adult development. We shall begin by discussing how researchers have conceptualized the period of time just beyond adolescence.

Emerging Adulthood: Process or Stage?

The developmental factors described in the previous chapter combine with the increasing heterogeneity in life choices to produce a great deal of diversity in developmental pathways. Recently, there has been increased interest in late adolescence as an important period of change, transition, and preparation for emerging adulthood. As I noted in Chapter 1, Jeffrey Arnett (2000, 2004, 2007) has argued that emerging adulthood is a developmental stage that is distinct both from late adolescence and from young adulthood. This claim is based on the observation that there is little demographic variation among adolescents aged 12 to 17, but considerably more after that. Until about age 18, nearly all (Western) adolescents are unmarried and live at home with one or both parents. Most also attend school. However, demographic diversity abounds in the years between 18 and 25 to 30. Most adolescents leave home around the age of 18 or 19, some

Adolescents, Families, and Social Development: How Teens Construct Their Worlds.   Judith G. Smetana
© 2011 Judith G. Smetana

to work and some to attend college. Some marry young, whereas for others marriage is greatly delayed. Some continue to live at home or become part of the "boomerang" generation, returning home after a period spent away, at college, or spent living on their own. Others establish their own households and live independently. This leads to varying educational, occupational, and psychosocial outcomes. But during the past 50 years, and particularly among young people in industrialized societies, there has been more widespread participation in post-secondary education and greater acceptance of premarital sex and cohabitation. The ages for entry into marriage and parenthood have been greatly delayed, too. These observations form the basis for Arnett's claim that emerging adulthood is a new period in life, which allows for the exploration of one's identity. Emerging adults have the luxury of exploring their options vis-à-vis love and work.

There are debates about whether emerging adulthood can rightfully be considered a "stage" of development. Studies of non-Western cultures and ethnic minorities in the United States suggest that this notion does not capture the considerable variation that exists within individuals and across cultures. For instance, in considering the experiences of Latin American youth, Galambos and Martinez (2007) describe emerging adulthood as "a pleasure for the privileged" (p. 109). In Latin America, a period of exploration of life choices, together with delayed marriage and parenthood, is an option only available to individuals from wealthy families living in the urban areas of the more developed countries. And subjective experiences of adulthood vary even among those who have the opportunity to explore educational and career options. For instance, in one study, the percentage of university students reporting that they had reached adulthood was more than twice as great in the United States than in China (Badger, Nelson, & Barry, 2006; Nelson & Chen, 2007). These types of observations prompted Hendry and Kloep (2007) to claim that emerging adulthood is "merely a description limited to a certain age cohort in certain societies at a certain historical time with particular socioeconomic conditions" (p. 76). In different societies there is wide variation in the perception of the age at which adulthood is attained. However, the criteria that youth view as necessary for adulthood appear to be similar in various regions of the world. These criteria include the ability to accept responsibility for the consequences of one's actions, to make decisions independently, to control one's emotions, and to achieve financial independence from parents (Barker & Galambos, 2005; Nelson, Badger, & Wu, 2004). But, whether we believe that emerging adulthood is a distinctive life stage or not, there are constants to the developmental tasks that young people face. During the third decade of life, individuals generally must establish new relationships with peers and romantic partners, settle into career choices, and perhaps adapt to new living arrangements. They must also gain increased independence, although the family continues to play a very important part in their development. They must establish a new equilibrium in their relationships with parents.

Relationships with Parents as Adolescence Concludes

Autonomy and attachment remain critical developmental issues as late adolescents leave home (Hauser & Greene, 1991; Holmbeck & Wandrei, 1993). Some researchers believe that it is difficult to establish mature relationships with parents during late adolescence and young adulthood until a certain degree of autonomy and individuation has been achieved. That is, there may be more alienation from parents in late adolescence than at either earlier or late ages, because the need for autonomy is greater than the need for dependence. In fact, at least in the United States, young adults who have the most frequent contact with parents, especially those who are living at home, are less close to their parents and have poorer psychological adjustment than those who have less contact (Dubas & Petersen, 1996; O'Connor, Allen, Bell, & Hauser, 1996). Also, better adjustment following high school graduation is associated with improvements in parent–adolescent relationships, especially for European American adolescents who attend residential colleges (Aseltine & Gore, 1993).

American youth who have moved away to college report less parent–adolescent conflict and disagreements and more supportive relationships with parents. They have closer relationships, better communication, and greater appreciation and respect for parents than early and middle adolescents do, who still reside at home (Aquilino, 1998; Furman & Buhrmester, 1992; Lefkowitz, 2005; Smetana, Metzger, & Campione-Barr, 2004). This is especially true for girls' perceptions of their relationships with their mothers. In my study of African American families, discussed extensively in Chapter 8, we found that African American late adolescent girls who had left home reported less negative interactions with mothers than girls in the process of leaving home for college. Moreover, African American girls who were living at home or were in transition out of the house reported more negative relationships with mothers than same-status boys did (Smetana, Metzger et al., 2004). Moving out of the parental home may have positive effects on adolescent adjustment and on parent–adolescent relationships because there is less opportunity for conflict over parental rules and expectations and greater opportunities for independent decision-making. The longer American students have been in college, the more likely they are to mention positive changes in the quality of their relationships with parents (Lefkowitz, 2005).

Transitions from Adolescence to Adulthood

The focus on emerging adulthood has led to a flurry of research, but this has consisted mostly of cross-sectional studies employing convenience samples of college students. There has been very little longitudinal research examining the transition from adolescence to adulthood. The few available studies (in Western contexts) of transitions to adulthood have focused primarily on work and romantic relationships. Developmental tasks wax and wane. As individuals gain competence in certain arenas, the challenges of that age diminish, and a new set of developmental challenges emerges. Managing parent–adolescent and peer relationships are stage-salient tasks of adolescence. Developing competence in romantic relationships and at work are the stage-salient tasks of young adulthood (Roisman, Masten, Coatsworth, & Tellegen, 2004).

Nevertheless, as revealed in several longitudinal studies, adolescents' relationships with parents set the stage for adult development. For instance, in their long-running study of individual and family psychological development, Stuart Hauser and his colleagues (Allen, Hauser, O'Connor, & Bell, 2002; Hauser, Allen, & Golden, 2006; Whitton et al., 2008) followed a sample of primarily middle-class and upper middle-class families from the period when teenagers were 14 years of age until they were in their early 30s. During adolescence, perceptions of self and other, as revealed in narratives about relationships, had a somewhat more negative tinge than they did in adulthood (Waldinger et al., 2002). As others have found when examining moral narratives from childhood through to adolescence (Wainryb, Brehl, & Matwin, 2005), these became more complex and elaborate over time. Both in adolescence and in young adulthood, the most frequently expressed wish was to be close to others. But, in adolescence, the next most frequently mentioned theme was the desire to be distant. This was transformed in young adulthood into a desire to be independent. Therefore, at both ages, individuals expressed concerns with individuality as well as with their connection with others. However, much as we have found in descriptions of self and personal issues, there was movement towards more positive and integrated perceptions.

In addition, there was impressive continuity in relationships between observed family interactions at age 16 and later interpersonal functioning. At the negative end of the spectrum, there was substantial continuity between adolescents' expressions of hostility during their family interactions and peer ratings of hostility nearly a decade later (Allen et al., 2002). This is much as I found in my study of African American families discussed in Chapter 8, where more general negativity in relationships with parents in middle adolescence predicted more negativity in those relationships in young adulthood.

Moreover, adolescents who had struggled more over autonomy in the family context directed more hostility to their peers at the age of 25 (Allen et al., 2002). In particular, the fathers' interfering with autonomy strivings during adolescence had a very powerful effect on later social development, even after controlling for the initial level of hostility of adolescents. Allen and his colleagues speculated that, when fathers undermine teenagers' social interactions, teens may come to believe that their autonomy is easily threatened. They may think that they cannot attain autonomy without hostile, distancing behavior in other social relationships.

Fathers may be particularly important in negotiating transitions in relationships beyond the home. Furthermore, there was significant continuity between interactions reflecting family conflict during middle adolescence and marital conflict resolution patterns 17 years later, when study participants were, on average, 31 years of age (Whitton et al., 2008). These findings provide compelling evidence that relationships with parents during adolescence set the stage for later social relationships, including those with life partners.

Several other longitudinal studies also show that family relationships during adolescence influence early adult romantic relationships. Rand Conger and his colleagues at Iowa State University and at the University of North Carolina at Chapel Hill (Conger, Cui, Bryant, & Elder, 2000) examined whether specific communication skills such as conflict management or problem solving, acquired in the context of parent–child relationships, influence the success or failure of later relationships. They followed a sample of European American largely rural families. Teenagers were observed interacting with their parents when they were 7th graders, and again 3 years later, in middle adolescence. The observations were extensive, focusing on sibling relationships, parental marital relationships, and parent–adolescent relationships. Eight years after the initial observations, the same youth (who were now in their early 20s) were observed interacting with a romantic partner. Earlier marital, sibling, and parent–adolescent relationships were all associated with the later behavior towards romantic partners. But, out of all of these different types of interactions, only the quality of the parent–adolescent relationship influenced the observed behavior with romantic partners. That is, more nurturant-involved parenting in early adolescence led to warmer, more supportive, and less hostile behaviors towards a romantic partner. In turn, this pattern was associated with having more satisfied, happier, and more committed romantic relationships. Conger and his colleagues believe that adolescents learn communication skills through their interactions with parents. These then influence the quality of romantic relationships and one's satisfaction with those relationships.

Shirley Feldman, Kris Gowen, and Lawrence Fisher (1998) also examined the role of family factors on young adults' intimacy in romantic relationships. They followed a group of primarily White adolescents and their parents for 6 years, from age 15 or 16 to the early 20s. They defined intimacy in terms of maintaining a healthy balance between autonomy and closeness. Young adults had happier love lives when their parents used more flexible control (which can be thought of as an aspect of authoritative parenting). They also expressed greater happiness when their family relationships were more cohesive and when there was greater family respect for privacy. (This can be conceptualized in terms of family members respecting the boundaries of their personal domains.) Interestingly, though, the effects of family respect for privacy differed for boys and girls. Respect for privacy predicted happiness in love for girls but unhappiness in love for boys.

These findings can be understood by reference to gender socialization. Women are very connected to others. Therefore they need to be encouraged to be more separate and autonomous in order to achieve balanced and successful romantic relationships. Respect for privacy is one dimension of this more autonomous orientation. In contrast, men's gender socialization already inclines them towards autonomy and separateness. Therefore they need to be encouraged to be more connected if they are to experience happy and satisfying romantic relationships.

Finally, in one of the most comprehensive studies of development from childhood to adulthood, psychologists at the University of Minnesota studied a cohort of American families from birth to adulthood (Sroufe, Egeland, Carlson, & Collins, 2005). Among the wealth of findings reported in this study, one comes across the observation that attachment security, or the quality of the infants' relationships with their caregiver, influenced romantic relationships at the age of 20 or 21. But parent–adolescent interactions, observed when adolescents were 13 years old, also contributed to the quality of later romantic relationships. Indeed, parent–child relationships during early adolescence (both parental support and parent–adolescent conflict resolution, each independently) accounted for much of the effect of earlier attachment relationships on the ability of romantic couples to resolve conflicts in their relationships. There were similar effects on hostility in romantic relationships (although competence in dealing with peers in childhood was also an important source of influence on later hostility). This indicates that well-functioning romantic relationships in emerging adulthood draw on the individuals' entire history of social interaction, although parent–adolescent relationships are a main contributor.

Continuity and Change in Social Development

These studies demonstrate that there is significant continuity between early childhood and adolescence in the quality of parent–child relationships. In turn, parent–adolescent relationships influence subsequent adult relationships, including both relationships with parents and with romantic partners. Adult social relationships build on prior experiences within and outside the family. According to W. Andrew Collins (2003), social relationships with parents, siblings, peers, and romantic partners unfold in distinct settings and follow different pathways during adolescence. Different relationships function in different ways. They have varying influences on the achievement of various developmental tasks, such as autonomy, individuation, and identity development. Collins believes that differentiation in social relationships is characteristic of adolescence. We have seen that new forms of peer social relationships, such as crowds, emerge and become influential during adolescence. We have also seen that adolescent–parent relationships move towards greater mutuality during adolescence. Parental control over decision-making gradually decreases (at varying rates in different domains), which results in greater adolescent control over decisions and greater compromises or transfers of authority in resolving conflicts. However, relationships become increasingly integrated during the early 20s. To have successful romantic relationships in young adulthood, individuals must integrate the competencies constructed from their diverse relationship experiences earlier on in life. In the previous chapter we saw a similar pattern emerging from the narratives of self and other that Waldinger and colleagues (2002) described. Conceptions of self and other became more integrated.

These claims are similar to the conclusions I drew in Chapter 12 about the development of social reasoning, as it emerges and transforms (and is transformed by) adolescent–parent relationships. The analyses of the different profiles of families – the frequent squabblers, the easy-going, and the tumultuous families described in Chapter 10 – show that adolescents' and parents' reasoning about conflicts and about parental authority is part and parcel of their social relationships. Adolescents construct, elaborate, and negotiate their social worlds in their interactions with parents, other important adults, siblings, and peers. As adolescents move into adulthood, struggling to achieve a balance between individuation and connectedness and between personal and parental authority over various aspects of their lives, the different strands of social reasoning examined throughout this book coalesce and become more integrated.

Throughout this whole book I have argued that adolescents – and parents – create meaning and construct their social worlds from their social interactions. It should be clear that these social interactions do not simply reflect the reproduction of culture or the adolescents' uncritical acceptance of parental standards, beliefs, and values. Adolescents continually recreate their culture through their social interactions. This may be particularly evident in the new fads and styles in dress, appearance, music, and recreation, which emerge from (or are heavily marketed to) today's adolescents. Adolescents also lead the way in terms of latching on to new technologies, including the emerging social media.

But these are not the only realms of innovation. We saw that adolescents' acceptance of adults' moral and conventional authority and rules is not unquestioning or absolute – nor should it be. Children evaluate parental moral and conventional norms and behaviors and do not simply accept them as given. Adolescents may challenge and resist the rules and expectations of the adult social world, an attitude that potentially leads them to modify and create new moral and social norms. To be fully autonomous moral beings, adolescents must apply principles of justice, welfare, and rights in ways that may differ from the expectations of particular parental, institutional, or societal authorities and environments. In addition, each generation constructs anew the social conventions of its society, a phenomenon that potentially leads to changes in cultural practices. Through social interactions, adolescents also negotiate and stake out a domain of personal choice, which allows them to exercise their agency, feel effective, express their identity, and develop some individuality. Youth in different cultures and in different generations find new modes of coordinating personal concepts, familial and societal conventions, and moral matters. Perhaps it is this reconstructive aspect of social development – with the ongoing questioning of the boundaries between the self and the social world – that makes parenting adolescents so challenging for each succeeding generation.

References

Abu-Lughod, L. (1993). *Writing women's worlds: Bedouin stories.* Berkeley: University of California Press.

Afifi, T., Caughlin, J., & Afifi, W. (2007). The dark side (and light side) of avoidance and secrets. In B. H. Spitzberg & W. R. Cupach (Eds.), *The dark side of interpersonal communication* (2nd ed., pp. 61–92). Mahwah, NJ: Erlbaum.

Allen, J. P., Hauser, S. T., O'Connor, T. G., & Bell, K. L. (2002). Prediction of peer-rated adult hostility from autonomy struggles in adolescent–family interactions. *Development and Psychopathology, 14,* 123–137.

Aquilino, W. S. (1998). From adolescent to young adult: A prospective study of parent–child relations during the transition to adulthood. *Journal of Marriage and the Family, 59,* 670–686.

Ardila-Rey, A., & Killen, M. (2001). Colombian preschool children's judgments about autonomy and conflict resolution in the classroom setting. *International Journal of Behavioral Development, 25,* 246–255.

Arim, R. G., Marshall, S. K., & Shapka, J. D. (2010). A domain-specific approach to adolescent reporting of parental control. *Journal of Adolescence, 33,* 355–366.

Arnett, J. J. (1999). Adolescent storm and stress, reconsidered. *American Psychologist, 54,* 317–326.

Arnett, J. J. (2000). Emerging adulthood: A theory of development from the late teens through the twenties. *American Psychologist, 55,* 469–480.

Arnett, J. J. (2004). *Emerging adulthood: The winding road from the late teens through the twenties.* New York: Oxford University Press.

Arnett, J. J. (2007). Emerging adulthood: What is it, and what is it good for? *Child Development Perspectives, 1,* 68–73.

Arsenio, W. F. (1988). Children's conceptions of the situational affective consequences of sociomoral events. *Child Development, 59,* 1611–1622.

Arsenio, W. F., & Lover, A. (1995). Children's conceptions of sociomoral affect: Happy victimizers, mixed emotions and other expectancies. In M. Killen & D. Hart (Eds.), *Morality in everyday life* (pp. 87–128). Cambridge, England: Cambridge University Press.

Arsenio, W. F., Gold, J., & Adams, E. (2006). Children's conceptions and displays of moral emotions. In M. Killen & J. G. Smetana (Eds.), *Handbook of moral development* (pp. 581–609). Mahwah, NJ: Erlbaum.

Adolescents, Families, and Social Development: How Teens Construct Their Worlds. Judith G. Smetana
© 2011 Judith G. Smetana

Aseltine, R. H., & Gore, S. (1993). Mental health and social adaptation following the transition from high school. *Journal of Research on Adolescence, 3*, 247–270.

Assadi, S. M., Smetana, J. G., Shahmansouri, N., & Mohammadi, M. R. (in press). Beliefs about parental authority, parenting styles, and adolescent–parent conflict among Iranian mothers of middle adolescents. *Parenting: Science and Practice.*

Badger, S., Nelson, L. J., & Barry, C. M. (2006). Perceptions of the transition to adulthood among Chinese and American emerging adults. *International Journal of Behavioural Development, 30*, 84–93.

Bai, M. (2008, August 6). Is Obama the end of Black politics? *New York Times Magazine.* Retrieved from http://www.nytimes.com/2008/08/10/magazine/10politics-t.html.

Baier, A. C. (1986). Trust and antitrust. *Ethics, 96*, 231–260.

Bakken, J., & Brown, B. B. (2010). Adolescent secretive behavior: African American and Hmong adolescents' strategies and justifications for managing parents' knowledge about peers. *Journal of Research on Adolescence, 20*, 359–388.

Baldwin, J. M. (1906). *Thought and things* (Vol. 1). London: Swan Sonnenschen.

Barbarin, O. A., McCandies, T., Coleman, C., & Hill, N. E. (2005). Family practices and school performance of African American children. In V. C. McLoyd, N. E. Hill, & K. A. Dodge (Eds.), *African American family life* (pp. 227–244). New York: Guilford Press.

Barber, B. K. (1996). Parental psychological control: Revisiting a neglected construct. *Child Development, 67*, 3296–3319.

Barber, B. K. (2002). *Intrusive parenting: How psychological control affects children and adolescents.* Washington, DC: American Psychological Association Press.

Barber, B. K., Olsen, J. E., & Shagle, S. C. (1994). Associations between parental psychological and behavioral control and youth internalized and externalized behaviors. *Child Development, 65*, 1120–1136.

Barber, B. K., Stolz, H. E., & Olsen, J. A. (2005). Parental support, psychological control, and behavioral control: Assessing relevance across time, method, and culture. *Monographs of the Society for Research in Child Development, 70* (4), 1–137.

Bargh, J. A., & Chartrand, T. L. (1999). The unbearable automaticity of being. *American Psychologist, 54*, 462–479.

Barker, E. T., & Galambos, N. L. (2005). Adolescents' implicit theories of maturity: Ages of adulthood, freedom, and fun. *Journal of Adolescent Research, 20*, 557–576.

Baumrind, D. (1971). Current patterns of parental authority. *Developmental Psychology Monographs, 4* (1, Part 2), 1–103.

Baumrind, D. (1978). Parental disciplinary patterns and social competence in children. *Youth and Society, 9*, 239–276.

Baumrind, D. (1989). Rearing competent children. In W. Damon (Ed.), *Child development today and tomorrow* (pp. 349–378). San Francisco: Jossey-Bass.

Baumrind, D. (1991a). Effective parenting during the early adolescent transition. In P. A. Cowan & E. M. Hetherington (Eds.), *Advances in family research* (Vol. 2, pp. 111–163). Hillsdale, NJ: Erlbaum.

Baumrind, D. (1991b). The influence of parenting style on adolescent competence and substance use. *Journal of Early Adolescence, 11*, 56–95.

Belkin, L. (2009, February 24). *Big lies, little lies, and the tooth fairy.* Retrieved from http://parenting.blogs.nytimes.com/2009/02/24/big-lies-little-lies-and-the-tooth-fairy/.

Belkin, L. (2009, May 14). *More teens say they like their parents*. Retrieved from http://parenting.blogs.nytimes.com/2009/05/14/more-teens-like-their-parents/.

Bell, R. Q. (1968). A reinterpretation of the direction of effects in studies of socialization. *Psychological Review, 75,* 81–95.

Bellah, R. N., Madsen, R., Sullivan, W. M., Swidler, A., & Tipton, S. M. (1985). *Habits of the heart: Individualism and commitment in American life.* New York: Harper and Row.

Benedict, R. (1934). *Patterns of culture.* Boston: Houghton Mifflin.

Benjamin, C. L. (1993). *Surviving your dog's adolescence: A positive training program.* New York: Wiley.

Benner, A. D., & Graham, S. (2009). The transition to high school as a developmental process among multiethnic urban youth. *Child Development, 80,* 356–376.

Bennett, W. J. (1992). *The de-valuing of America: The fight for our culture and our children.* New York: Free Press.

Bennett, W. J. (2001). *The broken hearth: Reversing the moral collapse of the American family.* New York: Doubleday.

Bersheid, E. (1985). Interpersonal attraction. In G. Lindsey & A. Aronson (Eds.), *Handbook of social psychology* (3rd ed., pp. 413–484). New York: Random House.

Bibby, R. (2009). *The emerging Millennials: How Canada's newest generation is responding to change and choice.* Lethbridge, Canada: Project Canada Books.

Billingsley, A. (1992). *Climbing Jacob's ladder: The enduring legacy of African–American families.* New York: Simon & Schuster.

Blos, P. (1962). *On adolescence: A psychoanalytic interpretation.* New York: Free Press.

Blos, P. (1967). The second individuation process of adolescence. *The Psychoanalytic Study of the Child, 22,* 162–186.

Blos, P. (1979). *The adolescent passage: Clinical studies.* Madison, CT: International Universities Press.

Bok, S. (1989). *Lying: Moral choice in public and private life.* New York: Vintage Books.

Boyd-Franklin, N. (1989). *Black families in therapy: A multi-systems approach.* New York: Guilford Press.

Boyd-Franklin, N., & Franklin, A. J. (2000). *Boys into men: Raising our African American teenage sons.* New York: Dutton.

Boykin, A. W. (1983). The academic performance of Afro-American children. In J. Spence (Ed.), *Achievement and achievement motives* (pp. 321–371). San Francisco: Freeman.

Boykin, A. W., & Toms, F. D. (1985). Black child socialization: A conceptual framework. In H. P. McAdoo & J. L. McAdoo (Eds.), *Black children: Social, educational, and parental environments* (pp. 33–51). Newbury Park, CA: Sage.

Braine, L. G., Pomerantz, E., Lorber, D., & Krantz, D. H. (1991). Conflicts with authority: Children's feelings, actions, and justifications. *Developmental Psychology, 27,* 829–840.

Brody, G. H., & Flor, D. L. (1998). Maternal resources, parenting practices, and child competence in rural, single-parent African American families. *Child Development, 69,* 803–816.

Bronte, C. (1949). *Jane Eyre [1847].* New York: Modern Library.

Broughton, J. (1978). The development of concepts of mind, self, reality, and knowledge. In W. Damon (Ed.), *Social cognition* (pp. 75–100). San Francisco: Jossey-Bass.

Brown, B. B., & Klute, C. (2003). Friendships, cliques, and crowds. In G. R. Adams & M. D. Berzonsky (Eds.), *Blackwell handbook of adolescence* (pp. 330–348). Oxford, England: Blackwell.

Brown, B. B., & Larson, J. (2009). Peer relationships in adolescence. In R. L. Lerner & L. Steinberg (Eds.), *Handbook of adolescent psychology* (3rd ed., Vol. 2, pp. 74–103). New York: John Wiley & Sons.

Brown, B. B., Bakken, J. P., Nguyen, J., & Von Bank, H. (2007). Sharing information about peer relations: Parent and adolescent opinions and behaviors in Hmong and African American families. In B. B. Brown & N. S. Mounts (Eds.), *Linking parents and family to adolescent peer relations: Ethnic and cultural considerations* (pp. 67–82). San Francisco: Jossey-Bass.

Brown, B. B., Mounts, N., Lamborn, S., & Steinberg, L. (1993). Parenting practices and peer group affiliation in adolescence. *Child Development, 64,* 467–482.

Buchanan, C. M. (2003). Mothers' generalized beliefs about adolescents: Links to expectations for a specific child. *Journal of Early Adolescence, 23,* 29–50.

Buchanan, C. M., & Hughes, J. L. (2009). Construction of social reality during adolescence: Can expecting storm and stress increase real or perceived storm and stress? *Journal of Research on Adolescence, 19,* 261–285.

Buhrmester, D., & Furman, W. (1990). Perceptions of sibling relationships during middle childhood and adolescence. *Child Development, 61,* 1387–1398.

Buhrmester, D., & Prager, K. (1995). Patterns and functions of self-disclosure during childhood and adolescence. In K. Rotenberg (Ed.), *Disclosure processes in children and adolescents* (pp. 10–56). Cambridge, England: Cambridge University Press.

Bulcroft, R. A., Carmody, D. C., & Bulcroft, K. A. (1996). Patterns of independence giving to adolescents: Variations by race, age, and gender of child. *Journal of Marriage and the Family, 58,* 866–883.

Buller, D. B., & Burgoon, J. K. (1994). Deception: Strategic and nonstrategic communication. In J. A. Daly & J. M. Wiemann (Eds.), *Strategic interpersonal communication* (pp. 191–223). Hillsdale, NJ: Erlbaum.

Bumpus, M. F., Crouter, A. C., & McHale, S. M. (2001). Parental autonomy granting during adolescence: Exploring gender differences in context. *Developmental Psychology, 37,* 164–173.

Buri, J. R. (1989). Self-esteem and appraisals of parental behavior. *Journal of Adolescent Research, 4,* 33–49.

Buri, J. R. (1991). Parental authority questionnaire. *Journal of Personality Assessment, 57,* 110–119.

Caldwell, E. (1996). *Teenagers! A bewildered parents' guide.* San Diego: Silvercat Publications.

Campione-Barr, N., & Smetana, J. G. (2009). *The impact of sibling ordinal status on adolescents' expectations for and actual behavioral autonomy.* Unpublished manuscript, University of Missouri–Columbia.

Campione-Barr, N., Smetana, J. G., & Bassett, K. M. (2009). *Subjective and observer ratings of parent–adolescent interactions with first- and later borns.* Unpublished manuscript, University of Missouri–Columbia.

Cauce, A. M., Hiraga, Y., Graves, D., Gonzales, N., Ryan-Finn, K., & Grove, K. (1996). African–American mothers and their adolescent daughters: Intimacy, autonomy, and conflict. In B. J. Leadbeater & N. Way (Eds.), *Urban girls: Resisting stereotypes, creating identities* (pp. 100–116). New York: New York University Press.

Chao, R. K. (1994). Beyond parental control and authoritarian parenting style: Understanding Chinese parenting through the cultural notion of training. *Child Development, 65,* 1111–1119.

Chao, R. K. (1995). Chinese and European American cultural models of the self reflected in mothers' child rearing beliefs. *Ethos, 23,* 328–354.

Chao, R. K. (2001). Extending research on the consequences of parenting style for Chinese Americans and European Americans. *Child Development, 72,* 1832–1843.

Chao, R. K., & Tseng, V. (2002). Parenting of Asians. In M. Bornstein (Ed.), *Handbook of parenting: Vol. 4. Social conditions and applied parenting* (2nd ed., pp. 59–93). Mahwah, NJ: Erlbaum.

Chen, L., Baker, S., Braver, E., & Li, G. (2000). Carrying passengers as a risk factor for crashes fatal to 16- and 17-year old drivers. *Journal of the American Medical Association, 283,* 1578–1582.

Cherney, I. D., & Shing, Y. L. (2008). Children's nurturance and self-determination rights: A cross-cultural perspective. *Journal of Social Issues, 64,* 835–856.

Chuang, S. S. (2006). Taiwanese–Canadian mothers' beliefs about personal freedom for their young children. *Social Development, 15,* 520–536.

Cohen-Sandler, R., & Silver, M. (2000). *"I'm not mad, I just hate you!" – A new understanding of mother daughter conflict.* New York: Penguin.

Colby, A., & Kohlberg, K. (Eds.). (1987). *The measurement of moral judgment* (Vols. 1–2). Cambridge, England: Cambridge University Press.

Coleman, J. S. (1961). *The adolescent society.* Glencoe, IL: Free Press.

Coley, R. L., Votruba-Drzal, E., & Schindler, H. S. (2009). Fathers' and mothers' parenting predicting and responding to adolescent sexual risk behaviors. *Child Development, 80,* 808–827.

Collins, W. A. (1995). Relationships and development: Family adaptation to individual change. In S. Shulman (Ed.), *Close relationships and socioecomotional development* (pp. 128–154). New York: Ablex.

Collins, W. A. (2003). More than myth: The developmental significance of romantic relationships during adolescence. *Journal of Research on Adolescence, 13,* 1–24.

Collins, W. A., & Laursen, B. (1992). Conflict and relationships during adolescence. In C. U. Shantz & W. W. Hartup (Eds.), *Conflict in child and adolescent development* (pp. 216–241). Cambridge, England: Cambridge University Press.

Collins, W. A., Gleason, T., & Sesma, A., Jr. (1997). Internalization, autonomy, and relationships; Development during adolescence. In J. E. Grusec & L. Kuczynski (Eds.), *Parenting and children's internalization of values: A handbook of contemporary theory* (pp. 78–99). New York: Wiley.

Conger, R. D., Cui, M., Bryant, C. M., & Elder, G. H., Jr. (2000). Competence in early adult romantic relationships: A developmental perspective on family influence. *Journal of Personality and Social Psychology, 79,* 224–237.

Coombs, H. S. (1998). *Teenage survival manual: Why parents act that way and other mysteries of mind and matter.* San Francisco: Halo Books.

Cox, J., Emans, S. J., & Bithoney, W. (1993). Sisters of teen mothers: Increased risk for adolescent parenthood. *Adolescent and Pediatric Gynecology, 6,* 138–142.

Crockenberg, S., & Litman, C. (1990). Autonomy as competence in 2-year olds: Maternal correlates of child defiance, compliance, and self-assertion. *Developmental Psychology, 26,* 961–971.

Crouter, A. C., & Head, M. R. (2002). Parental monitoring and knowledge of children. In M. Bornstein (Ed.), *Handbook of parenting: Vol. 3. Becoming and being a parent* (2nd ed., pp. 461–483). Mahwah, NJ: Erlbaum.

Crouter, A. C., & McHale, S. M. (1993). Temporal rhythms in family life: Seasonal variation in the relation between parental work and family processes. *Developmental Psychology, 29*, 198–205.

Crouter, A. C., McHale, S. M., & Bartko, W. T. (1993). Gender as an organizing feature in parent–child relationships. *Journal of Social Issues, 49*, 161–174.

Crouter, A. C., Bumpus, M. F., Davis, K. D., & McHale, S. M. (2005). How do parents learn about adolescents' experiences? Implications for parental knowledge and adolescent risky behavior. *Child Development, 76*, 869–882.

Crouter, A. C., Helms-Erikson, H., Updegraff, K., & McHale, S. M. (1999). Conditions underlying parents' knowledge about children's daily lives in middle childhood: Between- and within-family comparisons. *Child Development, 70*, 246–259.

Csikszentmihalyi, M., & Larson, R. (1984). *Being adolescent: Conflict and growth in the teenage years*. New York: Basic Books.

Cumsille, P., Darling, N., Flaherty, B. P., & Martinez, M. L. (2006). Chilean adolescents' beliefs about the legitimacy of parental authority: Individual and age-related difference. *International Journal of Behavioral Development. 30*, 97–106.

Cumsille, P., Darling, N., Flaherty, B. P., & Martinez, M. L. (2009). Heterogeneity and change in the patterning of adolescents' perceptions of the legitimacy of parental authority: A latent transition model. *Child Development, 80*, 418–432.

Daddis, C. (2008a). Influence of close friends on the boundaries of adolescent personal authority. *Journal of Research on Adolescence, 18*, 75–98.

Daddis, C. (2008b). Similarity between early and middle adolescent close friends' beliefs about personal jurisdiction. *Social Development, 17*, 1019–1038.

Daddis, C. (in press, a). Adolescent peer crowds and patterns of belief in the boundaries of personal authority. *Journal of Adolescence*.

Daddis, C. (in press, b). Desire for increased autonomy and adolescents' perceptions of peer autonomy: "Everyone else can; Why can't I?" *Child Development*.

Daddis, C., & Randolph, D. (2010). Dating and disclosure: Adolescent management of information regarding romantic involvement. *Journal of Adolescence, 33*, 309–320.

Daddis, C., & Smetana, J. G. (2005). Middle class African American families' expectations for adolescents' behavioral autonomy. *International Journal of Behavioral Development, 29*, 371–381.

Damon, W. (1977). *The social world of the child*. San Francisco: Jossey-Bass.

Damon, W., & Hart, D. (1988). *Self-understanding in childhood and adolescence*. Cambridge, MA: Harvard University Press.

Darity, W., Jr., & Nicholson, M. J. (2005). Racial wealth inequality and the Black family. In V. C. McLoyd, N. E. Hill, & K. A. Dodge (Eds.), *African American family life* (pp. 78–85). New York: Guilford Press.

Darling, N., & Steinberg, L. (1993). Parenting style as context: An integrative model. *Psychological Bulletin, 113*, 486–496.

Darling, N., Cumsille, P., & Martinez, M. L. (2007). Adolescents as active agents in the socialization process: Legitimacy of parental authority and obligation to obey as predictors of obedience. *Journal of Adolescence, 30*, 297–311.

Darling, N., Cumsille, P., & Martinez, M. L. (2008). Individual differences in adolescents' beliefs about the legitimacy of parental authority and their own obligation to obey: A longitudinal investigation. *Child Development, 79,* 1103–1118.

Darling, N., Cumsille, P., & Pena-Alampay, L. (2005). Rules, legitimacy of parental authority, and obligation to obey in Chile, the Philippines, and the United States. In J. G. Smetana (Ed.), *Changing boundaries of parental authority.* (pp. 47–60). San Francisco: Jossey-Bass.

Darling, N., Cumsille, P., Caldwell, L. L., & Dowdy, B. (2006). Predictors of adolescents' disclosure to parents and perceived parental knowledge: Between- and within-person differences. *Journal of Youth and Adolescence, 35,* 667–678.

Demos, J., & Demos, V. (1969). Adolescence in historical perspective. *Journal of Marriage and the Family, 31,* 632–638.

DePaulo, B. M., & Kashy, D. A. (1998). Everyday lies in close and casual relationships. *Journal of Personality and Social Psychology, 74,* 63–79.

DePaulo, B. M., Kashy, D. A., Kirkendol, S. E., Wyer, M. M., & Epstein, J. A. (1996). Lying in everyday life. *Journal of Personality and Social Psychology, 70,* 979–995.

Dishion, T. J., Nelson, S. E., & Bullock, B. M. (2004). Premature adolescent autonomy: Parent disengagement and deviant peer process in the amplification of problem behavior. *Journal of Adolescence, 27,* 515–530.

Dix, T. (1992). Parenting on behalf of the child: Empathic goals in the regulation of responsive parenting. In I. E. Siegel, A. V. McGillicuddy-DeLisi, & J. J. Goodnow (Eds.), *Parental belief systems: The psychological consequences for children* (2nd ed., pp. 319–346). Hillsdale, NJ: Erlbaum.

Dodge, K. A., McLoyd, V. C., & Lansford, J. E. (2005). The cultural context of physically disciplining children. In V. C. McLoyd, N. E. Hill, & K. A. Dodge (Eds.), *African American family life* (pp. 245–263). New York: Guilford Press.

Dornbusch, S. M., Ritter, P. L., Mont-Reynaud, R., & Chen, Z. (1990). Family decision-making and academic performance in a diverse high school population. *Journal of Adolescent Research, 5,* 143–160.

Douvan, E., & Adelson, J. (1966). *The adolescent experience.* New York: Wiley.

Dubas, J. S., & Petersen, A. C. (1996). Geographical distance from parents and adjustment during adolescence and young adulthood. In J. A. Graber & J. S. Dubas (Eds.), *Leaving home: Understanding the transition to adulthood* (pp. 3–19). San Francisco: Jossey-Bass.

Duffet, A., Johnson, J., & Farkas, S. (1999). *Kids these days '99: What Americans really think of the next generation.* New York: Public Agenda.

Dunn, J. (2006). Moral development in early childhood and social interaction in the family. In M. Killen & J. G. Smetana (Eds.), *Handbook of moral development* (pp. 331–350). Mahwah, NJ: Erlbaum.

Dworkin, R. (1978). *Taking rights seriously.* Cambridge, MA: Harvard University Press.

East, P. L. (1996). The younger sisters of childbearing adolescents: Their attitudes, expectations and behaviors. *Child Development, 67,* 267–282.

Eccles, J. S., Midgley, C., Wigfield, A., Buchanan, C. M., Reuman, D., Flanagan, C., & Mac Iver, D. (1993). Development during adolescence: The impact of stage-environment fit on adolescents' experiences in schools and families. *American Psychologist, 48,* 90–101.

Eid, M., & Diener, E. (2001). Norms for experiencing emotions in different cultures: Inter- and intranational differences. *Journal of Personality & Social Psychology, 81*, 869–885.

Emery, R. E. (1992). Family conflicts and their developmental implications: A conceptual analysis of meanings for the structure of relationships. In C. U. Shantz & W. W. Hartup (Eds.), *Conflict in child and adolescent development* (pp. 270–298). Cambridge, England: Cambridge University Press.

Engels, R. C. M. E., Finkenauer, C., & van Kooten, D. C. (2006). Lying behavior, family functioning, and adjustment in early adolescence. *Journal of Youth and Adolescence, 35*, 949–958.

Erikson, E. H. (1968). *Identity, youth, and crisis.* New York: Norton.

Etzioni, A. (1993). *The spirit of community: The reinvention of American society.* New York: Touchstone.

Feldman, S. S., & Quatman, T. (1988). Factors influencing age expectations for adolescent autonomy: A study of early adolescents and parents. *Journal of Early Adolescence, 8*, 325–343.

Feldman, S. S., & Rosenthal, D. A. (1990). The acculturation of autonomy expectations in Chinese high schoolers residing in two Western nations. *International Journal of Psychology, 25*, 259–281.

Feldman, S. S., & Wood, D. N. (1994). Parents' expectations for preadolescent sons' behavioral autonomy: A longitudinal study of correlates and outcomes. *Journal of Research on Adolescence, 4*, 45–70.

Feldman, S. S., Gowen, L. K., & Fisher, L. (1998). Family relationships and gender as predictors of romantic intimacy in young adults: A longitudinal study. *Journal of Research on Adolescence, 8*, 263–286.

Feldman, S. S., Rosenthal, D. A., Mont-Reynaud, R., Leung, K., & Lau, S. (1991). Ain't misbehavin': Adolescent values and family environments as correlates of misconduct in Australia, Hong Kong, and the United States. *Journal of Research on Adolescence, 1*, 109–134.

Finkenauer, C., Engels, R. C. M. E., & Meeus, W. (2002). Keeping secrets from parents: Advantages and disadvantages of secrecy in adolescence. *Journal of Youth and Adolescence, 2*, 123–136.

Finkenauer, C., Engels, R. C. M. E., Branje, S. J. T., & Meeus, W. (2004). Disclosure and relationship satisfaction in families. *Journal of Marriage and the Family, 66*, 195–209.

Finkenauer, C., Frijns, T., Engels, R. C. M. E., & Kerkhof, P. (2005). Perceiving conceal- ment in relationships between parents and adolescents: Links with parental behavior. *Personal Relationships, 12*, 387–406.

Flanagan, C. A., Stout, M., & Gallay, L. S. (2008). It's my body and none of your business: Developmental changes in adolescents' perceptions of rights concerning health. *Journal of Social Issues, 64*, 815–834.

Fletcher, A., Steinberg, L., & Williams-Wheeler, M. (2004). Parental influences on adolescent problem behavior: Revisiting Stattin and Kerr. *Child Development, 75*, 781–796.

Fogelman, K. (1976). (Ed.). *Britain's sixteen-year olds.* London: National Children's Bureau.

Fordham, S., & Ogbu, J. (1986). Black students' school success: Coping with the burden of "acting white." *Urban Review, 18*, 176–206.

Franklin, A. W., & Boyd-Franklin, N. (1985). A psychoeducational perspective on Black parenting. In H. P. McAdoo & J. W. McAdoo (Eds.), *Black children: Social, educational, and parental environments* (pp. 194–210). Newbury Park, CA: Sage.

Freud, A. (1966). *The ego and the mechanisms of defense [1937].* London: Hogarth Press.

Freud, S. (1953). *Three essays on the theory of sexuality [1905].* London: Hogarth Press.

Frijns, T., Keijsers, L., Branje, S., & Meeus, W. (2010). What parents don't know and how it might affect their children: Qualifying the disclosure–adjustment link. *Journal of Adolescence, 33,* 261–270.

Fuligni, A. J. (1998). Authority, autonomy, and parent–adolescent conflict and cohesion: A study of adolescents from Mexican, Chinese, Filipino, and European backgrounds. *Developmental Psychology, 34,* 782–792.

Fuligni, A. J., & Eccles, J. (1993). Perceived parent–child relationships and early adolescents' orientations toward peers. *Developmental Psychology, 29,* 622–632.

Fuligni, A. J., Hughes, D. L., & Way, N. (2009). Ethnicity and immigration. In R. L. Lerner & L. Steinberg (Eds.), *Handbook of adolescent psychology* (3rd ed., Vol. 2, pp. 527–569). New York: John Wiley & Sons.

Furman, W., & Buhrmester, D. (1985). Children's perceptions of the personal relationships in their social networks. *Developmental Psychology, 21,* 1016–1024.

Furman, W., & Buhrmester, D. (1992). Age and sex in perceptions of networks of personal relationships. *Child Development, 63,* 103–115.

Galambos, N. L., & Martinez, M. L. (2007). Poised for emerging adulthood in Latin America: A pleasure for the privileged. *Child Development Perspectives, 1,* 109–114.

Garcia Coll, C. T., & Pachter, L. M. (2002). Ethnic and minority parenting. In M. H. Bornstein (Ed.), *Handbook of parenting: Vol. 4. Social conditions and applied parenting* (pp. 1–20). Mahwah, NJ: Erlbaum.

Garcia Coll, C. T., Crnic, K., Lamberty, G., Wasik, B. H., Jenkins, R., Garcia, H.V., & McAdoo, H. P. (1996). An integrative model for the study of developmental competencies in minority children. *Child Development, 67,* 1891–1914.

Gaskell, E. (1995). *North and south [1855].* New York: Penguin.

Geertz, C. (1973). *The interpretation of cultures.* New York: Basic Books.

Geertz, C. (1975). On the nature of anthropological understanding. *American Scientist, 63,* 47–53.

Geertz, C. (1984). From the native's point of view. In R. A. Shweder & R. A. Levine (Eds.), *Culture theory: Essays on mind, self, and emotion* (123–136). Cambridge, England: Cambridge University Press.

Geertz, C. (1994, April 7). Life on the edge. *New York Review of Books,* pp. 3–4.

Gewirth, A. (1978). *Reason and morality.* Chicago: University of Chicago Press.

Gluck, B., & Rosenfeld, J. (2005). *How to survive your teenager.* Atlanta, GA: Hundreds of Heads Books, Inc.

Goffman, E. (1969). *Strategic interaction.* Philadelphia, PA: University of Pennsylvania Press.

Gonzales, N. A., German, M., Kim, S. Y., George, P., Fabrett, F. C., Millsap, R., & Dumka, L. E. (2008). Mexican American adolescents' cultural orientation, externalizing behavior and academic engagement: The role of traditional cultural values. *American Journal of Community Psychology, 41,* 151–164.

Goodnow, J. J., & Collins, W. A. (1990). *Development according to parents: The nature, sources, and consequences of parents' ideas*. Hillsdale, NJ: Erlbaum.

Graham, S. (1992). Most of the subjects were white and middle class: Trends in published research on African–Americans in selected APA journals, 1970–1989. *American Psychologist, 47,* 629–639.

Gralinski, H. H., & Kopp, C. B. (1993). Everyday rules for behavior: Mothers' requests to young children. *Developmental Psychology, 29,* 573–584.

Greenfield, P. M., & Cocking, R. R. (Eds.). (1994). *Cross-cultural roots of minority child development*. Hillsdale, NJ: Erlbaum.

Grolnick, W. S., & Pomerantz, E. (2009). Issues and challenges in studying parental control: Toward a new conceptualization. *Child Development Perspectives, 3,* 165–170.

Grusec, J. E. (2008). What is the nature of effective parenting: It depends. In M. Kerr, H. Stattin, & R. Engels (Eds.), *What can parents do? New insights in the role of parents in adolescent problem behavior* (pp. 239–257). West Sussex, England: Wiley.

Grusec, J. E., & Davidov, M. (2007). Socialization in the family: The role of parents. In J. E. Grusec & P. D. Hastings (Eds.), *Handbook of socialization: Theory and research* (pp. 284–381). New York: Guilford Press.

Grusec, J. E., & Goodnow, J. J. (1994). Impact of parental discipline methods on the child's internalization of values: A reconceptualization of current points of view. *Developmental Psychology, 30,* 4–19.

Grusec, J. E., Goodnow, J. J., & Kuczynski, L. (2000). New directions in analyses of parenting contributions to children's acquisition of values. *Child Development, 71,* 205–211.

Guerrero, L. K., & Afifi, W. A. (1995). What parents don't know: Topic avoidance in parent–child relationships. In T. J. Socha & G. H. Stamp (Eds.), *Parents, children, and communication: Frontiers of theory and research* (pp. 219–245). Mahwah, NJ: Erlbaum.

Gutman, L. M., & Eccles, J. (2007). Stage–environment fit during adolescence: Trajectories of family relations and adolescent outcomes. *Developmental Psychology, 43,* 522–537.

Haidt, J. (2001). The emotional dog and its rational tail: A social intuitionist approach to moral judgment. *Psychological Review, 108,* 814–834.

Hall, G. S. (1882, January). The moral and religious training of children. *Princeton Review,* pp. 26–48.

Hall, G. S. (1904). *Adolescence: Its psychology, and its relations to physiology, anthropology, sociology, sex, crime, religion and education* (Vols. 1–2). New York: Appleton.

Hardway, C., & Fuligni, A. J. (2006). Dimensions of family connectedness among adolescents with Mexican, Chinese, and European backgrounds. *Developmental Psychology, 42,* 1246–1258.

Harter, S. (1999). *The construction of the self*. New York: Guilford Press.

Harter, S. (2006). The self. In N. Eisenberg (Ed.), *Handbook of child psychology: Vol. 3. Social, emotional, and personality development* (6th ed., pp. 505–570). New York: Wiley.

Harter, S., & Monsour, A. (1992). Developmental analysis of conflict caused by opposing attributes in the adolescent self-portrait. *Developmental Psychology, 28,* 251–260.

Harter, S., Bresnick, S., Bouchey, H. A., & Whitesell, N. R. (1997). The development of multiple role-related selves during adolescence. *Development and Psychopathology, 9,* 835–854.

Harter, S., Marold, D. B., Whitesell, W. R., & Cobbs, G. (1996). A model of the effects of perceived parent and peer support on adolescent false self behavior. *Child Development, 67,* 360–374.

Hartup, W. W. (1989). Social relationships and their developmental significance. *American Psychologist, 44,* 120–126.

Harwood, R. L., Scholmerich, A., & Schulze, P. A. (2000). Homogeneity and heterogeneity in cultural belief systems. In S. Harkness, C. Raeff, & C. M. Super (Eds.), *New directions for child and adolescent development: Vol. 87. Variability in the social construction of the child* (pp. 41–57). San Francisco: Jossey-Bass.

Hasebe, Y., Nucci, L., & Nucci, M. S. (2004). Parental control of the personal domain and adolescent symptoms of psychopathology. *Child Development, 75,* 815–828.

Hastings, P., & Grusec, J. E. (1998). Parenting goals as organizers of responses to parent–child disagreements. *Developmental Psychology, 34,* 465–479.

Hatch, E. (1983). *Culture and morality: The relativity of values in anthropology.* New York: Columbia University Press.

Hatchett, S. J., & Jackson, J. S. (1993). African American extended kin systems. In H. P. McAdoo (Ed.), *Family ethnicity: Strength in diversity* (pp. 90–108). Newbury Park, CA: Sage.

Hauser, S. T., Allen, J. P., Golden, E. (2006). *Out of the woods: Tales of resilient teens.* Cambridge, MA: Harvard University Press.

Hauser, S. T., & Greene, W. M. (1991). Passages from late adolescence to early adulthood. In S. I. Greenspan & G. H. Pollock (Eds.), *The course of life: Vol. 4. Adolescence* (pp. 377–405). Madison, CT: International Universities Press.

Hawk, S. T., Keijsers, L., Hale, W. W., III, & Meeus, W. (2009). Mind your own business! Longitudinal relations between perceived privacy invasion and adolescent–parent conflict. *Journal of Family Psychology, 23,* 511–520.

Helwig, C. C. (1995). Adolescents' and young adults' conceptions of civil liberties: Freedom of speech and religion. *Child Development, 66,* 152–166.

Helwig, C. C. (1997). The role of agent and social context in judgments of freedom of speech and religion. *Child Development, 68,* 484–495.

Helwig, C. C. (1998). Children's conceptions of fair government and freedom of speech. *Child Development, 69,* 518–531.

Helwig, C. C. (2006). Rights, civil liberties, and democracy across cultures. In M. Killen & J. G. Smetana (Eds.), *Handbook of moral development* (pp. 185–210). Mahwah, NJ: Erlbaum.

Helwig, C. C. (2010, June). Autonomy, rights, and culture: Findings from recent research in mainland China as seen through the lens of self-determination theory and social domain theory. Paper presented at the annual meetings of the Jean Piaget Society, St. Louis, MO.

Helwig, C. C., To, S. K. L., Wang, Q., Liu, C., & Yang, S. (2010). *Evaluations of parental discipline involving reasoning, social comparisons, shaming, and love withdrawal.* Unpublished manuscript, University of Toronto.

Helwig, C. C, & Jasiobedzka, U. (2001). The relation between law and morality: Children's reasoning about socially beneficial and unjust laws. *Child Development, 72,* 1382–1393.

Helwig, C. C., Arnold, M. L., Tan, D., & Boyd, D. (2007). Mainland Chinese and Canadian adolescents' judgments and reasoning about the fairness of democratic and other forms of government. *Cognitive Development, 22,* 96–109.

Hendry, L. B., & Kloep, M. (2007). Conceptualizing emerging adulthood: Inspecting the emperor's new clothes? *Child Development Perspectives, 1,* 74–79.

Hill, J. (1988). Adapting to menarche: Familial control and conflict. In M. R. Gunnar & W. A. Collins (Eds.), *21st Minnesota Symposium on Child Psychology: Development during the transition to adolescence* (pp. 43–78). Hillsdale, NJ: Erlbaum.

Hill, J., & Holmbeck, G. (1987). Familial adaptation to pubertal change during adolescence. In R. M. Lerner & T. Foch (Eds.), *Biological–psychosocial interactions in early adolescence: A life-span perspective* (pp. 207–223). Hillsdale, NJ: Erlbaum.

Hill, N. E., Murry, V. M., & Anderson, V. D. (2005). Sociocultural contexts of African American families. In V. C. McLoyd, N. E. Hill, & K. A. Dodge (Eds.), *African American family life* (pp. 21–44). New York: Guilford Press.

Hofstede, G. (1980). *Culture's consequences: International differences in work-related values.* Beverly Hills, CA: Sage.

Hollos, M., Leis, P. E., & Turiel, E. (1986). Social reasoning in Ijo children and adolescents in Nigerian communities. *Journal of Cross-Cultural Psychology, 17,* 352–374.

Holloway, S. D. (1999). Divergent cultural models of child rearing and pedagogy in Japanese preschools. In E. Turiel (Ed.), *New directions for child development: Vol. 83. Development and cultural change: Reciprocal processes* (pp. 61–75). San Francisco: Jossey-Bass.

Holmbeck, G. N. (1996). A model of family relational transformations during the transition to adolescence: Parent–adolescent conflict and adaptation. In J. A. Graber, J. Brooks-Gunn, & A. C. Petersen (Eds.), *Transitions through adolescence: Interpersonal domains and context* (pp. 167–199). Mahwah, NJ: Erlbaum.

Holmbeck, G. N., & Hill, J. P. (1988). Storm and stress beliefs about adolescence: Prevalence, self-reported antecedents, and effects of an undergraduate course. *Journal of Youth and Adolescence, 17,* 285–307.

Holmbeck, G.N., & Wandrei, M. L. (1993). Individual and relational predictors of adjustment in first year college students. *Journal of Counseling Psychology, 40,* 73–78.

Horn, S. S. (2003). Adolescents' reasoning about exclusion from social groups. *Developmental Psychology, 39,* 71–84.

Horn, S. S., & Nucci, L. (2003). The multidimensionality of adolescents' beliefs about and attitudes toward gay and lesbian peers in school. *Equity and Excellence in Education, 36,* 136–147.

Jacob, T. (1975). Family interaction in disturbed and normal families: A methodological and substantive review. *Psychological Bulletin, 82,* 33–65.

James, W. (1899). *The principles of psychology.* London: Macmillan.

Jeffries, E. D. (2004). Experiences of trust with parents: A qualitative investigation of African American, Latino, and Asian American boys from low-income families. In N. Way & J. Y. Chu (Eds.), *Adolescent boys: Exploring diverse cultures of boyhood* (pp. 107–128). New York: New York University Press.

Jenkins, A. H. (1988). Black families: The nurturing of agency. In A. F. Edwards & J. Spurlock (Eds.), *Black families in crisis: The middle class* (pp. 115–128). New York: Brunner/Mazel.

Jensen, L. A., Arnett, J. J., Feldman, S. S., & Cauffman, E. (2004). The right to do wrong: Lying to parents among adolescents and emerging adults. *Journal of Youth and Adolescence, 33*, 101–112.

Johnston, L. D., O'Malley, P. M., Bachman, J. G., & Schulenberg, J. E. (2005). Monitoring the future: Overview of key findings. Retrieved from http://www.MonitoringTheFuture.org.

Josephson Institute. (2008). Report card on the ethics of American youth. Retrieved from http://charactercounts.org/programs/reportcard/index.html.

Kagitcibasi, C. (1996). The autonomous–relational self: A new synthesis. *European Psychologist, 1*, 180–186.

Kagitcibasi, C. (2005). Autonomy and relatedness in cultural context: Implications for self and family. *Journal of Cross-Cultural Psychology, 36*, 403–422.

Kakihara, F., & Tilton-Weaver, L. (2009). Adolescents' interpretations of parental control: Differentiated by domain and types of control. *Child Development, 80*, 1722–1738.

Kandel, D. B., & Lesser, G. S. (1972). *Youth in two worlds.* San Francisco: Jossey-Bass.

Kashy, D. A., & DePaulo, B. M. (1996). Who lies? *Journal of Personality and Social Psychology, 70*, 1037–1051.

Keijsers, L., Branje, S. J. T., VanderValk, I. E., & Meeus, W. (2010). Reciprocal effects between parental solicitation, parental control, adolescents' disclosure, and adolescent delinquency. *Journal of Research on Adolescence, 20*, 88–113.

Keijsers, L., Frijns, T., Branje, S. J., & Meeus, W. (2009). Developmental links of adolescent disclosure, parental solicitation, and control with delinquency: Moderation with parental support. *Developmental Psychology, 45*, 1314–1327.

Keijsers, L., Branje, S. J. T., Frijns, T., Finkenauer, C., & Meeus, W. (2010). Gender differences in keeping secrets from parents in adolescence. *Developmental Psychology, 46*, 293–298.

Kelley, M. L., Power, T. G., & Wimbush, D. D. (1992). Determinants of disciplinary practices in low-income Black mothers. *Child Development, 63*, 573–582.

Kerr, M., & Stattin, H. (2000). What parents know, how they know it, and several forms of adolescent adjustment: Further support for a reinterpretation of monitoring. *Developmental Psychology, 36*, 366–380.

Kerr, M., & Stattin, H. (2003). Parenting of adolescents: Action or reaction? In A. Booth & A. Crouter (Eds.), *Children's influence on family dynamics: The neglected side of family relationships* (pp. 121–151). Mahwah, NJ: Erlbaum.

Kerr, M., Stattin, H., & Burk, W. J. (2010). A reinterpretation of parental monitoring in longitudinal perspective. *Journal of Research on Adolescence, 20*, 39–64.

Kerr, M., Stattin, H., & Trost, K. (1999). To know you is to trust you: Parents' trust is rooted in child disclosure of information. *Journal of Adolescence, 22*, 737–752.

Keshavarz, F. (2007). *Jasmine and stars: Reading more than Lolita in Tehran.* Chapel Hill, NC: University of North Carolina Press.

Kett, J. (1977). *Rites of passage: Adolescence in America, 1790 to the present.* New York: Basic Books.

Killen, M., & Smetana, J. G. (1999). Social interactions in preschool classrooms and the development of young children's conceptions of the personal. *Child Development, 70*, 486–501.

Killen, M., & Sueyoshi, L. (1995). Conflict resolution in Japanese social interactions. *Early Education and Development, 6,* 317–334.

Killen, M., & Wainryb, C. (2000). Independence and interdependence in diverse cultural contexts. In S. Harkness, C. Raeff, & C. M. Super (Eds.), *New directions for child and adolescent development: Vol. 87. Variability in the social construction of the child* (pp. 5–21). San Francisco: Jossey-Bass.

Killen, M., Margie, N. G., & Sinno, S. (2006). Morality in the context of intergroup relationships. In M. Killen & J. G. Smetana (Eds.), *Handbook of moral development* (pp. 155–183). Mahwah, NJ: Erlbaum.

Killen, M., Breton, S., Ferguson, H., & Handler, K. (1994). Preschoolers' evaluations of teacher methods of intervention in social transgressions. *Merrill–Palmer Quarterly, 40,* 399–415.

Kim, J. M. (1998). Korean children's concepts of adult and peer authority and moral reasoning. *Developmental Psychology, 34,* 947–955.

Kim, J. M., & Turiel, E. (1996). Korean children's concepts of adult and peer authority. *Social Development, 5,* 310–329.

Kochanska, G., & Aksan, N. (2004). Conscience in childhood: Past, present, and future. *Merrill–Palmer Quarterly, 50,* 299–310.

Kochanska, G., Aksan, N., & Koenig, A. (1995). A longitudinal study of the roots of preschoolers' compliance: Committed compliance and emerging internalization. *Child Development, 66,* 1752–1769.

Kochman, T. (1981). *Black and white styles in conflict.* Chicago: University of Chicago Press.

Kohlberg, L. (1984). *Essays on moral development: Vol. 2. The psychology of moral development.* San Francisco: Harper and Row.

Kohut, H. (1978). *The search for the self: Selected writings (1950–1978).* New York: International University Press.

Kowal, A., & Kramer, L. (1997). Children's understanding of parental differential treatment. *Child Development, 68,* 113–126.

Krueger, A. (1994). *Focus groups: A practical guide for applied research.* Thousand Oaks, CA: Sage.

Kuczynski, L. (1984). Socialization goals and mother–child interaction: Strategies for long-term and short-term compliance. *Developmental Psychology, 20,* 1061–1073.

Kuczynski, L., & Navara, G. S. (2006). Sources of innovation and change in socialization, internalization and acculturation. In M. Killen & J. G. Smetana (Eds.), *Handbook of moral development* (pp. 299–327). Mahwah, NJ: Erlbaum.

Lagattuta, K. H., Nucci, L., & Bosacki, S. L. (2010). Bridging theory of mind and the personal domain: Children's reasoning about resistance to parental control. *Child Development, 81,* 616–635.

Lahat, A., Helwig, C. C., Yang, S., Tan, D., & Liu, C. (2009). Mainland Chinese adolescents' judgments and reasoning about self-determination and nurturance rights. *Social Development, 18,* 690–710.

Laird, R. D., & Marrero, M. D. (2010). Information management and behavior problems: Is concealing misbehavior necessarily a sign of trouble? *Journal of Adolescence, 33,* 297–308.

Laird, R. D., Pettit, G. S., Bates, J. E., & Dodge, K. A. (2003). Parents' monitoring-relevant knowledge and adolescents' delinquent behavior: Evidence of correlated developmental changes and reciprocal influences. *Child Development, 74,* 752–768.

Lamborn, S. D., Dornbusch, S. M., & Steinberg, L. (1996). Ethnicity and community context as moderators of the relations between family decision making and adolescent adjustment. *Child Development, 67,* 283–301.

Lansford, J. E., Chang, L., Dodge, K. A., Malone, P. S., Oburu, P., Palmerus, K., Bacchini, D., Pastorelli, C., Bombi, A. S., Zelli, A., Tapanya, S., Chaudhary, N., Deater-Deckard, K., Manke, B., & Quinn, N. (2005). Physical discipline and children's adjustment: Cultural normativeness as a moderator. *Child Development, 76,* 1234–1246.

Larson, R., & Richards, M. H. (1994). *Divergent realities: The emotional lives of mothers, fathers, and adolescents.* New York: Basic Books.

Lau, S., & Cheung, P. C. (1987). Relations between Chinese adolescents' perception of parental control and organization and their perception of parental warmth. *Developmental Psychology, 23,* 726–729.

Laupa, M. (1991). Children's reasoning about three authority attributes: Adult status, knowledge, and social position. *Developmental Psychology, 27,* 321–329.

Laupa, M., & Tse, P. (2005). Authority concepts among children and adolescents in the island of Macao. *Social Development, 14,* 652–663.

Laupa, M., & Turiel, E. (1986). Children's conceptions of adult and peer authority. *Child Development, 57,* 405–412.

Laursen, B., & Collins, W. A. (2009). Parent–child relationships during adolescence. In R. L. Lerner & L. Steinberg (Eds.), *Handbook of adolescent psychology* (3rd ed., Vol. 2, pp. 3–42). New York: John Wiley & Sons.

Laursen, B., & Koplas, A. L. (1995). What's important about important conflicts? Adolescents' perceptions of daily disagreements. *Merrill–Palmer Quarterly, 41,* 536–553.

Laursen, B., Coy, K., & Collins, W. A. (1998). Reconsidering changes in parent–child conflict across adolescence: A meta-analysis. *Child Development, 69,* 817–832.

Lefkowitz, E. S. (2005). "Things have gotten better": Developmental changes among emerging adults after the transition to university. *Journal of Adolescent Research, 20,* 40–63.

Lenhart, A. (2009, May 23). It's personal: Similarities and differences in online social network use between teens and adults. Pew Internet and American Life Project. Retrieved from http://www.pewInternet.org.

Lenhart, A., & Fox, S. (2006, July 19). A portrait of the Internet's new storytellers. Pew Internet and American Life Project. Retrieved from http://www.pewInternet. org.

Lenhart, A., Madden, M., Smith, A., & Macgill, A. (2007, Dec. 19). Teens and social media. Pew Internet and American Life Project. Retrieved from http://www.pewInternet. org.

LeVine, R., & White, M. (1986). *Human conditions: The cultural basis for educational development.* New York: Routledge & Kegan Paul.

Lickona, T. (1991). *Educating for character: How our schools can teach respect and responsibility.* New York: Bantam.

Lickona, T. (2004). *Character matters: How to help our children develop good judgment, integrity, and other essential virtues.* New York: Touchstone.

Lincoln, C. E., & Mamiya, L. H. (1990). *The Black church and the African American experience.* Durham, NC: Duke University Press.

Livingstone, S. (2008). Taking risky opportunities in youthful content creation: Teenagers' use of social networking sites for intimacy, privacy and self-expression. *New Media and Society, 10,* 393–411.

Lundell, L. J., Grusec, J. E., McShane, K. E., & Davidov, M. (2008). Adolescent–parent conflict: Adolescent goals, maternal perspective-taking, and conflict intensity. *Journal of Research on Adolescence, 18,* 555–571.

Luthar, S. S., & Latendresse, S. J. (2005a). Children of the affluent: Challenges to well-being. *Current Directions in Psychological Science, 14,* 49–53.

Luthar, S. S., & Latendresse, S. J. (2005b). Comparable "risks" at the socioeconomic status extremes: Preadolescents' perceptions of parenting. *Development and Psychopathology, 17,* 207–230.

Maccoby, E. E. (2007). Historical overview of socialization theory and research. In J. E. Grusec & P. D. Hastings (Eds.), *Handbook of socialization: Theory and research* (pp. 13–41). New York: Guilford Press.

Maccoby, E. E., & Martin, J. A. (1983). Socialization in the context of the family: Parent–child interaction. In E. M. Hetherington (Ed.), *Handbook of child psychology: Vol. 4. Socialization, personality, and social development* (pp. 1–102). New York: Wiley.

Madden, R. (1992). *Cultural factors and assumptions in social reasoning in India.* Unpublished doctoral dissertation, University of California, Berkeley.

Maggs, J. L., & Galambos, N. L. (1993). Alternative structural models for understanding adolescent problem behavior in two-earner families. *Journal of Early Adolescence, 13,* 79–101.

Mahler, M. S. (1979). *The selected papers of Margaret S. Mahler* (Vols. 1–2). New York: J. Aronson.

Markus, H. R., & Kitayama, S. (1991). Culture and the self: Implications for cognition, emotion, and motivation. *Psychological Bulletin, 98,* 224–253.

Markus, H. R., & Lin, L. R. (1999). Conflictways: Cultural diversity in the meanings and practices of conflict. In D. A. Prentice & D. T. Miller (Eds.), *Cultural divides: Understanding and overcoming group conflict* (pp. 302–333). New York: Russell Sage.

Markus, H. R., Mullally, P. R., & Kitayama, S. (1997). Diversity in modes of cultural participation. In U. Neisser & D. Jopling (Eds.), *The conceptual self in context: Culture, experience, self-understanding* (pp. 13–61). Cambridge, England: Cambridge University Press.

Marshall, S. K., Tilton-Weaver, L. C., & Bosdet, L. (2005). Information management: Considering adolescents' regulation of parental knowledge. *Journal of Adolescence, 28,* 633–647.

Mattis, J. S. (2005). Religion in African American life. In V. C. McLoyd, N. E. Hill, & K. A. Dodge (Eds.), *African American family life* (pp. 189–210). New York: Guilford Press.

McAdoo, H. (2002). African American parents. In M. Bornstein (Ed.), *Handbook of parenting: Vol. 4. Social conditions and applied parenting* (2nd ed., pp. 47–58). Mahwah, NJ: Erlbaum.

McLean, K. C., & Thorne, A. (2003). Late adolescents' self-defining memories about relationships. *Developmental Psychology, 39*, 635–645.

McLoyd, V. (1990). Minority children: Introduction to the Special Issue. *Child Development, 61*, 263–266.

Mernissi, F. (1994). *Dreams of trespass: Tales of a harem girlhood*. Reading, MA: Addison-Wesley.

Mill, J. S. (1968). *Utilitarianism [1863]*. New York: Washington Square Press.

Miller, J. G. (1994). Cultural diversity in the morality of caring: Individually oriented versus duty-based interpersonal moral codes. *Cross-Cultural Research: The Journal of Comparative Social Science, 28*, 3–39.

Miller, J. G. (1997). Agency and context in cultural psychology: Implications for moral theory. In H. D. Saltzstein (Ed.), *New directions for child development: Vol. 76. Culture as a context for moral development: New perspectives on the particular and the universal* (pp. 69–85). San Francisco: Jossey-Bass.

Miller, P. J., Fung, H., & Mintz, J. (1996). Self-construction through narrative practices: A Chinese and American comparison of early socialization. *Ethos, 24*, 237–280.

Min, A. (1994). *Red azalea*. New York: Random House.

Minuchin, S. (1974). *Families and family therapy*. Cambridge, MA: Harvard University Press.

Modell, J., & Goodman, M. (1990). Historical perspectives. In S. S. Feldman & G. R. Elliot (Eds.), *At the threshold: The developing adolescent* (pp. 93–122). Cambridge, MA: Harvard University Press.

Montemayor, R. (1983). Parents and adolescents in conflict: All families some of the time and some families most of the time. *Journal of Early Adolescence, 3*, 83–103.

Mosle, S. (2000, July 2). The vanity of volunteerism. *New York Times Sunday Magazine*. Retrieved from http://www.nytimes.com/2000/07/02/magazine/the-vanity-of-volunteerism.html.

Much, N., & Shweder, R. A. (1978). Speaking of rules: The analysis of culture in breach. In W. Damon (Ed.), *New directions for child development: Vol. 1. Moral development* (pp. 19–40). San Francisco: Jossey-Bass.

Murdock, G. P., & White, D. R. (1969). The standard cross-cultural sample. *Ethnology, 8*, 329–369.

Murdock, G. P., & Wilson, M. (1980). The standard cross-cultural sample and its codes. In H. B. Barry III & A. Schlegel (Eds.), *Cross-cultural samples and codes* (pp. 75–116). Pittsburgh, PA: University of Pittsburgh Press.

Nafisi, A. (2004). *Reading Lolita in Tehran: A memoir in books*. New York: Random House.

Nelson, L. J., & Chen, X. (2007). Emerging adulthood in China: The role of social and cultural factors. *Child Development Perspectives, 1*, 86–91.

Nelson, L. J., Badger, S., & Wu, B. (2004). The influence of culture in emerging adulthood: Perspectives of Chinese college students. *International Journal of Behavioral Development, 28*, 26–36.

Nguyen, J., Brown, B. B., Von Bank, H., & Bakken, J. P. (2007). "You know how Hmong parents are …": Culturally embedded negotiations of romantic relationships in Hmong immigrant families. Paper presented at the Society for Research in Child Development, Boston, MA.

Nisan, M. (1987). Moral norms and social conventions: A cross-cultural comparison. *Developmental Psychology, 23*, 719–725.

Nisbett, R. (2003). *The geography of thought: How Asians and Westerners think differently ... and why.* New York: The Free Press.

Noller, P., & Callan, V. J. (1990). Adolescents' perceptions of the nature of their communication with parents. *Journal of Youth and Adolescence, 19,* 349–362.

Nucci, L. P. (1977). *The personal domain: A domain distinct from morality and social convention.* Unpublished doctoral dissertation, University of California, Santa Cruz.

Nucci, L. P. (1981). The development of personal concepts: A domain distinct from moral or societal concepts. *Child Development, 52,* 118–121.

Nucci, L. P. (1984). Evaluating teachers as social agents: Students' ratings of domain appropriate and domain inappropriate teacher responses to transgressions. *American Educational Research Journal, 21,* 367–378.

Nucci, L. P. (1985). Children's conceptions of morality, social conventions, and religious prescription. In C. Harding (Ed.), *Moral dilemmas: Philosophical and psychological reconsiderations of the development of moral reasoning* (pp. 137–174). Chicago: Precedent Press.

Nucci, L. P. (1996). Morality and personal freedom. In E. S. Reed, E. Turiel, & T. Brown (Eds.), *Values and knowledge* (pp. 41–60). Mahwah, NJ: Erlbaum.

Nucci, L. P. (2001). *Education in the moral domain.* Cambridge, England: Cambridge University Press.

Nucci, L. P. (2008). *Nice is not enough: Facilitating moral development.* New York: Pearson.

Nucci, L. P., & Lee, J. (1993). Morality and personal autonomy. In G. G. Noam & T. Wren (Eds.), *The moral self: Building a better paradigm* (pp. 123–148). Cambridge, MA: MIT Press.

Nucci, L. P., & Smetana, J. G. (1996). Mothers' concepts of young children's areas of personal freedom. *Child Development, 67,* 1870–1886.

Nucci, L. P., & Turiel, E. (1978). Social interactions and the development of social concepts in preschool children. *Child Development, 49,* 400–407.

Nucci, L. P., & Turiel, E. (1993). God's word, religious rules, and their relation to Christian and Jewish children's concepts of morality. *Child Development, 64,* 1475–1491.

Nucci, L. P., & Turiel, E. (2000). The moral and the personal: Sources of social conflicts. In L. P. Nucci, G. B. Saxe, & E. Turiel (Eds.), *Culture, thought, and development* (pp. 115–137). Mahwah, NJ: Erlbaum.

Nucci, L. P., & Turiel, E. (2007). Development in the moral domain: The role of conflict and relationships in children's and adolescents' welfare and harm judgments. Paper presented at the Biennial Meetings of the Society for Research in Child Development, Boston, MA.

Nucci, L. P., & Turiel. E. (2009). Capturing the complexity of moral development and education. *Mind, Brain, and Education, 3,* 151–159.

Nucci, L. P., & Weber, E. K. (1995). Social interactions in the home and the development of young children's conceptions of the personal. *Child Development, 66,* 1438–1452.

Nucci, L. P., Camino, C., & Sapiro, C. M. (1996). Social class effects on Northeastern Brazilian children's conceptions of areas of personal choice and social regulation. *Child Development, 67,* 1223–1242.

Nucci, L. P., Guerra, N., & Lee, J. (1991). Adolescent judgments of the personal, prudential, and normative aspects of drug usage. *Developmental Psychology, 27,* 841–848.

Nucci, L. P., Killen, M., & Smetana, J. G. (1996). Autonomy and the personal: Negotiation and social reciprocity in adult–child social exchanges. In M. Killen (Ed.), *New directions for child development: Vol. 73. The influence of adult–child and peer interactions on children's autonomy and social competence* (pp. 7–24). San Francisco: Jossey-Bass.

Nussbaum, M. C. (1999). *Sex and social justice.* New York: Oxford University Press.

O'Connor, T. G., Allen, J. P., Bell, K. L., & Hauser, S. T. (1996). Adolescent–parent relationships and leaving home in young adulthood. In J. A. Graber & J. S. Dubas (Eds.), *Leaving home: Understanding the transition to adulthood* (pp. 39–52). San Francisco: Jossey-Bass.

Offer, D. (1969). *The psychological world of the teenager.* New York: Basic Books.

Offer, D., Ostrov, E., & Howard, K. (1981). *The adolescent: A psychological self-portrait.* New York: Basic Books.

Oyserman, D., Coon, H. M., & Kemmelmeier, M. (2002). Rethinking individualism and collectivism: Evaluation of theoretical assumptions and meta-analyses. *Psychological Bulletin, 128,* 3–72.

Parke, R. D., & Buriel, R. (2006). Socialization in the family: Ethnic and ecological perspectives. In N. Eisenberg (Ed.), *Handbook of child psychology: Vol. 3. Social, emotional, and personality development* (6th ed., pp. 429–504). New York: Wiley.

Parker-Pope, T. (2009, January 26). The myth of rampant teenager promiscuity. *New York Times.* Retrieved from http://www.nytimes.com/2009/01/27/health/27well.html.

Pempek, T. A., Yermolayeva, Y. A., & Calvert, S. L. (2009). College students' social networking experiences on Facebook. *Journal of Applied Developmental Psychology, 30,* 227–238.

Perkins, S. A., & Turiel, E. (2007). To lie or not to lie: To whom and under what circumstances. *Child Development, 78,* 609–621.

Pettit, G. S., & Laird, R. D. (2002). Psychological control and monitoring in early adolescence: The role of parental involvement and prior child adjustment. In B. K. Barber (Ed.), *Intrusive parenting: How psychological control affects children and adolescents* (pp. 97–123). Washington, DC: APA Press.

Phelan, T. W. (1998). *Surviving your adolescents: How to manage and let go of your 13–18 year olds* (2nd ed.). Glen Ellyn, IL: Child Management Press.

Phinney, J. S., & Landin, J. (1998). Research paradigms for studying ethnic minority families within and across groups. In V. C. McLoyd & L. Steinberg (Eds.), *Studying minority adolescents: Conceptual, methodological, and theoretical issues* (pp. 89–109). Mahwah, NJ: Erlbaum.

Phinney, J. S., Kim-Jo, T., Osorio, S., & Vilhjalmsdottir, P. (2005). Autonomy-relatedness in adolescent–parent disagreements: Ethnic and developmental factors. *Journal of Adolescent Research, 20,* 8–39.

Piaget, J. (1965). *The moral judgment of the child [1932].* Translated by M. Gabain. New York: Free Press.

Prinz, R. J., Foster, S. L., Kent, R. N., & O'Leary, K. D. (1979). Multivariate assessment of conflict in distressed and non-distressed mother–adolescent dyads. *Journal of Applied Behavior Analysis, 12,* 691–700.

Proulx, T., & Chandler, J. M. (2009). Jekyll and Hyde and me: Age-graded differences in conceptions of self-unity. *Human Development, 52,* 261–286.

Putnam, R. D. (2000). *Bowling alone: The collapse and revival of American community.* New York: Simon & Schuster.

Qin, L., Pomerantz, E. M., & Wang, Q. (2009). Are gains in decision-making autonomy during early adolescence beneficial for emotional functioning? The case of the United States and China. *Child Development, 80,* 1705–1721.

Raeff, C. (2006). *Always separate, always connected: Independence and interdependence in cultural contexts of development.* Mahwah, NJ: Erlbaum.

Rawls, J. (1971). *A theory of justice.* Cambridge, England: Cambridge University Press.

Robin, A. L., & Foster, S. L. (1989). *Negotiating parent–adolescent conflict: A behavioral-family systems approach.* New York: Guilford Press.

Roisman, G. I., Masten, A. S., Coatsworth, J. D., & Tellegen, A. (2004). Salient and emerging developmental tasks in the transition to adulthood. *Child Development, 75,* 123–133.

Rothbaum, F., Pott, M., Azuma, H., Miyake, K., & Weisz, J. (2000). The development of close relationships in Japan and the United States: Paths of symbiotic harmony and generative tension. *Child Development, 71,* 1121–1142.

Rowe, D. C., Rodgers, J. L., Meseck-Bushey, S., & St. John, C. (1989). Sexual behavior and nonsexual deviance: A sibling study of their relationship. *Developmental Psychology, 25,* 61–69.

Rutter, M. (1980). *Changing youth in a changing society.* Cambridge, MA: Harvard University Press.

Rutter, M., Graham, P., Chadwick, O. F. D., & Yule, W. (1976). Adolescent turmoil: Fact or fiction? *Journal of Child Psychology and Psychiatry, 17,* 35–56.

Ryan, R. M., & Deci, E. L. (2000). Self-determination theory and the facilitation of intrinsic motivation, social development, and well-being. *American Psychologist, 55,* 68–78.

Schaefer, E. S. (1965). A configurational analysis of children's reports of parental behaviors: An inventory. *Child Development, 36,* 417–424.

Scher, H. (2009). The lies we tell our kids. Retrieved from http://www.redbookmag.com/kids-family/lying-to-kids.

Schlegel, A. (2009). Cross-cultural issues in the study of adolescent development. In R. L. Lerner & L. Steinberg (Eds.), *Handbook of adolescent psychology* (3rd ed., Vol. 2, pp. 570–589). New York: John Wiley & Sons.

Schlegel, A., & Barry, H. B., III (1991). *Adolescence: An anthropological inquiry.* New York: Free Press.

Seligman, M. E. P., & Csikszentmihalyi, M. (2000). Positive psychology: An introduction. *American Psychologist, 55,* 5–14.

Selman, R. (1980). *The growth of interpersonal understanding: Developmental and clinical analyses.* New York: Academic Press.

Shanahan, L., McHale, S. M., Crouter, A. C., & Osgood, W. (2007). Warmth with mothers and fathers from middle childhood to late adolescence: Within- and between-families comparisons. *Developmental Psychology, 43,* 551–563.

Shanahan, L., McHale, S. M., Osgood, W., & Crouter, A. C. (2007). Conflict frequency with mothers and fathers from middle childhood to late adolescence: Within- and between-families comparisons. *Developmental Psychology, 43,* 539–550.

Shantz, C. U., & Hartup, W. H. (1992). Conflict and development: An introduction. In C. U. Shantz & W. H. Hartup (Eds.), *Conflict in child and adolescent development* (pp. 1–11). Cambridge, England: Cambridge University Press.

Shweder, R. A., & Bourne, E. J. (1984). Does the concept of the person vary cross-cultur-ally? In R. A. Shweder & R. A. Levine (Eds.), *Culture theory: Essays on mind, self, and emotion* (pp. 158–199). Cambridge, England: Cambridge University Press.

Shweder, R. A., Mahapatra, M., & Miller, J. G. (1987). Culture and moral development. In J. Kagan & S. Lamb (Eds.), *The emergence of morality in young children* (pp. 1–82). Chicago: University of Chicago Press.

Shweder, R. A., Goodnow, J. J., Hatano, G., LeVine, R. A., Markus, H., & Miller, P. (2006). The cultural psychology of development: One mind, many mentalities. In R. M. Lerner (Ed.), *Handbook of child psychology: Vol. 1. Theoretical models of human develop-ment* (6th ed., pp. 865–937). New York: Wiley.

Silverberg, S. B., & Steinberg, L. (1990). Psychological well-being of parents with early adolescent children. *Developmental Psychology, 26,* 658–666.

Sinha, D., & Tripathi, R. C. (1994). Individualism in a collectivist culture: A coexistence of opposites. In U. Kim, H. C. Triandis, C. Kagitcibasi, S. C. Choi, & G. Yoon (Eds.), *Individualism and collectivism: Theory, method, and applications* (pp. 123–136). Thousand Oaks, CA: Sage.

Small, S., Eastman, G., & Cornelius, S. (1988). Adolescent autonomy and parental stress. *Journal of Youth and Adolescence, 17,* 377–391.

Smetana, J. G. (1981). Preschool children's conceptions of moral and social rules. *Child Development, 52,* 1333–1336.

Smetana, J. G. (1983). Social–cognitive development: Domain distinctions and coordina-tions. *Developmental Review, 3,* 131–147.

Smetana, J. G. (1988a). Adolescents' and parents' conceptions of parental authority. *Child Development, 59,* 321–335.

Smetana, J. G. (1988b). Concepts of self and social convention: Adolescents' and parents' reasoning about hypothetical and actual family conflicts. In M. R. Gunnar and W. A. Collins (Eds.), *21st Minnesota Symposium on Child Psychology: Development during the transition to adolescence* (pp. 79–122). Hillsdale, NJ: Erlbaum.

Smetana, J. G. (1989a). Adolescents' and parents' reasoning about actual family conflict. *Child Development, 60,* 1052–1067.

Smetana, J. G. (1989b). Toddlers' social interactions in the context of moral and conven-tional transgressions in the home. *Developmental Psychology, 25,* 499–508.

Smetana, J. G. (1993a). Children's conceptions of social rules. In M. Bennett (Ed.), *The child as psychologist* (pp. 111–141). London: Simon & Schuster.

Smetana, J. G. (1993b). Conceptions of parental authority in divorced and married mothers and their adolescents. *Journal of Research in Adolescence, 3,* 19–40.

Smetana, J. G. (1995a). Parenting styles and conceptions of parental authority during adolescence. *Child Development, 66,* 299–316.

Smetana, J. G. (1995b). Morality in context: Abstractions, ambiguities, and applications. In R. Vasta (Ed.), *Annals of child development* (Vol. 10, pp. 83–130). London, England: Jessica Kingsley Publishers Ltd.

Smetana, J. G. (1996). Adolescent–parent conflict: Implications for adaptive and maladap-tive development. In D. Cicchetti & S. L. Toth (Eds.), *Rochester Symposium on Developmental Psychopathology: Vol. 7. Adolescence: Opportunities and challenges* (pp. 1–46). Rochester, NY: University of Rochester Press.

Smetana, J. G. (2000). Middle class African American adolescents' and parents' conceptions of parental authority and parenting practices: A longitudinal investigation. *Child Development, 71,* 1672–1686.

Smetana, J. G. (2006). Social domain theory: Consistencies and variations in children's moral and social judgments. In M. Killen & J. G. Smetana (Eds.), *Handbook of moral development* (pp. 119–154). Mahwah, NJ: Erlbaum.

Smetana, J. G., & Asquith, P. (1994). Adolescents' and parents' conceptions of parental authority and adolescent autonomy. *Child Development, 65,* 1147–1162.

Smetana, J. G., & Berent, R. (1993). Adolescents' and mothers' evaluations of justifications for disputes. *Journal of Adolescent Research, 8,* 252–273.

Smetana, J. G., & Braeges, J. L. (1990). The development of toddlers' moral and conventional judgments. *Merrill–Palmer Quarterly, 36,* 329–346.

Smetana, J. G., & Chuang, S. S. (2001). Middle class African American parents' conceptions of parenting in early adolescence. *Journal of Research on Adolescence, 11,* 177–198.

Smetana, J. G., & Daddis, C. (2002). Domain-specific antecedents of psychological control and parental monitoring: The role of parenting beliefs and practices. *Child Development, 73,* 563–580.

Smetana, J. G., & Metzger, A. (2008). Don't ask, don't tell (your mom and dad): Disclosure and nondisclosure in adolescent–parent relationships. In M. Kerr, H. Stattin, & R. C. M. E. Engels (Eds.), *What can parents do? New insights into the role of parents in adolescent problem behavior* (pp. 65–89). Chichester, England: John Wiley & Sons.

Smetana, J. G., Abernethy, A., & Harris, A. (2000). Adolescent–parent interactions in middle-class African American families: Longitudinal change and contextual variations. *Journal of Family Psychology, 14,* 458–474.

Smetana, J. G., Braeges, J. L., & Yau, J. (1991). Doing what you say and saying what you do: Reasoning about adolescent–parent conflict in interviews and interactions. *Journal of Adolescent Research, 6,* 276–295.

Smetana, J. G., Campione-Barr, N., & Daddis, C. (2004). Developmental and longitudinal antecedents of family decision-making: Defining health behavioral autonomy for African American adolescents. *Child Development, 75,* 1418–1434.

Smetana, J. G., Campione-Barr, N., & Metzger, A. (2006). Adolescent development in interpersonal and societal contexts. *Annual Review of Psychology, 57,* 255–284.

Smetana, J. G., Crean, H. F., & Campione-Barr, N. (2005). Adolescents' and parents' changing conceptions of parental authority. In J. G. Smetana (Ed.), *Changing boundaries of parental authority* (pp. 31–46). San Francisco: Jossey-Bass.

Smetana, J. G., Daddis, C., & Chuang, S. S. (2003). "Clean your room!": A longitudinal investigation of adolescent–parent conflict in middle class African American families. *Journal of Adolescent Research, 18,* 631–650.

Smetana, J. G., Kochanska, G., & Chuang, S. (2000). Mothers' conceptions of everyday rules for young toddlers: A longitudinal investigation of the effects of maternal reasoning and child temperament. *Merrill–Palmer Quarterly, 3,* 391–416.

Smetana, J. G., Metzger, A., & Campione-Barr, N. (2004). African American adolescents' relationships with parents: Developmental transitions and longitudinal patterns. *Child Development, 75,* 932–947.

Smetana, J. G., Schlagman, N., & Adams, P. (1993). Preschoolers' judgments about hypothetical and actual transgressions. *Child Development, 64,* 202–214.

Smetana, J. G., Yau, J., & Hanson, S. (1991). Conflict resolution in families with adolescents. *Journal of Research on Adolescence, 1*, 189–206.

Smetana, J. G., Metzger, A., Gettman, D. C., & Campione-Barr, N. (2006). Disclosure and secrecy in adolescent–parent relationships. *Child Development, 77*, 201–217.

Smetana, J. G., Villalobos, M., Rogge, R. D., & Tasopoulos-Chan, M. (2010). Keeping secrets from parents: Daily variations among poor, urban adolescents. *Journal of Adolescence, 33*, 321–331.

Smetana, J. G., Yau, J., Restrepo, A., & Braeges, J. L. (1991). Adolescent–parent conflict in married and divorced families. *Developmental Psychology, 27*, 1000–1010.

Smetana, J. G., Tasopoulos-Chan, M., Villalobos, M., Gettman, D. C., Campione-Barr, N., & Metzger, A. (2009). Adolescents' and parents' evaluations of helping versus fulfilling personal desires. *Child Development, 80*, 280–294.

Smetana, J. G., Villalobos, M., Rogge, R. D., Tasopoulos-Chan, M., & Gettman, D. C. (2009). Daily variations in African American, Latino, and European American adolescents' disclosure about their activities to parents. Unpublished manuscript, University of Rochester.

Smetana, J. G., Villalobos, M., Tasopoulos-Chan, M., Gettman, D. C., & Campione-Barr, N. (2009). Early and middle adolescents' disclosure to parents about activities in different domains. *Journal of Adolescence, 32*, 693–713.

Smith, C., & Denton, M. (2005). *Soul searching: The religious and spiritual lives of American teenagers.* New York: Oxford University Press.

Soenens, B., & Vansteenkiste, M. (2010). A theoretical upgrade of the concept of parental psychological control: Proposing new insights on the basis of self-determination theory. *Developmental Review, 30*, 74–79.

Soenens, B., Vansteenkiste, M., Luyckx, K., & Goossens, L. (2006). Parenting and adolescent problem behavior: An integrated model with adolescent self-disclosure and perceived parental knowledge as intervening variables. *Developmental Psychology, 42*, 305–318.

Song, M. J., Smetana, J. G., & Kim, S. Y. (1987). Korean children's conceptions of moral and conventional transgressions. *Developmental Psychology, 23*, 577–582.

Spiro, M. E. (1984). Some reflections on cultural determinism and relativism with special relevance to emotion and reason. In R. A. Shweder & R. A. Levine (Eds.), *Culture theory: Essays on mind, self, and emotion* (pp. 323–346). Cambridge, England: Cambridge University Press.

Spiro, M. E. (1986). Cultural relativism and the future of anthropology. *Cultural Anthropology, 1*, 259–286.

Spitz, R. A. (1957). *No and yes: On the genesis of human communication.* Madison, CT: International Universities Press.

Sroufe, L. A., Egeland, B., Carlson, E., & Collins, W. A. (2005). *The development of the person: The Minnesota study of risk and adaptation from birth to adulthood.* New York: Guilford Press.

Stattin, H., & Kerr, M. (2000). Parental monitoring: A reinterpretation. *Child Development, 71*, 1072–1085.

Steinberg, L. (1987). The impact of puberty on family relations: Effects of pubertal status and pubertal timing. *Developmental Psychology, 23*, 451–460.

Steinberg, L. (1990). Interdependency in the family: Autonomy, conflict, and harmony in the parent–adolescent relationship. In S. S. Feldman & G. R. Elliot (Eds.), *At the threshold: The developing adolescent* (pp. 255–276). Cambridge, MA: Harvard University Press.

Steinberg, L. (2001). We know some things: Parent–adolescent relations in retrospect and prospect. *Journal of Research on Adolescence, 11,* 1–19.

Steinberg, L. (2005). Cognitive and affective development in adolescence. *Trends in Cognitive Science, 9,* 69–74.

Steinberg, L. (2008). A social neuroscience perspective on adolescent risk-taking. *Developmental Review, 28,* 78–106.

Stolberg, S. G. (2010, February 9). Childhood obesity battle is taken up by First Lady. *New York Times.* Retrieved from http://www.nytimes.com/2010/02/10/health/nutrition/10obesity.html.

Strauss, C. (1992). Models and motives. In R. G. D'Andrade & C. Strauss (Eds.), *Human motives and cultural models* (pp. 1–20). Cambridge, England: Cambridge University Press.

Strauss, C. (2000). The culture concept and the individualism–collectivism debate: Dominant and alternative attributions for class in the United States. In L. P. Nucci, G. B. Saxe, & E. Turiel (Eds.), *Culture, thought, and development* (pp. 85–114). Mahwah, NJ: Erlbaum.

Subrahmanyam, K., Smahel, D., & Greenfield, P. (2006). Connecting developmental constructions to the Internet: Identity presentation and sexual exploration in online teen chat rooms. *Developmental Psychology, 42,* 395–406.

Tardif, T., & Miao, X. (2000). Developmental psychology in China. *International Journal of Behavioral Development, 24,* 68–72.

Tasopoulos-Chan, M., Smetana, J. G., & Yau, J. Y. (2009). How much do I tell thee? Strategic management of information with parents among American adolescents from Mexican, Chinese, and European backgrounds. *Journal of Family Psychology, 23,* 364–374.

Tatum, B. (1987). *Assimilation blues: Black families in a White community.* Westport, CT: Greenwood Press.

Tilton-Weaver, L. C., & Galambos, N. L. (2003). Adolescents' characteristics and parents' beliefs as predictors of parents' peer management behaviors. *Journal of Research on Adolescence, 13,* 269–300.

Ting-Toomey, S. (1994). Managing intimate conflict in intercultural personal relationships. In D. D. Cahn (Ed.), *Intimate conflict in interpersonal relationships* (pp. 44–77). Hillsdale, NJ: Erlbaum.

Tisak, M. (1986). Children's conceptions of parental authority. *Child Development, 57,* 166–176.

Tisak, M. (1993). Preschool children's judgments of moral and personal events involving physical harm and property damage. *Merrill–Palmer Quarterly, 39,* 375–390.

Tisak, M. S., & Turiel, E. (1988). Variation in seriousness of transgressions and children's moral and conventional concepts. *Developmental Psychology, 24,* 352–357.

Tisak, M. S., Nucci, L. P., & Jankowski, A. M. (1996). Preschool children's social interactions involving moral and prudential transgressions: An observational study. *Journal of Early Education and Development, 7,* 137–148.

Triandis, H. C. (1990). Cross-cultural studies of individualism and collectivism. In J. Berman (Ed.), *Nebraska Symposium on Motivation, 1989* (pp. 41–133). Lincoln, NE: University of Nebraska Press.

Triandis, H. C. (1995). *Individualism and collectivism*. Boulder, CO: Westview Press.

Triandis, H. C. (2001). Individualism–collectivism and personality. *Journal of Personality, 69,* 907–924.

Triandis, H. C., & Gelfand, M. J. (1998). Converging measurement of horizontal and vertical individualism and collectivism. *Journal of Personality and Social Psychology, 74,* 118–128.

Triandis, H. C., & Suh, E. M. (2002). Cultural influences on personality. *Annual Review of Psychology, 53,* 133–160.

Trujillo, M. (2000). *Why can't we talk? What teens would share if parents would listen: A book for teens.* Deerfield Beach, FL: Health Communications, Inc.

Turiel, E. (1978). Social regulation and domains of social concepts. In W. Damon (Ed.), *New directions for child development: Vol. 1. Social cognition* (pp. 45–74). San Francisco: Jossey-Bass.

Turiel, E. (1979). Distinct conceptual and developmental domains: Social convention and morality. In C. B. Keasey (Ed.), *Nebraska Symposium on Motivation* (pp. 77–116). Lincoln, NE: University of Nebraska Press.

Turiel, E. (1983). *The development of social knowledge: Morality and convention.* Cambridge, England: Cambridge University Press.

Turiel, E. (2002). *The culture of morality: Social development, context, and conflict.* Cambridge, England: Cambridge University Press.

Turiel, E. (2005). The many faces of parenting. In J. G. Smetana (Ed.), *Changing boundaries of parental authority* (pp. 79–88). San Francisco: Jossey-Bass.

Turiel, E. (2006). The development of morality. In N. Eisenberg (Ed.), *Handbook of child psychology, Volume 3: Social, emotional, and personality development* (6th ed., pp. 789–857). New York: Wiley.

Turiel, E. (2008). Thought about actions in social domains: Morality, social conventions, and social interactions. *Cognitive Development, 23,* 136–154.

Turiel, E., & Wainryb, C. (1998). Concepts of freedoms and rights in a traditional, hierarchically organized society. *British Journal of Developmental Psychology, 16,* 375–395.

Turiel, E., & Wainryb, C. (2000). Social life in cultures: Judgments, conflict, and subversion. *Child Development, 71,* 250–256.

Turiel, E., Hildebrandt, C., & Wainryb, C. (1991). Judging social issues: Difficulties, inconsistencies and consistencies. *Monographs of the Society for Research in Child Development, 56* (Serial No. 224).

Turiel, E., Killen, M., & Helwig, C. (1987). Morality: Its structure, functions, and vagaries. In J. Kagan & S. Lamb (Eds.), *The emergence of morality in young children* (pp. 155–243). Chicago: University of Chicago Press.

Tyson, K., Darity, W., & Castellino, D. R. (2005). It's not "a black thing." Understanding the burden of acting white and other dilemmas of high achievement. *American Sociological Review, 70,* 582–605.

Vendantam, S. (2007, February 19). Almost everyone lies, often seeing it as a kindness. *Washington Post,* p. A2.

Verkuyten, M., & Slooter, L. (2008). Muslim and non-Muslim adolescents' reasoning about freedom of speech and minority rights. *Child Development, 79,* 514–528.

Villalobos, M., & Smetana, J. G. (2009). *Latino values and Puerto Rican adolescents' disclosure and lying to parents.* Unpublished manuscript, University of Rochester.

Wainryb, C. (1991). Understanding differences in moral judgments: The role of informational assumptions. *Child Development, 62*, 840–851.

Wainryb, C. (1993). The application of moral judgments to other cultures: Relativism and universality. *Child Development, 64*, 924–933.

Wainryb, C. (1995). Reasoning about social conflicts in different cultures: Druze and Jewish children in Israel. *Child Development, 66*, 390–401.

Wainryb, C. (2006). Moral development in culture: Diversity, tolerance, and justice. In M. Killen & J. G. Smetana (Eds.), *Handbook of moral development* (pp. 185–210). Mahwah, NJ: Erlbaum.

Wainryb, C., & Turiel, E. (1993). Conceptual and informational features in moral decision-making. *Educational Psychologist, 28*, 205–218.

Wainryb, C., & Turiel, E. (1994). Dominance, subordination, and concepts of personal entitlements in cultural contexts. *Child Development, 66*, 390–401.

Wainryb, C., & Turiel, E. (1995). Diversity in social development: Between or within cultures? In M. Killen & D. Hart (Eds.), *Morality in everyday life: Developmental perspectives* (pp. 283–316). Cambridge, England: Cambridge University Press.

Wainryb, C., Brehl, B., & Matwin, S. (2005). Being hurt and hurting others: Children's narrative accounts and moral judgments of their own interpersonal conflicts. *Monographs of the Society for Research in Child Development, 70* (3), 1–114.

Wainryb, C., Shaw, L., Langley, M., Cottam, K., & Lewis, R. (2004). Children's thinking about diversity of belief in the early school years: Judgments of relativism, tolerance, and disagreeing persons. *Child Development, 75*, 687–703.

Waizenhofer, R. N., Buchanan, C. M., & Jackson-Newsom, J. (2004). Mothers' and fathers' knowledge of adolescents' daily activities: Its sources and its links with adolescent adjustment. *Journal of Marriage and the Family, 18*, 348–360.

Waldinger, R. J., Diguer, L., Guastella, F., Lefebvre, R. Allen, J. P., Luborsky, L., & Hauser, S. T. (2002). The same old song? Stability and change in relationship schemas from adolescence to young adulthood. *Journal of Youth and Adolescence, 31*, 17–29.

Wallis, C. (2008, September 26). What makes teenagers tick? *Time Magazine*. Retrieved from http://www.time.com/time/magazine/article/0,9171,994126-97,00.html.

Warner, J. (2009, January 29). The myth of teen innocence. *New York Times*. Retrieved from http://warner.blogs.nytimes.com/2009/01/.

White, M. (1993). *The material child: Coming of age in Japan and America*. New York: Free Press.

Whiteman, S. D., & Buchanan, C. M. (2002). Mothers' and children's expectations for adolescence: The impact of perceptions of an older sibling's experience. *Journal of Family Psychology, 16*, 157–171.

Whiteman, S. D., McHale, S.M., & Crouter, A.C. (2003). What parents learn from experience: The first child as a first draft? *Journal of Marriage and the Family, 65*, 608–621.

Whitton, S. W., Waldinger, R. J., Schulz, M. S., Allen, J. P., Crowell, J. A., & Hauser, S. T. (2008). Prospective associations from family-of-origin interactions and marital interactions and relationship adjustment. *Journal of Family Psychology, 22*, 274–286.

Wikan, U. (2002). *Generous betrayal: Politics of culture in the new Europe*. Chicago: University of Chicago Press.

Wiley, A. R., Rose, A. J., Burger, L. K., & Miller, P. J. (1998). Constructing autonomous selves through narrative practices: A comparative study of working-class and middle-class families. *Child Development, 69,* 833–847.

Wilson, J. Q. (1993). *The moral sense.* New York: Free Press.

Wilson, M. N., Cooke, D. Y., & Arrington, E. G. (1997). African American adolescents and academic achievement: Influences of parents and peers. In R. W. Taylor & M. C. Wang (Eds.), *Social and emotional adjustment and family relations in ethnic minority families* (pp. 145–155). Mahwah, NJ: Erlbaum.

Winfield, L. F. (1995). The knowledge base on resilience in African American adolescents. In L. J. Crockett & A. C. Crouter (Eds.), *Pathways through adolescence: Individual development in relation to social contexts* (pp. 87–118). Mahwah, NJ: Psychology Press.

Wolf, A. E. (2002). *Get out of my life – but first would you drive me and Cheryl to the mall? A parent's guide to the new teenager.* New York: Farrar Strauss Giroux.

Wray-Lake, L., McHale, S., & Crouter, N. (2010). Developmental patterns in decision-making autonomy across middle childhood and adolescence: European American parents' perspectives. *Child Development, 81,* 636–651.

Xu, F. (2000). *Chinese children's and mothers' concepts regarding morality, social convention and children's personal autonomy.* Unpublished doctoral dissertation, University of Illinois, Chicago.

Yamada, H. (2004). Japanese mothers' views of young children's areas of personal discretion. *Child Development, 75,* 164–179.

Yamada, H. (2009). Japanese children's reasoning about conflict with parents. *Social Development, 18,* 962–977.

Yau, J., & Smetana, J. G. (1996). Adolescent–parent conflict among Chinese adolescents in Hong Kong. *Child Development, 67,* 1262–1275.

Yau, J., & Smetana, J. G. (2003a). Adolescent–parent conflict in Hong Kong and Shenzhen: A comparison of youth in two cultural contexts. *International Journal of Behavioral Development, 27,* 201–211.

Yau, J., & Smetana, J. G. (2003b). Conceptions of moral, social–conventional, and personal events among Chinese preschoolers in Hong Kong. *Child Development, 74,* 647–658.

Yau, J., Smetana, J. G., & Metzger, A. (2009). Young Chinese children's authority concepts. *Social Development, 18,* 210–229.

Yau, J. Y., Tasopoulos-Chan, M., & Smetana, J. G. (2009). Disclosure to parents about everyday activities among American adolescents from Mexican, Chinese, and European backgrounds. *Child Development, 80,* 1481–1498.

Youniss, J. (1980). *Parents and peers in social development: A Sullivan–Piaget perspective.* Chicago: University of Chicago Press.

Youniss, J., & Smollar, J. (1985). *Adolescents' relations with mothers, fathers, and friends.* Chicago: University of Chicago Press.

Zhang, W., & Fuligni, A. J. (2006). Authority, autonomy, and family relationships among adolescents in urban and rural China. *Journal of Research on Adolescence, 16,* 527–537.

Zimmer-Gembeck, M. J., & Collins, W. A. (2003). Autonomy development during adolescence. In G. R. Adams & M. D. Berzonsky (Eds.), *Blackwell handbook of adolescence* (pp. 175–204). Oxford, England: Blackwell.

Author Index

Abernethy, A. 164
Abu-Lughod, L. 103, 107–8
Adams, E. 54
Adams, P. 50
Adelson, J. 19, 20–1, 22, 23, 36
Afifi, T. 220, 221
Afifi, W. A. 220, 222
Aksan, N. 32
Allen, J. P. 273, 274
Anderson, V. D. 140
Aquilino, W. S. 273
Ardila-Rey, A. 72, 111
Arim, R. G. 247
Arnett, J. J. 29, 120, 217, 271
Arnold, M. L. 114
Arrington, E. G. 157
Arsenio, W. F. 54–5
Aseltine, R. H. 273
Asquith, P. 78, 173–4, 176, 178, 180–1
Assadi, S. M. 185
Azuma, H. 99, 202, 224

Bachman, J. G. 40, 176
Badger, S. 272
Bai, M. 145
Baier, A. 218
Baker, S. 230
Bakken, J. P. 225, 227, 233, 235, 236–7
Baldwin, J. M. 71
Barbarin, O. A. 157
Barber, B. K. 199, 200
Bargh, J. A. 268
Barker, E. T. 272

Barry, H. B., III 6–8, 96
Bartko, W. T. 238
Bassett, K. M. 93
Bates, J. E. 242
Baumrind, D. 193–6, 198, 202–3, 213
Belkin, L. 6, 217
Bell, K. L. 273, 274
Bell, R. Q. 33
Bellah, R. N. 98, 100, 121
Benedict, R. 110
Benjamin, C. L. 3
Benner, A. D. 160
Bennett, W. J. 2, 8
Berent, R. 78
Bersheid, E. 102
Bibby, R. 5–6
Billingsley, A. 141, 144, 157
Bithoney, W. 92
Blos, P. 16–18, 23
Bok, S. 217, 230
Bosacki, S. 72
Bosdet, L. 220
Bouchey, H. A. 250
Bourne, E. J. 71
Boyd, D. 114
Boyd-Franklin, N. 143, 147
Boykin, A. W. 145
Braeges, J. L. 35, 50, 78, 258
Braine, L. G. 173, 174
Branje, S. J. T. 220, 221, 222, 244
Braver, E. 230
Brehl, B. 45, 274
Bresnick, S. 250

Adolescents, Families, and Social Development: How Teens Construct Their Worlds. Judith G. Smetana
© 2011 Judith G. Smetana

Subject Index